Y0-DJQ-011

EYES TOWARD THE SOUTH

The Civil War Saga of John Yates Beall

TO : JACK
3/24/16

by

RANDY KOCH

Randy Koch

INFINITY PUBLISHING

The cover, featuring Moses Ezekiel's sculpture in the Johnson's Island cemetery, was designed by Vanessa Koch. The portraits featuring John Yates Beall and Martha O'Bryan are courtesy of the Jefferson County Museum in Charles Town, West Virginia.

ISBN 0-7414-5855-5

Printed in the United States of America

This book is a work of historical fiction within which many real persons and events have been described. However, all of the dialogue, all of the non-historical persons, and many of the events, are a product of the author's imagination, making any resemblance of such characters to real people purely coincidental.

Published May 2010

INFINITY PUBLISHING
1094 New DeHaven Street, Suite 100
West Conshohocken, PA 19428-2713
Toll-free (877) BUY BOOK
Local Phone (610) 941-9999
Fax (610) 941-9959
Info@buybooksontheweb.com
www.buybooksontheweb.com

1 – COMMONWEALTH JUSTICE

"Oh, what could have been," sighed the old man before he stepped down the weathered stairs onto the dusty street. But he accepted, not in my time Lord, but in thine, shall thy will be done. Guard Hiram O'Bannon and jailer John Avis flanked him. Veteran Sheriff James Campbell followed several feet behind. Two walnut navy colt handles ominously rested above Campbell's thick belt. O'Bannon showed no sign of a weapon but everyone knew his buttoned coat concealed a capped and loaded revolver.

With the old man's defiant gray eyes becoming accustomed to the late morning sunlight he slowly squinted from left to right. Without hesitation his gaze passed over the coffin resting in the wagon. Time enough to examine that on the upcoming ride. Upon the old man's entry onto the street Virginia militia units suddenly scrambled about. Confusion momentarily reigned. Young infantrymen scampered to their assigned positions. Cavalrymen guided their skittish mounts into place. Fortunately most of the law-abiding citizens of Charles Town remained off the town streets as ordered.

"Captain, time to climb into the wagon," the guard said to the prisoner.

"I am ready, Mr. O'Bannon."

Before exiting the jail cell the guard pinioned the prisoner's arms. Several strands of course rope behind the old man's back constrained him at the elbows while permitting free use of the hands. Waiting for assistance into the wagon, the old man passed a note he had been tightly clutching to the guard.

"Thank you, sir," responded O'Bannon, slipping the note into his trousers pocket. One more keepsake from the old man, along with the personal bible he received minutes earlier.

Jailer Avis, who just accepted the old man's watch, set a worn porch chair to serve as a step behind the wagon. He supported the old man from behind while Sheriff Campbell and another passenger reached down and pulled the prisoner up. The old man strode three paces to the front of the cargo wagon's open bed. The prisoner pivoted and seated himself on the coffin. He allowed his eyes to gaze beyond the jail to the courthouse where the jury delivered its verdict less than five weeks ago. Although Virginia's court judged him guilty he consoled himself confident that the Almighty would deliver Virginia's sentence come judgment day.

General Taliaferro, commander of all troops, mounted his nervous white mare and signaled the Virginia Military Institute cadets to commence marching. O'Bannon sadly tipped his hat farewell to the old man he'd come to know intimately the last month and a half. When the two white draft horses lurched the wagon forward, the fourth passenger's right hand reached for the sideboard while he steadied the seated prisoner with his left.

"Thank you, Mr. Sadler," the old man politely acknowledged. He patted the top of the coffin and commented, "You make a fine piece of furniture. I always appreciate black walnut and am pleased you found choice lumber for my coffin. It is good though that you crate it in poplar," continued the old man, tapping the side of the shipping box with his foot.

"Why thank you, Mr. Brown, it is a pleasure to hear one's craftsmanship recognized. And if I may say so, you seem very calm today," the undertaker added.

"God is with me. I am ready to accept the task before me, yet it is difficult to part with friends, both longtime and newly made."

"You are a brave man, Captain Brown."

"Yes, my mother trained me so.

While Brown and Sadler casually conversed, the procession headed up South George Street. Civilians gradually appeared. Initially only faces peered around window curtains and through partially open doors but eventually curious citizens stood on porches with family members. Groups began congregating along the street. Several men displayed their finest Sunday apparel. More dressed in work clothes. Other bystanders wore rumpled clothing and reeked of alcohol from the previous night's revelry.

When the entourage turned east after a six block journey, Rebecca Hunter's farm appeared. Corn stubble covered a portion of her fields while pastureland comprised the remainder. The number of civilian onlookers near the field significantly diminished. Companies of infantry in loose order acted as scouts along the edge of the perimeter while nearby several men patrolled the area from horseback. An officer on a white horse cantered in one direction while his counterpart's black mount trotted in the other. Artillery pieces guarded both the interior and exterior grounds. Near the field's boundary the sentinels blocked the random accesses in the fence. Only military men and select civilian leaders entered the execution site.

In a soft but disgusted voice Brown uttered, "Why, are none but the military allowed in the inclosure? I am sorry citizens have been kept out."[1] Inside the fence the wagon rolled to a halt. Avis jumped three feet from the wagon onto the ground to assist the prisoner. Without the aid of steps, the old man's feet, protected only by red carpet slippers over white socks, hit the ground with a subtle thud. Almost fifteen hundred troops formed a hollow square around the gallows. Anticipation for the coming event intensified. The large military contingent stood ready to counteract the rumored attempts to disrupt the execution. Everyone remained on edge. The old man stood erect by the wagon, dressed in his black pants, vest, and frock coat which he wore the day federal troops under Colonel Robert E. Lee captured him over six weeks ago. He viewed the mountains with their summits barely touching a soft, lazy haze, and commented to Avis, "This is beautiful country. I've never taken the pleasure of observing it so."

Brown randomly perused the assembled troops, catching sight of a man directly to his front twenty yards beyond the scaffold. Positioned among the first row of the Virginia Military Institute cadets, and dressed in the same gray pants, red flannel shirt, and gray coat worn by the cadets, stood an elderly gentleman whose age exceeded the oldest cadet by forty years. Shaggy hair hung beneath his kepi. In a less serious setting the man would present a comical spectacle. Edmund Ruffin's and Brown's eyes met and locked. They glared at each other with identical stares of conviction, but conviction for utterly conflicting causes. Brown heard that Ruffin, a civilian but an honorary cadet for the day, would be permitted to witness the execution. Like Brown, only death would extinguish the passion burning within the fire eating soul of Mr. Ruffin. Brown's rapidly diminishing time forced him uncharacteristically to break eye contact with his adversary.

He focused upon arguably the most debonair individual assembled on the field. The man's trim moustache and black curly hair, accentuated by his dark features, created an image better suited for the stage than the militia. His physique transformed a rumpled gray uniform into well-fitting, tailored clothing. Unknown to Brown the man acting the part of a member of the Richmond Grays militia unit gained his admission twelve days earlier by purchasing pants from one member of the unit and a coat from another at the Richmond railway station. The locally popular young actor John Wilkes Booth refused to miss this historic event.

Brown turned his head to the left away from Booth and towards another militia group. This unit consisted of locals from Charles Town. The Botts Greys initially formed in the early daylight hours the morning following Brown's seizure of the armory. Though the insurrection took place eight miles to the east at Harpers Ferry, Brown's trial took place in the militia's hometown and county seat of Jefferson County. In sharp, crisp lines the Greys faced their leader, Captain Lawson Botts, who also had the distinction of representing the prosecution in the trial. Brown, for some unknown reason, studied the face of a young private, perhaps in his mid twenties, who peered rigidly ahead over the shoulders of those to his front. The soldier's youthful face exhibited signs of discipline that displaced the raw emotion visible on many others. Absent from the capture of Brown at the Ferry, the Botts Greys and John Yates Beall today experienced their first serious military activity. Their lines formed as practiced. No drill today. This was real. Adrenalin flowed throughout the unit. Beall's wide forehead and thickset jaw exemplified a man ready to perform his duty whether that obligation be mundane or dangerous. As Private Beall stood at attention, Brown turned to fulfill his destiny. The prisoner proudly ascended the scaffold steps followed by Avis and Sheriff Campbell. Standing on the platform Brown firmly shook each man's hands before he extended his forearms for his wrists to be bound.

"Thank you gentlemen for the kindness you have shown," Brown said sincerely.

"While it was our duty, it was also our pleasure," replied Avis.

Brown calmly stood several short paces before the gallows's trap door which beckoned him into eternity.

"Would you like a handkerchief to drop to signal me, sir?" questioned Campbell.

"No, I do not want it—but do not detain me any longer than is absolutely necessary."[2]

Standing high above the assembly the old man soberly absorbed his surroundings. With long, uncombed hair, six inches of ragged white beard, and penetrating steel gray eyes, Brown conjured the image of an Old Testament prophet about to pass judgment upon the multitude of sinners gathered below. His black slouch hat accompanied him hundreds of miles but would not travel his final few steps. Sheriff Campbell removed the hat, tossed it on the platform, and dropped a white hood over Brown's head. The condemned felt the course noose tighten around his neck beneath his beard. Two feet of slackened rope looped against his shoulder. Ironically, he realized he stood with his back to the north. Why should he not die with his face, though covered, toward his enemy?

"We need to move ahead over the door, sir."

"Please assist me, Mr. Avis, for I do not want to fall."

Commands to march and to countermarch reverberated across the field while unit commanders directed men into final position. All the while impatient for the door to drop the prisoner stood shrouded in the darkness of the hood with the noose snuggly fitting around his neck. From below Ruffin imagined he saw Brown's leg shaking but realized the balmy breeze floated the victim's baggy trousers to and fro. Although Ruffin respected Brown's courage he could not resist cynically mumbling, "Clothed like a field hand without even a cravat. Dresses like niggers, lives with niggers, fights beside niggers. Deserves to die like a nigger."

Booth stood mesmerized by the old man's composure. Momentarily he observed an excellent theatrical performance rather than a real life drama.

Opposite the Richmond Grays, Private Beall analyzed the scene, the justice about to be served, and the punishment demanded by an orderly society.

"Allsedy, sheriff," sounded a voice from below.

Campbell leaned over the rail, cocked his head, held his hand by his ear, and waited for General Taliaferro to repeat himself.

"All is ready Sheriff Campbell! The men are in position!" he shouted.

The sheriff hurriedly descended the step to assume his role of executioner, methodically grasped the razor sharp ax with both hands, raised it over his head, and glanced above at the trap door held in place by two hinges on one side and supported by the rope on the other. In one quick motion he severed the rope. The wooden door banged against the scaffold frame. Two legs dropped twenty-four inches into empty space before jerking to a stop. Avis heard the nauseating crack and witnessed Brown's elbows fling his forearms with clenched fists against his chest. Arms spasmodically lowered, dangling legs went limp, and labored breathing mercifully ceased.

Only the occasional whinny of the general's high-strung horse broke the chilling silence. The hooded body swayed gently in the soft breeze. The VMI Commandant's voice boomed out, "So perish all such enemies of Virginia! All such enemies of the Union! All such foes of the human race"[3]

The suspended body hung flaccidly for thirty-seven minutes before a staff of surgeons declared John Brown officially dead and allowed his remains to be lowered. Mr. Sadler respectfully positioned the body in the walnut coffin and secured the lid. He and Avis slid the shipping crate from the wagon.

Troops reformed for the return march. The VMI Cadets received the assignment to guard the wagon. Edmund Ruffin eagerly anticipated the opportunity to provide inquisitive citizens with his eyewitness account of the hanging. He would enjoy describing Virginia's retribution for meddlesome abolitionists. If the Yankees respected the law and the *Constitution,* which Ruffin seriously doubted, today's action might in the least keep them out of Virginia's affairs. Tomorrow he would depart for the daylong train journey to his southeastern Virginia plantation to repeat the story for new audiences. The cadets patiently stood waiting for the Richmond Grays to form.

The Grays served as the vanguard to clear the way for delivery of Brown's body to the Charles Town train station where his remains would be shipped to his widow waiting in Harpers Ferry. John Wilkes Booth fell in, impatient to leave the execution site. Although he detested all that Brown represented, watching the old man's hooded head abruptly yank to a stop unnerved the actor. Booth craved several glasses of strong bourbon to calm his nerves and obliterate the ghastly spectacle which drained the color from his face. He also needed time to refresh and change into proper apparel for tonight's social gatherings.

Sadler hammered the final nail into the shipping crate, signaling the Botts Greys to fall into formation at the rear of the procession. Duty was duty even in choking dust at the rear of the line. The sun shone from the western sky. Rumors of violence appeared unfounded. Hopefully John Brown's raid would soon shrink into an insignificant footnote in Virginia history. The *Constitution* created a law-abiding society with consequences for treasonous acts like those committed by the mentally unbalanced northerner. Beall yearned to retrieve his horse at the conclusion of today's responsibilities so that he could depart and indulge in a night's rest in the comfort of his own bed. Tomorrow he faced numerous postponed tasks which accumulated during the interruptions of the past month and a half.

While the procession marched to town Hiram O'Bannon sat outside the jail and reminisced of his time with the old man. The deed should be well over. He remembered he had yet to read the message Brown handed him. He pulled the paper from his trousers pocket and glanced over the words. Reading them again more slowly an unsettling feeling gnawed into his gut. Fearing it to be prophesy, praying it was not, O'Bannon reread the words once more.

"I John Brown am now quite certain that the crimes of this guilty land will never be purged away, but with Blood. I had as I now think vainly flattered myself that without very much bloodshed it might be accomplished."[4]

2 – RETURN TO NORMALCY

"Company halt!" Captain Lawson Botts shouted above the hoarse coughs of his men who attempted to clear their throats of the choking dust that engulfed them during their return march. A layer of fine, reddish-brown dirt coated everyone and everything. The grime covering weapons, clothes, and faces eliminated any designation of rank. John Beall wiped his face with his gloved hand. Streaks of fair-complexioned skin appeared. A sharp jab in his ribs interrupted the cleanup.

A lanky private in a loose fitting militia uniform impatiently asked, "Johnny, you think they'll turn us loose soon or we gonna hafta stand here the rest of the day?"

"Well Henry," Beall replied, "Captain Botts did inform us this morning of rumors of violence before, during, or after the execution. I suspect we'll be needed a while longer. In several hours Brown's body should be on the way to the Ferry. Then we'll probably be released from duty."

"Don't know why the wait Johnny; no trouble so far. A man would be fool to take on a thousand armed men, especially men ready to eliminate any more uninvited abolitionists. Besides I've had my fill of soldierun. Fall in! Fall out! Left face! About face! And I always end up where I started. I've had enough to last me a lifetime."

Beall quickly admonished his fellow private. "Henry, a treasonous though deranged old man invaded Virginia with the sole purpose of inflicting rebellion. It is and always remains our responsibility to take up arms, not as the aggressor mind you, but as the protector of our homeland. If we do not take this responsibility seriously, October's incident shall be repeated. But I must say, besides punishing the intruder today, we issued a message to the rest of the

Union that Virginia shall uphold her sovereign laws and those of the *Constitution*."

"My Johnny, you being such a quiet fella I thought you was a lawyer for a minute there."

"A life time ago, Henry."

Ignoring the inquisitive stare from his younger friend, Beall stiffened his posture before the Botts Greys marched down a side street. The unit separated from the main body and halted on Jefferson Street where Captain Botts addressed the unit. "Gentlemen, as your commander and on behalf of the Commonwealth of Virginia, I wish to thank you for your exemplary service not only today but since our sudden formation that memorable Monday seven weeks past. As stated earlier today, we were greatly concerned with rumors of interference from outsiders. It appears those rumors are either false or the charlatans who planned such activity are now in hiding, and have thus avoided the obvious fate. While threats exist, several of the more experienced units shall remain. The Botts Greys are now released until our next call to duty."

"Henry, you have your wish," chided Beall.

"Time to celebrate, Johnny. Good times in ol' Charles Town tonight. Let's head on over to the Jefferson House while there's still room," Henry said before he paused. "Sorry John. Forgot, you're not a drinking man."

"Henry, a man just lost his life. How can this be a time to celebrate?"

"That man was a criminal of the worst kind. I'm celebratin justice with most of the men in uniform, and many more that ain't. It'll be a good finish to a good day."

"Good day, Henry," John responded sarcastically. Bidding his companion farewell, he walked away desiring a quiet finish to a somber day.

He heard Henry mutter, "Some people a man will never figure out and Johnny Beall you're one of them."

At half past three John rode from the stable. Although the day's temperatures had been mild, in less than an hour the sun would disappear. A late autumn chill now filled the air but at a steady pace horse and rider would reach Walnut Grove by dark. His favorite mount, Jenny, trotted east down Main Street. He thought less of the day's events and more of the accumulated farm work especially with winter descending upon northern Virginia. The hands should have been going about their daily routine but they required someone to think for them whenever something irregular occurred, which usually happened several times a day. Most of his Negroes lived their entire lives on Walnut Grove although the Beall's inherited some from other estates. John also purchased a few. Most slave owners considered John and his mother, Janet, benevolent masters, in part because John's physical presence maintained daily productivity and all but eliminated harsh physical punishment.

When he rode past Jesse Blockly's cobbler shop John remembered that several pairs of shoes for his field hands were being repaired. No time to stop today. At the edge of town he passed the beef and hog broker's establishment, Redman & Gibson. Quantity and price usually had been agreed upon by the end of November. Not this year, compliments of Mr. Brown. Instinctively Jenny turned north onto Flowing Springs Road. She trotted past the field to the left which for fifty years periodically transformed into the race track. While not one to wager, John thrilled at the excitement of well-bred horses competing against one another. Perhaps sensing her owner's thoughts, the black mare's gait increased. "You think you're a race horse, girl! How quickly can we reach the mill?" After John tapped his heels into her flanks she galloped hard for five minutes.

He pulled her into a trot to cool down for the final ten minutes. Despite bare trees and a colorless landscape the rolling countryside always offered a sight to behold contrasted against the brilliant sunset. The road soon wove through Walnut Grove fields and orchards. Pruning fruit trees could begin anytime, with his supervision of course. To the west lay the original tract of land handed down from John's maternal grandfather. The crisp air and clear skies completely filled the western horizon with intense crimson hues above the drab fields. He gently tugged the reins, slowing Jenny's trot to a walk. He turned his head for one more view of God's brilliant colors about to disappear behind the western mountains. He guided Jenny down the farm lane and followed his vanishing shadow in the diminishing daylight. To his left beyond the dormant peach trees lay vacant vegetable fields while to his right only apple and pear trees dotted the countryside. Farther down the rolling slope to his left, about twenty-five yards off the lane, rested a two-story white structure, his only home since shortly after birth. A bundled figure inside the barn stood with a glowing lantern. He smiled at the only servant whom he permitted to handle the reins of a freshly ridden horse. Timothy showed the same compassion in preparing a horse for the stall at day's end that a mother displayed in lovingly preparing her child for bed.

"Massa John, I'm very glad you're back afore it gets too dark."

"I am too. I trust you'll feed her, water her, and wipe her down. Even the best livery in town doesn't give her the care you do. Good night, Timothy."

"Night, suh."

When John walked through the door his siblings and mother swarmed to greet him. His sister Mary, six years his senior, and his fifty-five year old mother, Janet, simultaneously greeted him with hugs. Twenty year old Annie, seventeen year old Beth, and thirteen year old Janie appeared next. Fifteen year old Will ran through the doorway shouting an array of questions.

Janet Beall immediately took control. "William, we are relieved your brother returns safely home but allow him to change out of that dirty uniform which he has worn, I am sure proudly, for the past week. During dinner all appropriate questions may be answered."

"But Mother?"

John interceded with a smile, "Will, you must learn that although the master operates the farm the mistress runs the household. I'll be down in a matter of minutes."

A short time later, refreshed but hungry, he strode down the steps. Why some men preferred the company in taverns to that of their own families far exceeded John's comprehension. He seated himself in the vacant seat at the head of the dining room table with Mary to his left where she sat even when Father lived. Annie filled the seat which John vacated with the passing. Beth and Janie faced each other across the middle of the table. Will, the only sibling still assigned to sit by his mother, excitedly asked, "Now Johnny! Tell us about the hanging of old man Brown!"

"William! The blessing first!" Mother admonished.

"Sorry Mother," Will apologized. He immediately turned to his brother and requested, "Go ahead with the blessing, Johnny," while he thought to himself, and keep it short.

Following the brief prayer, John though famished, politely responded to general inquiries from Mother in between bites of pickled tongue, fresh bread, cheese, and cinnamon apples. Hunger pangs vanished. Janet hesitantly nodded to her youngest son to begin the inquisition.

"Did you hear his neck snap when the door dropped? Did his legs shake?"

"William!"

"Mother, I do want to describe what happened," John said, smiling to her. He looked directly at his younger brother and in a rebuking tone added, "Though without the gruesome details for the ladies, Will."

John reviewed the events to his captive audience. "The day began somewhat like the Fourth of July might with scores of men in uniform filling the street. But I heard no jovial laughing or loud voices even before the units assembled. Everyone remained alert with the expectation of some sort of attempt to free the prisoner prior to his execution. Fear also existed, for whatever reason, that violent reprisals might be taken against Charles Town. Fortunately neither occurred. It seemed we accompanied the carriage of a deceased to the graveyard following a funeral in our journey to the scaffold. Visualize the procession with the condemned sitting on his own coffin, calmly conversing with the undertaker and guards. Understand no clergy attended. I understand Mr. Brown refused all offers because they were Virginians. I sat at Grandfather Yates's bedside vigil eight years ago before his spirit departed as I did with Father four years ago. The reverend's soothing words comforted us during their passings. I would assume John Brown would have welcomed such reassurance."

He continued. "We accept we are all sinners. I believe God showers all mankind with unfathomable mercy. Yet I question how John Brown, by his own admission of guilt in planning and committing these terrible crimes, can be a Christian? The physical sight of his execution was ghastly. Moral and spiritual concerns are complex. Does his family struggle with similar feelings? I pray that I never be involved with another execution. I am sorry I have little more to share. Tomorrow I must rise early and determine which tasks need immediate attention." With that John excused himself to imbibe in some much needed sleep.

Saturday's sun rose and set. Following a full country breakfast on Sunday the Bealls departed for worship services in Charles Town. Janet, with Mary handling the reins, sat on the covered carriage's front seat while the other three girls occupied the rear. A pair of brown draft horses pulled the carriage. John, mounted on Jenny, and Will, on his spirited pony, trotted along each side. Cold air vaporized the breath spewing from the chattering women. Bright sunshine and the lack of wind provided a pleasant first Sunday in December.

Feigning total seriousness Mary asked, "Johnny, do you think Sue Ellen O'Brien will swoon over you again for most of the service?"

"I would hope, Mary, that more reverent thoughts would fill your mind during worship than playing match maker for me," John curtly replied.

Ignoring his tone she continued. "At your age, Brother, a man should think about settling into a family life. You don't drink or spend late nights discussing politics in taverns with the so-called informed men that you know.

Besides Sue Ellen is attractive, intelligent, and comes from a family residing in Jefferson County for three generations. Folks say her great-grandfather surveyed the county with George Washington. If your older sister may be so bold, what is there not to like about the girl?"

"The girl aside, I am responsible for the operation of one of the finest farms in the area. The duties I perform on four hundred acres of orchards and fields, not to mention the livestock, limit my socializing with males, and females. Besides, Sue Ellen is, well, Sue Ellen." John lightly dug his boots into Jenny's sides attempting to extricate himself from the inquisition.

Sensing her son's irritation with his older sister's intrusion into his private life, Janet ended the dialogue, loudly saying, "John Yates Beall, when the right woman enters your life you will happily add her to the list of your overwhelming number of responsibilities." Feminine giggles broke the tension. Small talk amongst the women never ceased the remainder of the journey while John chose to ride silently a distance ahead, deep in thought.

Will secured the horses at the rail while John helped the ladies from the carriage. Zion Episcopal Church became one of the few distractions away from the farm which John allowed himself to engage. The family proceeded over the walkway which passed through the gate of the waist-high brick wall which surrounded the church grounds and cemetery. The year following Father's death John's activities at the church noticeably increased. He supervised construction of the masonry wall while strengthening his commitment to his congregation and satisfying his need to honor his father's memory.

When they neared the steps to the entrance a voice called from behind.

John turned to face William Redman. "Morning, Bill. You appear to have something of consequence to tell me."

"You are a perceptive man, John Beall. You left immediately after Captain Botts dismissed us Friday afternoon. I headed over to the tavern with several of the boys where word spread that George Turner's house and barns burned about noon while everyone was absorbed with the hanging. Assume you hadn't heard."

"No Bill, I haven't. Thanks for informing me. We'll talk later, my friend. Better get inside before the service begins. Don't want to embarrass Mother."

The Beall family advanced down the center aisle to their designated pew, smiling silent greetings to longtime friends and neighbors. Many of Jefferson County's socially elite attended the church including ancestors of George Washington. To their left and right, round fluted pillars supported the long balconies where Negroes observed the service.

During worship John's mind traveled back to Friday. George Turner had been one of the four civilians killed during John Brown's insurrection at Harpers Ferry. Was the fire on his estate accidental, or could it have been arson? Would Turner's Negroes intentionally commit such an act? Or could the fire be just a careless accident? Many questions regarding Brown's influence in the area remained unanswered. John's attention reverted to the conclusion of Reverend Charles Ambler's sermon.

"The entire Union's attention centered upon Jefferson County these past several weeks. Those living outside of Virginia already turn their attentions to concerns nearer their homes. Soon the events at Harpers Ferry become a distant memory to those people, but whenever our citizens travel near the arsenal at the Ferry, or encounter those brave men who the intruders held hostage, memories will revive. Whenever one travels past Rebecca Hunter's field unpleasant images will return. As Christians, we struggle as we study worldly events within a spiritual context. As your pastor I must remind you that our society survives because we adhere to the law. Just as Moses gave the *Ten Commandments* to the Israelites to obey, our founding fathers gave us the *Constitution* to obey. Even the New Testament, which speaks of love and forgiveness, references obedience and respect for authority. I close now, my people, with a reading from the New Testament Book of First Peter, chapter two, verses 13-15. '*Submit yourselves to every ordinance of man for the Lord's sake; whether it be to the king as supreme; or unto governors, or unto them that are sent by him for the punishment of evildoers, and for the praise of them that do well. For so is the will of God, that with well doing ye may put to silence the ignorance of foolish men.*' Amen."

A soft smile touched John's face before he stood for the closing hymn. Through adherence to man's law in unison with God's law, justice would prevail as always. The past seven weeks demonstrated evil men challenge the law, but if leaders such as Governor Wise, and common men such as John Beall responded to duty's call, the Virginia which he loved and honored would always triumph over lawless aggressors.

3 – NEW YEARS DAY, 1860

Another decade vanished with the arrival of 1860. Since the turn of the century social visits to friends and neighbors transformed New Years Day into one of America's most celebrated holidays. Jefferson County residents anticipated this holiday season since the conclusion of the John Brown episode. While five of Brown's followers were at large, two remained in the Jefferson County Jail awaiting their leader's fate. The December executions of Brown and five of his raiders had removed Charles Town from the national spotlight.

The Beall's New Years Day celebration would end as it had the past eight years, at Judge Lucas's Rion Hall. Before traveling there the Bealls partook in a celebration unique to their clan. Twenty-five years ago George and Janet Beall welcomed John Yates Beall into the world on January 1. John enjoyed the attention he received whenever a new year arrived although the boyish excitement for one's birthday long since disappeared. Janet meanwhile appreciated the opportunity to silently reminisce. Life seemed simpler that first day when she and George held John, with little Hezekiah and Mary at their sides. The Union was stronger too. Of course Andy Jackson was the president also. No president since managed to be elected for two terms. Folks say you can't stop progress. At her age, Janet sometimes wondered if better progress might be made going back rather than trudging forward. Enough reminiscing. "Time to depart for the Lucases. Who's going?" queried the Beall matriarch, still in control of her maturing family.

"I'm not going this year, Mother," Mary replied. Although traditionally on New Years Day unmarried women respectably made advances toward unattached men, John's single older sister chose to remain at home with Beth and

Janie, both of whom weren't feeling well. At age thirty, and not yet spoken for, Mary graciously acknowledged younger women more readily enticed the bachelors. Annie, on the other hand reached a delightful age to pursue an eligible bachelor. Will nervously looked forward to his first New Years experience, although ten years would pass before he, as a male, would be viewed as eligible. Janet always enjoyed the annual Lucas News Years gathering. And John had seen little of the judge's son, Dan, since they roomed together at the University of Virginia six years ago. Only the thought of Sue Ellen O'Brien's advances dampened John's spirits.

"Happy New Years Day, Missy Beall," greeted Timothy, standing by the hitched carriage waiting by the porch. Janet responded with a smile to the elderly servant, as John helped her into the rear seat while Will assisted Annie. Thirty-five minutes later the foursome turned off the Harpers Ferry turnpike onto the long lane which terminated at the Lucas Residence.

Rion Hall, constructed forty years earlier, still drew the envy of property owners throughout the county. Dormant ornamental cherry trees lined each side of the steep hundred yard pathway leading up to the stately two-story brick mansion. In four months the tree's pink petals again would gracefully welcome visitors. Several bare magnolias near the house would also explode with their fragrant brilliance to erase memories of another bland winter landscape. John, the prudent farmer, never justified trees which flowered but that did not bear fruit. During spring and summer an array of perennial flowers and dazzling shrubs complemented the home. Rion Hall, even shrouded by December's drab sky, and unadorned without colorful foliage, sat majestically as an architectural jewel upon the hilltop crown. Bright lights sparkled through the large first floor windows while candles glistened from the second floor glass. Several male servants stood ready to welcome visitors and escort guests inside. Others carefully folded the heavy woolen carriage blankets, stored them on the seats, and parked the vehicles. When the foursome stepped down and stretched, they observed female servants scurrying across the narrow porch below the upper balcony which connected the detached brick kitchen to the left of the main house. The aroma of steaming platters of assorted meats and dishes of hot food filled the air while kitchen servants disappeared into the rear of the mansion.

The guests ascended the steps to the front porch. A massive oak door with a detailed carving of a pineapple hospitably invited visitors to enter. The beveled sunburst transom above the door and two clear sidelites brightly illuminated the entry way. Neither too early nor too late the Bealls timed their arrival as expected of well-bred people. The hearty laughter of men, the chatter of women, and the giggles from teenage girls, blended with the scents of delicious foods which suppressed the stench of tobacco. The amalgamation rushed out with the gust of warm air when the door opened.

Virginia Lucas, the youngest daughter of the judge and his deceased wife, stood in the center of the impressive entry hall and greeted her guests. She smiled as she welcomed each new arrival. "Janet Beall, it's always so good to see you. You appear healthy as ever. Annie, are we searching for a beau today? John Beall, I so miss your visits since you left school and Daniel began practicing in Richmond. I do believe a good number of ladies await your arrival, Johnny." She then greeted Will. "Enjoy the evening. Your time shall arrive soon enough." Turning her head to the creak of the door's opening, Virginia concluded her welcome to the Bealls. "You know your way to the dining room. John, as you hear, the men congregate in the parlor. Janet, we shall visit later. Everyone have a pleasant celebration."

Each of the Bealls anticipated their next destination. Before several steps could be taken though, John cringed from the sound of a familiar feminine voice. "Why Mrs. Beall, how delightful to see you this evening. I pray the new year is healthy and prosperous for all of Virginia, especially Jefferson County. I must say it is a relief to ring out 1859, don't you agree?"

"Yes, Sue Ellen, I suspect everyone does," Janet politely answered.

Terminating her conversation with Janet, the young woman turned her attention briefly to Annie. "My, Miss Annie Beall, you are stunning tonight. Who's the lucky man?"

Without waiting for an answer or slowing to make eye contact with the youngest Beall she superficially commented, "My Will, you have grown." Uninhibited she added, "Some day you will become an appealing eligible bachelor like your brother." Sue Ellen O'Brien's tantalizing green eyes looked directly into the warm blue eyes of John Beall. He paused only because courtesy demanded such from a well-mannered gentleman.

John absorbed the approaching beauty. Auburn hair, gathered within the traditional net, touched the back of her bare neck. A narrow face accentuated her high cheek bones. A thin nose sculptured her attractive face. Lips parted to reveal pearly white teeth, making her sensuous smile all the more inviting. An emerald necklace and sizzling green jewels in her dangling earrings contrasted with her snow white skin while complimenting her lively eyes. Her striped amber and green satin dress followed the contours of her youthful figure from her exposed shoulders down to her waist before gracefully flowing to the floor. Billowing full length sleeves trimmed with white lace added a few years of sophistication to the twenty year old belle. While John failed to be enticed by the low yet tasteful neckline, Will couldn't refrain from staring at the fleshy cleavage. John knew that if a man only sought beauty this woman would be highly coveted but he craved more. And the aggressive comment she just uttered repelled rather than attracted him.

Politely nodding, John offered in a highly formal tone, "Good evening, Miss O'Brien. As usual you present yourself well. It is good to see you again. If you will be so kind as to excuse me, gentlemen patiently await my presence." With that he escaped her alluring gaze.

Janet gravitated to mature feminine companionship. Though Sue Ellen's age, Annie quickly surrounded herself with several longtime friends with whom she soon shared the latest gossip. Will chose to satisfy his young appetite. He surveyed the wide variety of eatables spread across the large dining room table and adjacent buffet. He bypassed the turtle soup but carefully selected roasted turkey with cranberry sauce, which he favored over boiled turkey with celery sauce. Pickled beets and winter squash covered more of his plate. A generous slice of ham and a ladle of baked apples covered the last visible design at the edge of the ornate china. One of his favorites, smoked tongue, added to the feast. Curried veal might initiate a second trip. The plum pudding certainly would. With surprising dexterity, especially with silverware in hand, he grasped a cup of champagne punch to wash everything down. To his relief he spied an empty chair near the far wall by several lads he knew well. A man could not concentrate on a meal such as this and share polite conversation with a girl.

While Will devoured the contents of his plate John followed the scent of cigar smoke to the rear parlor where groups of men clustered discussing the politics of the day. He moved forward until he spied Daniel Lucas in the group nearest the parlor opening. John extended his hand but Dan ignored it, stepped forward, and wrapped his arms around his former classmate. Everyone present witnessed the bond shared between the two men.

"Johnny, you do look well. What has it been, summer I believe, since we last met? I really planned to return sooner but the practice keeps me in Richmond. Have any ladies laid claim to you yet?"

"Dan, it was August, and no to your other question. Furthermore, at this point I have no one in whom I have an interest."

"My apologies," he answered with a grin. "I incorrectly concluded you share the same interest in Sue Ellen O'Brien which she obviously possesses for you. She certainly takes advantage of this holiday's tradition to make her intentions known."

"If there is one woman in this county who does not need New Years Day to make her intentions known it is Miss O'Brien," John rebutted. "Whenever I am in the same room as that woman a set of dark green eyes immediately cast upon me." Both men glanced through the parlor entryway into the spacious hall where Sue Ellen O'Brien's gaze rested John's case. "With that discussion concluded, I am sure we can find a topic of mutual interest."

Dan smoothly transitioned into a less delicate subject. "Has your farm been productive this year? My readings indicate that even with the war in Europe over, grain prices remain strong. You of course do not raise cotton, but its continued high price does increase the value of your Negroes. All commodities should continue to do well. Do you concur?"

Relieved to discuss anything beyond Miss O'Brien, John eagerly replied. "As you know, much of our produce remains in the valley, although recent construction of the railways allows me to ship produce to cities throughout Virginia and also up north. More of the grain fields deeper south are converting to cotton. Those of us producing grain should benefit. Simple economics—supply versus demand."

"You've always believed in planting a variety of crops. Do you continue committed to the conservative approach?"

"Dan, Grandfather Yates, being of English descent, adhered to conventional practices. Father descended from Scotch ancestors and also maintained a traditional philosophy. Our agricultural community respected both men. Except for my three years in Charlotte studying law, I developed my principles under their tutelage. Of course I'm committed to their conservative approach. Besides planting grain, and producing vegetables and fruit, I also raise hogs and beef for meat, sheep for wool, and harvest lumber from the wooded acreage. We're self-sufficient and therefore we weather most economic crises. I enjoy the successes farming brings even without the immense wealth which the legal profession would have provided," he jested with his good-natured smile.

Becoming serious, Dan queried, "Why did you really leave the university after three years of studying law? One more year," the attorney added while attempting to maintain a stoic expression, "and you could have entered the profession leading to instant wealth."

"Well friend, between you and I," John began, lowering his voice and moving closer to his former college roommate, "I respect the law tremendously, as did Grandfather Yates and Father. The elder of the two belonged to the Whig party after the demise of the Federalists while as you remember Father supported the Democrats ever since Andy Jackson's election. Both men believed the *Constitution* established the foundation for each of their respective parties. On rare occasions, heated discussion erupted amongst them upon which each cited the *Constitution* with the reverence of a preacher quoting scripture on Sunday morning. When the debate finally concluded the *Constitution* had been shredded by each man's opinions. I adamantly believe the document served us well these past seventy years. I studied it diligently for three years. I failed to wholeheartedly visualize a lifelong occupation which entailed dissecting the text which I so greatly respect, and in some instances interpret it with bias for the benefit of a client. But please, my good friend, do not take offence. I have nothing but respect for you as a man. You are the first person, and most likely the last, who receives an answer to the question just posed. I apologize for the dissertation. My rambling responses often confuse rather than clarify."

Dan placed his hands firmly on the other's shoulders and stared directly into his eyes. "Johnny, when friends posess mutual respect for each other, little can be said or done to tarnish the relationship. Now come, let me introduce you to a gentleman with whom you are not yet acquainted." Placing a hand on his friend's back, the barrister guided John over to three men engaged in pleasant conversation.

"Mr. Othello Rawson, permit me to introduce Mr. John Beall, an intimate friend from Charles Town, and also my roommate during the several years we attended the University of Virginia. Mr. Beall farms over four hundred acres of the most productive land in Jefferson County." Nodding toward Othello Rawson, Dan continued, "Mr. Rawson is highly recognized as a widely acclaimed attorney in Richmond. His popularity could lead to public office within our state government or to even to higher office in Washington." Both men momentarily sized up each other. Rawson clothed himself in colorful maroon and beige striped trousers and wore an unbuttoned, matching jacket over an orange vest which exposed a ruffled white shirt. A blue cravat around his neck completed his wardrobe. Though portly, Rawson's thick neck and broad shoulders hinted of a man with intimidating physical strength. His square jaw with stylish goatee, classic Roman nose, piercing blue eyes, and fiery red hair above his broad forehead, seemed to confirm this man could hold his own verbally against anyone and physically against most.

Before Dan acknowledged the remaining gentlemen, Othello interjected, "If requested, Mr. Lucas, I would be willing to serve our commonwealth in whatever capacity our fine citizens desire of me. As for a political future at the national level, a Virginian should set his eyes farther south than Washington."

The brash innuendo drew immediate attention from the audience. Lucas, with no desire to inhibit Rawson, acknowledged the other two familiar faces. "John, you're acquainted with Jacob Wilson, and you've developed an extended relationship with Hiram Keller.

"Mr. Wilson, Hiram, good to have the opportunity to benefit from your company again." Looking toward the new acquaintance, he commenced a cross examination by firmly asking, "Mr. Rawson, could you please clarify your statement for the benefit of all I assume?"

Othello Rawson spoke collectively to his captive audience but communicated in a mesmerizing manner in which

Lucas, Beall, Keller, and Wilson each believed the aspiring politician individually addressed him. “Gentlemen, as recently evidenced in the very county which we stand, northern abolitionists blatantly resorted to violence as a means of forcing not only their oppressive, but also their illegal designs upon us. South Carolina resisted their aggressive behavior in the past and shall in the future. The radical Yankee attitude only serves to fuse the deep south. Whereas thirty years ago South Carolina stood alone, today likeminded brothers surround her. During that so-called Nullification Crisis even the palmetto state’s southern neighbors politically distanced themselves from her. Mr. Jackson, our southern slaveholding president, threatened the use of force to terminate the standoff. Before the Carolinians responded to counteract federal aggression both parties saved face by reaching a subtle compromise. King Andrew claimed victory. South Carolina wisely realized the issue would be resolved in time but only after she built alliances. Today the economic lifeblood of the Union and the world, cotton, thrives from the Atlantic coast to Mexico. Travel throughout the lower south. The entire population astutely recognizes that our economy shall function more efficiently without northern interference.”

When Rawson paused to catch his breathe and mop the perspiration from his reddened brow, Hiram Keller grasped the opportunity to speak. Befitting his occupation as the area’s largest grain broker, dressed conservatively in solid brown trousers and coat, with a green vest and white shirt, he displayed a black and yellow plaid cravat around his neck. His slight five-foot-seven frame, trim moustache, receding hairline, and narrow bespectacled face gave all the impression of a man who derived success solely through the use of his mind. “Mr. Rawson, you harbor strong opinions. How do you propose to eliminate northern interference?”

“Sir, I shall not end northern aggression. One man alone, or even one state standing alone as South Carolina discovered, lacks the strength to remove the threat. Not I, my good man, but we,” he said as he paused to accentuate ‘we’ before continuing. "We, all honorable southerners, shall band together to form a republic of our own, reclaiming the intended government our forefathers so nobly entrusted to us."

The gracious host looked to the silent member of the group, a broad-shouldered man who towered over the others. The man Dan faced might even physically intimidate Othello Rawson. His ruddy completion, muscular body, and full head of coal black hair implied this young man could earn a living with his body if necessary. Although appropriately attired for the annual Lucas New Year's Day reception, he gave the impression of one more relaxed in less formal apparel in a more casual setting. Jacob Wilson operated the family's carriage shop in Harpers Ferry since his father's death in late 1857. Wilson cautiously made decisions, but once he committed never looked back. Before other area businesses successfully developed the practice, he rented surplus Negroes from local planters for fabrication laborers. Though never reluctant to physically instruct his workers, he learned to distance himself from manual tasks. If the business owner wished to attract a lady from the social circle from which he sought acceptance he must permit his newly hired foreman to direct the men.

"Mr. Rawson," Wilson bluntly asked, "what shall become of Virginia and the Union?"

"Son, I'm talking about a new southern union, one based on states rights. Without the wealth of cotton the Yankee states, even if they remain together, are destined to become a third rate economic power. Virginia either cowers and accepts a role as a southern member of a struggling new abolitionist northern confederation, or selects her rightful place of influence as the northern boundary for a recreated union operating within the constitutional framework our Virginia forefathers envisioned."

Wilson scrutinized the remark, and after a brief silence responded in a simplistic tone. "If the options are clear, Mr. Rawson, then Virginia's allegiance must be with the cotton states."

"Call me Othello, my boy," Rawson responded with a hearty laugh, already assuming he obtained one convert.

John garnered respect as a man who seldom spoke but whose words always deserved attention. The flushed face highlighting his penetrating blue eyes foretold Mr. Othello Rawson he needed to prepare for strong opposition to his vision. "Mr. Rawson, with your residence one hundred and fifty miles to the south, you cannot appreciate the tranquility which again descends upon Jefferson County since John Brown's execution."

"And Mr. Beall, you sir, being somewhat isolated from the opinion of mainstream Virginia, do not realize the fear that insane old man spread throughout our commonwealth and to our neighbors farther south. How much more blood must be shed before you unionists come to your senses?"

Beall sharply retorted, "I sir am a Virginian, not a unionist."

"But sir, I am a unionist," interrupted the grain dealer.

Rawson took an intimidating step toward the slight man. "Before the arrival of Mr. Beall you mentioned you hailed from Pennsylvania, Keller. How careless of me not to realize your sentiments would be with the abolitionists!"

Though Rawson dwarfed Keller the broker angrily responded, "Only a narrow minded fire-eater would consider them one in the same"

Dan enjoyed lively discussion but heated tempers now displaced civil debate. "Gentleman, we all respect men who show passion for their beliefs, but let all of us remember we are each Virginians holding the commonwealth's best interest close to our heart."

Tension evacuated from John's body, supplanted by calmness. If he could diffuse the existing emotion he could prevent the incident from escalating into an embarrassment for the Lucas family. "Gentlemen, as usual Dan is the perfect host. Let us continue but let us remain civil." Othello Rawson retreated a step and displayed a more relaxed posture. The redness left Hiram Keller's cheeks. Jacob Wilson retained his deadpan expression.

Dan Lucas breathed a huge sigh of relief. Attempting to maintain spirited but controlled conversation he asked no one in particular, "What is the outlook for the coming presidential canvas?"

Othello Rawson, transitioning to the role of diplomat, responded first. "Let us pray that most of the Union possesses the intelligence of Virginians, and leaves the Black Republican Seward in New York." All four listeners nodded with smiles of agreement more in recognition for the left handed apology to Keller rather than the statement's actual content.

Keller, a recognized local member of the Whig party, congenially added, "The Whig party is sadly all but dead. Consistent national leadership most always has been lacking. Henry Clay, God rest his soul, could have been a two-term president but never even got elected for one term. Our only two elected Whig presidents died before completing their first terms," continued Keller, referring to William Henry Harrison and Zachary Taylor. "General Scott, like Clay, proved a case of the right man at the wrong place, at the wrong time. Daniel Webster never could decide if he was a Democrat or Whig." Damn it, thought Keller after the last statement. He was thankful his careless mention of a known abolitionist had not offended Rawson. Turning to John he commented, "I hear, Mr. Beall, that your namesake, John Bell of Tennessee, might return to the Whigs for one last hurrah."

"Obviously you fellas keep better informed than I," chimed in Jacob Wilson. "With the visitors that pass through the Ferry I hear an assortment of names." Nodding to Rawson, he continued, "No one is brave enough, or Othello, should I say foolish enough to mention Seward's name or any Republican's. The Democracy bandies about names such as Robert Toombs and Howell Cobb of Georgia, Jeff Davis of Mississippi, and of course that brilliant architect of the Kansas-Nebraska Act, Stephen Douglas." The carriage shop owner uncharacteristically spoke with contempt and rolled his eyes when he uttered Douglas's name.

"Johnny, sometimes you persist in keeping your thoughts to yourself. I'm not just referring to affairs of the heart, my friend," Dan jested. "Who do expect to be elected?"

Beall paused, took a deep breath, and cast a smirk toward his friend which communicated he would settle a score with him later. "Powerful men within each party lock horns fighting for the top prize. When the dust settles the man left standing may not become the best leader, or the most electable. He might have called in political favors or promised influential government positions in exchange for support. In order to keep Seward at home, which we all desire, we must elect another man, not likely a Whig, but more probably a Democrat. Jacob spoke of several capable candidates. However, he failed to mention my choice, John C. Breckinridge. The Democracy draws more supporters than all other parties combined. Our sitting vice-president understands the role of the head of the executive branch of government. The years Breckinridge served in the House of Representatives provided a legislative background. The man's an attorney, which adds judicial knowledge. He served as an officer in the Mexican War." John purposely neglected to mention Breckinridge saw no action in the conflict. "The man, although a former slave holder, garners respect among northern Democrats. His moderate views attract the segment of the population who changes party allegiance every other election. From my readings Breckinridge is an honest, confident man who will not be compromised. Though we all know," he continued with a wide, cynical grin, "that no man seeks the office but the office seeks the man. The vice-president's greatest drawback is he truly will not seek the office."

Othello Rawson, in the spirit of the good natured discussion evolving stepped forward with his extended hand. "Bravo, Johnny Beall! For the quiet agriculturist you profess to be, your exceptional oratorical skills offered a preeminent nominating speech for John C. Breckinridge of Kentucky for the next president of these United States. However, with much regret I cannot second your nomination until I trust that a slave holder can indeed gain the White House. While five of our first seven Presidents owned Negro property, and remember four of those five were Virginians, only three of the past eight possessed them. The last of those three elected, gained the office sixteen years ago," he added in reference to Louisiana's Zachary Taylor's election in 1844. "With all due respect, John, I recognize and admire the attributes of Mr. Breckinridge, but I fear the growing northern population, with its increasing number of foreign born immigrants, shall never again allow us to elect a president from a slave holding state."

John grasped his opportunity to even the score for the verbal joust Dan commenced several minutes earlier. "Daniel Lucas, as esteemed host of this gathering, and also the chap who introduced this topic of discussion, the sole responsibility to look into the future rests with you."

"Johnny, if only blessed with half the wisdom of you gentleman, and twice the foresight, I would be honored to offer the name. I only call upon our Lord to endow us with a Democratic candidate who appeals to all. A splintered party could grant us the man we least desire." Realizing the discussion could become volatile again he tactfully added, "We must have confidence our party leaders possess the same concern."

Dan excused himself to acknowledge other guests. The four remaining men bid each other adieu so they might mingle with other acquaintances. John avoided the opposite sex until he departed with his mother and sister. The two ladies and Will conversed nonstop the duration of the ride home. Dialogue revolved exclusively around which new couples paired with each other, and of course food.

John's thoughts returned to the fiery discussion that almost burned out of control. Strong, differing opinions supplied the fuel. Othello Rawson lit the match. Dan Lucas doused the flames before damage occurred. John added additional water to prevent it from reigniting. With their carriage rolling toward Walnut Grove, he concluded tonight's discussion between five men with assorted views represented a microcosm of the Union. Othello Rawson stood firmly for the separatist faction while Hiram Keller stood by the Union at all cost. Jacob Wilson symbolized the vast number of citizens sorting through each faction's vast propaganda. Fortunately the country abounded with men who like Daniel Lucas and John Beall could impact others and offer an open-minded spirit of compromise, within the government the Union's founders so skillfully crafted.

4 – JULY FOURTH, 1860

How Father would marvel. Six hands with adequate supervision completed the wheat harvest in four days utilizing the McCormick reaper. Last year, similar acreage required thirteen hands and seven days. With the grain pulverized into flour at the family's grist mill John partook of the July 4th celebration free from any pressing concerns.

He could do without marching through town in the fancy Botts Greys dress uniform, although when his unit marched past, his mother and sisters proudly waved. Will stood alongside anticipating his opportunity to join when he reached legal age in two years. The parade ended and the unit dispersed. Duty completed. Across the way in the front of Easterly's Emporium stood Lillian Keller with her gloved hand resting on her husband's arm. Hiram's friendly wave beckoned John across the street.

"Hello, Mrs. Keller," he acknowledged. While not well acquainted with Hiram's wife, John recalled his mother always referred to her as a sweet, God-fearing woman.

"Good to see you again, Mr. Beall. Is that your mother over there in front of Drum's Confectionary? Enjoy the holiday," Mrs. Keller said before she excused herself and pulled her dress up several inches so as not to drag it in the dust of Main Street.

Watching her cross the thoroughfare John commented, "You are a fortunate man Hiram Keller."

"Thank you. I count my blessings. A loving wife and good children offer a unique tranquility. I do pray peace continues in this land of ours."

"Any other thought today borders on blasphemy."

Concern showed on Hiram's face. "What can men such as you and I do? A huge majority of the Union wishes for peace while arrogant fire-eaters and holier-than-thou abolitionists refuse to utter the word 'compromise'. Both extremist factions assume their strength far exceeds that of their irrational opponents."

"Hiram, what do you know of Lincoln? Seward assumed himself to be the Republican nominee, as did we."

"John, we know the man only served in the U.S. House of Representatives for a single two-year term. Other than that, he's just held some state offices, and earned his living as an Illinois attorney. One has to believe if elected old Honest Abe," paused Keller displaying an obvious expression of sarcasm, "will be nothing more than a Republican marionette, sad to say. I approve of John Bell and his Constitutional Unionists platform. Probably just a new name for the slowly expiring Whig party. Since I was, or I guess I still am one, I can more thoroughly comment on him. He lacks both strong deep south support and ample northern support; therefore I acquiesce to any moderate Democratic candidate over a radical Republican, if only to subdue the country's emotions. I see the secessionist Democrats appear to have seconded your New Year's Day nomination of Breckinridge. Very astute, John."

"Thank you, Hiram. Several months ago the Democracy owned this election. Maybe Breckinridge will not be the overwhelming choice for whom to cast a ballot but in the southern two-thirds of the Union, Lincoln will be the man to vote against. You've judiciously implied the Whigs now gasp for their last breaths but I fear they shall still draw some anti-Lincoln ballots. Douglas siphons sorely needed northern votes away from Breckinridge. Lincoln wins by default. Rumors circulate of the Democrats uniting and putting forth a compromise candidate but first Douglas and Breckinridge must step down. Nobody with his eyes set on the top prize walks away and concedes the title to the other."

"John, since the colonies united, the country always looked to Virginia for guidance. Do you really believe that she, and Kentucky, Maryland, and North Carolina, along with Tennessee, shall watch idly as the Union dissolves?"

"Hiram, when we speak of Virginia, we must consider the Othello Rawsons in our analysis. Not all Virginians desire like verdicts in this case. I only pray God grants us the wisdom to preserve our land."

"John, I dread choosing between the Union and Virginia."

"Choosing between Virginia and the Union would be an unenviable task for me also," concluded John before he bid Hiram a friendly farewell.

Ambling away, Beall reflected upon the subtle but diverse loyalties evident between two seemingly like-minded citizens. Keller spoke of choices and led by referring to the Union while John conversely initially alluded to Virginia. Merely semantics? He shrugged his shoulders and decided to enjoy the balance of the beautiful July day. Events play out regardless of any one man's actions. A year from now the same festivities and similar discussions most likely will prevail. Life in the serene valley will continue. After all, this always was and always will be the Virginia he's known and loved. Now for a refreshing glass of lemonade, some appetizing food, and pray to God no encounters with Sue Ellen O'Brien.

The balance of July Fourth passed without additional political discussions relevant to the potential election crisis facing the Union in four short months. Nonetheless he realized America's oldest and most populous political party faced severe division while the infant Republican camp possessed strong unity. And the Whig Party, or whatever it renamed itself, refused to completely fade away. The Union's constitutional structure mandated periodic elections for the orderly transfer or retention of executive power every four years. Eighteen prior presidential elections showcased the founding father's wisdom. Would 1860 illustrate to the world the destined failure of America's eighty-four year old experiment? If only this year's election could be bypassed, the Union could avoid drinking from the cup set before it. No one could imagine the duration of intense suffering that lay ahead until that cup finally sat empty.

5 – NEW YEARS 1861

"John Yates Beall, rise and shine! Happy birthday," Mother's voice resounded through the closed bedroom door.

"Happy New Years Day, Mother," politely replied her groggy son who had arrived home yesterday from a business trip in Iowa. Twenty-six years old today. Would he be graced with Miss Sue Ellen O'Brien at the annual Lucas gathering? He rose from bed leaving that thought behind.

Years of repetitive activities become the traditions which build heritage. Especially in the south these oft repeated customs became akin to religious rituals. "And many returns," resounded the family chorus as the intimate family celebration concluded.

The verse usually signaled the highly anticipated departure for the New Years Day open house. Today unexplained melancholy overwhelmed John. He lamented that he had long taken the precious day for granted. Despite the presidential election results he possessed faith in Virginia's ability to right the Union ship through the upcoming rough waters. Yet he could not emit the uneasiness within him. Only one remedy! He sprang to his feet envisioning the calming presence of his good friend. "Let's move family." Peering through the window, he added, "I see Timothy has guided the team from the barn."

Virginia Lucas greeted her guests in the mansion's elegantly decorated reception hall. After exchanging pleasantries the Beall's sought out friends and acquaintances. On his first step toward the library John froze at the sound of that dreaded feminine voice.

"Mr. Beall, fit and handsome as ever."

"Good evening, Miss O'Brien." Sue Ellen's innate vibrancy accentuated the beautiful creature whom men in the valley coveted. John might be gradually joining their number although he refused to admit such. He responded with a sincerity absent in the past, "You present yourself well this New Year's Day." Actually she appeared stunning, standing below the bright chandelier in her low cut burgundy gown, enhanced by dangling ruby earrings and a sparkling diamond necklace shimmering against her soft white skin.

"Mr. John Beall, for a learned individual, your vocabulary for greeting a lady remains somewhat limited," she replied with an innocent yet seductive smile.

Tonight her aggressive forwardness failed to alienate him. He responded with an unusually warm smile. "Miss Sue Ellen O'Brien, all that my words lack in quantity is compensated with my sincerity." Instantly an uncomfortable redness burned across his cheeks and forehead. Adding to his discomfort, he realized he never before uttered Miss O'Brien's first name. Nor had he addressed her with genuine affection. He extricated himself with typical male elegance.

"Miss O'Brien, if you will be kind enough to excuse me, I have gentlemen awaiting me in the parlor."

"Certainly, Mr. Beall. The concerns of the world await you." Her sensuous smile and penetrating eyes followed him during his retreat.

A wide grin crossed Dan's face. Rion Hall's young host grasped the opportunity to verbally jab his friend. "I pray we did not inhibit your deep discussion with Miss O'Brien, or is it Sue Ellen now?"

"She remains Miss O'Brien."

"You say 'remains' in a very tentative manner, John."

"If I respond to your interrogation, counselor, shall I be assured this cross examination ceases?"

"Of course, my friend. Please proceed," encouraged the attorney, gesturing with extended forearms waist high with palms open.

Following a stiff, theatrical bow, the defendant commenced. "Miss O'Brien remains the salutation by which I address the lady. Despite the fact I am getting on in years," he continued with a fictitious smirk, "I have no intentions of changing the relationship." He terminated the awkward discussion while questioning the honesty of his own reply.

He freed himself by waving to the elder gentleman several paces beyond Dan. "Judge Lucas, if my memory serves me correctly you were absent last year."

"Absolutely correct, John. My daughter and son hosted the festivities last year. I felt obligated to greet Governor Letcher's train when he arrived in Richmond to commence his term. Although I preferred the companionship of family, friends, and neighbors, our newly elected governor also deserved my support. This year, unfortunately due to our disjointed Democracy, we await the further development of issues created by our sister states to the south."

The comment attracted the familiar faces of Hiram Keller and Jacob Wilson. "Pleasure to welcome you both again at Rion Hall," greeted the younger Lucas.

"Thank you Dan," Hiram replied before acknowledging Judge Lucas. Glancing around the room, he added, "I haven't heard, excuse me, I haven't seen Othello Rawson. Might he be joining us this evening?"

With a hint of contempt the judge answered, "Daniel's acquaintance is in Charleston where he belongs, celebrating another misguided South Carolinian temper tantrum."

Jacob Wilson, a man of few words, respectfully challenged Judge Lucas. "Sir, many folks passing through the Ferry anticipate that Carolina's two neighbors, Georgia and Florida, along with Mississippi, Alabama, Louisiana, and even Texas might, as you say, throw a tantrum."

"If that occurs, Wilson, we shall witness the beginning of the dissolution of our Union," interjected Keller.

Judge William Lucas regained the floor and initiated a thorough dissertation. "You younger gentlemen entered this world after South Carolina's futile attempt to depart from the Union thirty years ago. At the time, President Jackson rattled some sabers while contemplating military action. Adjacent Georgia and North Carolina vehemently opposed South Carolina. As you would surmise, our commonwealth influenced the national government to seek compromise. To hear Jackson's, or his hot headed adversary's version, you would conclude neither party backed away. And that, boys, is the essence of our political system. Compromise! Nobody loses! Few in the north and few in the south desire the escalation of current emotions. The states with the most to lose if the current condition gets out of hand—Maryland, Kentucky, and our Virginia, will rally the vast majority to isolate the abolitionists and secessionists. Tempers shall cool. By New Years Day 1861 compromise shall have again settled a crisis."

"Judge Lucas, do you believe the *Constitution* sanctions secession?" queried Beall.

"Johnny, despite our current dilemma, your theoretical question never shall be addressed. Today South Carolina believes the entire lower south backs her. The leaders of those states must soon realize that a loose confederation lacking railroads, industry, northern trading partners, and most importantly a strong military, cannot survive. Only our stable Union prevents France from moving north against us to enlarge her Mexican empire. Of even far greater concern is the disproportionate slave population within those states far to the south. The upper south has two to three Negroes for every white man. In the deep south, with its cotton economy, only one white man might reside for every seven Negroes, very few of which are not slaves. The threat of an imperialistic slave-free Mexico on the Texas border generates far more concern than the ramblings of Yankee abolitionists hundreds of miles away."

"Johnny," continued the judge, "I have side-stepped but have not overlooked your question. I am not exceptionally well versed as to the entry into the Union of the other colonies. I know when Virginia joined in the formation of our Union she consented with the proviso that she enter upon her terms. Documentation exists that she may depart at her pleasure. But this is irrelevant. Neither now nor shall there exist in the foreseeable future any benefit for our exiting this current arrangement. I admire Buchanan for calmly staying the course. Our newly elected, politically-naïve backwoods president might utter some radical rhetoric, but rest assured gentlemen, that Seward, aided by experienced political trainers, shall soon have Mr. Lincoln performing tolerably for the next four years until a competent man ascends to the position."

"Johnny, I assume Mr. Breckinridge's showing disappointed you," interjected Dan.

"Disappointed? Yes. Surprised? No. But the vice-president's failure to carry his native Kentucky puzzles me. If the small-minded, so-called Little Giant from Illinois withdrew in favor of Breckinridge, only the New England abolitionists and a few southern fire-eaters would have been unhappy. Now we have a president who only forty percent of the Union supports. Without Douglas siphoning votes, Breckinridge would have gained valuable northern electoral votes. Bell would have been less effective. And while technically separated from us today, I daresay that South Carolina would still remain a member of the Union if we had a southern Democrat as our president."

Keller immediately challenged the rationale. "The man finished third in votes. How do you assume a candidate who receives roughly twenty percent of the popular vote can beat a man who obtains forty percent, the same man who also gains about two-thirds of the electoral vote?"

"Hiram, many a good man, you included," continued John with a soft smile, "requests more fact in support of my view. Breckinridge did receive only about one-fifth of the ballots cast. An in-depth analysis confirms he also received votes evenly distributed from throughout the country, a feat no one else accomplished. He received over a quarter of a million votes from the sparsely populated deep south, almost three hundred thousand from the north, and over three hundred thousand from the border states. I dare anyone to dispute that only he offered universal appeal. With two choices instead of four the canvas rhetoric dissolves into two transparent options. Does a man vote for the continuation of a system whereby the prosperity of the last eighty years continues or does he settle for the dangerous, uncharted path being opened by an inexperienced trail blazer?"

"Johnny, I realize you have your reasons for bypassing a law career, but son, you speak with a simple eloquence that we all admire, backed by logical conclusions derived from concrete thinking," said the elder Lucas beaming with pride for the boy he watched grow and mature along side his son.

"Thank you, Sir," replied John, gratified by the praise spewing from the respected judge. "I do appreciate your compliment and your insight. I rest assured listening to your views, as I am sure do these other gentlemen, that cooler heads shall prevail, and the crisis shall resolve itself." Looking to Jacob Wilson, he added, "Sounds like we only need focus on increasing crop prices so that I might purchase a new carriage."

"No focus on the affairs of the heart, Johnny?" Dan jested.

"No my dear friend, not with the farm to run," replied John, rolling his eyes. The evening continued well into the night before farewells were finally exchanged.

John's practiced handling of the team's reins maneuvered the carriage down Rion Hall's steep drive. He concentrated on guiding the horses while remaining oblivious to the female chatter. Judge Lucas's calming words of reassurance, coupled with the clear, starry night, displaced his earlier melancholy with a welcome serenity. Perhaps the image of the dark-haired beauty contributed to that emotion. Did he desire her for merely an appealing woman he could learn to love, or did she attract him as the lady with whose love he could share his life. With prospects for a peaceful and prosperous 1861, Miss Sue Ellen O'Brien might in the very least be addressed as Sue Ellen on January 1, 1862.

6 – FRIDAY, APRIL 12, 1861

Four sharp chimes from Saint Michael's belfry shattered the silence. Nervous bodies jerked with surprise. Good natured snickers from fellow soldiers followed. A man old enough to be the grandfather of most men assembled shook his head, smiled, and calmly reassured them. "Settle boys. Clock makes that noise at four in the morning, every morning."

"Mr. Ruffin, this isn't any morning. All hell's to break loose anytime now unless the Yankees surrender Fort Sumter," replied one tense young man.

Sixty-seven year old Edmund Ruffin removed his black, wide-brimmed militia hat, pushed his long, shaggy gray hair behind his ears, and repositioned his hat. "I know, son. I've been waiting for this day long before you were out of short britches. Sure would like to view some fireworks before sun-up, but when General Beauregard's ready the order to commence firing will be issued."

Despite the pleasant night, Ruffin, the renowned agriculturalist and sometime novelist, tossed a blanket over his shoulders, concealing his dark blue Palmetto Guard uniform jacket. He joined a half dozen youngsters sprawled across the lawn several rods behind the artillery pieces. He reclined against a tree while wrapping part of his cover underneath his blue trousers to protect them from the heavy spring dew.

"Mr. Ruffin, why are you here, being a Virginian and all?" inquired a fair-skinned lad, fruitlessly attempting to start a moustache.

The facial hair needed aging, fertilizer, or both, thought the elderly gentleman. "My granddaddy fought in the rebellion for independence eighty years ago. My pa watched Redcoats burn their house and barn. Though Pa was only seven at the time he attempted to stop the arsonists.

They cruelly struck him and rode away with their haughty laughs. Pa taught me we inherited the responsibility to prevent such arrogance and oppression from ever returning to Virginia. I've preached to the cowering lily livers in Richmond, to no avail. They want compromise to maintain peace. You want your grandchildren facing juries of their peers or juries born of black slave stock? That's what damn Yankee abolitionists call compromise. Remember after John Brown's invasion that both the governors of Ohio and Iowa refused to extradite the anarchists, displaying the Republican's total disregard for the *Constitution.* Virginia's esteemed governor and our sacred commonwealth's legislators crawl to negotiate with a federal government headed by an abolitionist president. I'm here to honor my granddaddy. I'm here to respect the memory of my pa. And I'm here out of admiration for you South Carolinians who are a credit to the entire white race. That being said, I'm also here to piously petition our Lord for support as we strike back at the despot's boot raised to crush us. Our actions here in Charleston must bring Virginia to her senses. It is my privilege to serve beside you gentlemen since your captain so graciously invited me to join. In fact, I..." an earth-rattling blast interrupted him. Everyone stared at the signal shot brilliantly arcing over Fort Sumter.

"To your pieces, men," barked the captain's piercing voice. "Mr. Ruffin, you, sir, receive the honor of pulling the first lanyard from our battery. Fire at will."

The old man yanked the cord with such force that his free hand needed to shoot up to keep his hat atop his head. The booming barrage of artillery fire reverberating throughout the harbor muted the chorus of cheers which followed. Evil thunder from the guns blending with the cosmic light display drew swarms of citizens to rooftops and the waterfront. None of the ecstatic audience watching this prelude to war could fathom the four years of death and destruction that would rip the land apart until the curtain finally dropped ending an American tragedy the likes of never witnessed before.

7 – WAR COMES TO VIRGINIA

Four hundred miles to the north in Jefferson County a feeling of caution supplanted the wild exuberance engulfing South Carolina. The afternoon following the bombardment of Fort Sumter, John and his mother bounced along in their wagon laden with assorted supplies purchased in Charles Town. Janet disguised her concern while exuding calm optimism that soon eroded her son's anxiety. "Mother, do you believe this translates into armed conflict?"

She answered guardedly, "There are storm clouds on the horizon. Hopefully though, the Lord sees fit to blow them away. You've heard prior to your birth the Union experienced such a crisis, I believe in '32. As you know, bloodshed was avoided. In 1850 during Zachary Taylor's presidency fear of war again abounded. Maybe our Lord intervened with the president's untimely death to prevent a tragic conflict. Of course you remember the violence in Kansas, but," she paused with a frustrated sigh, "we've seen lawlessness increase the farther one migrates west. Brown's raid at the Ferry cast more darkness across the Union. Unfortunately four of our local citizens died but it could have been worse. I earnestly trust that our commonwealth, comprised of rational, civilized men such as you John, shall prevail and blow the storm clouds out to sea."

He hoped some day to possess a positive outlook that would allow him to stifle feelings of uncertainty in others. Today he settled for Mother's strength as he guided the reins with his left hand while he firmly placed his right one over both hers and squeezed tightly. They both hoped for steady, controlled receding of the precarious situation brought on by actions beyond their control.

Unfortunately, instead of stability returning, a tempest of spontaneous decisions in Washington and in

Richmond brought a cataclysmic collision to Jefferson County. In the late afternoon of April 18, Private John Beall marched with a large contingent of militia from Charles Town toward Harpers Ferry. To his left trudged Henry Schmitt. To his right tramped Augustus Hummrickhouse. Fifty yards to their front rode Jefferson County Militia Colonel William Allen on his handsome bay mare. Robert Allen, who was his aide and also his nephew, trotted along on a brown and white spotted gelding. The spring sun peering just over their left shoulders warmed their backs as they marched. Unseasoned troops awkwardly collided when Colonel Allen signaled the column to halt. Most of the men immediately dropped down at the road's edge.

"Boys, I just ain't cut out to be a soldier. We been marching well over an hour, covered about three mile, and only bout half way there. If God intended our legs to travel this far He'd a given us four instead of two," commented Henry holding up four fingers on his left hand and two on his right.

"And you'd be complaining about the cuisine. We'd hear the hay's too dry or there's not enough oats," Augustus chided with a laugh, slapping his thigh, totally enthralled by his own sense of humor.

"Gentleman," John began, following a long, satisfying drink from his canteen, "we could well face battle when we reach the Ferry. Time to get serious. Aren't either of you somewhat apprehensive of our potential encounter?"

"Johnny, does that big word you just used mean scared?" replied Gus, staring inquisitively into the sky, removing his hat, and scratching his dark black hair. He slowly drawled, "Then yes, I'd be ap-per-sensible." He quickly bellowed, "Only if I was a Yankee!" The remark brought forth hearty laugher from Beall's comrades.

Realizing the two lads had not yet reached age twenty he attempted to suppress his frustration. While all three owned the same rank, he assumed a mentoring role. "Boys, soldiers die in war, or at the very least face horrific injury."

"We know, Johnny. I discussed the very thing with Henry before you fell in at Charles Town. I only yearn for the courage not to turn tail and run. Dishonoring the family would be worse than getting wounded or even kilt." Beall realized he drastically underestimated the maturity level of the two. Gus added, "Pa told me a week ago that politicians talk but nothing ever comes of it. Guess this hike confirms that Virginia really did quit the Union."

"Your pa's not the only intelligent man who missed the mark. When the Virginia convention met earlier, nearly two-thirds of the delegates opposed secession," replied John. "Although our friends in South Carolina, or should I now say our brothers in arms, terminated the stalemate at Fort Sumter, our Virginia desired to navigate her own course. Much to my chagrin that inept Republican president blundered on every occasion. He first displayed his incompetence by ordering the resupply of Sumter. He far exceeded that act of stupidity this past Monday when he requested 75,000 troops from each state that remained in the Union. In essence, he invited Virginia, and for that matter Maryland, Tennessee, Kentucky, and North Carolina to join the Confederacy. The only rational motive from this irrational president must be that he plans to force out all slave states and liberate the Negroes before he coerces us back into the Union as free states." Briefly the name Breckinridge entered John's mind. Remorsefully he forced it to exit.

The conversation ended when Colonel Allen ordered the ranks to reform. The ten minute respite revived the men but they soon realized that the lowering sun no longer warmed their bodies clothed in the sweat soaked uniforms. Two hours later they reached the base of Bolivar Heights. Again the men fell out of formation and sprawled along the periphery of the road.

John remained on his feet casually meandering about while straddling strewn military accoutrements and outstretched legs. His wandering ceased when he reached earshot distance of the commanding officers. Colonel Allen conferred with an officer unfamiliar to Beall. Allen's aide stood silently along side. Nearby two men dressed in Federal uniforms and armed with muskets stood talking with a man in civilian attire. The unknown officer with a captain's rank, shorter than average, and appearing to weigh about 140 pounds, had an unassuming air about him, but his penetrating ebony eyes and deep olive skin implied that more comprised this man of slight build. Emotional voices attracted the bystanders' attention.

In a stressful tone Colonel Allen spoke nervously to the captain. "If we attack in the manner which you suggest we face a defensive force of over four hundred well-armed men, each proficient in the use of their weapons. We only command two hundred and fifty ill-trained militia, plus your squad of cavalry, Captain Ashby. Such an advance will be suicidal."

Impatiently shifting his weight from one foot to another, Captain Turner Ashby pointed to the civilian and aggressively rebutted. "Colonel, with all due respect, this armory worker described the unrest in town. Citizens are rioting. The only confirmed force consists of a skittish lieutenant with less than fifty experienced troops. You suppose large numbers of armory workers shall flock to support the Federals. You assume too much. Have you not listened to this loyal Virginian?" asked Ashby, nodding to the civilian worker.

"Colonel, sir," pleaded the civilian, "most armory workers are Jefferson County boys, loyal to Virginia. After Old Abe's call for troops we convinced the Unionists to skedaddle. We can't allow the Yanks to remove the muskets or destroy our armory."

"Colonel, we was in the U.S. army this morning. We made our choice when we surrendered to join you. There's many a boy ready to exchange uniforms," interjected one of the men wearing the regular U.S. Army uniform. The Federal picket had chosen to immediately surrender in order to fight for his native Virginia.

Two fearful images raced through William Allen's mind. He first conjured the vision of an attack against a superior, strongly entrenched force and an unsuccessful assault ending with a field littered with bloody, dying men; people he knew as friends and neighbors. He also imagined a humiliated colonel whom townspeople labeled a coward because he held back. Dishonor or death? A Virginia gentleman selects the latter if only to evade the former. With an artificial air of confidence the colonel spoke loudly, "We shall shortly move ahead, but cautiously." Beall strode briskly back to his position, possessing first hand information instead of here-say.

"Where you been Johnny," queried Henry.

"What'd you hear?" demanded Gus.

"Nothing boys. Can't a man relieve himself without being cross-examined?" The troops trudged up the road toward the crest of the hill, anticipating their descent directly into to the face of the enemy. Beall nearly froze in his tracks when he absorbed the term enemy! Virginia's political adversary is now her military enemy. An uneasy chill entered his body.

While Ashby and Allen finalized their plan on the crest fifteen minutes march away from their destination, United States Army Lieutenant Roger Jones conferred with his sergeants near the shore of the Potomac. The thirty-one year old officer faced danger throughout his career. He knew the Texas plains, he understood Comanche combat tactics, but urban warfare against fellow Americans proved unsettling. Jones realized his refusal to accept the transfer of additional troops to his command several weeks ago proved a poor decision. An hour ago the lieutenant instructed his sergeants to fill mattresses with gun powder, place them in the arsenals and manufacturing buildings, and prepare to ignite them. A segment of his troops positioned themselves at the gate to ward off hostile advances from enemy militia or civilians. The locals surmised the true intent of the Federal activity since visible powder trailed from outside the building entrances leading to explosives inside. At 9:00 p.m.

Jones ordered the powder fuses lit and proceeded to retreat from Virginia across the railroad bridge over the Potomac into Maryland.

Colonel Allen's and Captain Ashby's concluding strategy session abruptly ended when the sky to the east illuminated with a roar. Ashby galloped away screaming a savage yell, leading his horse soldiers toward the action. In a matter of moments the captain atop his beautiful black stallion returned to Allen. "They fired the armory. Get your troops into town now. No sign of Federals. The fires must be extinguished immediately. With a tip of his hat the cavalier wheeled his horse, dug spurs into its flanks, and thundered away with his mount's mane flowing through the air.

Thick smoke increased as the militia advanced into town. Flames leaped from buildings into the sky to greet them as they raced down the road's steep slope. The disgusting odor and choking smoke of burned structures and exploded gunpowder intensified. Instead of fighting enemy troops, the militia found themselves combating the destructive flames ignited by their foe. While their wool militia uniforms grew uncomfortably heavy with perspiration they afforded the firefighters protection from the scorching heat. Muskets salvaged by citizens following the Federal retreat littered the street. Stinging beads of sweat rolling into Beall's eyes quickly evaporated from his forehead once he neared the blaze. His back ached. Feeling faint he reached for his canteen only to recall he'd emptied it half an hour ago. While refilling a bucket to douse the fire he took a swig of its murky contents. The muddy river water's bitter smoky flavor gagged him. Water splattered to the ground from his mouth. He forced another mouthful down. Better a little nauseated then overcome by heat. Mercifully the inferno subsided in several hours with the aid of civilians manning pumps and hoses. The fatigued men persisted in shrinking the fire's perimeter. The troops battled another three hours before being released from their firefighting responsibility. Beall and his comrades wobbled fifty yards before collapsing near the Shenandoah's shore. Day break's first rays gradually roused the troops. An acrid, foul stench prohibited their return to sleep. John rolled over, sat up, and saw Gus staring at him with a huge grin. As Henry slowly awakened he jerked up at the sound of a boisterous laugh.

"What's so funny, Gus," demanded John.

"Us. Last night we worked liked field hands. Today we are field hands."

Still exhausted, Henry needed sleep, not Gus's humor. He glared at Gus preparing to confront him. All three men stared at one another. Combustible laughter echoed in unison from deep within each man who stared at the others' blackened faces. Tears of laughter rolled down cheeks. Moments like these shared by sleep-deprived men surviving traumatic experiences began building the bonds which would carry them through the perilous years ahead. The three stood, stretched, and stepped toward several half empty water buckets. Soon black grime dripped from their faces and hands. The brightness of the rising sun allowed the men to survey the surroundings.

Henry lifted his arm to sniff his sleeve. "Even if Ma gets the dirt out of these clothes I doubt if the smell ever disappears. Shucks, if we do end up in battle the other fellas will smell us well before we get close."

"Henry," replied Gus, never missing an opportunity to interject his own brand of humor, "if they catch the scent of the likes of us they'll assume the devil with all his legions is advancing straight from hell. They'll skedaddle before we get a shot off. We could capture Washington City with this aroma." Gus's comment even received a smile from the habitually sedate Beall.

John closely examined the smoldering arsenal, with scores of muskets remaining within. The fire also destroyed the carpenters' shop. Luckily the stock turning shop and storehouse survived, though a number of finished musket stocks were lost. Had every explosion transformed into a fire catastrophic losses would have ensued. Shattered window glass littered the ground outside the buildings. Apparently the explosive force inside many buildings prevented flames from igniting. Eventually the militia learned that besides preventing the fire from spreading beyond the armory buildings, they preserved valuable gun manufacturing machinery destined for shipment south. They also retrieved components for over two thousand weapons from various buildings.

Standing between Gus and Henry, John stared at the undamaged firehouse, once John Brown's fortress. Then he gazed at the railroad bridge over which Lieutenant Roger Jones and his troops exited Virginia and Harpers Ferry. "Gentlemen, that's the same bridge John Brown traveled over to enter Virginia and Harpers Ferry barely eighteen months ago." Beall shuddered with the realization that the war the old man so desired to bring to Virginia had arrived.

8 – THE ALARM SOUNDS

John relaxed in Walnut Grove's serene fall setting while enjoying his second visit home since he, Will, and many of the Botts Greys mustered into the Army of Northern Virginia on May 12. Much to his chagrin, his only other visit home occurred late in July during a brief leave to finalize a business transaction. That arrival in Jefferson County coincided with the eruption at Manassas Junction, the initial large scale battle of the war. He sped south only to discover that the remnants of the Federal troops had scattered to the safety of Washington. He swore he would never depart camp whenever rumors of battle existed, although such rumors had circulated since the end of May.

"Johnny, you should've seen the Yanks run from the field," younger brother Will exclaimed, greeting his brother with a bear hug. "The 2nd Virginia now belongs to what folks call the Stonewall Brigade for the time we stood like a stone wall by General Jackson with our artillery and saved the day. I swear, some of those Northern boys moved faster than a rabbit fleeing a hound."

Missing the only battle of the war stung enough, but hearing the firsthand account from a younger brother only added salt to the wound. Three months later, except for minor border skirmishes or raids, both armies appeared content to settle into winter and organize for spring. In good conscience John now visited his family when the opportunity arose to return to Charles Town with an ill comrade, Private Augustus Hummrickhouse.

Mary initiated a short walk through the orchard with her three younger sisters on the crisp autumn eve so that Janet and her son could benefit from several precious moments alone. Janie slammed the back door shut and rushed down the porch steps through the damp grass to catch up with her three sisters. John sat peacefully at the kitchen table, absorbing the simple pleasures of home he realized he so cherished since the advent of the war. The radiating heat of the stove. The aroma of tonight's stew blending with the scent of apple butter canned earlier in the day. And Mother, as she walked from the hallway to join him. The table lamp's soft illumination combined with the shimmering twilight rays from the window, casting an angelic glow upon her face.

Her warm maternal smile appeared when she compassionately asked, "How is Augustus?"

"He should recover and return to camp after the first of the year. I don't know what caused his illness. Some fellows have difficulty adjusting to the crowded camps. Others are unaccustomed to the food. Good water might be our most crucial deficiency. I've witnessed, though rarely, soldiers taking ill one day, and God rest their souls, having their bodies shipped home three days later. But don't concern yourself with Gus. That good natured Dutchman is too jovial to pass on just yet."

"I'm pleased to hear that," replied Janet with a sigh of relief. She folded her hands together, resting them upon the blue and white checkered tablecloth. "Now, tell me about your brother. Is he eating well? Does he attempt to stay warm and dry? And does he realize he's in the middle of a war with people shooting at each other?"

John never before sensed this degree of anxiety within his mother. "Which question do you want me to answer first?" he asked. He smiled and without waiting for a reply responded with carefully chosen words. "Mother," he slowly began while collecting his thoughts, "my little brother's adjusted well. I wanted him to travel here with Gus but he insisted I come, and not of noble heart," interjected John with a wide grin. "He thoroughly enjoys military life. During Will's first eighteen years, whether we care to admit it, folks outside his peer group knew him as the youngest Beall boy or John's little brother. The army, aside from rank, treats men as equals. He glories in the fact we're both privates. No more taking direction from older brother. You've raised him to come inside out of the rain. When's he ever missed a meal? We both have funds to purchase food to supplement the somewhat bland camp diet. And Will possesses common sense. His towering stature and quick wit make him a favorite with his fellow soldiers. As for the war itself, I question if the North desires anything more than to harass us near the border. They may settle for assaulting us only in their newspapers. In any case, another battle like Manassas and we'll capture Washington City, send Abe slinking back to Illinois, and end this war. Before it's over I realize more blood might be shed. Of course property will be destroyed and commerce interrupted, but the issues with the North shall be resolved once and for all. And your boys under God's care shall return without a scratch."

"I sincerely pray you are correct, Son," she responded with concern.

"Mother, you spend an inordinate amount of time worrying about the girls, Will, and me. Despite not mentioning his name I believe you keep Hezekiah in your prayers too. Let's talk about you. John placed his hands over his mother's and looked into her deep blue eyes, her gift to him. He stared at a face which several months ago lacked the new wrinkles embedded in her forehead and around her eyes. Her carefully groomed hair uncharacteristically displayed several loose wisps above her left brow. Her predominantly sandy brown hair now showed isolated streaks of gray. He squeezed her warm hands. "Walnut Grove has been without male direction much of the growing season. You are a very capable woman but being here alone and defenseless against invasion or slave revolt deeply concerns me. I really believe…"

"John Yates Beall! A minute ago you told me not to worry about Will or you!" she admonished. "You implied this conflict will soon end. As for a slave revolt, we've always been good to our people. Except for disciplinary reasons we've never separated families. Physical punishment's been used very sparingly. True, Solomon fled north in June but we obtained him when he was twelve. Many of our Negroes were born here. This is their home. Why leave, and go where?" John only laughed and shook his head several times. If the bar ever permitted women to become attorneys many a male lawyer's shingle would come down. He winced as she delivered the final salvo. "And mounted rangers and militia provide protection if Negroes get it in their heads to cause mischief."

John roared with laughter.

"What's so funny?" she challenged, before her affectionate smile returned. "You show total lack of respect for your mother."

John paused in appreciation for the aging woman before him wearing a green and blue plaid woolen dress with a simple white lace collar accentuating her determined Southern face. He replied, "The North shall never defeat the Confederacy. I doubt it can even prevail against Virginia. What I find so humorous is my vision of the poor Yankee who attempts to take on the daughter of John Yates or his namesake grandson." Chairs creaked back across the painted hardwood floor. Mother and son rose and joined together in a long, warm embrace conveying the utmost confidence each possessed in the other to perform their duties and survive the dangers ahead. They separated with the sounds of the laughter and chatter of the Beall sisters opening the door. Dampness along the hems of their lengthy dresses confirmed heavy dew already descended over the farm.

While removing her faded red shawl Mary asked, "When do you return to the 2nd Virginia, John?"

"Tomorrow morning. I hope to arrive in camp by Thursday. Three days of hard riding with this limited daylight should get us there."

Janie quickly added, "Beth helped me knit socks and scarves for you and Will. Don't leave without them."

John walked over to his youngest sister and gently kissed her forehead twice. "A thank you kiss from Will and one from me. I'll pack them tonight before I go to bed." He received an affectionate hug from his sisters before he climbed the stairs for a peaceful night's sleep.

The following morning he lay in bed absorbing the sounds, smells, and feel of home. The secure warmth of his familiar bed, pillows, and linens enveloped him. How many weeks or even months before he could again spend a night in this tranquil setting? The call of duty finally broke the bonds which shackled him to his pleasant surroundings. He swung his legs over the edge of his bed and pulled Janie's new socks over the bottom of his underdrawers. He stood, stretched, and buttoned his red and beige checkered shirt up to the neck. He stepped into his heavy blue woolen trousers, and slid the tops of his green suspenders over his shoulders, which he covered with his black vest. He felt fortunate as he reached for his knee-high custom crafted boots which he purchased from Jesse Blockley. Many a soldier in the regiment wore poorly-manufactured, uncomfortable government brogans. In his recently issued, black-tarred knapsack he stuffed extra clothes, a sewing kit, a razor, a mirror, soap, and other assorted items. Besides writing materials he tossed in *Ivanhoe, Julius Cesar*, and of course the *Bible*. Holding his kepi, bulging knapsack, and his Botts Greys frayed frock coat he descended the stairs. A new coat should be issued after his return to camp. By the kitchen door, near his rifle and military accoutrements, he laid his coat, knapsack, and kepi. While he devoured a hearty breakfast of ham, eggs, biscuits, apples, and coffee, his mother and sisters talked incessantly until he rose to bid everyone farewell.

"Give Will my love," requested Annie.

"Travel safely," cautioned Beth.

"Shoot me a Yankee," shouted Janie much to Mother's chagrin. "And don't forget the socks and scarves."

Mary grasped the pause in conversation to say, "We'll be praying for you."

Janet stood silently enjoying her family's interaction until John looked at her and asked, "Are you sure if Timothy accompanies me to camp that it will not cause you hardship? He could be gone almost a week."

"I would rather be without Timothy for seven days than without that extra horse he'll bring back."

"Very well, Mother," he replied before he hugged everyone and moved toward his belongings by the door. "Remember what Father always said, 'Better catch the daylight before it escapes,' and the light is escaping."

"Did you remember my socks?" Janie inquired. John carefully drew up his trouser legs as if wading through a stream and exposed the new socks. "What about the red scarf I knitted too? Where's that?" she demanded.

With an embarrassed expression he began searching. After a minute's hunt he turned with an impish grin and pulled the missing item from his frock coat sleeve with the dexterity of a magician.

"Oh, Johnny, I'm going to miss you so much," Janie yelled as she ran and threw her arms around him. Looking him square in the eyes she rapidly repeated, "Oh I love you so much! I love you so much! Be careful."

Timothy stood outside with Jenny. John slid up onto her saddle while Timothy mounted a roan. The soldier attached his cartridge box and belt to the saddle. He stored his canteen in the leather bag under his blanket roll. A sling loosely attached to his musket allowed him to hang his gun behind his back. Mother walked out the door with a bulging haversack and a carpet bag stuffed with goods only a mother would send. "Mother, how am I supposed to travel efficiently with this excess baggage," he complained.

"Between you and Timothy you'll manage, won't you Timothy."

"We will Miz Janet. Yez we will," he affirmatively replied as expected.

She looked to her son. "I'm sure your camp can use whatever you don't consume on the journey or whatever Timothy feels he won't need for the return trip."

"Yes Mother," replied John stiffly, fighting the urge to salute her. The pair shook the horses' reins to begin their journey when everyone turned, startled by the thunder of hoofs racing down the lane from the west. George Ranson, on his beautiful tan mount Goldie, galloped beside Benjamin Molar, who bounced up and down on his dapple gray gelding. An inquisitive expression grew on John's face when he observed his two friends, fully armed and attired in their ornate Botts Greys militia uniforms.

"Definitely not a social visit at this hour. What's happening, fellows?"

Ranson quickly blurted, "Johnny, Pa says Colonel Ashby's called out the militia to support his rangers to stop the Federals. I rousted Ben. That's when he told me you were home on leave."

"George, slow down! Stop the Federals from what?" demanded John.

"The Federals, under Colonel Geary," interrupted Ben with less emotion, "are stealing the wheat in Herr's granary at the Ferry and taking it to Maryland. You know Turner Ashby, not in his backyard. The Yankees been a loading the barge since last Tuesday. I hear Herr encouraged them to take it so Virginia won't get it. Damn Unionist. He can go to hell with his grain."

John glanced toward the women folks.

"Sorry, Mrs. Beall, Miss Anne, and ladies," Ben apologized with a tip of his hat. Having been enamored for some time with Annie only added to his embarrassment.

"Where do we report?" questioned John.

"We're to meet Seth Henderson and James Burell at Halltown," interjected George. "This could be a good one. Glad you're home for it Johnny!"

"Lord no!" shrieked Janet, clasping her hand to her forehead.

"Mother, God will take care of me," comforted John while reaching down and squeezing her shoulder. "Timothy, you remain here. We can leave our horses with the Miller's or Henderson's." He extended his haversack and carpetbag for Beth to take. Janet intercepted them, hastily removed half the contents from the haversack, refilled it with half the contents from the carpetbag, and pressed it back into her son's hand. He obediently tied it to his saddle. End of discussion.

"See you soon ladies. Watch over them until I return Timothy," shouted John, tapping Jenny's flanks with his spurs. A minute later only a cloud of dust remained from the trio speeding east down the lane's gentle slope towards the farm road leading into Halltown.

When the men galloped to the right onto the road, they slowed to a canter riding three abreast so as not to prematurely fatigue their horses. An almost adolescent babble caused by the excitement of the day flowed endlessly from George who seemingly carried on a conversation with himself. Between the thumping of hoofs and preoccupation with all that lay ahead John absorbed little of what anyone said. Three months ago when he passed the edge of the field hospital near Manassas, he experienced the flip side of battlefield glory. True, in the encounter the South obtained an overwhelming military victory, but even the one-sided win extracted a high price. Northern casualties were estimated at over 3000. The Southerners reported less than 1500 including 387 killed; 1,071 wounded, many beyond gruesome description; and only 13 missing. After that experience John never used the word "glorious" to describe death for those killed on the battlefield. With a clear conscience he substituted "honorable" for this war, his war, which revolved around honor. His honor bound him to defend his family, his land, and his native Virginia. The third generation Virginia farmer felt duty-bound to protect the ancestral lands his father and grandfather passed down to him. The cavalier blood pumping through young Beall's veins also had circulated through his namesake and maternal grandfather's, John Yates. Years ago the stain of an insult had been addressed by the original American patriarch in a duel shortly after his arrival in America. Although Yates received a wound in the duel he vanquished forever the stain while retaining his honor. John Yates Beall now prepared for his baptism under fire, standing before Mars not as a reckless man seeking glory but as an honorable warrior striving to sustain honor.

October's sun already warmed the morning air. A twenty minute jaunt brought them to Halltown. Along the way rich agricultural fields and orchards, many now harvested, lay upon the rolling landscape in all directions. Halltown, more a crossroads than a town, sat midway between Harpers Ferry and Charles Town. The B & O Railroad siding and nearby grist mill offered the illusion that more existed to Halltown than actually did, although scattered frame houses with well-kept out buildings confirmed the railroad contributed to the prosperity of Jefferson County. When the three men dismounted, Mr. Miller, a farmer who struck up a lasting friendship two years ago with vocal Southern rights extremist Edmund Ruffin, rushed from his porch to greet the new arrivals. Seth Henderson and James Burell followed.

"Saul, come here boy," Miller yelled, looking back toward the large barn behind his two story house. A sturdy Negro lad, clad in second hand trousers and shirt, a sack coat, an out of season straw hat, and ill-fitting shoes, advanced at an even step after closing the gate.

"Boy, get a move on here," Miller ordered. "Take Master Beall's, Molar's, and Ranson's horses to the barn, wipe 'em down good, fetch 'em water, and give 'em plenty of hay."

"No need for that, sir. Mine's well fed, and I suspect so are the others'."

"Johnny, that's polite of you to say, but although I'm too old to fight I'm not too old to support you men. Want the saddles off?" Answering his own question the elderly man stated, "No, it won't take that long to whip those thieving Yankees. On second thought, the way those boys run you might be chasing them on foot until sundown," Miller concluded with a deep hearty laugh.

John silently nodded when Mr. Miller lead the horses to the Negro stable hand. With eyes looking down, Saul walked away tightly grasping the reins. Groups of militia infantry, from pairs to clusters of eight, continued marching into Halltown. Barren fields transformed into staging grounds for portions of two regiments formed with over several hundred men awaiting their mission. In mid afternoon a uniformed rider trotting in from the east at a steady pace appeared beyond the scattered troops. Soon Captain Josiah Albert sat atop his horse directly before the foot soldiers. Albert's beautiful buckskin mare, Shenandoah, casually swung her black tail back and forth as her rider prepared to speak.

With the attentive eyes and ears of all present Captain Albert began. "Virginia's warriors, Colonel Ashby orders us to prepare to march after midnight to this side of Bolivar Heights to stage a dawn assault against the Northern invader who pilfers Jefferson County wheat from Herr's granary. Colonel Ashby commands the operation and shall issue specific orders to officers upon our arrival. Trust assured that even as I speak his rangers reconnoiter enemy positions so as to formulate a successful plan of action. Men, if we do not halt the charlatans tomorrow, our fields, our homes, and dare I say even our families shall be overrun by these Northern barbarians. Organize within your regimental companies. Fill your canteens. Secure ammunition. Try to rest. And absolutely no fires! Remember our prompt, secret arrival is imperative for tomorrow's success."

Two subordinate officers joined Captain Albert at which time he spun Shenandoah towards the east. The trio rode away and received a unified "hurrah" which echoed throughout the assembled troops. Beall's mind returned to his march six months ago. Would events transpire similar to those or would tomorrow, October 16, be destined to produce memorable events for these inexperienced, ill-equipped men?

Four miles to the east, Union Colonel John Geary dismounted and strode over to the middle-aged man watching civilians load wheat onto the barge, which Major Gould floated several miles down the Shenandoah from Sandy Hook to Harpers Ferry. By day's end tomorrow the grain laden flat boat would cross the river into friendlier territory.

Removing his right glove Geary warmly shook hands with the civilian. “Good day, Mr. Herr. The United States Army deeply appreciates your assistance with our removal of your wheat to the secure borders of Maryland. We receive numerous sightings of mounted Rebel irregulars operating in the vicinity. I am certain they will steal it if we do not remove it.”

Surveying the surroundings Abraham Herr smiled. “Da rumors become more and more dat da Secesh vill take my grain. Vas afraid day interfere here today but since you hire townsmen to shovel grain and load da boat you have more soldiers to protect us.”

Beaming with confidence Geary replied, “We have six hundred United States regulars to insure the loading continues efficiently and with minimal danger. The men you observe here by the mill belong to the 13th Massachusetts. Members of their regiment also guard the Maryland bridge and parts of the river shore,” added the colonel, motioning to the south along the Shenandoah. We have the 3rd Wisconsin camped above the town with pickets stationed on Bolivar Heights to detect incursions from the west. In the event an ill-advised attempt is made to interrupt our task the United States Army shall most assuredly prevail.”

“Ya, dat very goodt. Da Rebs, day take me to Richmond because I be a Union man. Dis beautiful little village is now dreary empty shadow of its old self. Kaput! Put it back together, Colonel.”

Placing his hands on Herr’s shoulders, Geary said, “With troops like mine, loyal citizens such as you, and God’s helping hand, may we return to our normal lives again.” The colonel walked away leaving the mill owner with the encouraging words of comfort.

Deep within his bosom John Geary knew war, especially in border towns, simmered with mixed allegiances until it boiled over into confrontation ending with ruthless, bloody violence. The colonel witnessed first hand such brutality while he governed the Kansas Territory in 1856. He tactfully extinguished the flames burning toward the territorial powder keg and gradually removed the fuse before returning east. Quelling conflict on paths once trod by John Brown was becoming a dangerous vocation. With a sad feeling of remorse for Herr, Geary mounted his horse. The Dutchman successfully operated his mill since 1848. Within the past several years he constructed a new brick foundry adjacent to his mill. Geary only hoped the man avoided physical harm. He encouraged Herr to depart Virginia when Northern forces redeployed on the Maryland side of the Potomac. The Rebs would probably take their vengeance once the Yankees vacated the town. Geary would depart as the third Union commander in six months from the town which the Southerners had controlled twice in that period. The tough old crout Herr probably was ornery enough to get through this ordeal. At least by tomorrow Colonel Geary would be out of this desolate little village.

9 – FORWARD MARCH

When the day's march ended, the sun barely peered over the mountaintops to the west. Men sprawled in groups of six to ten. Ben, George, Seth, James, and a handful of other familiar faces devoured the ham, bread, and apples which Janet Beall had shoved into the haversack. John caught up on the lives of friends he hadn't encountered since spring. Ben Molar remained in Jefferson County bringing in the fall harvest and slaughtering several hogs for his ailing father. A sufficient store of food, plus some much needed cash, would see his family through the winter. If the war continued another year Ben received Mr. Molar's blessing to join the 2nd Virginia. George Ranson's father, the Confederate agent for conscription and supply in Jefferson County, preferred that his headstrong son remain close to home serving the local militia. Mr. Ranson anticipated the need for a strong home guard since Jefferson County rested adjacent to the enemy border. Seth Hendersen, a slender, bushy-haired lad with the reputation of one of the finest horsemen in the area, impatiently awaited the separation of Ashby's unit into an independent command apart from Colonel McDonald. Only then would Ashby have the freedom to aggressively fight the war as he saw fit.

James Burell still possessed the wild, sometimes vicious streak which locals cautiously avoided. Throughout the region folks also recognized his skills as an avid hunter. Rumors circulated that the blond-haired marksman already spilled the blood of Federal soldiers unfortunate enough to become separated from their main body, and local Unionists who too vocally expressed their support for the North.

Beall hoped for several hours of sleep as the sky darkened. George's skittishness prevented that desire from being fulfilled since he conversed with anyone who would listen. “I fervently hope this won’t be another one of those empty marches like we had last spring. Member? By the time we got to the Ferry the Yanks set their fires and high-tailed it cross the river.”

“That’s reason enough for me join the cavalry. Two sets of legs‘ill git you there quicker then one,” chimed in Seth.

“Fellows,” interjected John, “let’s just hope we’re up to the task in the morning. Few, if any of us, have faced enemy fire. Although each man reacts differently, if we stick together we shall drive the intruder back across the river.”

“Knowing it could be kill or be killed tomorrow brings a serious tone to this business doesn’t it,” added Ben somewhat apprehensively. “Taking the life of another man seems so unnatural but honor dictates we perform the task.”

As the conversation slowed, Beall could not help but reflect upon the cynical smile crossing Burell’s face with Ben’s mention of taking a life. John’s thoughts meandered south to Will. He chuckled softly, visualizing the expression on his little brother’s face once his younger sibling understood he bypassed an opportunity for action a stone’s throw from home.

A lieutenant roused the troops about half past two in the morning. The low drone of hushed voices throughout the night had prevented sustained sleep. A bright moon cast light over the field, aiding the men gathering their blankets, hats, weapons, and military accoutrements. John stood, stretched, and prepared to fall into line. The company commander, Julius Maddox, who had been a close friend of John’s older brother Hezekiah, approached the young private.

“Johnny Beall, good you’re here. ‘Tis our great fortune you’re home on leave. I know you missed Manassas but you’ve spent six months under Jackson in the regular army, and many a day and night with men who participated in that victory. You know many of the boys here, all of them good men, but none ever having been in a battle or ever having seen its aftermath. They need the benefit of any experience we can share. You and I also realize the Yanks are better armed. Laddie, most of us only carry old 1816 flintlocks! Glad you brought your '42. Stick close to me; I'll place the younger fellows with you."

When the militia began moving down the road, Private Beall remained within several rods of Captain Maddox. Except for the thumping of feet, the scattered rattle of gear, and the occasional muffled curse from a stumbling man, the militia moved forward with little noise. Everyone understood the necessity of the element of surprise in their dawn attack. The bright moon-lit sky illuminating the road also posed a threat for early detection by enemy scouts. Undetected and a mile from Bolivar Heights, the unit halted. Maddox dismounted and motioned for John to follow. The captain left the road and followed a wooded path terminating in a clearing fifty yards north of the thoroughfare.

Ten paces to the right of a covered wagon eight officers clustered around a crude table, constructed of planks resting upon two barrels. They peered at an unfurled map held open by several rocks on each end, and illuminated by four short candles. Maddox cautiously joined the outer circle of junior officers. Beall inched closer to hear the voices. The flickering candles reflecting upon the faces near the flame emitted a glow akin to that characteristically radiating from holy men preparing for a sacred mission. By contrast, the unquestioned leader of the operation, Lieutenant Colonel Turner Ashby, with his swarthy complexion, white teeth framed between his upturned moustache and flowing black beard, and fiery black eyes which released the inferno which blazed from within, conjured images of Satan's emissary sent to wreak destruction upon a naive mankind. Ashby issued instructions with an atypical soft-spoken, even-toned voice.

"I have stationed Colonel Griffin to our south across the Shenandoah on Loudon Heights with cannon and sharpshooters. He shall silence artillery on the ground above the Ferry and also on the heights beyond the Potomac. A detachment of cavalry and more marksmen are stationed to protect the low ground below Griffin. They shall press forward when practicable. To support our advance in the center I've assigned Captain Avirett to man the rifled gun while Captain Comfield mans the twenty-four pound columbiad." Moving his gloved finger over the map Ashby continued. "Movement shall commence at daybreak with artillery fire followed by the cavalry charge which I shall lead on our left from the wooded area on Bolivar Heights. The advance of our infantry from our center and on our right shall immediately follow. Captain Turner's cavalry shall support the center division of our infantry as it moves up the Charles Town Pike. Captain Wingfield's responsibility shall be our right. Our initial assault should scatter the pickets, create chaos, and send the Yankees camped on lower Bolivar racing down the backside of the hill in confusion toward the river. Wingfield's advance down Shenandoah Street either captures the enemy or drives him across the bridge. After we reclaim our wheat we shall partake of a late breakfast prepared courtesy of our Northern hosts. Any questions?" Looking toward the junior officers he added, "Be certain your companies form up in proper position. At the sound of our big guns I shall advance followed by our infantry." With agile cat-like movements Ashby strode away, pounced atop his chiseled white stallion, and disappeared from sight into the darkness.

Maddox stepped back into Beall, knocking both men off balance. "Excuse me, Johnny. Guess I'm already preoccupied with the upcoming battle."

"No harm, sir. What's my assignment?"

"Just before the assault I'll determine precisely where to place you." As they walked Maddox awkwardly asked, "Heard anything recently from Hezekiah?"

"I visited him in Iowa in December. Mother's received several letters, the last in late spring. That's all. Don't know if he's fighting, or with whom, but trust he remains a Virginian at heart."

"Let's hope so," replied the captain. When they reached the company, Maddox quickly gathered his three lieutenants to review their responsibilities. Soon thereafter the entire force completed the last leg of the march and deployed to their assigned position.

The militia anxiously crouched in the swale near the road while they stared east toward the enemy and the gradually lightening sky. Ashby posted the cavalry assigned to lead the charge about a quarter mile back behind the bend where nervous horses could be neither seen nor heard. Maddox assigned a half dozen green militia to Beall. The need to maintain silence prevented introductions but in the dim light he recognized several faces. One resembled a boy with whom Will associated, but today the innocent lad seemed a year or two younger than John's brother. The youth appeared barely old enough to fight though all volunteers claimed to be of age. Several boys sprouted substantial growths of facial hair, ranging from shaggy beards to well-groomed goatees. Two appeared to possess virgin faces yet untouched by the blade of a razor. All possessed eyes sparkling with excitement in anticipation of the adventure ahead. They received instructions to stay low while loading muskets and expressly not to prime the pan or to cock the flint hammers of their firearms.

Barely past seven the sun's rays began silhouetting long shadows falling toward the Rebel forces. The Confederate guns on the heights to Beall's right shattered the tranquil morning with an adrenalin-injecting roar. He sprang to assemble on the highway. To the left the echoing of hammering hooves blended with the demonic shrieks emanating from Ashby's riders. Blue clad pickets scattered with only several pausing to fire poorly aimed shots. The remainder either raced away without looking back or flattened themselves on the cool, dew-soaked, ground. The rout commenced. Lead elements of Rebel militia raced forward for fifty yards until one man raised his rifle and fired his gun at a fleeing Federal. Instantly a sheet of flame roared from the muskets of a score of undisciplined infantrymen in the lead militia column who abruptly stopped to fire. Beall and the second column advanced through the haze created by the unwarranted small arms fire. Without warning the big

Federal guns reverberated with ear piercing fury to the Confederate left. Shells exploded harmlessly a hundred yards to the front. Clouds of gray dust and debris flew upwards well beyond Ashby's advancing troops. In all directions the sights and sounds of war induced havoc at incomprehensible speeds for Beall and the inexperienced troops near him. At the first sound of Union artillery, dozens of Southern boys dove to the ground and hugged the turf, searching for sanctuary from this horrific new experience. Gradually the lads regained their composure, calmed by Beall and other familiar comrades advancing upon the battlefield. Shortly all but a few terrorized souls rose to their feet and prodded towards the climax of another humiliating defeat for the blue clad invaders.

Atop the plateau where ten minutes earlier Union troops casually enjoyed a hot breakfast around a warm campfire chaos reigned. Spine chilling fear spread like wildfire as panic-stricken comrades retreated, confusing artillery fire from both armies thundered, Rebel cavalrymen with gleaming sabers neared the base of the hill, and a vast sea of enemy militia rolled toward the hill separating the main Federal force from its foe.

Amid the confusion Colonel Geary appeared. His calming, confident presence immediately injected a semblance of order within his men. He quickly reached a beneficial observation point and digested the unfolding panorama. The initial assault cleared many of Geary's pickets from the field. Rebel cavalry rapidly continued their brisk advance on the Union right, followed in the center by three columns of enemy infantry with flags unfurled, marching steadily towards the Yankees. Geary called his officers together to arrange his counter attack.

Unruffled by the sounds of battle the Union colonel spoke in a loud, clear, composed voice. He looked directly into the eyes of Captain Henry Bertram of the 3rd Wisconsin. The slightly-built, dark-haired captain displayed the defiant glare commanders seek in crucial times of battle. Geary issued simple instructions to Bertram. "Major Gould is overseeing the firing of Captain Tompkins's Rhode Island battery from the Maryland Heights and also commands the infantry along the river. Sounds like his guns are already slowing the Reb's. Bertram, you move ahead with your company to our left to stall their movement along the river." The captain nodded in acknowledgement and hurriedly departed. Geary turned his gaze toward the unfolding enemy advance before making eye contact with Lieutenant Moses O'Brien, also with the 3rd Wisconsin. The emotional red-headed Irishman, with blue eyes flaring with excitement, leaned forward and listened intently to Geary shout, "You sir, are to take the road directly to our front. The captain will support if..." Just then an enemy shell exploded thirty yards to their right, showering the officers with dust. Several nearby soldiers dove for cover behind rocks and trees. The officers coolly brushed off the dirt while listening to Geary continue speaking. "As I was saying before our interruption, Bertram will support if practicable. Turning toward to a short, stout officer from the 13th Massachusetts, the colonel pointed to the road leading down into the town. "Captain Shriber, take up a defensive position along the old rifle works on the island to deter the enemy should he choose to ford the river." With a crisp New England salute Shriber sauntered away. Geary completed his instructions for the counterattack by instructing another 13th Massachusetts lieutenant to fall in behind the two Wisconsin companies and support them as needed. An accepting nod by the youthful, clean-shaven officer convinced Geary his men were ready. "Forward boys! Drive the attackers from our field." The colonel pivoted and hustled to settle his nearby reserves who remained scattered defensively about the plateau.

On the lower slope of Bolivar Heights, Beall advanced with the center Confederate column continuing to steadily move forward. Federal cannon fired at Confederate artillery on Loudon Heights, and also randomly lobbed shells in advance of the Virginia militia. The initial experience with artillery minutes before educated the raw Rebel troops that a big gun's intimating bark often preceded only a toothless bite. Captain Maddox swung his ornate sword above his head and jubilantly screamed to his reformed militia, "Forward men of Jefferson County, on to victory!"

Maddox's men resumed their advance until without warning the center of the Southern battle line abruptly halted at the sight of the men in blue methodically descending to meet them. Confused Rebel troops rapidly parted when they heard shouts from behind. They cleared a path upon the realization that their artillery prepared to stall the Yankees' movement. Captain Comfield strategically placed his twenty-four pounder south of an abandoned brick house resting on the lower slope of the heights. In that position the house shielded the gun from enemy fire on the heights to the north but allowed the Rebel cannon a position to spray death amongst advancing Wisconsin troops. Captain Avirett placed his small, long-ranged rifled piece nearby to compliment Comfield's larger gun.

Beall knelt in the safety of a small swale and turned to smile confidently at the young charges placed under his wings. Ben and George impatiently readied themselves on John's right. Seth flanked his left. "Where's Jimmy Burrell," John shouted above the commotion to his friends. Seth's inaudible response forced John to scream the question louder. Ben motioned over to their left where Ashby's cavalry congregated. Jimmy's familiar figure, with a euphoric but sinister smile across his face, sat atop an unfamiliar mount that apparently lost its original rider.

"Should be me instead of him," complained Seth to George. "I can outride him any day of the week, 'cept I'd never desert you boys."

A bright flash of flame crackled from the left of the Yankee battle line. A cloud of hazy smoke obscured the blue-clad rifleman. The nauseating splintering of bone followed by a youthful shriek formulated from the blending of unbearable pain and intense fear. Beall glanced back to sympathetically gawk at one of his young charges rocking back and forth on his side while clutching his right knee with both hands. The jagged hole in the youngster's trousers revealed protruding bone fragments barely visible beneath the steady glistening crimson flow streaming through the boy's fingers. All color drained from the lad's fair cheeks as his eyes rolled shut before he mercifully passed out oblivious to the battle raging all around. Bertram's Wisconsin badgers made their presence felt a hundred yards away. O'Brien's men, to Bertram's right, opened fire from the same distance. Comfield's unit hurriedly positioned its big gun to answer the challenge posed by Federal infantry, especially since the ancient flintlocks in the hands of the green Virginia militia proved no match against percussion cap muskets in the hands of trained Federal troops. With a tug of the cannon lanyard the Rebels more than equalized the fire power. The canister round exploded within the columbiad's barrel, spitting thirty-two one-ounce lead spheres spewing forth agony into O'Brien's company, and bringing forth screams even horrific to the ears of the Southern foe. Before the cannon's path sprawled half a dozen mangled bodies, some still, others writhing in excruciating pain. Small arms fire popped from line to line. After fifteen minutes of sustained fire from the Northerners the Confederates begrudgingly redeployed a hundred yards to the rear which brought a pause in firing. The Federals congregated for twenty minutes near the brick house before assembling into battle formation and moving forward.

Beall turned to offer words of encouragement to the green boys maturing into veterans during the fighting's progression. A damp paste of sweat, dirt, powder residue, and blood spatters coated virgin faces with the battlefield's hellacious grime. Young eyes, innocent only hours earlier, stared knowingly ahead at the line of forty blue-clad advancing soldiers. The short, quiet interlude before the assault abruptly terminated with the spontaneous crackle of Yankee musket fire.

Beall calmly shouted instructions. "Hold your fire until they get closer. A good first shot from each of us'ill stall their attack. Aim high. We hold this ground together.

Reload quickly but efficiently. If they make it through the gully, fix bayonets. Give 'em the steel. Drive 'em back."

From John's left he heard George mumble, "Here we go again, Johnny! I'm beside you."

Beall heard something to his right from Seth. Twisting his head to listen, John froze. Seth lay crumpled on the ground, eyes wide open, without expression on his placid face. Red spurts of blood from Seth's neck stopped. His statuesque stare gazed forever into eternity. Protecting one's homeland and family instills undeniable determination within a man; the sight of a comrade dying in battle releases the demon only retribution recalls. Beall's awareness of danger evaporated with Seth Hendersen's life. Much to his chagrin he observed the thirty-two pounder being withdrawn for fear of capture. In their haste to turn the piece the Rebel gunners snapped the axel on the obsolete carriage supporting the heavy gun. The artillerymen instantly proceeded to spike it to prevent its use against them if captured by the Yankees.

"Fire one more round, then fix bayonets," Beall ordered. Engulfed by a haze of black musket smoke and the chaos of battle both sides became oblivious to any defined battle line. Beall's militia twisted bayonets onto the ends of their gun barrels when a murderous rifle fire to their left tore into the Union right flank. One man's body spun one-hundred-eighty degrees before spreading over the ground like a comforter draped over a bed. Another blue-clad soldier's leg bent ghoulishly to his left instead of forward when his lower leg shattered and dropped him on the ground. A third man's forward movement abruptly stopped before he dropped backwards without a visible attempt to break his fall. The firing spewed from a Rebel militia line concealed from both Beall's unit and the Yankees. The Virginians prepared to carry the day when thunder clapped from their rear.

"What the...," muttered Beall jumping out of formation with his men. The big gun was disabled. The little gun had been removed. Beall squinted through the smoke and smiled. Captain Turner's cavalry galloped through the parting Rebel line toward astounded Federals. Swirling sabers banished by devil-may-care riders reversed the blue troops' movement, forcing them to race to the sanctuary of the brick house to regroup. Had O'Brien and Bertram not ordered a score of disciplined Northern soldiers to pause, fire, and empty several Rebel cavalry saddles, Turner's charge would have prevailed. The riders veered to the left leaving Beall and the militia to resume their attack. The fighting digressed into a series of small skirmishes. John found himself separated from George but accompanied by his young companions. With pandemonium spreading over the battlefield John gathered his small squad.

He observed groups of four or five U.S. troops forty yards ahead slowly backing away from the brick house towards the safety of Union lines. Well-positioned Federal soldiers further up the slope provided protective fire. Remembering Seth's motionless body lying with its face staring skyward, John spoke. "Men, do we let them effortlessly slither away into their lines to wreak havoc upon us another day or do we bury them here, now! Virginia must be preserved for Virginians. Who's with me?"

The young soldiers looked confidently ahead, prepared to follow their fearless leader. "Very good, men. Two of you to each side of me an arm's length apart and a pace back. Once we move follow my lead. If I advance, follow. If I stop to fire, fire also. Stay low. Don't hurry your shots. We're just going rabbit hunting-slow, plump, blue ones. Think of us positioned on a large clock face. You can all tell time can't you?" Soft chuckles indicated a break in the tension. "We're on the six. The brick house rests on the nine. If we reach the two they've lost their cover. We must first control the four before repositioning on the three. Follow me to the four and the house will soon be ours." With that five men lowered their heads and sprinted along the swale toward their first goal. Lead balls whistled overhead or ripped up the turf. Beall's squad reached its first objective before the enemy could reload. Several unprotected Yankees stood within range. Beall moved forward several paces to obtain a more advantageous firing lane. He knelt, effortlessly aimed, cocked, and fired his weapon. The intended victim jumped when the shot, wide of the target, fractured a brick which blew apart from the corner of the house. Shots erupted from Beall's left and right followed by musket smoke drifting above. Beall's confidence grew with the realization his men followed him. He reloaded, aimed, cocked, and fired again. The instant he pulled the trigger the heavyset soldier in his sights moved. A nearby tree received the slug destined to perforate the portly Yankee. Beall reloaded, took aim a third time, and shouted, "This one's for you Seth." Sighting a stationary enemy soldier, he ever so slowly squeezed the trigger. John's torso jerked. Pain seared his rib cage as his chest ripped apart. He tumbled forward with his shoulder absorbing the painful repercussion of his discharging musket.

John Yates Beall lay face down on a quiet battlefield, slowly regaining consciousness. Excruciating pain knifed through the right side of his chest the instant he attempted to roll over. He struggled instead to slowly raise his head, viewing neither Virginia militia nor Federal troops. He squinted at the glaring sun resting directly overhead. He estimated he received his wound several hours ago. He realized he occupied the precarious ground between two combatant forces, though neither friend nor foe roamed nearby. He grasped his weapon and inched along the ground toward the bullet riddled brick sanctuary. Enduring agonizing pain he crawled towards the unoccupied house which both armies coveted hours earlier. With his back resting against the wall and his legs stretched out on the ground he reached for his canteen. Thankfully the sloshing inside the wooden container indicated water remained. Tightness in his chest inhibited his ability to swallow; still he forced two mouthfuls down his throat. The warm water tasted sweeter than any cool water ever obtained from the well back home. After ten minutes he sensed he must reach his lines before fighting resumed. Using his gun as a staff he struggled to his feet and staggered half a mile through high grass before collapsing. Lying there semiconsciously he thought he heard the thud of several sets of hooves. Surreally he imagined a cloudy conversation between an unfamiliar voice and a familiar one.

"Let's dump 'em here," said the familiar voice.

"Then what?"

"I'll appropriately prepare them for their maker, that's what."

"How you gonna do that?"

"Shut up and watch!" the familiar voice sharply demanded.

Several moments later John dreamed he heard the unknown voice utter, "My God, let's get out of here."

Beall lay semiconsciously awhile longer before he looked in the direction of the voices. No horses or men, just an illusion. Oddly though, one voice sounded like, no, couldn't have been. One more swig of water, then on the move again.

Painfully he pulled himself to his feet, and forced himself to take the first miserable step. For you Mother, he thought, as one foot slowly lead the other. The crackle of distant rifle fire shattered the silence, causing John to peer over his shoulder while he staggered several more feet. He tripped and fell forward, moaning in agony when the ground smashed his throbbing chest. As he knelt to regain his feet he discovered he had fallen into an unfathomable sight more horrific than any yet witnessed on this disastrous day. Blood-soaked blue uniforms littered the ground. He gagged at the sight of four completely naked bodies strewn about. Their legs lay together with arms stretched perpendicular to the torsos. Disfiguring bayonet wounds appeared to have been inflicted after the men expired. Short, crude, desecrating slices even serrated the open palms of one man. Regurgitating acid burned Beall's throat when he realized that some sick soul sought to symbolize a crucifixion. No human beings deserved this, not even Yankees. He began to understand the difference between soldiers and guerrillas.

God help him if he ever digressed to the latter. An exploding artillery shot prodded him to continue his grueling trek.

He struggled to his feet, took a step, and another. One more step. Left, right, left, right. An hour later John heard voices. When he stumbled onto Halltown Road several riders appeared. He raised his arm to secure aid, slipped to his knees, and passed out in the dusty road.

Three riders sped to the fallen man. One hopped off his horse, looked up at the other two, and dejectedly shook his head. "Yep, he's one of ours. In really bad shape. Doubt if he'll make it. Get him on your horse, Aaron. We'll see if the doc's at camp yet." Another rider dismounted and roughly helped push the limp body up on the third horse while its rider tugged from above. Unconscious moans filled the air throughout the ride. Ten minutes later Beall lay incoherently covered with a dirty blanket.

An elderly man approached the doctor tending the wounded. Andrew Hunter, the well-known attorney who prosecuted John Brown two years earlier, rode out with his spring wagon to transport the wounded more comfortably. The irony that Brown's raid transpired exactly two years ago to the day did not escape the lawyer.

"Doctor, who do you want moved first?"

"Take your choice, Mr. Hunter, although the two over there are probably beyond help," replied the doctor motioning in Beall's direction. He glanced at the pair of motionless bodies and raced over when he recognized one.

"Dear God, this is Johnny Beall. Get him in the wagon!" Hunter exclaimed. "I'll take him to Janet before darkness sets in."

Pulling Hunter aside the doctor solemnly whispered, "Are you sure. He's really bad. Several ribs are damaged. The round penetrated his right lung. And he's coughing blood." Placing his hand on Hunter's forearm the doctor pleaded, "Why not take someone possessing a chance?"

Andrew Hunter defiantly jerked his arm away and harshly responded, "Because I owe it to his mother, his four sisters, and the departed soul of his fine father. If he dies, he dies at home."

Thirty minutes later Timothy walked out of the barn at the sounds of hooves and creaking wagon wheels. He peered into the wagon. The moment he recognized its contents he uncontrollably shook and sobbed. Hunter left the helpless groom by the wagon. He climbed the porch steps, opened the door without knocking, and encountered Mary. His solemn face conveyed the tragic words soon to follow. "It's Johnny. He's wounded. Severely. Where's your mother?"

"I heard!" screamed Janet entering the kitchen and racing through the back door behind Mary. Janie, Beth, and Annie followed on Mother's heels. Timothy, regaining his composure, and Andrew Hunter aided by Janet and Mary, gently carried John onto the parlor couch. Mary and Janet removed the bloody coat and vest, and stained, sweaty shirt. Mary winced at the bullet hole before she indiscriminately tossed the clothing to the floor.

"The doctor said the bullet pierced his lung after grazing his ribs. Since the round wasn't deeply embedded, Doc removed it." Hunter said.

Janet and Mary continued to comfort the patient. Annie, with tear-streaked face, hugged a crying Janie. Beth stood in a trance alone in the corner staring expressionlessly at her brother. The Beall women prepared for a long night, one they knew not whether they wanted to end.

10 – RECOVERY

Time stood still since that tragic event two weeks earlier. With each passing day, the burgundy floral wallpaper and heavy gold drapes shrunk the walls of the converted parlor confining John. His mother and sisters pampered him at every opportunity, inadvertently fostering his mood of melancholy with the extensive care they provided. An increasing number of waking hours permitted him the occasion to read books and newspapers without interruption. However, boredom eventually overcame him without alternatives to challenge his mind. Conversations with family members offered minimal diversions, for discussions digressed to either the weather or the lack of significant war news. During the day unanticipated visions of Seth's eternally expressionless eyes haunted him while at night unsettling images of the desecrated Yankees reappeared. Despite war's horrors he yearned to return to the 2nd Virginia, participate in the concluding action of the war, and in the process regain the male companionship he sorely lacked.

With his left arm he reached for the half-filled water glass resting by the white pitcher atop the small, pink marble topped table beside his makeshift bed. He winced the instant jagged pain shot through the right side of his chest into his shoulder. Would he ever heal? His throbbing chest indicated a lengthy recovery. He closed his eyes in the vain attempt to foresee his future. A drab curtain concealed the stage upon which the next act would play. He reflected upon his performance during the preceding scene. He possessed a sense of pride recalling his leadership of young, unskilled troops in battle. He smiled, recalling the willingness with which they followed him. He ascertained the four lads accompanying him on his final assault escaped injury. How he longed for the opportunity to lead again.

A knock on the door jolted him back to the present. Mary's enthusiastic voice called out, "Johnny, if you are up to it I have a guest to see you."

Besides a visit from the doctor which John barely remembered, and a brief visit from Andrew Hunter two days ago, the only male contact John encountered arrived with the daily well wishes and assurances of Timothy. The wounded soldier eagerly replied to his sister, "Send him in now."

"Ah, he's a she," Mary replied awkwardly. "Are you presentable?"

"Well, I'm," aw, what the heck he thought, any new face would be a welcome change, although he could not fathom whose. "Certainly, send her in."

Mary opened the door for the slender form of Miss Sue Ellen O'Brien to enter. The visitor's bright pink cotton dress with white collar accentuated her narrow neck which supported her head with a slight aristocratic tilt. Her narrow beige bonnet concealed hair twisted in a bun atop her head. A blue ribbon drawn loosely around her neck held the bonnet in place, complementing her thin face. In her usual forward manner, though inappropriately, Miss O'Brien removed her gloves. Mary left the door open and departed, totally aware the spider prepared to spin her web. Sue Ellen glided toward the patient, set a straight chair aside the bed, and gracefully settled herself.

"Oh, Johnny, how good to see you in the safety of your own home. Imagine, you could be in some disgusting prison constantly harassed by those Yankee devils," she said, wincing and resting her hand on her forehead. She grasped his hand and exclaimed with a wide-eyed expression, "Or heaven forbid, even worse." Amazing how the warm, loving grasp of a mother or a sister lacked the soft, sensuous touch of an attractive member of the opposite sex.

"Thank you, Sue Ellen." He never addressed her by her first name before yet it seemed as natural as her bare hand upon his.

Leaning back with a more proper feminine posture she continued resting her hand over his. In a pious tone she said, "I prayed to our caring Lord for your recovery since becoming aware of your dreadful injury. I am thankful for his benevolent response."

"I too am thankful but I am far from a complete recovery. As you know, the round partially entered my lung. Several of our relations suffered from consumption. The wound only amplifies the potential for the infliction to appear." Embarrassment welled within him. He barely knew this woman, certainly not intimately enough to speak of his innermost fears. And he most certainly desired no woman's sympathy.

Intuitively Sue Ellen smoothly steered the conversation toward a different path. "Everyone says this evil war the abolitionists cast upon us shall end by summer. What are your plans then?"

Where is this going, he wondered? "My primary focus remains to regain my health so that I may participate in the climax. After that I'll return home and confront the Negro issue."

In a condescending tone she bluntly stated, "When we win there shall be no Negro issue. The abolitionists shall be barred from our land with their high and mighty ideas of emancipation."

"Miss O'Brien, I respectfully beg to differ." Did use of her last name imply he wished to deter the familiarity she assumed with him? "Whether the North attacked us or not, we would have had to deal with the issue soon enough, although now we shall on our own terms. Agriculture becomes more mechanized. We completed the grain harvest using the reaper in a fraction of the time with fewer hands. With little uncleared, tillable land available in Virginia, the need for common field hands decreases. If we have no work for them, economics dictates we cannot feed, cloth, and house them. Some suggest we lease them to factories in the cities. The practice exists in Richmond but Dan Lucas tells me the arrangement provides little control after the workday because they live unsupervised in company housing. Some even earn extra income after they fulfill their contracted hours. In that setting they are only a step away from freedom. We'll also face economic hardship when our investment's value drops. Remember, lenders accept them as collateral too."

Sue Ellen interrupted, "Can't we ship them farther south? Cotton and sugar planters pay large sums for labor. And Poppa says new lands will become available to the west."

"That's a sound observation," John replied. A smile crossed her face as she absorbed the compliment. He would learn more existed above her shoulders than a pretty little face. Her proud glow faded when he said, "But mechanization shall eventually reach cotton just as it now begins impacting sugar production. And who's to say lands beyond Texas and Arkansas choose to join the Confederacy. The dilemma should concern us more. We shall require domestic labor, stable hands, and a few Negroes to perform menial tasks unsuited for white men. But as I said, the need for high priced field hands already diminishes. If no work exists here or to the south where do we send them? Freedmen balked at being shipped back to Africa as I imagine would our Negroes on Walnut Grove. Crises evolve when men, black or white, with hungry families to feed, lack work. We must…"

"Scores of unmanageable darkies roaming the area!" Sue Ellen gasped. "It's terrifying enough as it is now for a white woman to encounter a freed Negro! How shall we cope if they all roam about unsupervised?"

"As I said, this is a real dilemma. The high and mighty Yankees demand we free them but refuse to accept them in the north. Some men with whom I've discussed the issue suggest as your father does that we export them beyond Texas but I've addressed that questionable solution. A more practical alternative depends upon the growth of a strong new nation. Lush lands await development in the Caribbean, Mexico, and beyond. These primitive regions attract labor tolerant of hot climates but do not require strong mental capacity. A free labor force might be effective, but not as profitable or benevolent as our current institution. Several expeditions to obtain these lands failed in the past. Between ineffective commanders, a spineless president, Yankee interference, and European objections, the attempts for southern expansion came to naught. A vibrant, economically sound Confederacy with a strong military, befriended by Europe, and absent of Yankee interference enhances our satisfactory resolution of the issue."

John reached for his water glass only to experience reoccurring pain shooting through his body. To no avail he failed to suppress his grimace.

"Forgive me if my visit fatigues you," Sue Ellen said, while batting her eyelashes.

"If so, I tire delightfully."

"I really must go, but if I may be so forward, I must first ask," she innocently said with a pause. When did Sue Ellen ever ask permission to be forward? He nodded for her to continue. "Do you ever look beyond the day to day activities of operating your estate and consider other interests?"

He recognized the path she now traveled but felt up to a mental joust even though he overmatched her. "I have considered investing in several manufacturing facilities in Richmond. Land speculation intrigues me too. In fact, six years ago, Mary and I just arrived in New York when we received the message to return home due to Father's brief illness and subsequent death which prevented our trip to Iowa for possible land purchases. I believe God desired that I remain in Jefferson County although I now do own several parcels in Iowa."

"And live out your life as a lonely bachelor forever!" she impatiently blurted out.

Checkmate, he thought. Not much challenge in this match. Still this woman, with whom he was growing more comfortable, deserved a sincere response. Placing his right hand over hers which rested upon his left hand, he intently locked his warm blue eyes with her sparkling green eyes.

“Sometime—yes, in the immediate future—no. A great deal of effort shall be required to stabilize and grow Jefferson County after the war, in the least a year or two. I must be prepared to devote time and energy if duty calls. I adamantly declare,” he emphasized in an admonishing tone, “that no consideration of other thoughts shall be entertained until the Yankees leave Virginia, and accept and formally recognize our commonwealth as a member of a new and sovereign country. For the war’s duration my only commitment remains to Virginia. A man on the battlefield needs no distraction to dilute his focus while fighting for freedom.” He graciously added, “Even if that distraction be a Jefferson County belle of Irish descent.”

A broad smile rolled across Sue Ellen’s face. In her heart she new him to be an honest, forthright gentleman. She accepted his lack of commitment to her, understanding she only competed with Virginia. And two or three months remained for her to ingratiate herself with him before he returned to the army. His unwillingness to commit to her made him all the more appealing.

When they heard Janet’s footsteps approach hands quickly separated. “So kind of you to visit, Sue Ellen. John greatly appreciates your company. The same familiar faces day after day do little to stimulate the mind.”

“Don’t say that Mother. You know without your care, and that of my sisters, my improvement would be stifled.”

“Thank you, Son.” Turning to Sue Ellen she asked, “May I serve you any refreshment.”

“I fear I must decline. With these uncertain times Poppa prefers I visit only briefly so that I have ample daylight to journey on well-traveled highways.”

“We can’t be too cautious, can we? I am so glad you have the opportunity to see John before he travels south to continue his recovery.”

Sue Ellen’s head whirled toward him when she absorbed the words. “Travel south! How far? When?”

“I’m so sorry Sue Ellen,” replied Janet coming to her son’s defense. “I thought John informed you the doctor believes for a thorough and expedient recovery that a winter spent in a warmer climate shall be beneficial. We've encouraged him, and he recently, though reluctantly, consented. We'll miss his presence on New Years Day for the first time ever. None of the men who grace my life shall be present unless Will manages a leave, which remains doubtful," she sadly said before she walked away.

"John Beall! Why didn't you inform me rather than embarrass me in front of your mother?"

"Miss O'Brien, I planned to inform you earlier, but if you recall, we became enthralled in a complex dialogue. Do you believe I would fail to extend to you the common courtesy of communicating my short term plans? I would have offered such to any visitor."

So I'm just any visitor she thought. Fighting the natural desire to respond defensively she grasped the offensive, utilized her innate charm, and managed to follow his lead. "Mr. Beall, I have no doubts your intentions represent your high moral character. Forgive my atypical outburst. I should have better controlled my disappointment upon realizing I shall not have opportunity for numerous visits prior to your return to our army." With the flicker of her eyelashes in harmony with her subtle smile she softly begged, "Can you find it in your heart to forgive this mammoth transgression?"

"Miss O'Brien, I forgive your commission of this minor indiscretion." His soft blue eyes indicated sincere exoneration.

As she rose to depart Sue Ellen leaned over to leave an affectionate kiss upon his forehead, and perhaps by design, perhaps by chance, she managed to bring her chest to within fractions of an inch of touching his hand. John understood he dealt with one enticing woman.

"Johnny Beall, I look forward to seeing you again, whether before your departure or after your return."

"As do I, Sue Ellen."

Alone again John pondered a future opportunity to visit with her. He firmly believed couples should avoid involvement until the conflict ended. War placed personal lives on hold, necessary when combatants truly desired victory. Chivalrous Virginians understood this sacrifice. Hedonistic Yankees never would, precisely the foundation upon which the South shall prevail. John drifted into a peaceful nap, realizing his departure before her next visit presented the optimum course of action for both their benefits.

In the following days he began to rise and walk throughout the house. His seeping wound required the daily changing of bandages but three weeks after his wounding he ventured outside and into the barn where he chatted with Timothy. Several days later he even managed a twenty minute stroll through the orchard. Four weeks to the day of the Bolivar Heights action found him seated with Mother and Janie, partaking of a midday meal of roast pork, carrots, and stewed apples. The other girls had taken the wagon into town for supplies to purchase provisions before wartime inflation drove prices even higher.

Mother casually inquired, "Have you given thought to your departure date?"

"I hope to sufficiently heal first. Although the entire journey to Tallahassee should be completed by rail, unplanned events could dictate travel on horseback."

"Florida's so far away," interjected Janie. "Why go there? Georgia or South Carolina's closer."

"You are absolutely correct my dear sister but the farther south I travel the warmer the climate. The warmer the climate the sooner I recover. The sooner I recover the sooner I return to General Jackson and Will, and whip the Yankees for good."

"And maybe get shot again!" Janie curtly replied.

"Janeta Beall, neither your brother nor I shall tolerate that sort of talk," Janet scolded.

"Mother, if she possesses such fears she should articulate them." Looking compassionately at his youngest sister he continued speaking. "Janie, every soldier understands he might be wounded during battle. We acknowledge the risk of death. None of us expect it." He paused before he whispered, "I'm sure Seth didn't." He proudly stated, "But feel blessed, my dear sister, that you live in a society where honor-bound men respond to the call to arms when their families and homes are threatened. Never believe death on the battlefield, nor any death for that matter is glorious." Pausing he added, "Except for that death on the cross so many centuries ago. But death on the battlefield can be noble. If my life on earth ends prematurely, which I do not intend to allow, you shall experience immense sadness but you must not grieve for me. You need to look beyond to your unborn children, to their children, and the great-grandchildren you may never know. Smile and visualize the wonderful land preserved for them with every drop of Virginian blood shed in this time, in my time, in your time."

A tear rolled down Janie's cheek. With a loud chuckle, John reached over and squeezed her shoulder. "Fear not, I'm an experienced soldier now. This wound taught me the wisdom of recognizing when to duck."

Her face brightened. At fifteen she felt ashamed she failed to control her emotions. Janet suddenly looked out the window toward the sound of hooves thudding down the lane. The girls shouldn't be back yet. No creek of wagon wheels to be heard. Boots thumping on the wooden porch preceded a sharp knock on the door.

11 – AN ABRUPT DEPARTURE

"Why George Ranson," Janet warmly greeted the newcomer. "you're just in time for dinner. Pull up a chair." Turning to her youngest daughter she said, "Janie, fill a plate for him."

Hanging his coat and hat on the pegs by the door George eagerly obliged.

"What brings you here, friend?" asked John. "Haven't seen you since, well, a month ago."

"Partly social, partly business. I apologize for not getting over sooner. After the battle, folks said you weren't up ta seeun visitors right off. Pa also had me working with the partisans to gather information and keep an eye on the Yankees. Got to help burn down old Herr's mill. Served him right. The old coot's just fortunate he wasn't around or things might have gotten a bit hot for him too."

"George, please," admonished Janet casting her eyes toward Janie.

"Sorry, Mrs. Beall got carried away with the update. Anyways, the real purpose for my visit, though I wanted to see you too, Johnny, is military. Ever since that lying Geary fabricated the tale that our boys stripped, mutilated, and even crucified dead Yankees, old Banks has been rambling on how there will be, I think his exact words were, 'debts to repay.' Several scouts report rumors filtering from the Federal camp indicating Yankee troops will be roaming the countryside next week trying to flush out partisans and will treat them as guerrillas, which means hanging. Anyone caught harboring a guerrilla could have their property confiscated or destroyed."

"I cannot believe the enemy stoops to such disgraceful tactics to subdue us," said Janet with a contempt-laced voice. "Implying Virginians desecrate human bodies is ludicrous. Mr. Lincoln reaches to depths even once unfathomable for him, but that should be expected since his war is going so badly." John never witnessed such a vile expression across his mother's face. He avoided shattering her misconception that only honorable Virginians waged war against the Yankees.

"As I was saying Mrs. Beall, by the way this is an excellent meal," said George swallowing another mouthful. "With the Federals looking for retribution it's probably best for all of you if Johnny clears out. The fact he's part of the 2nd might be questioned by some lieutenant or captain trying to set an example and impress his colonel. If you leave within a day or two you should be safe. Wait much longer and who knows?"

"If I catch the ten o'clock train tomorrow morning I could be in Richmond sometime the following day. I hope to visit briefly with Dan, find Will, and then journey to Charleston and Savannah before traveling to my final destination."

"Savannah! That's almost in Florida isn't it, Johnny?"

"Last time I checked it was George."

"Why you going way down there? Not enough pretty ladies in Virginia to nurse you back to health?" he joked.

"There are more than enough here," replied John with memories of Sue Ellen's visit flashing through his mind. "The doctor believes my partially perforated lung will better heal in a warm, sunny climate rather than in the cold, damp weather we experience here. In spring I'll rejoin the 2nd, help whip the Yankees, and return here to plant my crops."

Less than twenty-four hours later John made himself comfortable in the Winchester & Potomac coach. Shortly he'd be in Winchester where he'd arrange transportation to Strasburg. From there he'd switch lines twice before arriving in Richmond. He wore the new shirt Mother insisted upon. She destroyed his bloodstained battle shirt. His uniform now consisted of his repaired frock coat and cleaned trousers. God only knows where his kepi lay. Rifle and accouterments accompanied him although he planned to store them with Dan. He carried enough food to feed four men on a two day journey. He simply smiled and expressed appreciation rather than decline Mother's offering. He'd locate Will and unload, rather disperse, the excess bounty.

Janie, Annie, and Beth openly cried when he said his farewells in the kitchen. Mother gave him a long, warm hug. Her tears would come late that night in the privacy of her room away from her daughters. Mary accompanied him to the station, gave him a sisterly hug, and stoically waved as his train departed the station.

12 – A SLOW, INFORMATIVE JOURNEY

The train chugged through Berkley County with John eerily pondering when he might return to Jefferson County. He regretted failing to bid Sue Ellen farewell, not for romantic motive, but purely as a courtesy. For the time being he wished to distance himself from the relationship she believed existed although he held an obligation to express his appreciation for her visit. During his upcoming convalescence in Florida he would compose a concise note, a well-thought-out epistle without any hint of hidden meaning for which the fairer sex was so inclined to search.

Exhausted from the day's exertion he kept to himself and rested. After enduring an hour in the smoke filled coach, caused by a loose-fitting woodstove door, the relieved passengers departed the train following their twenty-mile journey. At the Winchester station he joined two dozen people seeking transportation. A stagecoach driver informed the group his vehicle would depart shortly in order to reach Strasburg for the 9 p.m. train to Manassas. Upon hearing of the eight dollar rate per person in gold, many passengers angrily threatened to commandeer his vehicle and without remorse inflict bodily harm upon him. With revolver drawn, the town's middle aged sheriff interceded much to the disgust of several disgruntled complainers.

The peace officer stared at two men presumed to be merchants, though by the condition of their clothes, somewhat unsuccessful. He bluntly stated, "If that's unsatisfactory to you gents you can lodge in the jail tonight for disturbing the peace and pay a ten dollar fine in the morning."

"Apologies, Sheriff," quickly acquiesced one of them. The peddlers realized the lawman received a cut from the lucrative venture.

Having his audience's full attention the law officer continued in an authoritative tone. "For those willing to wait, or who are short on funds, the hotel across the way puts you up and feeds you for six bits, four to a room of course."

"Naturally," a cynical voice muttered from the rear of the crowd. The visitors acknowledged the town sheriff benefited from much of the town's commerce.

The officer continued ineptly sympathizing with the travelers. "If you folks will be kind enough to let me continue, teamsters leave for Strasburg at first light tomorrow with room on their wagons at a dollar a head. You should arrive by afternoon with plenty of time to catch the 9:00 train tomorrow evening or possibly the 3:00 afternoon departure." All but three passengers headed out the door toward the hotel. A woman wearing a worn blue dress, tightly-tied blue bonnet, and simple gray homespun coat, stood anxiously by, holding a bulging carpet bag. Her age and resolute disposition reminded John of Mother.

The other passenger, a well-dressed man in his middle thirties, appearing to have missed very few meals lately, spoke up. "Four dollars now and another twelve if you really do get us there for the nine o'clock train tonight."

An insincere expression of hurt crossed the coachman's face. "Sir I'm an honest man making an honest living. You greatly offend me when you question my integrity."

"And sir," replied the portly passenger, pompously grasping the labels of his expensive coat, "I am a highly successful entrepreneur cognizant that talk is cheap." He paused before sarcastically adding, "Especially talk from a man who profits from the war at the expense of loyal Virginians."

Something in the man's demeanor caused John to wonder if this wasn't the pot calling the kettle black.

The coachman looked to John and to the elderly woman and barked, "Are you two coming along?"

John already felt weak from the day's exertion or he would confront the coachman's rudeness. He only said, "Yes, let's get going."

"And you ma'm?" asked the coachman.

"Sir, I only have thirteen dollars. I'm traveling to Strasburg to bring my son home from a battle injury he received three weeks ago. Could you see it in your heart to reduce the rate?"

"Sorry ma'm, in fairness to the others, a rate's a rate. Besides, thought the army gave the wounded transportation home."

"Only by rail," she said with a frown. "And Yankees control the rails from Harpers Ferry to Maryland where we live. Please sir?"

"What kind of patriot are you?" the well-attired passenger challenged.

The red-faced coachman stepped forward with clenched fists and blurted out, "I've had enough of your high-filuting, uppity attitude. We'll settle..."

"Now Nehemiah," interrupted the sheriff, "the gentleman is paying us, I mean you a double fare. Let him have his say and then get moving. These two men have to be on the road."

"And this dear sweet lady too," interrupted John, removing her fare from his pocket. He handed it directly to the sheriff who smiled with relief when the foursome headed to the stagecoach.

"Son, I don't know how to thank you," said the woman with heartfelt gratitude.

"I trust that were my mother in a similar situation a like kindness would be extended," replied John with a tip of his hat.

At the end of the very uncomfortable four-hour ride the woman bid farewell to her traveling companions and scurried toward the small hotel to see her boy.

"Mr. Beall, please join me for dinner, regardless of how modest the meal may be," offered John's fellow traveler. While he only desired to rest before resuming the grueling night of rail travel John accepted the invitation to better pass the time. Soon the two men dined on over-cooked mutton, mushy sweet potatoes, strong coffee, and a small dish of a fresh apple cobbler.

"I certainly appreciate your company this evening, Mr. Beall. I dine alone too often. You seemed somewhat subdued on the carriage ride. You mentioned you recently suffered a wound. I also believe you mentioned your vocation is agriculture."

"Yes, Mr. Higgins, although agriculture temporarily is in the past tense until the conflict concludes this spring."

"I do pray you are correct as do all Virginians. Politics tend to become complicated. Lincoln says he desires to welcome us back into the Union but too much blood already has been shed and Virginia harbors no wish to return. If she and possibly Tennessee, and let us say North Carolina did accept such a reunion the cotton states would remain estranged. Northern troops would march through the commonwealth and the events of last spring would replay again. Unfortunately the radicals residing in both the North and South covet the opportunity to structure their national governments as they see fit. The Yankees castigate slavery. Those after power insincerely wave the abolition banner only to gain antislavery support. Our staunch secessionists to the south condemn damned abolitionists to grasp for the occasion to become bigger players on a larger stage. This war revolves around power. Those without it will sacrifice many a good boy's life for it; those with it will continue forfeiting lives to keep it. The Europeans also watch the game unfold. Once the French and English determine who holds the better cards they'll pull up a chair along side the obvious winner, boasting they planned such allegiances since day one. We both know politicians prolong the misery for their own self-serving benefit." Higgins gregariously laughed and added, "Which means this conflict continues longer than most suspect."

"Then I expect I'll be wearing a uniform longer than originally anticipated. What shall you be doing, Mr. Higgins?" John casually questioned.

"By vocation I am a merchant. As a lad I learned the dry goods trade. Later I discovered livestock, especially prime horses, could be transported rather quickly and turned at a larger profit to boot. Next I tried trading in niggers. Made only a modest profit first go around because the best buck of the bunch broke for the river before we subdued him. Don't know if the black son of a bitch drowned or escaped. I didn't cotton to losing $1500 dollars on account of some unpredictable darkie. Speaking of cotton, that's what I've been doing the past four years. Suffered a setback when I started but I am now quite proficient," Higgins replied with a gloating smirk.

"How do you occupy your days now, sir? The Yankees blockade the coast, and President Davis seems anxious to assist them by imposing his export embargo on cotton. With all due respect, you're out of business."

"Mr. Beall, what is your most profitable crop?"

"Under ideal conditions, apples."

"What happens to prices when a harsh frost enters the valley as the blossoms form?"

"Apples and cider sell at higher prices in the fall."

"Exactly! The Yankees and our not so astute Confederate president both drive up the price of cotton. Supply and demand—simple economics. He who finds a means to supply receives handsome rewards."

John cynically stated, "Sir, you imply you break the law for personal gain."

Higgins smiled softly and confidently responded, "Mr. Beall, your supposition is logical. I take a substantial risk for a modest profit to provide our young country with what she most needs, manufactured goods from Europe, not to mention strong commercial ties with the continent. Astute Southerners realize that which escapes our idealistic political leaders. Well-equipped and well-fed men win battles. Food and war materials cost money. Trade with Europe transforms our cotton into weapons, shot, powder, and uniforms. Man for man one of our boys can whip two or three Yankees provided we equally equip our troops. I may go against Jeff Davis's policy today but mark my words, within twelve months he'll be willing to ship all the cotton we produce."

John flourished in a black and white world. This man capitalized in gray. John visualized the stripped, desecrated Yankee bodies he tripped over that fateful October day. Yes, he began understanding the longer the war continued the grayer it would become. Strong commitment to his duty would be the only path leading John away from the gray uncertainty. Politely he offered, "Issues do become complicated, do they not Mr. Higgins?"

"Unfortunately they do, Mr. Beall, and not of our choosing." Gazing out the window at the darkened sky Higgins removed his watch from his vest pocket, squinted at the piece in the dim light, and said, "Mr. Beall, if you ever become interested in this sort of commerce remember the parting words of advice from old Winfred Higgins—he who controls shipping controls price." With a slight grin and nod of his head the merchant ambled towards the door with Beall at his side.

Feeding the ego of the other man while satisfying his own curiosity John asked, "How does one control shipping?"

Higgins reveled in responding to his companion's inquiries. "Despite the traps set by the Yankees along the coast numerous options exist for men willing to take initiative. England presently builds sleek, fast, shallow-draft boats to outrun the Federals and elude their blockade. Several successful round trips and you've paid for your vessel free and clear, but," cautioned Higgins with a wave of the index finger, "the risk of capture always exists."

Upon entering the Manassas Gap passenger coach the pair discovered only single seats remained unoccupied. "Mr. Higgins, thank you for the informative evening." The merchant responded with a like farewell and advanced toward the front to a vacant seat.

John seated himself beside a middle aged man dressed in work clothes, who opened his eyes to mumble "good evening" and then leaned back and shut them. John appreciated the opportunity for much-needed sleep. When his chest began throbbing he felt drips of seepage from his wound trickle through his bandage and down his abdomen. With the journey's progression smoke from the stove subtly crept throughout the coach, provoking John to cough and wince while reminding him his fractured ribs would require weeks to heal. His back ached from the long, exhausting day. His head drooped as he slipped into a welcome slumber.

The passenger coach's jolting stop awakened him with a rude jerk. The conductor bellowed, "Everyone off. End of the line. The southbound midnight train departs in forty-five minutes. The northbound run leaves at half past twelve."

John exited the railcar and plodded toward the Orange and Alexandria Railroad station half a block away. Gazing up, he paused to absorb the serenity of the star-lit sky. The line at the ticket counter extended out through the doors onto the covered boardwalk. John waved to Higgins who chose to visit the tavern instead of waiting in line. Less than twenty minute later John boarded the passenger coach for uninterrupted sleep until the locomotive wrenched him forward with its departure. Two minutes later he again slept soundly. At 3:45 a.m. he pulled his fatigued body up to again transfer rail lines. Although he considered purchasing a hot breakfast before the train departed at 6:00 a.m., he opted for a seat in the Virginia Central Railroad station, fearing he might doze off if away from the station, and thus miss his connection. He consumed an early morning meal of ham, day old biscuits, apples, and cider, all from the complimentary cuisine Mother thrust into his arms yesterday morning. The train departed Gordonsville and chugged east toward the brightening sky. He avoided the aggravation of another transfer by spending two extra dollars and not switching to the Richmond, Fredericksburg, and Potomac Line when the Virginia Central crossed its tracks. He succumbed to sleep with the train winding towards Richmond through picturesque rolling countryside. At 11:00 a.m. he stood on the front porch of Dan Lucas's Richmond townhouse at the corner of Canal and Eighth Streets.

The sharp clanging of the door knocker summoned a longtime servant with wooly gray hair cropped close to his head. His dark ebony face contrasted his sparkling white teeth. The Lucases always possessed well-maintained people.

With a sincere smile the domestic welcomed John. "Massa Beall, Massa Daniel told me to expect you. He got your telegram yesterday afternoon. General Wise has him busy til late this afternoon doin what Lord only knows. Nothing much a happening with the war now days. Did hear you was shot bad. Glad to see you're alright. Let me take your things and show you to your room. You hungry or thirsty?"

"Thank you, Reuben, but I'll rest for awhile. Frequently transferring rail lines proved extremely strenuous. Wake me by four."

After a week's rest in Richmond, courtesy of his friend, John boarded a train headed southwest. While in the city he purchased new clothes. He left his uniform, musket, and accoutrements with Dan, expecting to reclaim them upon his return in the spring. He was taken back by the inflated prices from the dry goods store, almost three times higher than prewar prices. With Christmas only several weeks away holiday shoppers crowded businesses establishments, albeit with a more diverse mixture of people than John previously remembered in Richmond. The thriving Virginia capital expanded in all directions with its transformation into a national capital. While grateful for the week's hospitality and Dan's company, plus the opportunity to visit Will, John experienced relief upon departing the city. He now traveled at a leisurely pace with imminent danger from Yankees far to the north. He prayed for his mother's and his sisters' safety. Late in the afternoon he transferred from the Richmond and York Railroad to the North Carolina Line. Arriving in

Greensboro he spent a relaxing evening before he departed for Columbia the following day. Via the Wilmington & Manchester and then the South Carolina Railroad he migrated to Charleston. While in the port city he hoped to visit Fort Sumter and of course anticipated dining upon the excellent coastal cuisine. He also desired to board the sleek cargo ships that Higgins spoke of, now referred to as blockade runners. Eventually he would travel to Savannah aboard the Charleston & Savannah Rail system. He hoped to reach Tallahassee by New Years Day.

Whereas Richmond experienced unmanageable growth the past six months, Charleston, the city the Yankees blamed for initiating the war, remained the charmingly southern city John anticipated. Recent mild weather and ample rainfall brightened the green lawns of the stately mansions along the waterfront in an area known as the Battery. John obtained lodging in the quaint but elegant Planters' Hotel near the market. Exuberance emanated from local citizens although eight months passed since Fort Sumter's fall. An abundance of high priced European wines and liquors continued feeding the euphoria, especially among those who had dreamed of their separation from the Union for over thirty years. Imported apparel and perfumes filled store shelves. John could not imagine a more robust economy. During his five day stay he roamed the waterfront while recuperating in the agreeable, mild sunny climate. He engaged in enlightening conversations with sea captains whenever the opportunity arose. Much to his surprise, his prior perception of a pompous Winfred Higgins rapidly transformed into admiration for the astute businessman involved in enterprise greatly aiding the war effort. Too much coastline existed for the sparse Federal navy to patrol. Inordinate numbers of Yankee vessels would be required for the impossible task of sealing the Confederate coast. And European shipyards christened ships faster than the Yankees could capture them. John recognized control of the rivers and seas to be equally essential to the successes on land for Confederate victory. The chameleon conflict continued turning assorted shades of gray, an especially dark shade of gray now, the hue of camouflaging blockade runners' hulls against the horizon above the sea.

Early on December 16, John boarded the train for the morning journey to Savannah. Precisely two months ago he suffered his wound. Bandages now required changing only every third day. Reoccurring pain periodically revisited his chest. An ever present nagging cough still accompanied him. His lack of stamina proved most disconcerting although he continued planning for a complete recovery within two months.

Arriving in Savannah he rediscovered much of the costal ambiance he left in Charleston while he acknowledged that due to Fort Sumter's capitulation an atmosphere existed in the South Carolinian harbor unique to all other Southern cities. He enjoyed a daily routine of sleeping late, dining at midday on sumptuous seafood, and traversing the waterfront to quench his thirst for knowledge of blockade runners. Maritime adventure appeared more enticing with each passing day.

During his four days in Savannah he grew progressively enamored with the lucrative blockade running business. Reclining on his bed before an evening meal, he recognized that the adventuresome activity gradually lured him away from his duty with the 2nd Virginia. Grandfather Yates's and Father's presence surrounded him as he considered his future. His responsibility lay with the army. While success demanded Southern control of the seas, Will and the 2nd Virginia depended on each man's commitment. When God healed him, John would follow his conscience back to Virginia.

The following day the Savannah, Albany, & Gulf locomotive pulled away from the Georgia station. Christmas in Florida. Who'd have thought last year this time? He dreaded another thirty-six hours of jostling over rough rail beds. Warmer temperatures eliminated the inconvenience of the poorly vented stoves, but necessitated the opening of windows for ventilation, forcing passengers to contend with dirty, hot ashes flying into the coach. Mother always said many folks had larger burdens to carry then her family. Could he really complain while enjoying these late December balmy temperatures?

Journeying deeper south John was about to encounter a couple who would impact the balance of his life. The congenial pair sat directly across from him. Their thick southern accents indicated dialects from Louisiana? A deep yellow traveling dress, sewn from expensive cloth, covered the middle aged woman's rotund, matronly body. Green gloves covered her thick fingers. A pale blue bonnet outlined her round, white face. Beside her sat a slender man, at least a decade her senior and perhaps a fraction short of six feet tall. Wisps of thinning gray hair protruded below a wide brimmed hat. Expensive boots stopped at the knee of finely tailored black trousers. His gray coat of similar quality covered a crisp white shirt. A blue cravat completed his attire.

"Good day, son," he pleasantly said with a soft smile. "If I may be so bold as to introduce myself, I'm General R.W. Williams."

John shielded his surprise. Most officers arrogantly displayed their rank on military uniforms. Pompous men flaunted their positions, arrayed in a variety of gaudy outfits. John suppressed a smile, remembering the simple dress of the exceedingly competent Stonewall Jackson. "Pleased to meet you, sir," graciously responded the younger man leaning forward to firmly shake the general's hand. I'm John Beall." He unsuccessfully concealed an agonizing wince when he leaned back.

"My dear boy, you appear to be in pain," the woman commented with motherly concern.

"My apologies, Mr. Beall, this is my dear wife, Mrs. Williams."

With a tip of the hat John responded. "Very pleased to make your acquaintance also. Where is your destination?" Change the topic. Avoid the injury. Circumvent John's least favorite topic of conversation, himself. Well done.

"You appear injured. May we assist in your comfort?"

"Not really ma'm, only need time to heal."

"Would it be an imposition to inquire as to the nature and circumstances?"

John found himself recounting the battle for the wheat barge. With deep interest General Williams politely offered strategic alternatives which might have provided greater success while humbly acknowledging the value of hindsight. He admitted his days of military service ended with the Mexican War. Between naps, stops, and meals the trio discussed a vast array of topics. With each conversation their familiarity increased. John learned the general owned a large plantation on the coast in southwestern Mississippi. An in-depth discussion ensued focusing upon the similarities and differences encountered while operating a farm in the upper south and a plantation in the lower south. Talk of the war's prospects eventually transpired. The Mississippian declared that while he staunchly supported the Richmond government he never voted for Mr. Davis for senator. The Williamses listened attentively to John's firsthand knowledge of Harpers Ferry, Brown's raid, and details of the abolitionist's subsequent execution.

The general freely offered, "Had the South shown backbone and demanded punishment for the influential abolitionists supporting the lunatic, war might have been averted, although the South shall be imminently better off independent of northern interference."

"It's all in the Lord's hands, my dear," interjected Mrs. Williams, patting her husband's arm. "God's will be done."

"Amen to that!" replied John. Soon a highly charged three-way discussion of religion evolved.

After thirty-three hours of travel the threesome transferred to the spur connecting passengers with the Florida, Atlantic & Gulf Central Railroad, and on to Tallahassee. John shook his head upon realizing he traveled eleven rail lines since departing Charles Town.

When the train commenced its final leg of the journey John anticipated the end of rail travel in Tallahassee, regardless of the available accommodations. The Williamses planned to depart the following morning with one more brief train ride to the coast where they would board a ship to arrive home Christmas Eve day. Both encouraged him to spend the Christmas holiday at their plantation. Though the older couple seemed like family, he felt uncomfortable intruding upon them, or so he told himself. In reality he lacked the stamina of the spry planter and his wife. They eventually coerced a commitment from him to follow three days later to their plantation near Pascagoula, Mississippi, and participate in their annual New Years Day celebration.

13 – JANUARY 1, 1862

John yawned, rose, and stretched, following a sound night's sleep at Mossy Oaks Plantation. He opened the window and inhaled the invigorating seacoast air. Spanish moss dripping from the live oaks dangled in the soft breeze, creating an illusion of life on an enchanted land. Negroes mulled about their quarters, anticipating their final day away from work this holiday season. Today's meal for the slaves, though not as elaborate as the Christmas feast, offered deviation far beyond a normal day's fare. Beyond the slaves' dwellings lay the estate's vast cotton fields. The small number of cattle gazing in the pasture and the hogs confined in the pen were raised solely for consumption on the plantation. Williams also produced a variety of grains, fruit, and vegetables to supplement their diet. However, the general's economic survival rested solely with the export of cotton. Raised in an agricultural environment which respected diversity, John questioned the merits of a one crop operation. As his thoughts drifted to Virginia he paused to gaze at the bright eastern sky, wondering if the same brilliant sun illuminated Walnut Grove.

He leisurely conversed with the general at breakfast before excusing himself for a morning horseback ride. Mounted on a beautiful butternut stallion he meandered along Mossy Oaks's irregular coastal shoreline. Upon John's arrival he and General Williams traversed the estate to familiarize the guest with the property. This New Years morning John desired solitude while coping with his first bout of homesickness since bidding his family adieu. Until today the opportunity for exploring new geography, discussing current events with engaging individuals, and savoring the gracious hospitality of newfound friends overshadowed the void of family. Today he realized he'd long taken family traditions for granted. Last year the annual ritual of recognizing his birthday began and ended as naturally as the rising and setting of the sun. Arriving and departing Rion Hall, with the interlude of fellowship and hospitality, disappeared with like commonality. When, if ever, would everyone gather for a pleasant celebration? All believed war, if it really transpired, would conclude before the fall harvest. The young soldier gazed down, realizing his scant shadow indicated it to be noontime. He lightly shook the reins, tickled his mount's flanks with his spurs, and cantered toward the house to prepare for New Years Day in the deep south.

While indulging in an early afternoon nap in his second floor room John heard the voices of guests. He preferred entering after more guests arrived but without portraying the image of a standoffish northerner. Odd, in Florida and Mississippi residents asked about conditions up north when referring to Virginia. He would provide no occasion for the general's guests to compare him to a Yankee. At half past two he forced himself to descend the ornate curved stairway to partake in the festivities. Early enough to avoid a grand entrance, late enough to avoid the role of unofficial greeter. Subconsciously a silent prayer passed through his mind. Lord, please grant me protection from unattached, aggressive southern belles who might become infatuated with a single Confederate soldier recuperating from wounds far from home. Inconspicuously perusing the spacious hallway, John breathed a sigh of relief. A cluster of ladies well beyond his age congregated in the dining room. Two young belles standing in the spacious hallway appeared to be escorted by uniformed gentlemen. Several affluent planters entertained the remaining young women. John felt at ease, realizing that the light gray jacket and trousers which he purchased in Savannah blended nicely with the local attire. His new blue vest accented his eyes. A gold cravat manifested the festive atmosphere.

General Williams immediately greeted him. Resting his right hand on John's left shoulder he guided his guest through the hallway to the parlor. The two passed through open French doors onto a wide veranda protected by a sloping roof covered with green wooden shingles. A mild saltwater breeze lazily carried toward them the aroma of a young pig roasting over hot coals. A circle of four gentlemen separated and widened to accommodate the pair.

"Gentlemen I'm pleased to introduce our guest, Private John Beall, recovering in the sunny south from a near fatal wound suffered while driving the Yankees into Maryland from his native Virginia." Williams began introductions on John's right. "Meet Mr. Thaddeus Thompson, owner of the finest cotton plantation in southern Mississippi. Next we have the Reverend Andrew Watson. He's served our congregation for how long Reverend, sixteen years now?" The preacher shook his balding head affirmatively while peering over his spectacles. "Captain Romulus Washington ships our cotton. Excuse me." The general paused with a sheepish grin. "Romulus shipped our cotton until President Davis banned its export. Next we have Colonel Ethan Larue who formed a Louisiana regiment and suffered a dreadful wound at Manassas." John politely extended his hand toward the colonel's before he awkwardly noticed Larue's empty right sleeve. Larue automatically slid his left palm over John's right hand.

"My apologies sir, I did not realize that..."

Larue curtly interrupted, "Unless you're a damn Yankee there's nothing to apologize for. Those nigger-loving bastards did this. I killed four blue bellies myself before they dragged me off the field. I return next week. I'll chase 'em out of Virgini for you. How many you killed so far?"

"Unfortunately none. We fought a small skirmish with our militia led by Colonel Turner Ashby." John hoped Ashby's name might add credibility to the action although he detested battle tales which disintegrated into egotistical coup counts. Yet he maintained an obligation to pay homage for the sake of his fallen comrade who fought his only battle that day.

"Damn shame you had only a marauder leading a passel of civilians playing soldier." Turning sharply so his empty sleeve subtly fluttered Larue asked in a challenging tone, "Where's that severe wound of yours boy, and when, or should I ask if you are going back?"

"Ethan, I've welcomed this honorable lad into my home to recover while experiencing our pleasant climate and warm hospitality. I hope you choose to contribute to the latter," finished Williams, flushed with embarrassment.

John found himself in the awkward position of defending his honor without disrupting the social gathering. Holding an open right palm towards his host, John calmly responded. He assumed a relaxed posture and directly faced Larue. "Colonel, I deeply regretted my absence during the Manassas affair. As you may recollect, rumors of action persisted since early June. Providence chose that I not be present." Larue rolled his eyes as John continued. "I missed fighting alongside my brother and the 2nd Virginia, part of what folks refer to as the Stonewall Brigade. You're familiar with their feats?" he asked with a tinge of contempt. Larue nodded his head in response. John added, "The Virginia and Jefferson County men present that day all fought honorably."

"Ah, Virginia, how shall we ever obtain independence without her leading us to victory," Larue replied with scathing sarcasm.

John continued, "My first action, the one in which I received my wound, occurred on the two year anniversary of John Brown's raid. God lead me home to Jefferson County. I prepared to return to my regiment when duty called. Due to my training under General Jackson, a captain assigned me to lead raw militia. While assaulting a Yankee position I received my wound. Remorse at the loss of a boyhood friend who perished that day continues following me. Though not as bountiful as the blood shed at Manassas, we bled just as loyally as any man at Manassas. May I add for the goal of Southern independence we all share? I hope I responded satisfactorily to a fellow brother in arms." Bad choice of words thought John after the colonel excused himself for another glass of brandy.

"Well done, lad," remarked Thaddeus Thompson. "You responded as a true southern gentleman."

"We all fight for freedom from Yankee domination. About time everyone realizes that," added Romulus Washington.

"I regret your first encounter with Ethan," consoled the reverend. "Time was the fellow drew crowds with his magnetic personality. Several years ago rumors began circulating that his beautiful young wife was loosing interest in her older spouse. As war fever spread Larue recruited his regiment. Like many others anticipating a speedy war which showered glory on men in uniform, Ethan visualized a hero's welcome and a rekindling of the spark that he once shared with Mrs. Larue. The bitter warrior arrived home convinced an undesirable man departing with two arms returned even less appealing with only one. Her absence today confirms such. I beg you not to judge the man too harshly Mr. Beall."

"Reverend Watson, rest assured I make no judgment upon Colonel Larue. We each have crosses to bear but that man shoulders more than most. Wounds such as his tend to draw the showers of pity which I trust the colonel detests. Today the man not only suffers from the wound to his arm but also from the rupture of his heart. I fortunately escape the complexities of involvement with the fairer sex and pledge to avoid such entanglements until this war concludes."

"Spoken like a true Christian gentleman. Enough of Ethan. How do like this part of our country?"

John paused while comprehending the stunning revelation. He never assimilated that Mississippi, Louisiana, or Texas for that matter, so far from home, with different climates, customs, and cotton or sugar driven economies, belonged to the Confederacy for which he and others already shed blood, whereas Maryland and Pennsylvania, with similar cultures and traditions to Virginia, elected to sever all ties.

"Good Reverend," John grinned, "I stand here partaking of the Williams's gracious hospitality while enjoying your pleasant conversation. I absorb balmy temperatures this January first on this beautiful mansion's veranda while clothed in late spring apparel by Virginia standards. You question if I care for this part of the country? Sir, you must suspect that only an insincere soul would respond in the negative." His closing comment produced hearty laughter from the others.

General Williams encouraged his guests to migrate to the dining room. "John, you must sample our fine Mississippi cuisine. Our roast hog, if I dare say so, is the talk of the county. Corn, okra, rice, tomatoes, along with oysters, shrimp, and catfish all grace the table. For those longing for sweets we offer assorted cakes and Mammy Ruth's pecan pie. Of course we provide an enticing champagne punch to welcome in the New Year. In fact, come inside as I perform our annual New Years Day toast."

The guests, holding crystal glasses filled with the bubbly beverage, gathered in the spacious hallway as their host ascended several stairs. "Honored guests, Mrs. Williams and I thank you for graciously accepting the invitation to our annual New Years Day festivities. Reflect upon the past year. Acknowledge the uncertainty we faced a year ago. Only South Carolina stood alone against Yankee oppression. Soon six states, including Mississippi, joined hands with her. Yankee aggression continued, bringing our sisters to our north into our noble adventure. Our united Confederacy, as evidenced by Manassas and numerous other encounters, displayed on the field of battle for the world to observe the unequaled bravery of our Southern knights who led us to innumerable successes. The future holds unimagined prosperity as we permanently shed the bonds of northern tyranny." Unrestrained applause and cheers roared from the guests. "To our future," toasted the general as glasses emptied. "In conclusion, I ask each of you to warmly welcome our guest, the brave lad whose blood soaks Virginia's soil from our quest for freedom. Mr. John Beall, I must acknowledge, turns twenty-seven today." Good natured cheers for a speech followed.

Flushed with embarrassment but out of courtesy, John joined General Williams on the stairs. "Thank you all, especially my kind hosts, for welcoming this sojourner so warmly. One always reminisces of days gone by as he covets the presence of absent friends and family on festive occasions. A portion of my heart yearns for my mother and four sisters on our farm, or should I now say plantation, in Virginia. Part of my heart desires companionship with my fellow soldiers, including my brother Will, who camps near Richmond with General Jackson, preparing for the spring offensive to whip the Yankees." He paused for the erupting roar to subside. "My heart seeks companionship with lifelong friends with whom I warmed myself from the chill of the northern Virginia winter each New Years Day. In the years to come though, my newfound friends, my heart shall forever hold open a chamber for you as I fondly remember the gracious welcome I received this first day in 1862. Thank you."

When John finished, General Williams signaled his trio of Negro string musicians to play. A slow, soft symphonic version of "Dixie" floated through the room as guests dispersed into smaller clusters throughout the mansion. Williams sharply shouted in mimic of his musicians' dialect, "Boys! Dat ain't no waltz you is a playing. Pick up da pace and put some thusiasm into it." Immediately a loud toe tapping rendition exploded. Guests recongregated. Male and female voices alike blared out the spirited unofficial Confederate national anthem. At the conclusion a surge of thirsty gentlemen rushed for glasses of liquid refreshment. Laughter and loud voices echoed throughout Mossy Oaks. John wondered if this revelry represented the typical Mississippi celebration or if perhaps today's emotions sprouted from war fever?

After the final guest departed John unwound with a rare second glass of wine while the general partook of a full glass of brandy from the crystal decanter. "How do you view your coming year, John? Do your plans remain on schedule?"

"God willing my wound heals, I plan to follow my army wherever it goes. I realized today that while fighting for Virginia I fight for much more. I fight for the *Constitution* which Washington, Jefferson, and even northerners such as Franklin adopted years ago. The original document, which southern apathy permitted to become eroded by northern irresponsibility, must be restored. The guns fired on Fort Sumter awoke us all. When Lincoln called for troops from Virginia to subdue our cousins he abolished the apathy within us. A man must follow his loyalties. Other than my family residing within the path of warring armies I have no obligations." John bid his hosts good evening and ascended the stairs with an inner peace enveloping him at the conclusion of this festive day far from family and friends. He counted himself blessed for the gift of the Williams's friendship. His tranquility evaporated as he pondered when he might experience this holiday at home.

14 – A CHANGE IN PLANS

The spirited buckskin John rode kicked up dirt as it trotted along the road. Overcast skies matched his mood. Already the first week of March. His slow healing wound stalled his return to Virginia. More disconcerting, he continued lacking stamina for even moderate walks. After exercising thirty minutes he became exhausted, not very conducive to the demands of Stonewall Jackson's foot cavalry as the boys termed themselves. While yearning for the fight, he realized partaking of the Williamses' generous hospitality would pave the speediest pathway to recovery. Upon reaching the barn the groom Gideon reached for the reins. John dismounted and wiped his brow.

"Glad you's back, Massa Beall. Miz Susan's kin from Nashville, all da wayz from Tennessee is here. The genrel, he a looking forward to introducing you."

John shoved his riding gloves into his hip pocket and reluctantly trudged up the stone path leading to the mansion. The reserved Virginian would display impeccable manners but he possessed no overwhelming desire to engage in polite conversation with members of the opposite gender. Pleasantries would be exchanged, his wound would become a topic, and dialogue would revolve around him. However, their insight into the disappointing setbacks the South encountered in Tennessee would prove enlightening. The newcomers, two school teachers as John recalled, escaped Nashville prior to Yankee occupation. He intended to refresh himself before formally meeting the guests. Handing his hat to Jacque, he moved toward the stairs. The servant thwarted his escape by loudly asking, "Pleasant ride, Massa Beall?"

The young man grimaced when Mrs. Williams's voice requested his presence in the parlor. He entered staring at his mud spattered boots before looking up to his hostess for an introduction to the visitors. Seated before him on the flowered loveseat sat a woman wearing a dark green cotton dress with long billowing sleeves terminating at the wrists. White lace cuffs matched the lace collar accentuating an ordinary neck supporting a slender face displaying prominent high cheekbones. She possessed slender lips, a classic nose, and caring hazel eyes that had witnessed both joy and sorrow. Narrow eyebrows matched her silky auburn hair which she parted in the center and held tightly behind her head beneath an inconspicuous net. The tilt of her head displayed a refined woman of sound character. Certainly not a typical school marm; John guesstimated her age near his.

"Mr. John Beall, may I introduce my dear cousin Miss Martha O'Brien." As John stepped forward with a short bow she stood and exhibited her slender but adequately endowed figure. His height exceeded hers by several inches. The mesmerized young man gawked awkwardly. She lacked the dazzling beauty which turned the heads as she passed but she appeared a mature, secure woman rather than a fragile belle clamoring for attention and responding to insincere flattery. Before him stood a woman whose wholesome attractiveness complimented a sincere character emanating from within. John would have consumed his life searching for her had he realized such a creature existed.

"Mr. Beall," sounded the uncharacteristically impatient but amused voice of Mrs. Williams. The infatuated young man realized his hostess attempted to introduce the other guest. Martha's lips slightly quivered as she suppressed a smile. "Mr. Beall, may I introduce my other cousin, Miss Frances O'Brien, or as we informally refer to her, Miss Fanny O'Brien."

John bowed and smiled at the other woman. Though noticeably older, perhaps more so than his sister Mary, John recognized the family resemblance between the sisters. "Did you say O'Brien?" blurted John.

"Why yes," replied Fanny, looking inquisitively toward him.

Feeling a need to promptly respond, John with the vision of Sue Ellen O'Brien wedged in his mind, stumbled through a reply. "A young lady I knew from my home in Charles Town carried a like surname."

Martha, who traditionally remained subdued in mixed company, surprised her sister by asking to the chagrin of the young Virginian, "A fond acquaintance of yours, Mr. Beall?"

"Just the good friend of a man I know very well, Miss O'Brien." A slight smile crossed his face with the technically honest response any competent attorney would appreciate. His reddening neck and cheeks implied a less than forthright answer. "May I again express pleasure in meeting both of you. I must now make myself presentable for dinner when perhaps I shall learn firsthand of conditions in Tennessee." With that he exited toward the stairway and breathed a huge sigh of relief.

In his room he stared at his meager wardrobe. No one ever accused him of being a dandy. Fortunately his purchase of the more formal light-gray coat and trousers in Charleston complimented his two sets of dark traveling clothes. Recently he also purchased an extra pair of boots. The six cravats and two vests offered a flexible wardrobe. After tediously analyzing all possible combinations he selected a maroon vest and gold cravat to accentuate his gray coat and dark trousers. Thank God Mother or Mary could not see him fussing. He slowly opened the door, took a deep breath, and stepped into the hallway. Feminine chatter interspersed randomly by the general's voice indicated everyone awaited him in the dining room.

He seated himself on the far side of the table between the Williamess who sat at the ends while the O'Brien sisters sat across from him. The general commenced with the prayer. "Dear Lord, your humble servants beseech you to bless our gathering this evening. We thank thee for Susan's cousins' safe arrival after travel through miles of hostile territory. We pray you shall soon return tranquility to thy peace loving people. Consecrate thy bounty before us as we partake of thy abundant blessings, in your dear Son's name, Amen."

"And may I add a special thank you to Cousin Susan, for welcoming Martha and I into the sanctuary of your home."

"This humble guest from Virginia again states his appreciation for your generous hospitality," John added, while Martha wondered if anyone humbly descended from the commonwealth.

A gray-haired, small-framed female servant with deep ebony complexion, carrying a platter laden with roasted chicken preceded a much younger mulatto girl holding two steaming bowls of vegetables. They served the female guests and Mrs. Williams, then John, and finally the host. Martha and Fanny filled their tea cups while the other three sparingly drank wine.

"Miss O'Brien, please favor us with details of your journey. I understand your trip became somewhat harrowing?" asked John, glancing from sister to sister while wondering who would respond.

Fanny began. "Although remaining optimistic even after the fall of Fort Henry, once Donaldson fell, Sister and I realized the peril any decent woman faced from hoards of common, mean-spirited Yankee invaders, loosely supervised by drunken officers, all unable to distinguish refined southern ladies from the female trash they associate with in their backwoods little towns." Martha softly patted her sister's hand as Fannie continued. "Fearing a digression into total panic with each passing day, Sister and I hastily packed limited belongings and boarded a crowded southbound train to Decatur. Upon our arrival the station transferring us onto the Memphis & Charleston Line greeted us with a scene of utter chaos. Since no seats remained we gained passage south to Jackson on military supply wagons, guarded by a unit of brave Confederate cavalry. Despite our army's setback here in the west Sister and I traveled securely in the company of the escort of the noble horsemen. The most talented Union cavalry trooper presents no match for the least of our mounted cavaliers. In Jackson we obtained passage to Vicksburg on the Southern Mississippi Railroad. We hoped to continue travel by rail to New Orleans but met with no success. Following the prudent suggestions of our astute major in charge of the supply wagons we found ample space on a river steamer destined for New Orleans. A short steamer ride transported us here."

"Did you encounter enemy troops?"

"Not directly but while traveling with the supply wagons shots barked in the distance as our scouts fired on horsemen failing to halt as ordered. Probably Yankee deserters. Praise God none of our boys were injured, but enough of our adventures. Cousin Susan informs us that your journey, while rather mundane, exemplified the inadequacy of our rail system. However, Mr. Beall, a near fatal wound received several months ago precipitated your travel. If not too gruesome, Sister and I desire to learn more."

Had to happen sooner or later, thought John. "By chance I brought an ill comrade home two days before the unexpected conflict at Bolivar Heights. We naturally took offence to the Yankees violating Virginia soil, especially for the sole purpose of stealing Jefferson County wheat. I found myself leading a group of brave, youthful, but inexperienced militia against a Yankee position when I received the wound to my breast."

With wide-eyed enthusiasm, Martha enthusiastically interjected, "and a glorious victory for our brave boys?"

She immediately realized her response improper when John paused and gazed expressionlessly to the ceiling, visualizing the mutilated Union bodies and Seth's cold stare. He bluntly replied, "With all due respect, Miss O'Brien, when fought by honorable men victory may be noble but, no glory exists in battle regardless of the outcome." Recognizing her hurtful expression, he added, "But your enthusiastic support is deeply appreciated."

Channeling the conversation into another direction, the general asked, "When this conflict ceases in the not too distance future, what paths shall you young folks pursue?"

"I'm consigned to return to Nashville to reopen the academy, the only realistic option at my age. Share your thoughts, Sister," Fanny said, turning to Martha.

"I have no immediate prospects beyond teaching at the academy." As John dissected her ambiguous comment, Martha broke his thought by asking, "And you, Mr. Beall?"

"I anticipate returning to my farm. With the retention of sufficient Negroes, increased supervision and retraining shall be required in the short term. I eagerly yearn for the reunion with my family. Unforeseen responsibilities may fall upon us as our new nation evolves. Virginia's prominence, as exhibited after the first revolution, may require special participation from her citizens."

"Thank God for Virginia, less our cause be lost," Martha cynically jested with a roll of her eyes. Fanny began realizing her sister's unusual behavior implied Martha may possess more than a passing interest for this young soldier.

John's face reddened as he ineptly struggled to overcome his perceived arrogance. "Please permit me to clarify, Miss O'Brien. I do not actively indulge in politics. Those men thrive on the gray. I prefer black and white. 'Tis perhaps my rationale for leaving the university a year prior to completion of my legal studies." Martha's' intrigue with this gentleman expanded with each passing comment. Everyone exchanged light conversation the remainder of the meal.

"Shall we proceed to the parlor for musical entertainment presented by our two talented pianists?" asked Susan Williams.

The ladies stood and awaited escort to the parlor. The Williamses and John relaxed to a variety of songs from the likes of the renowned Charles Grobe to the lesser known Stephen Foster. Martha and Fanny alternately performed four renditions until the audience joined in a songfest. The accomplished duet added their voices to the other three as verses from two recently composed songs, "The Bonnie Blue Flag" and "Maryland, My Maryland" echoed through the room. Enthusiasm heightened with the singing of their unofficial national anthem, "Dixie", ironically written in

1859 by a northerner from Ohio who débuted the music in New York City. "Amazing Grace" concluded the singing.

Fanny cast a sideways glance to Cousin Susan and fashioned a yawn. "If you'll excuse me, I shall retire for the evening."

Mrs. Williams quickly added, "As shall I. In the not so distant past I too enjoyed the youth of Cousin Martha and Mr. Beall, when the call for an evening's rest arrived several hours later."

General Williams took a step toward the brandy decanter summoning him from the white marble topped table, before he noticed his spouse's eyes directing him toward the stairway. "Ah, yes, age overcomes us all too quickly." He casually stated to Martha and John, "You young folks feel free to become better acquainted." Proper manners dictated that both acquiesce to their host's wishes. John relaxed in a beige wing chair while Martha sat to his left on the patterned loveseat. Both, fearing an awkward period of silence, simultaneously spoke and then laughed.

"You first, Mr. Beall."

"Ma'm, a gentleman always defers to a lady," replied John with a nod and a warm smile.

Engulfed in her enticing radiance, Martha said, "While dining, you mentioned your family but conversation never returned to the topic. Please tell me more."

"My pleasure, Miss O'Brien, providing you respond in kind." She nodded affirmatively for him to proceed. "Father entered heaven's gates almost seven years ago. I continually yearn for his companionship and guidance. Mother remains the lone soul whom I trust my innermost thoughts. After Father passed the responsibility of operating our farm fell upon Mother and me. Our closeness continued growing since. I truly hate the hardship this war places upon her although I thank God my sister Mary, six years my senior, remains at home. She reminds me a great deal of your sister. Miss Fanny seems very devoted to you. My sister Beth, now twenty, is a quiet, loving creature. Annie, four years younger than I, is a spirited beauty of a girl, with many suitors. I proudly declare such attention has not gone to her head. I really miss our baby, Janeta, whom we refer to as Janie. I say baby but she's almost sixteen." Laughing softly and shaking his head he added, "And changing so rapidly."

"You are the only male in the family?"

"Thank goodness, no! My older brother, Hezekiah, should be…, almost twenty-nine now. He's a businessman in Iowa. In fact Mary and I journeyed by rail to visit him when Father's illness struck. My plans to engage in land speculation in Iowa finally materialized a few years ago but ended abruptly with the advent of the war. Several years before Father's death, while I attended the university, Hezekiah up and left for Iowa. Father, as tradition dictated, expected his eldest son to oversee the farm's operation. He envisioned me becoming a lawyer. Though Father showed disappointment with my decision to leave school we continued on agreeable terms. I gather Hezekiah's departure, or 'abandonment' as Father once stated, was less than amicable. I suspect his migration to a free state further aggravated Father. Hezekiah maintains he predicated his destination solely on cheap land rather than the slavery issue."

"He's your only brother?"

"Heavens no!" John replied with a hearty laugh. Martha inquisitively raised her eyebrows. "The unaccounted for sibling is my little brother Will." John paused with a slight grin. "More appropriately, he's my seventeen year old brother who towers above me. I should probably refer to him as William, Mother's formal choice whenever he needs correction. She seldom calls him Will if that better portrays him." John caught himself momentarily ignoring Martha as his thoughts drifted toward his loved ones in Virginia. "I do apologize, Miss O'Brien. I sorely miss them all, including Father. I trust you will, er would enjoy them were you ever to encounter them." He transitioned into, "now your family." Martha continued absorbing the sincere sentiment emanating from this man.

"Before I commence, tell me, where is Will now?"

"As I mentioned earlier this evening, Will and I joined the 2nd Virginia in May. I presume he's encamped in Virginia. Enough of my family; your narrative please."

"At age nine I suffered the loss of my father. He served mankind as a physician. Ten years later Mother joined Poppa. If my ciphering is correct the year your father also passed, in 1855?" John shook his head affirmatively. "In '47 we lost my older brother Laurence, whom I adored. His character appears to have resembled that of your younger brother. Laurence was eighteen." John sensed she suppressed tears as she continued. "Our most heartbreaking loss occurred with the tragic death of my dear sister Susan, just barely three. I was eight at the time. She was my constant companion. Melancholy overtakes me whenever I think of the years we shall miss together." Martha's throat burned. Poorly controlled tears rolled down her cheeks as she searched for something to absorb them. John advanced with handkerchief in hand and cautiously seated himself beside her, careful to maintain a respectful distance. "Please sir, accept my apology for my improper display of emotion in the presence of a new acquaintance."

Why did she carry the name O'Brien, he wondered, as Sue Ellen's image reappeared? "Miss O'Brien, I feel honored to offer you assistance; we are both refugees courtesy of northern aggression. May I ask if Miss Fanny is your only surviving family?"

Martha's face brightened. "To my great fortune, no! I am blessed with George, four years my senior, who supplies clothing to our troops, and my younger brother Joe, who attached himself to me upon Susan's death. He remains my confidant. As we grew older the two-year gap in our ages dissolved. Regretfully when I joined Fanny our visits together diminished. He currently serves in Tennessee under General Bragg. And that, dear sir, is the family of Martha O'Brien."

Buoyant for a continuation of the evening and assuming Martha to be well-read, John asked, "Miss O'Brien, which writers do you favor?"

"I enjoy many authors. Lately I've commenced re-reading Sir Walter Scott as our current political situation offers better interpretation of his works."

"Aye! I enjoy Scott too. *Ivanhoe* always travels with me. I again read *Waverly*, compliments of our gracious host." The young man lifted his gaze from Martha to the mahogany bookshelves bearing leather bound titles with gilded letters. "I appreciate my library, although modest in comparison to the general's vast selection of fine volumes. May I ask your indulgence in allowing me to read a poem of Scott's which I rediscovered several days ago?"

She warmly smiled gesturing the affirmative.

Returning with a book he sat nearer her. He opened the volume and extended the right portion for Martha to hold while he supported the left. His trouser leg covered the wide hem of her dress. The enamored Virginian only hoped she could not sense the amplified beating of his heart when his arm made casual contact with hers. "My father's lines connect to that of a distant kinsman, Rob Roy, who fought beside Viscount Dundee, whom Scott portrays in *Bonny Dundee*," John said before he initiated the reading.

"To the Lords of the convention 'twas Clavers who spoke
Ere the King's crown shall fall there are crowns to be broke;
So let each Cavalier who loves honour and me,
Come follow the bonnet of Bonny Dundee.
Come fill up my cup, come fill up my can'
Come saddle your horses, and call up your men;
Come open the West Port and let met gang free,
And it's room for the bonnets of Bonny Dundee!"

As the young man reached the eleventh and final verse he boldly articulated,

"He waved his proud hand, the trumpets were blown,
The kettle-drums clashed and the horseman rode on,

Till on Ravelston's cliffs and Clemiston's lee
Died away the wild war-notes of Bonny Dundee.
Come fill up cup, come fill up my can,
Come saddle the horses, and call up the men,
Come open your gates, and let me go free,
For it's up for the bonnets of Bonny Dundee."

"Mr. Beall, for the even-mannered person your temperament professes you to be, you read with the thundering conviction of an experienced orator," she said as her eyes floated lazily to meet his, before teasingly adding with a sheepish grin, "I question whether a simple Irish lass such as I am worthy of the presence of a distinguished nobleman descended from the legendary Rob Roy MacGregor?"

Recognizing the tone of the question to be more playful than challenging, young Mr. Beall, far from experienced in engaging in conversion with members of the opposite sex, struggled for a sincere, proper response. "Miss O'Brien, may I compare myself to the overwhelming greenery that explodes throughout the countryside with the advent of spring while you my lady represent the blossoms of the season that follow and deservedly become the center piece of the enchanting season. It is I who lacks worthiness in your presence." As John silently queried as to from where he pulled that response, he observed Martha's soft white face transform into a bright red, the same hue now flushing his own.

Eager to extricate herself from the awkward situation she asked, "Mr. Beall, I have a poem, recently joined with tune, which I wish to share."

"Please do."

"A young Canadian teacher authored the verse several years past while enamored with a young lady. Perhaps my common vocation with the writer resulted in my emotional tie to his work. She slowly began singing.

"I wandered today to the hill, Maggie

To watch the scene below
The creek and the old rusty mill, Maggie
Where we sat in the long long ago
The green grove is gone from the hill, Maggie
Where first the daisies had sprung
The old rusty mill is now still, Maggie
Since you and I were young

A city so silent and lone, Maggie
Where the young and the gay and the best
In polished white mansions of stone, Maggie
Have each found a place of rest
Is built where the birds used to play, Maggie
And join in the songs that were sung
For we sang just as a gay as they did, Maggie
When you and I were young

They say I am feeble with age, Maggie
My steps are less sprightly than then
My face is a well written page, Maggie
But time, time alone, was the pen
They say we are aged and grey, Maggie
As spray by the white breakers flung
But to me you're as fair as you were, Maggie
When you and I were young."

"Beautifully done, Miss O'Brien," John exclaimed with soft applause. "Does your memory include numerous works?"

"Very few secular works, though I humbly admit to a large repertoire of biblical verses."

John's infatuation continued as she casually acknowledged her strong faith. He reverently replied, "As do I. We must compare common interest in verses."

Martha clasped her hand over her mouth to politely cover a long-suppressed yawn. "Mr. Beall, I eagerly anticipate such discussion, especially with you. However," she said as she stood, "the day has been long and tiresome excluding the latter part of the evening of course. I really must retire."

What now? Did she mutually share his affection? He longed to wrap his muscular arms around her slender body and draw her close, preceding a passionate, unbridled kiss. Perhaps because of the man's sense of propriety but more as a result of this soldier's lack of courage in affairs of the heart he stepped back, bent over, grasped and gently touched the top of her bare hand with his lips. He quickly released his grip. Eyes briefly locked. Each formally bid the other good evening. John stared longingly as she gracefully glided up the staircase.

Martha entered her room and prepared for bed, relieved Fanny already slept. She desired no inquisition at this hour, especially while she sorted through her tangled emotions. She just climbed into bed when her silent evening prayers were abruptly interrupted. "Sister, did you enjoy a pleasant conversation with the charming Mr. Beall?"

Thank God darkness concealed Martha's blushed face. "My dear Fanny, I so apologize for waking you."

"Don't fret. Despite a totally exhausted body my mind continues imagining the dire conditions in Nashville, which inhibits my sleep."

"After the strenuous demands of the last several days I doubt I shall endure such inhibitions," Martha answered, emitting a fabricated yawn.

"As always, Martha, I respect your wishes. Please answer my question in order that we may both welcome our much needed slumber."

Fanny, always the stern academy mistress who assumed the role of surrogate mother in 1855, would receive her answer. Tonight! "Mr. Beall and I casually discussed a variety of subjects such as notable persons, family, and literature. You know, no intrusive subjects, just superficial conversation between casual acquaintances."

"So the confident, aggressive Virginian proved the perfect gentleman upon your first encounter together?"

Too much so, thought Martha, who longed for more than a polite, generic touch of his lips upon her hand. "I suspect you assumed Mr. Beall's direct communication style portrayed a less than congenial man. And you say first encounter as if more shall ensue. In a matter of weeks he shall travel east to rejoin the war effort, wherever that may lead, while for you and me, my dear sister, the future remains more uncertain. I exhibited common courtesy one offers to a wounded soldier convalescing far from home."

"Good night, Martha,' concluded Fanny with a tone indicating she interpreted more than her younger sister communicated.

Across the hallway John climbed into bed, engulfed with fresh emotions completely foreign to him. Sue Ellen O'Brien aroused emotion, but Martha O'Brien, why dear Lord did you send me another O'Brien? He desired to define his relationship with Martha within the bold black-lined boundaries by which he lived. These definitive lines faded into an obscure fog of gray. Could it be war's uncertainty? Was it his boast to avoid romantic entanglement while serving the army? He owed no moral obligation to the other O'Brien, Sue Ellen. Or did he fear this proper young woman from Tennessee felt no affection for him, but rather as an extended member of the Williams family obligatorily offered hospitality. With these questions unanswered he fell into a restless sleep.

15 – CLARIFICATION

Bright sunshine illuminated the dining room while a subtle saltwater breeze gently billowed the drapes, as the mansion filled with mild, refreshing morning air. John leisurely conversed with the Williamses. Much to his relief neither host nor hostess alluded to Martha. He just had set his fork on his empty plate when the O'Brien sisters entered.

"Did you sleep well?" asked their cousin Susan.

"Delightfully," replied Martha.

"Too long," added Fanny. "Forgive any inconvenience we've created."

"Nonsense! After the ordeal you suffered I'm surprised you are both awake at this hour. Since all of our guests are present, the general and I wish to make an announcement. Next Friday we are hosting a reception in honor of you three. The invitations are already prepared for our servants to deliver."

The trio simultaneously read an invitation's flowing script.

"The General and Mrs. R.W. Williams graciously request your presence on Friday, March 14, to officially welcome our dear cousins, Miss Fanny O'Bryan and Miss Martha O'Bryan, recently arrived, following a harrowing journey to avoid the suppressive Yankee invaders in Nashville. We also provide the opportunity to bid farewell to our young soldier from Virginia, Mr. John Beall, as his wound nears healing, thereby permitting his imminent return to action in a matter of weeks. Please respond when practical."

Laughing aloud, John mumbled something about, "Thank you lord."

"What is so humorous Mr. Beall.?" Fanny curiously asked.

"I assumed you spelled your name o, b, r, i, e, n—not o, b, r, y, a, n. I mentioned a person I know is acquainted with an O'Brien, but she spells her name differently," he replied, thankful more than spelling distinguished the two. "Enough of that subject."

"Not so quickly," commented Martha with burst of laughter.

"I prefer not to pursue the topic," John bluntly retorted.

Ignoring his request she said, "I find humor in a man who finds comedy with two different but commonly accepted spellings of a familiar surname. Yet this same man fails to spell his name in conjunction with proper pronunciation. How does your spelling of b, e, a, l, l, receive the pronunciation of b, e, l, l?"

"I really do not know. It's always been what it's always been. God only knows more profound issues exist than that of the spelling of one's name." Everyone smiled when conversion turned to plans for the upcoming reception.

16 – A DAY TO REMEMBER

Two perfectly matched roans pulled the carriage along Martha's favorite lane on the plantation. While he preferred the path following the gulf coast's irregular contour with its view of the alluring sea, she delighted in the winding trail through moss-draped live oaks, past freshly planted cotton fields, over rolling pastures, and along a meandering stream. He staged the setting this last Saturday in March for her. Every day following the Williamess' reception the couple partook of afternoon excursions through the charming countryside. These outings provided occasion to share their innermost thoughts. Both supported their homeland, whether that be Virginia or Tennessee. The concept of a new nation remained alien. Martha could not picture Kentucky forming the Confederacy's northern border any more than John could accept Maryland's separation, although rumors persisted that both states would eventually be drawn away from the Union. John's vision for the Confederacy differed somewhat from Martha's, yet neither's view conflicted with the other's. John focused upon the new government's structure and the steps necessary to improve trade. Internal transportation improvements plus sound foreign relations with European powers took precedence. Coexistence with the Yankees after an acceptable peace settlement would prove beneficial to the South and also the North. Martha believed state and central governments needed to recognize the necessity of an all encompassing and more demanding public education in a rapidly changing society. She even advocated literacy for the Negroes. John disagreed but chose not to voice his feelings too adamantly. Martha acknowledged the merit of private education for the more affluent members of society to maintain distinction between the classes.

Yesterday they discussed slavery. Neither believed the issue one of moral right or wrong. They agreed submissive Negroes deserved and generally received humane treatment. They shared the belief that races with limited intellect faired better under the paternalistic system that evolved throughout the decades. They expressed anger at the Yankee's self-righteous position on the slavery issue.

They learned of each other's strong religious faith. The two well-read individuals shared intriguing insights which enhanced their understanding of God which in turn led to deeper appreciation for one another. They looked ahead to the war's conclusion, confident God supported the South's pure agrarian society. John and Martha accepted without question the life and fate God chose for each of them. Martha confided of her childhood fear that whenever utopia neared a person or event would cause it to vanish. John trusted God rewarded just, faithful people. Quietly recognizing the enveloping attraction between them, neither chose to discuss the future—until today.

John halted the carriage on the narrow wooden bridge with the slow moving stream bubbling beneath. Wild crabapples awakened by gentle spring temperatures released their appealing fragrance as pink blossoms dropped below and floated away with the passing current. Mid afternoon sun warmed the air. John clasped Martha's hand as his eyes met hers. His rehearsed words came slowly, hesitantly.

"Miss Martha, a man such as I never became obsessed with finding a wife because I never knew until you entered my life for whom I searched. You are a profoundly unusual lady gifted with all the qualities a man could desire. Your external beauty only surpasses your internal loveliness. You're a fine Christian woman of high moral character devoted to our Lord. You're a compassionate…." Martha tenderly placed her fingers to his lips as tears of joy flowed down her cheeks.

"John Yates Beall, I yearned for your proposal since the day I met you. Do you realize how many hours of sleep I have been deprived of on your account?" she asked with a giggle.

"Fewer than I," he rebutted with a grin.

He grasped her hands in his and leaned forward to kiss her. She dropped his hands, wrapped her arms around him, and drew him nearer. His searching tongue explored her sensuous mouth. His embrace pulled them tightly together. Their passionate kiss paused abruptly when her bonnet knocked off his brimmed hat. Eagerly he loosened the ribbon holding her bonnet in place, dropped it to the carriage floor, and gently caressed her neck. For several euphoric moments two hearts beat as one. Knowing this to be the extent of their physical love until marriage they reluctantly separated. "Time to return, my dear." He handed Martha her bonnet, placed his hat upon his head, and reached for the reins.

"If we must," she replied as the carriage wheels gradually rolled ahead, beginning the twenty minute return ride. She shifted closer to him, slid her arm through his, tightly squeezed his hand, and rested her head against his shoulder. He relaxed as her familiar perfumed scent drifted to him.

After several minutes of bouncing along she shyly spoke. "You've stated in the past that a soldier better performs his duty without the responsibility of a wife. Do you continue to adhere to that viewpoint? With an uncertain conclusion to this war, when can we, when shall we marry?"

"My dear Martha, the slow healing of my wound, and the moderate return of my strength cloud my future. If my health permits I must depart in early April for the spring action. But while I face an obligation to the army I also possess a new obligation to you. I long pondered purchasing a privateering vessel in England in order to support our cause by capturing essential supplies for the South while compromising Yankee shipping." He pulled the team to a halt. She released his hand, sat erectly, and stared attentively into his deep blue eyes. He rested both hands firmly on her shoulders and continued, "We could marry shortly and depart to England immediately thereafter. Cousins of mine near London will gladly welcome us. While we anticipate cessation of hostilities by year's end the recent defeats in Tennessee give rise to concern for a lengthier conflict. If so, I shall perform all the more admirably confident my loving wife resides safely in Europe. I fear if per chance war enters a third year traditional honor between warring parties shall deteriorate. I already observed numerous such behaviors from the Yankees and unfortunately isolated acts from our people. Upon achieving victory you and I shall return to a comfortable life in the peaceful serenity of Jefferson County."

Martha extended her arms and tightly gripped his forearms. Unexplained fierceness he never witnessed burned within her eyes. "I refuse to become your mistress!"

His cheeks flared at the puzzling admonishment. "Martha, my love, did you not hear of my honest intentions to marry you in a proper Christian ceremony?"

With his full attention, she slowly and tenderly elaborated, utilizing skills necessary to patiently explain abstract concepts to young students. Her matronly smile, similar to Mother's, further added confusion. "John Beall, you are a highly principled man whose compliance with duty encompasses his entire soul and being. Recognition of responsibility, whether to vocation, family, country, or God, defines you. You should comprehend your focus must be Virginia, to which you first swore allegiance. No man adequately serves two masters, particularly you. I have no reservations as to your devotion to me. Not initially, maybe in a matter of months, but more likely years from now, you shall look back to this time, to this decision, and regret that you abandoned your responsibility as the honorable warrior you swore to become. I shall become the illicit temptress from the Garden of Eden who corrupted your moral fiber. If I permit this I lose the man I love, the man you could not survive without being."

His throat burned as his eyes moistened for the first time since Father's death. He drew her tightly against him, convinced indeed their hearts beat as one. "Martha, how very blessed I am to be gifted with a woman who knows me better than do I."

"As appropriately it should be," she teased.

Mingling the newness of spring with the freshness of their lives together cast a dreamlike aura over them as their carriage rattled along the path. They agreed to keep their plans to themselves until circumstances dictated to the contrary. Martha especially desired to inform Fanny at a proper time, but significantly prior to a public announcement. John preferred to remain silent with his family until the war's end.

At dinner General Williams, totally oblivious to the fresh glow about Martha, and the sheepish grins John cast her way, addressed his usual topics. Unobserved smiles shared between Susan and Fanny indicated their feminine intuitiveness detected the markedly different relationship between John and Martha.

The general rambled on. "Cotton prices abroad continue steeply rising. Won't benefit us if Richmond doesn't come to its senses and allow us to ship it. Temperature and rainfall this spring are ideal. Also heard today the Yankees are building strength in Tennessee near Pittsburg Landing. General Johnston's presumed to be grouping nearby on the Mississippi side of the border, maybe in Corinth. Time for old Albert Sidney Johnston to strike. Of course he may be letting Grant sit, grow bored, and get drunk. Then he'll catch him unprepared. I imagine Pierre Beauregard's pacing back and forth like a gamecock anxious for a fight. That old Creole and his Louisiana boys just a soon rather rout the Yanks and capture the whiskey before that one-win-wonder Grant drinks it all." Williams paused for a hardy laugh with John joining him. The woman feigned amusement, albeit only polite accommodation. "Forgive me John. I also read of fighting in Virginia at a place called Kernstown. Are you familiar with it?"

"Kernstown! That's in Berkley County. It joins Jefferson County to the west, a leisurely day's ride from home. Any details on units involved or casualties?"

The general reached behind to the buffet and began browsing through the paper. "Says here that though outnumbered three to one, General Jackson assaulted Shields's Yankees, inflicting heavy casualties upon the enemy while Southern losses were moderate. It alludes to Northern designs to incorporate several northeastern counties including Jefferson and Berkley within the proposed creation of a new state composed of Virginia's Unionist northwestern counties, which received a crushing blow. I've heard no such rumors of any such formation. What do you know, my boy?"

Anger cascaded through John. He pushed back his chair, stood, and threw his napkin to the table. The other four sat silently stunned by the outburst. Uncontrollable rage poured forth as he ranted. "My homeland shall never suffer the degradation of the shredding of its identity and heritage, and be kidnapped by the vile, mercenary Unionist counties to our west. Every drop of my blood and that of every honorable Jefferson County man shall drain from us before such atrocity occurs." Somewhat embarrassed he seated himself and begged, "Please forgive my emotional outburst. General Williams, you did say that Jackson led our troops?"

"No need for apologies, John. A lesser reaction to an affront to one's honor would raise concern for a man's moral fiber. Our enemy lacks that character which shall carry us through to victory despite the odds. Ah, yes, in response to your inquiry, Jackson commanded our troops."

"Then Will faces action again. I must join him soon whether or not I am totally healed."

Susan, concerned for John's health but also cognizant of the relationship fostering between her young cousin and the soldier, asked, "Is it wise to depart before you attain full strength? Will not you better support our efforts if you return as a completely healed warrior?"

"With all due respect Mrs. Williams, the scenario you suggest sounds most enticing, though not practicable. I shall consent to delay only until the end of April but I must depart before May."

"My, dear," General Williams began, as he slowly spewed forth his lengthy rationale. "We all desire this noble lad remain safely here with us just as thousands of families throughout our beloved South wish to protect their young men. But for our country to survive we must send our brave young knights into harms way to preserve the treasure entrusted to us. Son, my heart yearns for you to remain but my soul recognizes your answer to the call to duty."

"I appreciate your words, sir. I do find cause to enjoy the peacefulness of your fine estate." John stood and asked, "Does anyone care to join me for an evening stroll?"

Even General Williams understood John only desired one companion for a leisurely walk. Martha slowly rose and innocently said, "If no one else wishes the exercise I shall be delighted to accompany you." Together they strolled through the flowering grounds of Mossy Oaks.

The lively chirping of birds building nests filled the air. Balmy daytime temperatures gradually eroded with the setting sun. John coveted the opportunity to relive his magnificent afternoon with Martha. Life's most cherished moments fleet all too swiftly only to be retained in the mind as fading, treasured memories. The lady from Tennessee and the gentleman from Virginia silently meandered about, arm in arm.

John initiated the conversation. "Thank you so very much, Martha."

"What did I do to warrant gratitude?" she asked, with her inquisitive, sparkling eyes wide open.

His eyes transfixed upon hers. "Several hours ago, under the spell of a beautiful woman to whom I swore lifelong devotion, I selfishly offered a life away from the strife and suffering of my countrymen while you and I sailed to the safety of England on the premise of better serving the South. That undertaking would benefit the Confederacy but in a self-serving manner. You predicted mental anguish if I failed to share the pain and sacrifices of my fellow Virginians. You spoke of months or years before I might recognize the shortcoming. Your astute prophesy prevented the burden of regret from descending upon me this afternoon with the recent news from Virginia. God sent you as my angel to temper this strong-willed man and for that I thank you and our Lord."

They clung together in a warm embrace as the gulf air dissipated the mild temperatures of the day. A suppressing stillness enveloped their beings. Sooner than a cotton plant drops its blossoms they would part. John to dangers unknown, Martha to destinations uncertain, both in the midst of the ninety day war about to enter its thirteenth month. As John escorted Martha inside he hoped a relevant message from Reverend Watson tomorrow might place all at ease.

17 – SHILOH

John hoped by sleeping an additional hour each morning and by taking vigorous walks every afternoon that his stamina would increase. To his dismay the strenuous walks only impeded the healing of his wound. He preferred strength to the absence of pain. His regimen lessened treasured time with Martha but the two relaxed in the late afternoons on the veranda and promenaded over the grounds in the evenings. On the second Thursday in April John descended the stairs hungering for a hearty breakfast. Light, but forced conversation, all but ceased as four sullen faces unconsciously stared at him as he seated himself and looked to Martha. "What's wrong?"

General Williams held the special edition of yesterday's April 9th newspaper which Reverend Watson's servant delivered earlier. "On Sunday General Johnston's forces clashed with the enemy north of Corinth where the Union soldiers camped at Pittsburg Landing. The papers call it the Battle of Shiloh, ironically because our initial assault commenced near a church of that name. An estimated 10,000 casualties! No one anticipated this kind of bloodshed!"

John sat dazed with hands clasped beneath his chin and index fingers resting on his nose. He hesitantly broke the silence. "How many of those causalities did we absorb?"

"John, those 10,000 are ours. General Johnston is dead. Thank goodness for Beauregard. His presence, I am convinced, stabilized the troops upon the commanding general's death. Our scouts estimate the Yankees lost as many as 15,000 men."

"Impossible!" John blurted out. "That's combined casualties of 25,000. Reports, a month after the battle at Manassas, confirmed combined casualties of only 5,000."

"Though difficult to comprehend I fear the figures to be accurate. This battle may be the harbinger of a more brutal and costly fight for independence than we anticipated."

John picked at his serving of eggs. With his appetite obliterated he bluntly stated, "I must depart for Virginia. Today! I shall pack immediately."

Totally unprepared for his abrupt decision Martha's uncontrolled sobs filled the room. Fanny and Susan squeezed her hands in an unsuccessful attempt to sooth her. John briefly rested his hand on her shoulder, mumbled something about "talk before I leave," and disappeared upstairs. In less than fifteen minutes he tromped downstairs dressed in traveling clothes and holding a carpet bag in each hand. The women still remained in the dining room consoling Martha while General Williams secluded himself in the parlor with an early glass of brandy. John tactfully interrupted the ladies to request that Martha join him. Briskly they walked beyond the eyes and the ears of those inside.

"My dear Martha, I have rehearsed the many words I wished to leave with you when we separated. Words now are so inadequate. Hold me tightly as I shall hold you. Let me feel the warmth that I never knew existed before I found you nor I shall I ever feel again until we reunite. Wherever I venture, your radiance, your soul shall always accompany me."

She softly sobbed and pressed her fingers deeply into his arms. "John Beall, I love you with all my heart. To the end of time you shall be in my first waking thought. Damn this cruel war."

Neither ever uttered a profane word in the presence of the other. John slowly relinquished her and looked into those teary hazel eyes, reddened from her emotional outburst. "Our Lord does operate in mysterious ways. Do you realize that without this miserable, tragic, cruel war you and I would never have met? Look to the east at the rising sun, where I go to fight for a new day. As your day begins each morning, rise knowing I am already experiencing the same day. And as I watch the sun travel westward I take pleasure knowing its rays still warm you and bring light into your world. Parting is painful but our reunion shall be all the more joyous. Come see me off. After a long passionate kiss which promised of things to come, the two young lovers returned to the mansion.

Following sentimental farewells, promises to write, and commitments to travel safely, John climbed into the carriage with General Williams and traveled to the boat dock. At noon the whistle shrieked and the steamer churned away from the landing. Private Beall stood at the rail and fondly waved to the general.

18 – AT SEA

With the sound of the stream engine's rhythmic drone John drifted into an eerie trance. He sprawled on the aft deck away from the passenger cabin's idle chatter. With the sun's rays warming him on the bright, cloudless afternoon, he pulled his hat's wide brim low to his forehead and closed his eyes. Two months ago nothing warmed him like the brilliant sun. Today it heated him solely externally; only Martha's radiance could remove the chill from within. After twenty-seven years he understood the fulfillment of discovering the mate destined for him. This morning fate extracted its toll for that gift. Memories of Martha obliterated all other thoughts entering his mind. The ship's shrill whistle jolted his body back to reality. He placed his hand against his aching chest, now housing an unhealed lung and a damaged heart. After the vessel banged into the wharf, the deck hands scrambled to tie the ship fast. John grabbed his bags and meandered over to join the line of disembarking passengers. No hurry. Still undecided. Should he endure the punishing thousand mile Confederate rail journey to Richmond or would sea travel terminating in Wilmington, North Carolina, followed by a brief rail trip to Richmond prove more viable? He gazed to the gulf's beckoning waters before strolling to the steamship office to book passage for the more appealing maritime route.

With downcast eyes he dejectedly walked away upon learning the next scheduled departure to the east shoved off in two days. He haphazardly ambled into the path of a gentleman walking at full stride. "My apologies sir," John offered while stooping to retrieve the bags he dropped. "A preoccupied mind on a busy walkway is careless and rude."

"May I be so bold as to inquire the origin of your preoccupation?" asked the slender fellow with a warm smile, friendly brown eyes, and a trim, dark moustache which accentuated his weathered face.

"I'm traveling to Richmond to rejoin the 2nd Virginia with General Jackson. Already experienced our fine rail system," John added with sarcasm. "I preferred a steamship to Wilmington. Nothing leaves for several days. Guess I'll suffer another tedious train journey."

"Never met one of Stonewall's men that lacked spunk. You keen on adventure and a little danger if it aggravates the Yankees and gets you to Wilmington? My ship departs at dusk."

With a smile John replied, "Be my guest for a brief meal, provide the details, and I could very well join you."

"Name's Cooper, Captain Ashley Cooper. The mates call me Captain. My friends call me Ash, the blockaders call me… We won't address that yet. You call me Ash, Mister…?

"Apologies again. I'm John Beall. Most folks call me John. Close friends call me Johnny. I'd be honored if you called me Johnny, also."

"Johnny it is," responded Captain Cooper with a slap on his new acquaintance's back before they migrated to the tavern.

Two hours later, with his gear stowed below, John stood on the deck of the *Mobile Maiden* and watched the crew scurry about. The prospect of traveling on Ashley Cooper's sixth voyage rekindled Beall's intrigue with maritime adventure. This evening the *Maiden's* hull carried 600 bales of western cotton, currently valued at $700 per bale in England. Upon reaching the foreign port of Nassau the cotton would be exchanged for European arms and luxuries. A more perilous leg through the Union blockade to Wilmington would follow. A hero's welcome in North Carolina awaited the crew upon surviving the blockade's gauntlet. Payment in gold plus a hull brimming with eastern cotton bound for Nassau would be exchanged for more European goods and war material. The lengthier return journey to Mobile presented fewer Union war vessels to avoid, and cotton, regardless of origin, sold at the same price in Nassau. Cooper contented himself with spreading the risk between the Atlantic and Gulf but certainly held no desire to cross the Atlantic to Europe.

Every waking moment John observed the dashing ship's captain. To the Virginian's good fortune Ash developed a genuine fondness for the young soldier, gloried in the role of mentor, and never tired of the novice's constant barrage of questions. The aspiring student studied the art of utilizing sails to augment steam power. Other valuable lessons focused on tides, navigational equipment, star constellations, maritime law interrupted by the Yankees, maritime law interpreted by the civilized world, and proper storage of cargo. The discussion of coal occupied another hour. The costly hard anthracite coal saved many a vessel from Federal detection. Soft coal produced highly visible black smoke plumes while hard coal burned more efficiently and emitted a nearly invisible residue.

They also reviewed weaponry. Ash concealed a six-inch rifled cannon on the bow of the *Maiden* while a four-inch rifled gun rested on the stern. Below deck the captain shared thoughts on appropriate side arms in the event of hand-to-hand fighting. He shook his head and made light of the man who carried a revolver and spare cylinders.

"Johnny, when your enemy's near and you've just emptied your revolver I don't suspect he'll pause, take a sip of water, watch you change cylinders, and then resume the fight. I prefer two loaded Colt's in my belt and another in my hand." Pausing to laugh his eyes sparkled with delight at the recollection of one of his former sailors. "Several months back a foot soldier tired of all that marching showed up saying his army enlistment was up. Boy looked healthy to me so I've got to believe the lad could've been a deserter, though not a concern of mine. I need bodies who take orders. In any case, he's carrying this fancy three-foot sword. I only imagined how he'd perform in close quarters with his ornate, over-sized weapon."

Ash bent over, lifted his trouser leg, and unsheathed a gleaming weapon with a double-edged blade separated from the handle by an ample hilt. “Men of experience tell me to always carry a knife in your boot.” He motioned John to follow him to the small armory near his cabin, unlocked the door, and walked past the musket racks to a worn wooden chest. Lifting the lid, he stooped and retrieved a sharp hatchet. “This proves as valuable as a brace of loaded revolvers. Utilized effectively it breaks down doors, aids a man scaling a hull, and severs an adversary’s hand from the arm in a split second.”

John winced at the vision of the ghastly injury. “To this point you say you’ve avoided altercations of any sort?”

That I have. ‘Tis more noble to be intelligent, than ‘tis to mistake bravery for foolhardiness. I derive profits for delivering goods, not killing Yankees. Besides, our cargo is more valuable to the South than several dead Union sailors, particularly if they’re only niggers.”

The education continued with John learning that a horizon with low lying dark clouds camouflaged a vessel while a bright horizon illuminated the ship’s silhouette. Incoming storms provided refuge for vessels fleeing a pursuer but aided the Yankees in setting traps for unsuspecting blockade runners.

Cooper’s smooth management of his thirty sailors proved the supreme lesson repeatedly taught throughout the journey. John marveled at the manner in which Ashley anticipated events before they occurred, with men positioned to effortlessly perform the task at hand. The disciplined crew functioned as a cohesive team motivated by ten per cent fear of their leader, forty per cent respect for him, and maybe ten percent loyalty for each other or their cause. The balance came from rewards reaped from a profitable voyage.

Six days after their departure they reached New Providence Island, centered in the Bahamas Islands about 300 miles northeast of Key West. The ship bumped against the wharf signaling their arrival to the bustling port city of Nassau. Negro stevedores wrestled with 1000 pound cotton bales which they transferred from the hull of one vessel, stacked briefly on the dock, and reloaded in the hull of another vessel destined for Europe. John never observed such thriving commercial activity in one location. Soon after their arrival Captain Cooper reboarded the *Maiden* with an immaculately dressed man wearing white trousers with a matching coat, and sporting a wide brim white straw hat to protect his fair-skinned, slight features. "John Beall, it's my pleasure to introduce my friend and long time business associate, Reginald Silverman, from, as he is fond of saying, across the pond in London. Hovering near Reggie, as Ash informally referred to the Englishman, stood a well-built man towering a head over everyone in the vicinity. His powerful arms folded over his chest above two polished revolvers which he displayed shoved into his belt. An eight inch worn wooden knife handle conspicuously protruded from his left boot. A nasty scar ran below his left eye across his deep Latin skin until the blemish disappeared into a dark black beard. The giant's solemn glare convinced John that the man gained employment for skills incompatible with a congenial demeanor. Laborers hustling to and fro also exhibited numerous scars. These disfiguring marks portrayed the rough element laboring along the wharfs.

John courteously exchanged greetings with Silverman while cautiously eyeing the Brit's bodyguard. "Good to meet you sir. From all Ashley tells me you two operate a thriving business that serves both of our nations well. If not for my enlistment in the army I would certainly entertain such an enterprise."

"Ashley mentioned you suffered a ghastly wound. Trust the healing goes well. The South needs every able bodied man available to throw back the Yankees. I hear the North recruits the bloody Irish and barbaric Dutchmen immediately upon their feet touching shore in New York." A tinge of guilt for his long absence crept into John with Silversmith's comment.

Empty wagons creaked to a halt adjacent to the *Mobile Maiden.* Speaking in a precise British dialect Silversmith concluded the conversation. "Our wagons shall unload your cotton and transfer your European merchandise immediately so you lads may be off. Captain Cooper desires a departure before the moon brightens the sky. Good to make your acquaintance, John Beall."

"The feeling's mutual Reggie Silversmith." With that the Englishman and his protector wound through the waterfront activity to arrange delivery of the goods destined for North Carolina.

Late that afternoon the *Mobile Maiden* departed Nassau under partly cloudy skies for another leg along the perilous route. Below the *Maiden's* deck lay a carefully stacked cargo of 1200 Enfield rifles, 1500 bayonets, 800 uniforms, a dozen rifled cannon barrels, several kegs of powder, cases of percussion caps, and small crates with hundreds of rounds of ammunition, in addition to assorted accoutrements. The continual flow of war material bolstered moral for the out-manned Rebel army. Always the affable gentleman, Ashley remembered to cater to the pleasures of the civilians far from the battle lines. His merchandise destined for the good citizens of the South included cases of fine European wine, bottles of French perfume, yards of fabric from the best mills of England, delicious chocolates, and expensive caviar. Before expenses the round trip grossed the captain almost $300,000. As the war continued expenses escalated. Ash long believed coal suppliers manipulated the price and supply of the sought after hard coal. The decreasing availability of competent seaman and the shortage of longshoreman inflated labor costs. And the Yankees were finding limited success as occasional blockade runners laden with valuable cargo failed to avoid capture.

John stretched out on his bed in the cabin the captain so generously provided. As he shut his eyes to partake in much needed sleep the inviting hazel eyes of Martha and her warm, appealing smile filtered into his mind. Could he have stayed several days longer with her? Should he have? Abruptly his thoughts traveled to Will and the 2nd. Recent feelings of guilt overshadowed the pain of his unhealed wound. Deep within he accepted his responsibility of a soldier first, followed eventually by that of a husband, and probably never of a sailor. He cherished these final days on the sea to which he had grown so fond. He drifted to sleep, absorbed the following uneventful day at sea, and rose for the voyage's concluding day scheduled to culminate in Wilmington that evening.

Selfishly John hoped the *Mobil Maiden* would glide across the Atlantic under clear skies and over calm seas warmed by balmy temperatures. Realistically he recognized rolling seas covered with gray skies would hinder detection by Yankee blockaders. Beyond the horizon many lessons learned on the voyage would soon be put into practice.

Early in the evening John entered the wheelhouse. "Appears we're making excellent time, Ash. Another couple hours before we reach Wilmington?"

"Hopefully," responded the captain with a forced smile while gazing at the overcast horizon. "Provided we don't steam right into the Yankees. The South loses more ships approaching Wilmington than any other port. If rumors of New Orleans's capture prove accurate the closing of harbors in Wilmington and Charleston shall become key Federal objectives. If we're detected you're welcome to observe at your own risk but stay clear of my men." The sharp tone of Cooper's order sent a shiver down John's spine.

Taking several steps back he calmly replied, "Ash, I'll shadow you at a distance per you request but if you need me to perform any task, any at all, I'm at your service."

"You're above deck because I can count on you," Ashley stiffly responded. He turned his attention toward the gray horizon merging with the dark sea as day transformed into night.

Not a man spoke as the side-wheeler guided only by compass churned through the darkness. Two dozen sets of eyes scanned the 360 degrees circumventing their ship. After an hour of uneventful sailing a shout came from the aft deck, "Ship to the starboard!"

John turned his head to the right in unison with the wheelhouse crew. “Damn you, Smitty,” Cooper yelled, “haven’t you learned the difference between a rolling wave and Yankee blockader? You’re more nervous than a virgin on her wedding night.”

“Sorry, Cap’n, I just, well, I thought…”

“One more thought like that,” Cooper interrupted, “and you’ll be shoveling coal in the boiler room.” The captain detested false alarms. Took the edge off. With each erroneous warning the men relaxed until they assumed every unidentified shape was a rolling sea swell or a nearing land mass.

Several minutes later a huge wave a hundred yards to the left transformed into a ship. Friend or foe? Anchored or moving? If running, in which direction? Captain Cooper slowed the engines bringing the mighty side wheel clanking to a stop. Low visibility limited vision. Rolling seas slapping against the *Maiden* obscured distant sounds, leaving the crew with the solitary consolation that the other vessel experienced similar handicaps. Cooper focused his expensive German binoculars upon the unidentified vessel just as she turned toward him. No merchant dared approach another vessel. Had to be a Yankee!

“Full speed a head!” he screamed. His ship lurched forward. “We’ll try to out run ‘em first,” he yelled. John stood silently with his chest pounding. Momentarily the hunted pulled away from the hunter but steadily lost separation as the Union Navy vessel attained full speed. Yankee cannon thundered. A round splashed far off the mark beyond eyesight of the crew. “They’ll get closer each time they sight their pieces,” Ashley mumbled subconsciously. A flash of light preceded the rumble of another blast. A geyser shot up thirty yards astern. “A little more elevation and we’re in dire trouble. Might have to lighten the load.” The third explosion illuminated the sky. The round sprayed saltwater over the deck.

John caught himself whispering, “And deliver us from evil, for thine is the kingdom, and the power…” Three spontaneous, sharp blasts interrupted his prayer. The cloud covered sky contained glaring orange muzzle flashes to their front for several long seconds. "Ash?" John began to exclaim. How could they escape Yankees to and fro. The crew's confusing unified cheer drowned his question. "What the…" he began to ask again, only to be cut off by the beaming captain.

"Johnny, I knew we neared the inlet, just unsure how close. Our artillery from the fort confirms we made it." Pointing to the rear he added, "Look at those Yankee bastards run from our shore guns." John watched the Union naval vessel melt into the darkness.

Five minutes later the Rebel fort received a rousing cheer from the crew of the *Maiden* as she churned past up the Cape Fear River. Five hours after entering the waterway the blockade runner bumped into the dock. Cooper stayed with his ship while his crew scampered towards the taverns for refreshment and female companionship. Physically drained but mentally alert John attempted to sleep in the three remaining hours of darkness. He finally drifted off, faintly recounting the blur of events thrust upon him the past eight days.

By six-thirty dock activity extinguished all opportunity for further rest. He climbed to the deck where he spied Ash tranquilly gazing at the wharf while clutching a steaming cup of hot coffee. "Jones, fetch another cup for Mr. Beall," ordered the captain as his crewman scampered below and reappeared seconds later with the simmering brew. "Thank you, Mr. Jones. Besides the captain's pleasant company and the peacefulness of the sea I shall certainly miss your coffee." Before sipping the beverage he deeply inhaled, inviting the appealing aroma to filter through his nostrils.

An hour later with carpetbags resting at his feet, John bid Ashley a fond farewell. "Don't know how to show appreciation for all you've done." The two maintained a firm hand clasp a bit longer than customary, warmly staring into each other's eyes. "I won't ever forget you and all that you taught me. I hate to leave the sea behind but duty looms larger than the sea.

"You continue favoring that wound a bit. A few more voyages on the *Maiden* and you'll be mended good as new Johnny."

"Don't tempt me my good friend. As I said duty calls and," he sheepishly grinned, "I'm technically AWOL. We don't want Old Stonewall to shoot me as a deserter do we?"

"That we don't, Private Beall," laughed Ashley with a gentle slap on the back. "So long and God's speed, Johnny."

"And may the Lord guide you on many a productive voyage," John said before turning toward the railway station.

19 – LAST DAYS AS A SOLDIER

Two weeks later John waved farewell to his friend who stood on the platform at the Richmond Central Rail station. As the locomotive steamed ahead each succeeding car jolted forward with a loud clank. John closed his eyes, leaned back, and took pleasure in lounging on a coach seat all to himself. Instead of agonizing over the short rail journey to Gordonsville he reminisced of the fortnight he'd visited with Dan.

The two shared news of their respective families along with details of war's affect upon their kinfolk. Escalating prices, substantially higher than the inflated amounts he observed six months ago, appalled John although he now acknowledged the risk taken by those who braved the Yankee blockade. He described his experience on the inadequate Southern rail system. While aware of deficiencies with Confederate transportation Dan failed to comprehend the severity until John offered his account.

Hours of dialogue evolved around the conduct of the war. John conveyed the disenchantment of western planters, isolated and neglected by the Richmond government. Media coverage focusing primarily upon the east emphasized the validity of his claim, especially the minimal reporting of the Southern loss of control of the Tennessee River followed by the capitulation of New Orleans. These critical setbacks threatened the essential circulation of the Confederacy's lifeblood, the western waterways. The impact of total Yankees domination of the Mississippi seemed unfathomable. Travel near Mobile grew more perilous also.

When discussions returned to the battlefields both men bemoaned the shocking number of casualties the escalating war produced. Significant victories had eluded the Confederacy since Manassas. Now McClellan's spring campaign gained a foothold in southeastern Virginia, perilously close to Richmond. Dan confidently assumed even the Yankees lacked man power and resources to occupy captured Rebel territory while simultaneously advancing deeper into Virginia. Ineffective Yankee generals and their inept commander-in-chief also faced a severe challenge against a more than capable General Joe Johnston.

On the lighter side the duo frequented Richmond's finer restaurants and attended concerts in addition to viewing two theatrical presentations. An extravagant lifestyle amongst the city's affluent citizens continued.

Dan badgered his friend to remain in Richmond for a complete recovery, unaware of Martha's ever present radiant image pushing John to fulfill his duty and bring a timely conclusion to the war. Dan might have more graciously accepted the refusal had John shared his relationship with Martha. For the time being he preferred that no one know of Miss Martha O'Bryan, including his own family.

The train rolling through the greening countryside gradually rocked him to sleep, and only interrupted him at periodic stops where passengers departed and boarded. He disembarked in Gordonsville to spend the evening at a local hotel before purchasing a mount to visit an aunt living in Madison County.

The horse trotted along the dusty road while John mulled over Richmond's offer to become involved in a different kind of warfare behind enemy lines. Officials erroneously assumed he possessed the character of a man capable of forsaking traditional values to participate in an operation unorthodox at the best, dishonorable at the worst. He politely responded he would prudently evaluate the proposal before rendering a decision.

He remained with his aunt several weeks while resting and performing assorted tasks until rumors surfaced that Jackson moved toward Winchester and intended to recapture Harpers Ferry. With horse and rider refreshed, John departed for an eighty-five mile ride to Charles Town before first light on the 25th of May. Gambling on Jackson's' ability to rid

Jefferson County of Yankee occupation John stayed on the east side of the Blue Ridge Mountains. A lone civilian traveling in western Virginia could easily fall prey to unforgiving Yankees, overly cautious Southerners, or blood thirsty guerrillas roaming the area. Night travel allowed safer movement but John chose to advance through the unfamiliar leg of his journey while fresh and alert. His loaded pistol hung within easy reach over the front of his saddle should he need fire power to back away from, or win a confrontation. A five shot .31 caliber pocket pistol stuffed into his boot increased his fire power to eleven rounds without reloading. Anyone foolish enough to prey upon him might well become the hunted.

He rested and watered his horse in the early afternoon before remounting to continue north. If Jackson had cleared the area of Yankees, Mother would find herself setting another place for dinner this evening. John slowed his pace, remembering Ashley Cooper's axiom to move cautiously along the last and most perilous leg of a journey. John rode from the forested landscape into fertile farm lands while noticing green shoots of sprouting corn breaking through the ground. Sweet scented clover blossomed in hay fields. The sorghum thrived too. Had it really been two years since he directed the spring planting? Spirea bushes hung low with white-flowering branches adorning the gate of the small farm house he passed. Nearer the dwelling, pale blue hydrangeas further brightened the homestead. He crossed a bridge spanning a rapidly moving stream while fragrances of the season and sounds of rushing water filled the mild spring air. His thoughts returned to the far away setting where in the not too distant past he held his beloved Martha after proposing to her. Only two short months since that memorable day? Time to temporarily wipe that image from his mind. A man could get killed not tending to business at hand. Ten minutes later he followed a dirt road leading into an area with a thick tree canopy overhead. Sounds of a huge body of marching men reached his ears. He abruptly yanked the reins. He cautiously dismounted and peered through the foliage to the turnpike connecting Charles Town with Harpers Ferry. A long, dirty, dejected column of blue clad soldiers, with drooping shoulders and heads down, trudged east to the Ferry. Mounted officers whacked random stragglers with the flats of their swords. Accoutrements cast along the roadside gave evidence of a hurried, disorganized retreat. Never could accuse the Yankees of a lack of benevolence. Maybe not tonight but soon the donated blankets, coats, and packs would find a home with deprived Southern boys.

Within fifteen minutes Union troops evaporated into the heights to the east. For an hour John watched the sun drop before vigilantly leading his horse across the pike. Silence blanketed the area. Not a sound from man or beast. The ebb and flow of heavy-handed Yankee occupation encouraged citizens to remain in their homes after dark. John guardedly traveled the familiar back road to his home which he last traveled in the bed of Andrew Hunter's wagon. Only a short, comfortable ride now. A melancholy shroud enveloped him. So near the farm with so many pleasant memories, but so close to proximity of his horrific wounding, on the same ground where Seth lay with his blind stare. Not far from the four desecrated Yankee bodies. Had providence prevented his participation on that dreadful day he would never…, pausing in mid-thought tranquility overwhelmed him. He would never have met Martha. Sensing an anxious rider, his worn mount increased her gait the final mile to the barn. When John entered, Timothy hesitantly approached before recognizing his master. John touched his fingers to his lips signaling the groom to remain silent.

"Let me surprise Mother."

"But Masser John, you..."

"Timothy, silence please," he barked before he hurried to the back door with the old Negro close behind mumbling something.

John opened the door in eager anticipation of the unexpected reunion with his family. After two short steps a sharp voice startled him, demanding, "Halt or I'll shoot!"

Simultaneously a revolver clicked into position ready to fire. He froze until to his relief he distinguished Mary silhouetted by the low light of the flickering lamp Mother held.

Mary shrieked upon recognizing her long-absent brother. "John Yates Beall, I almost shot you." Turning to Timothy she glared and spewed forth her wrath upon the cowering servant. "And you didn't warn him!"

"Mary, he tried. I didn't permit him to finish. I wanted to surprise everyone." He laughed nervously and offered, "That I obviously did." Lack of reciprocating smiles concerned him. "What's wrong?"

"I needs to tend to Massa's horse," the groom said before exiting.

"Night, Timothy," the three replied.

Beth, Annie, and Janie added to the excited voices ringing through the farm house. After hugs and greetings John settled into his designated seat at the table eager to devour a plate set of fresh greens, pickled tongue, and canned peaches.

When Mother turned up the lamp John winced at her worn face. Mary explained, "Since you departed we suffered the humiliation of Yankee occupation. Fences became firewood. Livestock disappeared. Yankee soldiers appeared at our door at all hours expecting a meal from our dwindling stores. Several citizens discovered to deny them invited trouble. If poorly controlled Union troops under incompetent officers weren't enough concern, we faced additional dangers from their deserters who answered to no one."

While it pains me to say," Mother interjected, "many of our so-called partisans really comprise roaming bands of thieves stealing whatever pleases them under the guise of serving the Confederacy. Thank God Father isn't alive watching the demise of southern chivalry."

"Mother, don't let the actions of a handful of self-serving ruffians weaken your faith in southern honor. Our resolve remains strong. I observed the exodus of the beaten, retreating Yankees to Maryland. General Jackson shall prevent their return. Have you heard from Will?"

"Your brother certainly's not the disciplined letter writer you are; he corresponds more like your older brother. William's messages arrive every five or six weeks. Wherever Jackson goes so goes your brother. Hopefully he'll visit once the general establishes camp nearby. Your brother's experienced what he refers to as a mild case of camp fever. Nothing serious. While involved with numerous actions he's suffered nary a scratch in battle."

"Anything from Hezekiah?"

"Two letters since you departed. One about Christmas and the other the end of March. He avoids involvement with the war. Sounds like many of the westerners view the conflict as an eastern issue. If the Union initiates a draft I pray he returns south although we now draft men too. He's probably poisoned with Yankee prejudice from living in Iowa for ten years. I wonder if we'll ever see him again. What do you plan, John?" Mother leaned forward with her forearms resting upon the table, hands folded together, and eyes locked directly on him as she conveyed an expectation of a sincere answer.

He pushed his chair away from the table and assumed a relaxed posture with a lower leg resting over a thigh. "Nothing's changed. I traveled south to accelerate my healing and thanks to the hospitality of some very fine people, as I wrote, I improved." No need to mention Martha yet. "During my journey south and throughout my return trip north," he paused to ponder the realization that he now too thought of Virginia as the north. "Excuse my deviation. As I was about to say, during my travels I encountered individuals involved with maritime shipping of war material. While intrigued by the opportunity my commitment remains to the 2nd and the defense of Virginia's soil. No longer content to await complete healing I plan to report for duty to Colonel Allen within the week. Hopefully we'll see Will first." No need sharing the option presented to him in Richmond.

"Your wound's not healed yet!" blurted Annie.

"Very close but not completely. Today's lengthy ride slightly aggravated it."

Mother's tired face emphasized her demand to, "Remove your shirt so I may examine you."

"Now, Mother?"

"Yes, now. All of us tended you as you lay in your bed near death."

Why protest? Outnumbered five to one. Gingerly he removed his vest and unbuttoned his shirt. He drew back his sleeve with his left hand. When he realized his shirt absorbed a splotch of moist blood through the bandage his look of surprise matched the expressions of astonishment upon the other faces.

"You're rejoining the army within the week, with an unhealed wound!" Mother screeched. "What doctor shall approve that?"

How could he explain all that transpired, particularly his commitment to Martha, especially when they knew nothing of her? Return to service, perform his duty, and promptly end this war, followed by the sweet reunion with Martha after which his family could meet his future wife. He stammered through a weak rationalization about "men with far more serious ailments continue to serve," and abruptly terminated the conversation by saying, "I've experienced a tedious day. I'll change my bandage upstairs, a task to which I've become adept, so if you'll excuse me I anticipate a very good night's sleep in the comfort of my own bed." Within twenty minutes he slept peacefully oblivious to the forthcoming turn of events.

John acquiesced in part to Mother's expectations for several days. The continuous aroma of favorite foods, the familiarity of home, and the pampering by five loving women softened the immediacy of the military commitment. However, John promised himself a return to duty within the week, a pledge he kept to himself. No value in disrupting the tranquil setting. He adamantly demanded that no one, especially Sue Ellen O'Brien, know of his return. His puzzled family quietly consented to his request although he feared the ever present slave grapevine would spread news of his arrival.

A day and a half after his return he rocked lazily in the old chair on the back porch. He gazed across the rolling patchwork of productive fields which benefited from the spring's mild temperatures and ample rainfall. Today's light rain further greened the landscape. He hoped the precipitation would disappear before his visit to camp in the morning. He planned to return home in the evening and officially rejoin his regiment the day after tomorrow unless he unexpectedly chose his other option. John didn't relish reacclimating to military life in the midst of a lengthy damp spell, especially after enjoying the easy life these past two days. His wound aggravated him less today then ever as his time home paid desired dividends. Today's rare solitude allowed his mind to drift south to the warm, smiling face he yearned to view. His thoughts vanished when a wagon rattled down the lane. Timothy pushed the team harder than usual. He stepped down from the wagon and walked briskly toward the porch at a pace rare for the old man. John frowned. Even simple tasks such as wiping down a wet team seemed to be neglected without constant supervision.

Before John admonished the servant, Timothy spoke. "Masser John, General Jackson, he's a leavin the Ferry, headed back south through Winchester. Folks say Yankees from Maryland and up the valley are a tryin to trap him. That old fox'ill ave none of dat. I know you fixed to catch up with em so I come back as quick as I could. Had to wait for our horse soldiers to pass. They didn't want nobody leavin town. Afraid of Yankee spies carryin information. I left anyhow. They was none too happy. Them boys sure knows how to cuss," he said, displaying a wide grin.

John looked into his slave's eyes and gripped his shoulders. "As usual your loyalty is unquestioned. I trust you'll watch after everyone."

"Massa John, you know I will."

"That I do, Timothy."

John pivoted and entered the house to explain his sudden departure. The women comforted each other while he climbed the stairs to gather his belongings.

Armed with his two revolvers, loaded down with an excess of food and extra clothes, Private John Beall climbed on a spirited dapple gray mount and cantered up the lane towards town. The steady drizzle dissipated although thick, threatening clouds hovered above. In Charles Town, John confirmed Timothy's report that Jackson's main force had a half day's lead. He decided to head due south across the Jefferson County line into Clarke County and spend the evening at his uncle's mansion, Mansfield. He said a pleasant goodbye to his relation and rode away the following morning intent upon intersecting Jackson's army. He ended the day at a Mr. Kaufman's house as moderate rain fell. Much to his dismay he awoke in the morning to sheets of rain thrust from a blowing wind hammering against the house. He craved rest but feared the rising streams. Further delay could place half the Yankee army between him and the 2nd. Reluctantly he bid farewell to his gracious host and mounted for a soaking journey. At noon he approached a familiar ford near a small town along the pike. He anticipated crossing the gently flowing tributary before it had swollen into a raging torrent with overflowing banks which prevented his passage. He detoured due south into the driving rain, trusting he paralleled Jackson's movement. Periodically the intensity of the storm converted his protective raingear into a funnel which channeled chilling rain into his clothing beneath his waterproof. His fatigued back amplified the throbbing pain reverberating throughout his chest. The presence of passing blue clad soldiers added further stress. Fortunately the miserable weather eliminated questioning by drenched Yankees plodding through the quagmire.

About mid-afternoon the weather cleared. John neared a white one-story farm house, with several sturdy outbuildings including a large barn. He paused and dismounted to water his horse from the worn wooden trough near the fence gate. He froze at the sounds of a column of blue clad infantry appearing at the bend beyond the house. He suppressed an initial impulse to gallop away. At that range he provided an inviting target to the Yankees armed with deadly accurate Springfield muskets. The alarm of several shots could alert the scores of Union troops already swarming the area. He quickly tied his horse and entered the gate while shielding his bags. He meandered lazily into the barn. Inside he quickly concealed his belongings and revolvers beneath a hay stack. He took several steps before remembering his 2nd Virginia leave papers. He concealed them in a crevice between boards in a horse stall. A moment later, assuming the role of simple farmer, he walked outside, grabbed a pitchfork, and began tossing hay to hungry cattle. He hoped no one remained inside the home to spoil his ruse. Rumors abounded that without conscience Yankees in occupied Virginia hung anyone suspected of subversive activity; he shuddered acknowledging he fit the bill. The first column of sodden soldiers marched past without even glancing at the disguised Rebel in their midst.

A soldier in the next column jeered, “Down here thought only niggers did such work, or they all run off on you, boy?” John smiled, turned, and speared another clump of hay. Fortunately they missed the grimace across his face. He slowed his pace but rhythmically continued performing the task. Mercifully the mounted rear guard appeared. His heart raced when a detachment of six horse soldiers dismounted outside the fence.

A mud-splattered lieutenant ordered a private to water his horse. He entered the gate with two others, each armed with threatening carbines. He strode assertively toward John. He stopped several paces from him.

“Lieutenant,” John asked in an irritated tone as he motioned to their point of entry, “could you please have your men close that gate? I’ve enough to do without chasing cattle halfway cross Shenandoah County.”

The lieutenant looked back and jerked his head in the direction of the open gate. One of the three men watering horses outside the corral responded immediately. Well-disciplined. Probably a competent officer. The 5'10" cavalryman towered several intimidating inches above John. The Yankee's broad forehead lay below shocks of red hair streaked with wisps of gray. A trim red moustache separated a classic Roman nose from stern lips. Cold blue eyes surveyed John from head to toe and then studied the horse tied to the fence. "Seen any of your troops pass today?"

"My troops? Don't know what you mean," John answered guardedly.

"Come, come, my boy. Many of you feint allegiance to the Union by day and become cowardly bushwhackers after the sun drops. You might be one of them."

Beall refused to be baited by the condescending tone of the Yankee about John's age. "Lieutenant, with all due respect, I wish the damn war never started, and I'll sure as hell be glad when it's over. That being said I do want the Union restored, with or without the darkies. That issue doesn't affect us since we don't own any."

"We? Who's we?"

John had no idea who lived here or where their allegiance might lay. Darn, they could be inside watching the inquisition ready to betray him at any moment. "My family of course. Hard working, honest white men. An astute man such as you realizes both armies recruited heavily from the valley. I believed it my responsibility to maintain the farm so folks here bouts could eat." Hopefully the vague answer deflected conversation from John's newly adopted family.

"Spent your entire life on this farm I take it?"

An improper response to this question could bring fatal ramifications. "Mostly, except for several years at the university. What occupation did the war draw you from, Lieutenant?"

"I supervised crews of lumbermen in upstate New York." Not to be distracted, he continued. "One bit of curiosity, Mister...?"

"Lewis, John Lewis." He hoped the empty shipping crate in the barn for a C. R. Lewis belonged to the owner of the property.

"Well, John Lewis," began the officer in a skeptical tone while glancing over his shoulder to John's horse, "I question why a man spending his entire life around livestock would let a good mount remain tied outside with the saddle atop a damp blanket."

If he only kept his pocket pistol in his boot he might take out these three and hope for the best with the other trio. "You've rightfully embarrassed me, sir. I snuck into town hoping to find a letter from my sweetheart residing in Lynchburg. Inclement weather delayed my return. Hoping to feed and settle the cattle, I carelessly neglected my horse. Love does strange things to a man."

"Must have been some letter."

The type of private letter this ill-mannered Yankee would ask to see and read aloud for entertainment. "Unfortunately the flooding delayed her epistle to me."

"Mr. Lewis," continued the lieutenant with the interrogation.

Just then an elderly man limped from the house accompanied by his mate. Fortunately the couple's age allowed them to pass for John's parents. He hoped a delayed appearance implied they had no desire to interact with Yankee soldiers unless a good Southern boy direly required assistance.

"What's the problem here, sir?" The old man demanded. "Hard enough to get a good day's work out of this boy without all this distraction."

"Just doing their duty, Pa. Looking out for your interest too. This gentleman's concerned I didn't tend to the horse before I fed the cows. Of course I appreciate a cavalryman's concern for well-cared horse flesh. Should remember what you always say, 'Johnny Lewis, first things first.' Remember telling your son Johnny that?"

The man John assumed to be C.R. Lewis answered knowingly with a smile, "Yes, I recall preaching such time and again to my boy Johnny."

Though not completely satisfied the officer loudly ordered, "Mount up men, we've got Johnny Rebs to catch."

Use of his name proceeding Rebs did not escape John who accompanied the troopers through the gate to their horses. As they mounted John unwound the reins of his horse from the fence post and led it inside the corral.

"Good day, John Lewis, until we meet again."

"That would be my pleasure," John firmly answered.

The Northern soldiers faded into the distance when a firm voice with the long forgotten tone of George Beall demanded, "Who exactly are you son?"

"John," he paused displaying his soft, warm smile accentuating his disarming blue eyes. "John Beall of Jefferson County." Enough information volunteered until he knew these folks' loyalties, although he suspected identical ones to his. "Thank you for interrupting the inquiring Union officer."

"God damn Yankees! Just be…"

"Charles, that's the Lord's name you take in vain!" the woman interrupted. "I'm not prepared to turn the other cheek but neither shall I tolerate your use of profanity, especially when prompted by those ungodly people."

"Yes, Agnes," Charles Lewis obediently replied. "Just because they have more men, not better men mind you, and told us what to do for the past eighty years, they believe it their privilege to rule over us forever. Most Virginians preferred to remain in the Union until that fool president demanded our boys fight our brothers to the south. Lincoln wanted Virginian troops; he got them, cept their rifle barrels pointed at him." A high pitched laugh erupted from the old man before he asked, "Where you exactly been, John Beall, and where you going?"

John recounted his past fourteen months. He sprinkled in details of the John Brown affair to which Agnes shook her head and muttered, "And he professed to be a Christian man."

John continued his narrative when Mrs. Lewis suddenly interrupted, "Why John, I assumed that dampness on your shirt came from the rain! You're bleeding."

"It's an old wound slowly improving, Mrs. Lewis. I'll pump some water, wash it, clean the bandages, and change my shirt. If you folks allow me, I'll bed down out here for the night before continuing my journey tomorrow."

"You'll do nothing of the sort," she flatly stated. "Charles, show the boy to the spare room."

"Really, Mrs. Lewis, I insist that I avoid placing you in danger, especially if that nosy lieutenant returns."

"How would a mother explain leaving her son sleeping in the barn for the night?"

Charles grinned as someone else lost a verbal battle with his wife. He simply said, "Agnes has a point, you know."

Within the hour John enjoyed the hospitality of newfound friends. After a supper of reheated beef stew, fresh baked bread, recently prepared strawberry jam, and slightly fermented apple cider, he relaxed at the table with Charles while Agnes washed the white dishes. Exhaustion forced John to retire early to the beckoning bed.

In no time he slept soundly. Images of a host of heavenly angels brightened the sky, all surrounding the surreal form of Martha. John reached for her as she extended her hands to him. The enveloping illumination grew brighter until John awoke, discovering morning's light indicated it well past dawn. He started to rise, only to drop back into the bed with a groan. He reluctantly digested the message transmitted by his body.

Six days earlier he rode eighty demanding miles to Jefferson County. After several days of pampering he embarked toward the 2nd Virginia. His first day's travel concluded with a relaxing evening with relatives, followed by a second day ending at Mr. Kaufman's. Yesterday soaked him to the bone. Pitching hay, albeit briefly, reminded him of muscles long forgotten. Now, after a good night's sleep in a comfortable bed, preceded by an excellent evening meal, he lay paralyzed from exhaustion. Physically worthless from several demanding days interspersed with total relaxation. Before his injury John relished forced marches under Jackson's driving leadership. Those challenging excursions paled in comparison to the strenuous movements now accomplished by Jackson's foot cavalry. Despite the call for duty soundly beckoning from within his soul, he accepted that a return to his unit remained in the distant future, if ever.

Now what? He longed to hold Martha, to kiss her, to be with her, but his reappearance would proclaim his selfishness. He lived for her approval, the absence of which would shatter all that bonded them together. A return to Jefferson County evaporated with the Confederate withdrawal from that war torn landscape. Several months ago he eliminated relocation to England from consideration because Martha adamantly opposed it. He laid in bed thinking of his loved ones—Martha, Mother, Mary, Beth, Annie, Janie, and Will, when his thoughts turned to his brother Hezekiah.

He pondered the Confederacy's need for operations behind Union lines, especially since the South lacked recent battlefield successes. Iowa, as evidenced by her response to Lincoln's call for troops, remained solidly pro-Union. However, many folks there continued going about life much as they did prior to the commencement of hostilities. Since he had traveled there in late 1860 to finalize land transactions he possessed familiarity with the region. That knowledge initiated the proposal from Richmond officials to consider traveling to operate beyond the Mississippi. His obligation to serve the 2nd could only be fulfilled with a sound body. Perhaps an opportunity to serve Virginia would evolve after he healed. At that moment John committed himself to reaching Iowa, mending his body, and serving the Confederacy. He confidently rose and dressed, devoured Agnes Lewis's hearty breakfast, and headed to the barn to saddle up. Before mounting he clasped Mr. Lewis's hand between his while he leaned down to kiss Mrs. Lewis on the cheek. Once atop his spirited horse he sentimentally said, "Thank you for everything, Pa. Take care, Mother Lewis."

"God's speed, Johnny Lewis," responded Charles.

When the horse turned towards the road John witnessed a tear trickling down Agnes Lewis's cheek as she softly said, "May God travel with you, Son."

Forty-eight miserable hours of travel in the rain preceded several pleasant days of mild, sunny weather. John finally reached Uniontown, Maryland, ten miles south of the Pennsylvania border. In Virginia he traveled in constant fear of encountering Union troops. The last fifty miles through Union territory proved stress free. When he recalled the hardships inflicted upon his homeland by the Northern invaders he bristled as he passed through their unscathed land. If the horrors of war spilled north the self-righteous Yankees might not be so committed to the plague of death which they had spawned.

20 – A JOURNEY WEST

John wore a satisfying smile as he settled into his seat. Nothing like a profitable horse trade to bring a man pleasure. Two hundred dollars for an animal he purchased three years earlier for one-and-a-quarter. Granted, the animal would command two hundred and fifty dollars in Virginia, but with inflated Confederate currency. The sale's newly issued greenbacks would spend well in Iowa.

As the train rolled west he watched the picturesque scenery glide past his window. Trimmed orchards, productive grain fields, and acres of pastures dotted with grazing livestock intertwined to weave a patchwork quilt which covered the hills and valleys of eastern Pennsylvania. The cloudless blue sky served as a backdrop for the glistening sun casting its soothing warmth across the landscape. The tranquility of the peaceful northern countryside gradually gnawed at him as he contrasted his native homeland, scared by the two warring armies' brutal tug-of-war. Each passing mile widened the disparity. If the Northern citizens experienced the deprivations Southerners suffered they might not be so content to continue the conflict. Before his journey ended John would travel through one enormous grain field stretching from Cleveland to the Mississippi River, interrupted only by numerous small towns and the growing cities of Toledo and Chicago.

At various stops he shook his head in amazement at the number of healthy white males out of uniform going about day-to-day civilian activities. In the South a white man either served in the military or directly contributed in a capacity tangibly supporting the war effort. His train passed a continuous procession of eastbound locomotives pulling flat cars loaded with gleaming new artillery pieces, box cars jammed with war materials, and passenger coaches carrying scores of green soldiers about to encounter the horrors of war.

Though awed by the military genius of Jackson, Beauregard, and Johnston, his travels through the North created an awareness of the endless resources available to the Yankees. During his thousand mile trek he would observe a first hand demonstration of the Northern rail system's amazingly efficient operation. Limited rail line changes occurred in part due to the North's utilization of standardized gauged track throughout their system.

He observed an extremely depressing scene between Cleveland and Toledo. A group of eleven Confederate officers, including several hindered by debilitating battle wounds, exited their coach and transferred to a spur leading a dozen miles north to a prison camp on an island in Lake Erie. As his train later neared Chicago scores of prisoners began filling vacant freight cars. Melancholy expressions upon unkempt faces tore at him, knowing that these men traveled farther from home and deeper into the land from which they fought to divorce themselves.

John's spirit's rose the first evening in Chicago. Kentucky natives Abe Lincoln and Jeff Davis, both born in 1809, had migrated west at a young age, with Davis landing in Mississippi and Lincoln settling in Illinois. To John's surprise many of Chicago's citizens showered their state's adopted son with anything but love. Democratic watering holes echoed with profane condemnation of Honest Abe. Criticism grew proportionately with the consumption of liquid refreshment. "Nigger-loving butcher," repeatedly resounded throughout the establishments.

In a hotel saloon John located an open table in the rear of the establishment near a pair of men dressed in fine business attire. While inconspicuously listening to their conversation he overheard several comments referencing the Knights of the Golden Circle spewing from the mouth of one well-lubricated merchant. On occasion the man's companion squeezed through the expensive fabric of the speaker's upper arm causing him to yelp and mumble a slurred reply.

"Damn it Michael, that hurts!"

"Not as much as me fist in your face if I hear those words again, Claudius."

"You worry too much. No Republican swine frequent this fine establishment. Management sees to that."

The man referred to as Michael quickly rebutted. "Lincoln knows the war's going poorly. He's planted spies throughout to lockup the likes of any Democrat opposing him. Reference to the Knights only simplifies the task. Shut up and have another drink or two." Claudius's flowing dissertation digressed into unrecognizable gibberish to even the most attentive listener. Thirty minutes later Michael escorted his wobbly charge into the hotel lobby and up the stairs.

John then recalled overhearing a conversation while rolling through Indiana, in which two men with low voices mentioned the organization. The Knights of the Golden Circle sprouted in the early 50's. Currently the loosely-defined secret Confederate society with strong roots in Indiana sprouted branches throughout the Old Northwest. Membership numbers rumored to be in the thousands. One man whispered the society even thrived in the prison camps with the support of sympathetic northern peace Democrats. This supposition implied opposition to the war in the North might exceed that from the South.

The following day he indulged in the pleasant June weather with a leisurely stroll along the windy city's shoreline. The morning bustle pushed him along the sidewalks at a pace even uncommon in the thriving ports of Charleston and Savannah. His hurried walk terminated at the perimeter fence of the Camp Douglas prison camp. Guilt descended while he helplessly observed the aimless meanderings of several thousand incarcerated prisoners. He yearned to do something, anything. In frustration he shrugged his shoulders. Sharp pain shot through his chest. The blasted constant reminder. Would he ever heal? Several paces to his right John overheard a mother lecture a young lad wearing short pants, a light-summer coat, and an oversized drooping cap which covered the eyebrows.

"Willie, these heathen Rebel prisoners are locked up because they broke the laws of the United States and of God. The vile disgusting creatures killed your uncle Frederick and wounded your papa."

Beall glanced over to challenge the lies the woman's son ingested but instead lazily carried his gaze through the woman and beyond. He reluctantly walked away just as the lad shouted, "Dirty Rebs, hope you all rot in there."

John's walk progressed along the waterfront. He so desired to impose comeuppance for these self-righteous Yankee citizens, particularly a sweeter retribution if delivered by the hands of these brave men who, with such dignity, endured insults from insensitive women and children. Once Northerners suffered the edge of the sword slice across their land the war assuredly would cease. The freshly conceived thought of unleashing thousands of Confederate prisoners to pour forth their wrath upon the enemy's homeland slowly nurtured.

An exploration of the lakeshore added nutrients to the germinating concept. He opened a casual conversation with a businessman gazing at the harbor. "Sir, this is my first visit to this fair city since the secesh attacked Fort Sumter. I see numerous artillery pieces protecting this port from invasion if the Rebels ever possess the brashness to attack. I am appalled to observe only one armed military vessel. Is that sufficient to ward off an assault?"

"One naval boat to protect Chicago?" the man responded in a condescending tone. "Where you from?"

"Forgive me. I'm John Yates from the southern part of the state. With the Mississippi closed I'm investigating shipping grain through the lakes rather than via the mercenary railroads." He paused with a sheepish expression, grinned, and said, "I pray that you are not a railroader."

Smiling ear-to-ear the well-built fellow with a ruddy complexion vigorously shook John's hand. "Heavens no man. Deal in livestock. Feel your pain with the railroads, though when my stock reaches the yards the army takes possession and pays the freight. Name's Keegan McIntosh. Where you'd say you're out of?"

Claiming the lower part of the state explained John's southern drawl but selecting a specific town might reveal deceit if McIntosh possessed familiarity with the locale. "Down on the river." He then pointed to the dock and questioned, "Why your puzzlement with my inquiry concerning the naval steamship?"

"Apologies, Mr. Yates isn't it?" McIntosh asked as John nodded affirmatively. "You asked if a lone ship adequately protects Chicago. My friend, you observe the only ship on Lake Michigan; hell, the only warship on the Great Lakes thanks to our outdated treaty with the limeys."

"Only one legitimate warship cruises between Chicago and Buffalo?" clarified the astounded Southerner. "This concerns me," John commented with feigned worry while thinking it concerns him that he couldn't take advantage of the situation.

McIntosh pulled a timepiece from his vest pocket, politely smiled, and terminated the brief conversation. Parts of a puzzle lay scattered about John's mind. Were supplementary pieces forthcoming or had they already arrived scattered randomly about awaiting proper arrangement by a preordained individual? He wandered throughout the warm afternoon, struggling to arrange the pieces. Early in the evening he passed the Wigwam, the massive convention hall where the Republicans nominated Lincoln and thrust the terrible war upon the nation.

Across the street well-dressed men entered a spacious hotel lobby. John followed with hopes of dining in a Republican establishment. Moments later he perused the appetizing menu, pleased he discovered a gathering site for vocal Republicans.

To his right sat four fashionably attired Yankee entrepreneurs. Portly waistlines indicated this bloody war provided a plentiful dining table for many. Listening intently, John presented the perception of a lone diner engrossed in his own thoughts.

"Sounds like McClellan might be celebrating July Fourth with a grand review in Richmond, especially with Joe Johnston out of the fight," commented a balding gent refilling his wine glass.

"Don't count those chicks before they hatch, Zebulon," countered a heavily bearded dining partner. "Just when the Rebels become most vulnerable our tentative Democratic general retreats and requests more troops. Mark my words."

"Luscious, what are the Rebs using for a general nowadays? Last I heard Jackson was still occupied in the Shenandoah Valley."

"Hell Zeb, they could dress a scarecrow in gray, put gold stars on its shoulders, pin some braid to its hat, stick it on a horse, and General George would race to the rear trembling in fear. Man's a typical gutless Democrat scared to fight."

"Luscious makes a valid point, Zeb," interjected the third companion with a chuckle, while the fourth sat quietly soaking up more wine than conversation. The third member straightened in his seat and earnestly continued. "We need a man like Ben Butler. You hear what he did in New Orleans?" Two heads shook back and forth simultaneously while another stared somberly at an empty wine bottle. "Seems a cocky Southern boy thought he'd be a man by pulling down the stars and stripes from atop the custom house. General dealt with the damned traitor by immediately stringing him up in the square. They say the culprit kicked and screamed like a true Southern gentleman." Raucous laughter erupted from the table. "That's the kind of man we need to end the war in the east. Hang 'em all I say."

John picked at the remainder of his lake trout. The vindictive war became harsher by the day. Both sides possessed men desiring to use the guise of war to commit brutal acts. Ironically these men distanced themselves from the battlefield where honorable men, yes, honorable men on both sides shed blood. He reviewed all he learned in Chicago during his leisurely walk to his hotel. Clandestine Knights of the Golden Circle apparently possessed hundreds of members throughout the North awaiting the opportunity to wreak havoc throughout the Yankee homeland. Besides Camp Douglas on the shoreline of Lake Michigan, John remembered the prison in northern Ohio. Battle tested veterans patiently awaited freedom. Only a single armed naval vessel to protect the entire shoreline from Chicago to Buffalo. The Democratic Party's dissent of the war and its apparent divisiveness shocked him. The atrocity committed by the Yankee military in New Orleans appalled him. Such ruthless acts only strengthened Southern resolve rather than subdued it. Before retiring for his final night in Chicago, John sat at the desk in his spacious room and composed a brief letter to Martha.

My Dearest Martha,

I am sure the fragrant blooms of Mossy Oaks orchards have transformed into the tiny fruits that all shall enjoy upon maturity during harvest season. Like those blooms, the flower of my love for you is constantly growing into something of value and substance. I regret not writing since my abrupt departure several months past, but my slow healing wound combined with unexpected events greatly altered my plans. I long to hear from you but my current situation prohibits such. As the opportunity arises I shall communicate. My thoughts of you only depart as I prepare for sleep with the setting sun. They return again with its rising golden glow, warming the day for me much as do my thoughts of you.

My travels throughout the North confirm no reconciliation between our two warring countries shall occur. From a woman and her son on the street to Republican businessmen dining in a fine hotel I observe bitter hatred displaces the brotherly love, which for so long bound our former Union together. I pray the warring factions, through the grace of God, may soon permanently separate without further unnecessary bloodshed which shall only open more wounds which shall fester for generations to come.

I must close, my dear, for my journey to points unknown continues tomorrow. I pray this finds you and those close to you well.

Yours forever,
John Yates

He turned down the lamp, draped his clothes over a chair, and climbed into bed, oblivious to the buzzing city noise below his third story window.

21 – REUNION

The day's lengthy rail travel terminated in East Dubuque, Illinois. John eagerly stood by the rail of the *Mississippi Princess*, as the side-wheeler ferry crossed the river to Iowa. He peered below the wide brimmed hat shading his eyes from the low sun's glaring rays shattering over the gently flowing water. Fighting fatigue, he hoped to settle into a hotel before dark.

Following a leisurely hotel breakfast John meandered over to the livery stable to inquire as to the availability of horses. He perused the over-priced, limited selection. He might have no choice but to pay two-and-a-quarter for half the mount he sold in Maryland for two hundred. He returned briefly to his room before walking to Bissell Brothers Grocery where Hezekiah last worked. Exiting the Jefferson Hotel he paused to inhale the refreshing morning air. Dubuque lay nestled between a towering bluff to the west and the wide, powerful Mississippi River to the east. In the distance bluffs also rose to the north. He turned his attention to the activity on the waterfront where an assortment of earthen and wooden piers provided dockage to a variety of vessels. A boardwalk extended over sloughs and inlets to the river's edge, although no one promenaded at this hour of the day. Sprouting from the ground near this side of the water's edge climbed a cylindrical, stone shot tower that once manufactured lead bullets. He trekked several blocks up 7th Street to the Main Street intersection where he paused. A block away the sun's rays reflected brightly from the third story of the white custom house walls, constructed with stone and accented by circle top windows. Raised lower sashes of several windows drew in cool air before the heat of the June day arrived. To his front he noticed increased growth in the young trees in Washington Park since his previous visit. He smiled recalling the countless number of northern streets, bridges, buildings, and parks carrying the name of the country's first president. When the South gained her independence would the names change or would the Yankees acknowledge the contributions of Washington and so many other Virginians in uniting the colonies eighty-six years earlier. He pivoted right for the one block walk remaining to Bissell Brothers. He again observed in amazement the number of able bodied white men not in uniform. A large portion of the Northern populace apparently possessed no overwhelming desire to volunteer for Lincoln's war. He glanced to the church spires piercing the heavens above Dubuque. How could Northerners consider themselves God-fearing and contribute to the misery inflicted upon the South?

The open door to Bissell Brothers Grocery welcomed the fresh morning air before activity on the dusty street forced its closing. Plentiful inventory filled the store. A bushel of apples sat near the door. Maybe the last of the previous fall crop removed from cold storage. Probably soft too, he thought while resisting the urge to pick one up and squeeze it. Canned goods abounded on the shelves behind the long pine counter. Barrels of flour, sugar, and salt pork sat to the side. No shortage of coffee either. Prices for flour and pork seemed astonishingly low compared to Virginia. Coffee and sugar, more expensive than several years back, also cost considerably less than in Virginia. A large glass jar with plump pickles sat on one end of the counter while smaller jars filled with penny candy occupied the other. Cotton bolts at inflated prices lay scattered about. To the rear of the store a man John immediately recognized sat examining stacks of papers. Invoices in one pile, bills of lading in the other.

"With you in a minute," acknowledged the clerk insincerely, demonstrating more of a concern with sorting through paperwork than selling merchandise.

"That any way to treat your first customer of the day?" John demanded.

The man at the desk aggressively started to rise to address the source of the interruption. He began to reply in an irritated tone, looked up, and stopped in mid sentence. "Damn it Johnny, you sound just like an impatient Yankee!" He advanced and warmly hugged his brother before he abruptly released his hold when a grimace raked John's face. "You're the last person I expected to see. Tell me about your wound. Mother's letter in January indicated you were on the mend and were recuperating down south. Didn't hear any more so I assumed you returned to the army." An agonized expression crossed Hezekiah's face. "The rest of the family alright?"

"Thank God, yes everyone's safe and sound as of several weeks back, though my dang wound's over half a year old and still unhealed. Supposed to be fighting with Will and the 2nd now but the blasted injury drains me of the strength I so long took for granted. You're the first person I'm admitting my concern of ever returning to my previous health. A setting far away from the war seems an ideal location from which to recuperate." John hesitated, then pointedly asked, "Where do your allegiances lie?"

"With the Democrats, the peace Democrats. Traveled west to purchase cheap land and avoid all the controversy brewing in Virginia. Told you of my relief when the mad man Brown returned east, though God only knows my shock when word of his action in Jefferson County spread to us. Figured his swift execution buried the issue. Would've if we elected someone other than the damned Republican dictator. His war nearly killed off the land business. Now he's promoting something called the Homestead Act. Wants to give land away. Just another scheme to settle more ground to create more free states to keep the Republicans in power. Simply put he's trading land for votes. With the Mississippi closed the railroad companies that encouraged Lincoln to initiate the war now rape the farmers something fierce. Fortunately grain prices are slowly getting better. Hope I don't get drafted and have to abandon all this. If I'm forced to wear a uniform it sure as hell won't be the damned blue one!"

John grasped his older brother's shoulders and looked intently into Hezekiah's dark brown eyes. "Your politics have been a source of concern, especially with your developing northern dialect."

"Johnny, you're the one with a misplaced tongue. How will you explain to townsfolk your Virginia gentleman's drawl?"

John grinned. "Mr. Beall, I'd like to introduce myself to you. I'm John Yates, grain broker from southern Indiana, down state by the river. If folks consign grain to me, for a modest fee I'll ship it east, obtain top prices for the wheat, and bargain rates from the railroad. Hope to locate different employment though to avoid dealing any longer with the thieving Yankees back east. Sound believable?"

"It'll do. Any prospects for work?"

"Nothing definite. Hope someone utilizes my abilities soon."

After thirty minutes of conversation consisting primarily of small talk Hezekiah suggested they meet for supper. He returned to his stacks of paper while his brother departed for his hotel. At the Jefferson House desk a clerk handed John a room key and a sealed envelope. In privacy he hurriedly ripped it open and read the brief message directing him to travel to Cascade, locate Thomas Chew, and inquire about a recent opening for a grist mill manager. At the Cascade Post Office a letter of introduction would be waiting for John Yates, the pseudonym he requested his Richmond connections use if he migrated to Iowa. The Confederate officials reacted promptly to the coded message he telegraphed eight days ago to a contact in Washington. To no avail John sought to determine who delivered the message.

To his relief, when he rushed back to Bissell's he found Hezekiah still pouring over paperwork at his roll-top desk, with no co-workers or customers in the store. Inquisitively the clerk looked up. "Johnny, back again?"

"Did you mention my arrival to anyone?"

"No, why?"

"The less you know the safer for us both. If anyone asks, tell them that I'm John Yates, a former grain broker interviewing for a position in Cascade. I'll explain at dinner."

He returned to his hotel where he dined on a light meal of ham, peas, and coffee while reading the *Dubuque Herald* to better familiarize himself with the sentiments of the area. By coincidence he noticed a posting of the open position at Chew's Mill in the paper. He remembered the *Herald's* name surfaced during his conference in Richmond. He revisited the livery and rented a horse with the proviso that he could purchase it if it met his expectations.

After a satisfying ride he leisurely walked to his hotel. Lengthening late afternoon shadows spread across the primary thoroughfare which he traversed. He stopped to study the panorama leading to the river where the Irish and Germans lived. Foreigners created their own neighborhoods catering specifically to ethnic needs. He resumed his walk toward his lodging in the more desirable section of town as evidenced by the three story buildings lining both sides of the street. The district housed upscale businesses, hotels, restaurants, and saloons. The sights, sounds, and smells permeating the air from the other direction nearer the river reconfirmed the waterfront district undeniably served immigrants rather than Americans. When he unlocked the door to his second story room a bright red prairie sky blazing above the bluff drew him to the panorama framed by his window. He opened the sash and welcomed the fresh air into his chamber. He poured water into the wash basin, splashed some on his face, slipped on his brown dress coat, and left to greet Hezekiah in the main dining room. The brothers casually conversed while munching on mouthfuls of fresh bread laden with rich butter and thick savory strawberry jam, which they washed down with a rather low quality white wine. John feasted upon pheasant topped with fresh creamed peas and onions, with a side of boiled potatoes. Hezekiah predictably ordered red meat, a succulent venison roast with carrots and potatoes.

When the waiter disappeared Hezekiah broached the subject of his brother's mysterious second visit. John replied by answering, "For the South to win, a new kind of warfare behind the lines might be required to augment our military efforts. What do you know of Thomas Chew and his mill in Cascade?"

"Only that he's a successful businessman highly respected throughout the county. Why?"

"I hope to assume management of his gristmill and in some manner aid our cause."

Hezekiah bluntly replied, "A hot, dusty environment for a man with an unhealed lung!"

"I've said enough, probably too much." John abruptly closed the discussion.

During a brief, awkward interlude of silence John casually observed the other diners. Several tables accommodated young couples more concerned with their companions than their meals. By contrast older couples scattered throughout bestowed their attention upon their entrees. An animated conversation flowing from a pair of gentlemen two tables away garnered John's attention. Customary dining room clatter muffled portions of the loud conversation, particularly the words of the man with his back toward them. A sturdy man facing John spoke with an evident Irish brogue. A platter of boiled ham, cabbage, carrots, and potatoes substantiated the assumption of his lineage. A quick refill of a rapidly drained whiskey glass confirmed such conjecture. A broad forehead rested above two piercing, deep-set blue eyes. Light brown hair sprouted half way down the sides of his head below his bare crown. Side locks curled over the man's ears, touching his collar at the neck. No facial hair concealed his light complexioned face and nothing masked the thoughts swirling within the man's mind as audible phrases spewing forth provided insights into his convictions. "Abolition Abe, Republican despot, senseless war, ostracized Democrats, elimination of freedom of speech, restricted freedom of press."

From across the table his companion grasped the orator's hand to settle the vocal speaker whose face had reddened deeper than an Iowa sunset. Despite poor acoustics the interested listener distinctly heard the man with his back to him say, "My dear friend Dennis, you must prudently select your words. Unlike your print type, spoken words can never be reset." Turning his head to survey the room, he succinctly added, "Always remain conscious Kirkwood's and Hoxie's spies eavesdrop on you, anxious to fabricate a reason to lock you up and shut down your paper. You also…"

John failed to hear the balance of the sentence as the voice lowered. He recognized Kirkwood as the Republican governor who two years earlier illegally blocked the extradition of a John Brown raider who fled to Iowa after the debacle in Harpers Ferry. John mentally catalogued the unfamiliar name of the other for future reference, unaware of the individual's impending arrival.

"Marshal Hoxie, don't you have enough good people to harass in Des Moines," the Irishman challenged the broad shouldered gentleman entering the dining area.

John sized up the new arrival advancing toward the man called Dennis. His head of ample dark hair, combed back, concealed part of his ears. Several rows of wrinkles below his eyes implied lack of proper rest, constant exposure to the sun, heavy drinking, or any combination of the three. A well-groomed full beard broadened his face. As the marshal moved closer Beall noticed his holstered revolver, most certainly a '44 in these parts and most assuredly loaded, capped, and ready for action.

"Dennis Mahony, you still free? Surprised my men haven't jailed you and your secesh traitor friends. God knows you've broken the law scores of times; problem is don't know when. But you Mics'ill slip up, especially those of you with the Rebel arrogance. Before long the sheets of lies you publish will cease rolling from your blasphemous presses."

"You're more than welcome to try to stop me, Herbert Hoxie, of course legally within the *Constitution* our founders composed without your skewed interpretation," rebutted Mahony, rising to confront his adversary.

The newspaper editor's dining mate forcefully yanked him back into his seat. "The marshal's got nothing on you Dennis unless you permit him to bait you as he's trying now."

"Listen to your friend, Mahony. I'd hate to miss dinner just to throw your secesh carcass in jail, especially knowing that time shall arrive soon enough." Staring about the entire room he threatened, "Also anyone else with your tainted views." John's discomfort grew when the lawman's eyes suspiciously locked on him briefly before he returned his banter to the newspaperman. "Later, Mahony. I'm lodging at an establishment selective of its clientele, but I'll be around." With that U.S. Marshal Herbert M. Hoxie strutted from the dining room towards the hotel exit. Beall possessed no desire to encounter that man again.

When John exited he tipped his hat, smiled, and said, "Good evening, gentlemen," as he passed Mahony's table. In the lobby the brothers bid each other a warm farewell, with Hezekiah warning his brother to maintain vigilance. Their parting handshake would lead the casual observer to assume the pair to be good acquaintances rather than fond siblings.

22 – CASCADE, IOWA

At daybreak, with the sun to his back, John unhurriedly rode twenty miles to the southwest. Upon arriving in Cascade he immediately visited the post office and claimed his letter of recommendation. He familiarized himself with its contents as he guided his horse over the bridge crossing the North Fork of the Maquoketa River at the east edge of town near the mill. He dismounted to the roar of rushing water slapping forcefully against the gigantic waterwheel powering the grinders which pulverized wheat into flour. A solid foundation of irregular light colored stones at water level supported the three floored clapboard building. One gabled side of the structure faced the water, with three windows per story above the waterwheel. The east side mirrored the west except on the first floor a lone window separated the man door from the set of hinged freight doors. Above the entrance bold black letters painted over a pale yellow background read "Thomas Chew Mill". Horses tied to overgrown vegetation nearby indicated someone's presence. The water's deafening sound greeted him when he lifted the latch and pushed the door open. He decided to head upstairs with hopes of encountering someone. He paused after several steps when above the thundering water's crash, heated voices reached his ears. He started to announce his presence when the conversation became audible.

"Don't care the consequences. We must discourage enlistments."

"You realize there's Union men looking for such interference all over this part of the state. Democrats don't get a fair shake in Des Moines either. Sides, you got no wife or family to feed."

"That's just the starch in the pudding. You got a good farm, a good Christian wife, and two fine boys fourteen and sixteen, not to mention your two young daughters. If men keep enlisting, this damn war lasts for years. Draft rumors may become a reality, forcing men against their will to fight, fight to free a bunch of worthless niggers to come north and pollute our towns and cities. You want your boys killed and maimed just to bring the darkies north and keep the Republicans in power. You see what Yankee railroads do to crop profits."

"You got a point there, Jonas."

The crux of the conversation began coming into focus when a sharp voice boomed from behind. "What the hell you doing?" John instinctively turned to confront his antagonist only to stare into the threatening muzzles of a double-barreled shotgun. A nervous thumb clicked both hammers back. Thumping footsteps preceded the creaking door opening from above. "Once more, what you doing here?" the gunman growled.

Before John answered, two men, one with a drawn pistol, appeared. He sharply ordered, "Ezekiel, give us room to come down. You was to be watching the door!" Glaring at John he added, "Try anything and old Zeke'ill blast you like the unwelcome rodent you are. Now move!"

At the foot of the stairs Ezekiel's excuses commenced. "Jonas, nature called so I was taking a leak behind the bushes when this feller rode up. Wasn't gonna piss all over myself and come a running half-buttoned. Didn't figure he'd dismount. I…"

"That's your problem, Zeke, you don't figure. Now shut up and let me decide what to do with him," he said, staring at his prisoner before casting a glance back to Ezekiel. "What if Chew showed up? Never mind," Jonas roughly admonished. Returning his attention to his captive, he menacingly pointed his revolver. "Exactly who are you and why you spying on us?"

John measured his response. These men shared many of his views but disagreeing with one's government and violently opposing it were two distinct courses of action. If these men discovered his true identity he could easily become a pawn for ingratiating these men with local officials. With a calm disarming voice he confidently answered, "I apologize for my unannounced arrival. I'm John Yates, from southern Indiana." Probably inappropriate time for a hand shake he thought. "Spent much of my life in the grain business—harvester, dealer, and mill operator, the latter of which brings me here. Position's still vacant?"

Jonas's head bobbed up and down. "Continue. Why'd you leave Indiana?" The trio's leader looked to Ezekiel and instructed, "Sit on the steps outside and alert me if anyone passes down the road. Go ahead Mister..." He skeptically paused, "Yates?"

John comprehended the seriousness of the situation. "I understand a man's disdain for another sneaking about listening to private conversation. In these times even disconnected phrases are woven into untrue sentences. I had my fill of such back home. Made a good living dealing with folks on both sides of the Ohio. Awoke one morning and found it unacceptable to associate with folks to the south. Being a Democrat I'd suddenly found myself labeled a traitor. Didn't start this war. Didn't want this war. Be damned if I have to be part of this blasted conflict. Figured to locate farther west and leave politics behind. You probably surmise I figure bout as good as Zekiel," John added with a soft smile. Jonas suppressed a smirk as John continued. "I suspect wherever people dwell politics follow. For instance, that crazy abolitionist they hung in Virginia several years back, he stirred things out here too, I understand. Heard he murdered, was it six unarmed men in Kansas?"

"Something like that."

"Well to continue,"

The door suddenly swung open alarming all three. Standing in the doorway with his back to them, Ezekiel bellowed, "Mr. Chew, how you doing today, sir?"

Jonas shoved his short barreled handgun into his pocket while whispering, "I'll trust you for now. You cross me and you're a dead man. Understand?"

John nodded his head.

Thomas Chew walked to the entrance. "Ezekiel, you shouted like I am an old man going deaf. Passing by and saw the four horses. What's going on in here?" When the mill owner walked inside and saw two familiar faces he offered a confused smile. "Jonas, Gilbert. Thought maybe the Knights of the Golden Circle was holding a secret lodge meeting inside my mill," he jested. "Though doubt it would be in broad daylight. Besides, with you men no need to concern myself with such thoughts." Stepping towards John he asked, "Who might you be?"

"I'm John Yates from Ill…," a muffled cough covered his inconsistency. "Excuse me, as I was saying, I'm John Yates from Indiana. I've traveled west to distance myself from the strife back east and humbly offer my services for the gristmill manager's position. I even possess a letter of recommendation," John added, reaching into his coat pocket. "I read your notice in yesterday's *Dubuque Herald*. I assume the position remains unfilled. Hope experience is an asset," he grinned.

The slender businessman with graying hair and trim moustache, true to his New England upbringing, completely ignored John's attempt at humor. "*The Herald's* run by the Southern sympathizer, Dennis Mahony. Why you reading that rubbish?"

"It's the first paper I happened to lay hands upon. With all due respect, sir, you chose to post the opening in the publication."

"Well, ah yes," he stammered, thinking this fellow might be the man for the position. Not arrogant but not easily intimidated. "You mentioned experience?"

"Yes, sir, as I told these kind gentlemen who passed by as I stood outside admiring your mill, and who graciously showed me the grinding stone, I've harvested grain, brokered grain, and supervised over a dozen men in a mill. My recommendation verifies such.

"Hope you didn't mind us bringing Mr. Yates through, Mr. Chew?" asked Jonas displaying an apologetic expression of humility, totally unfamiliar to John.

"Heavens, no Jonas, I'm extremely grateful you graciously extended our hospitality to this gentleman. If your letter of recommendation confirms all you claim, and we reach equitable terms Mr. Yates, the position is yours."

"I trust you to be a fair man who treats me justly," responded John with a firm handshake.

"Very well, we shall finalize the details before dinner this evening." The gathering subsequently broke up with Chew and Beall riding into town while the others traveled opposite directions.

After establishing John at a local rooming house a block off the main thoroughfare the pair backtracked over the bridge and rode up a shallow rise to the Chew residence. While wrapping the reins around the hitching post, John admired the town's newest and most elegant mansion. Several large oak trees shaded the manicured front lawn. Numerous younger trees grew on either side of the masonry dwelling. The two followed the walkway laid with irregular unused stones from the house construction. Strolling up the path John closely examined the ornate exterior wooden trim. A black wrought iron fence surrounding the grounds added quaintness to the Victorian structure. Upon entering the front reception area Chew summoned Gertrude. The blonde-haired, blue-eyed maid spoke in broken English with a distinct Germanic accent. After handing the maid their hats, Chew ordered, "Have Clarence unsaddle and tend to Zeus." North or south, men of means obtained people to look after their simplest needs. "And notify Mrs. Chew we shall have a guest dining with us."

In the parlor the pair just consummated their business arrangement when Margaret Chew entered the parlor, paused, and stared momentarily at John with an expression of far away remembrance.

"Margaret, is something the matter?" asked her husband.

Gazing at their guest she asked, "Sir, have I previously met you?"

He vaguely remembered the woman from years ago, his recollection in part enhanced by Hezekiah mentioning that John might encounter her. Margaret Chew, formerly the maiden Margaret Bemis, spent a week in Charles Town with her parents some fifteen years ago prior to their journey west. He nervously doubted she would remember him, then only a lad of twelve. Looking to his host he replied, "I regret as of yet I have the pleasure of meeting Mrs. Chew."

"Forgive me, my dear, this is my newly-hired mill manager, Mr. Yates." Now if we may advance to the dining room Gertrude shall assist Agnes in serving the meal."

Before exiting the parlor Mrs. Chew asked, "Did you originally hail from northern Virginia Mr. Yates? That name is prevalent beyond the Potomac near Harpers Ferry, and your dialect resonates similarly with those native to that vicinity."

John incorrectly assumed his maternal grandfather's name would trigger no recognition. He politely answered, "Sorry ma'm, heard from a close companion who hailed from that area that its beautiful country. I anticipate visiting after this dreadful war."

"Dreadful it is. I hold a degree of sympathy for the South due to my Maryland heritage." She looked lovingly to her husband and affectionately patted his arm. "Mr. Chew and I do not discuss the politics of the war. Such discussion would only disrupt our harmonious eleven years of wedded bliss. Do you have a wife or sweetheart Mr. Yates?" she asked with a soft smile.

"Regretfully no, Mrs. Chew."

To shield his new manager from Margaret's potential matchmaking, Mr. Chew ushered the trio into the dining room. The balance of their conversation centered primarily upon eastern Iowa's economy and an appraisal of John's subordinates. Several hours later he mounted his horse and waved farewell to his gracious hosts who stood arm in arm on the porch steps.

Thomas contentedly commented to Margaret, "We're blessed, my dear. I was at a loss as to where I might locate a competent replacement for Joseph Weidman when he departed last Saturday to enlist without giving fair notice. I'm still puzzled why he didn't join a company of Dubuque County boys. In any case, by fortunate coincidence Providence has delivered a man with qualifications far beyond Weidman's."

"Thomas, he seems like a personable young man. Perhaps we might offer him the use of a third floor room. His accessibility to you could be of benefit for the business, and he would avoid living in a boarding house overcrowded with immigrants."

Thomas nodded agreeably, smiled, and replied, "Perhaps providing you with ample opportunity to pair him with an eligible maiden."

Meanwhile, John's first few weeks rushed past. Familiarity with a mill's operation permitted his transition to transpire seamlessly. No one scrutinized the likable young man proficiently running Chew's mill. John ingratiated himself with local citizenry while studying the fragile political landscape. Although Republicans ruled the roost throughout most of the state, much of Dubuque County, to which Cascade belonged, contained a dominant heterogeneous blend of Democrats. Most of these folks outwardly supported the war effort. A significant but peaceful minority subtly opposed the war. Rumors circulated a less visible segment devoted itself to terminating the war by whatever means. This contingent detested the Republicans who in two short years usurped power from the people. John impatiently awaited contact from Richmond, hoping for communication to better grasp the degree of unrest in Dubuque County. Independence Day offered such an opportunity.

Cascade's Fourth of July celebration commenced following Sunday worship services. Enthusiasm exhibited by the locals, or lack there of, could serve as a barometer for the challenge before him. Folks milled about Main Street until an ancient cannon in the center of town ceremoniously bellowed the inauguration of festivities. Mayor Geoffrey Hogan stood near the temporary wooden platform draped with red, white, and blue bunting. John stationed himself near the trio he initially encountered at the mill. Gilbert Smith held the hand of a fidgety daughter while his wife grasped the hand of their youngest who constantly whined to be held for a better view. Ezekiel Stein all but ignored the noticeably plain woman accompanying him while he conversed with Jonas Swenson, who forced a polite, insincere smile towards Beall.

Ascending the platform the mayor garnered everyone's attention. "Citizens of Cascade and visitors from afar, welcome to our annual Fourth of July celebration, our sixteenth since joining the Union. As our forefathers bled to lay the foundation for this bastion of freedom, we recognize the torch now passes to our generation to continue building this noble nation whose future rests here in the west. This year ultimately draws us nearer to the triumphant conclusion of our conflict as evidenced by successes at Fort Henry, Fort Donelson, and Shiloh."

"He means useless slaughter," chirped Stein. His mortified companion frowned and tugged at his sleeve. He glanced at her, looked over to Jonas, and snickered. The mayor droned on, pausing only occasionally to wipe the beads of perspiration from his low forehead and pudgy cheeks.

After ten minutes of rhetorical ramblings, the speaker mercifully concluded, "Let us now humbly recognize the bravery of the many patriotic souls from Dubuque County serving in our army. We ask the Almighty for a safe and speedy return of all. The fading sounds of treasonous shouts uttered by Rebels at Manassas one year past are totally muffled by our victorious rally round the flag." The town's brass band on cue began its rendition of "The Battle Cry of Freedom" followed by other patriotic favorites.

Between selections Jonas squeezed in a sarcastic barb for the amusement of those nearby before blaring brass silenced him. "And I spose the Rebs holding Vicksburg is just a hallucination."

After the band concluded the citizenry scattered to partake in the numerous festive activities. John watched Smith's wife pull him in the opposite direction from his two companions and mutter, "Don't need more problems than we got already. You stay away from Zeke and Jonas."

Was Swenson merely the local loud mouth, or actually a man who without hesitation would place himself in danger to support the principles he so freely espoused? Could the dimwitted Stein become an asset? If clandestine activities developed, men following orders without question would prove essential. By late afternoon John satisfied his appetite while mingling with familiar acquaintances before he returned to his room to rest for tomorrow's wagons laden with freshly harvested grain. He recognized the urgency of tactfully extricating himself from the Chew residence. While they allowed him sufficient privacy, he feared if operations evolved that he must be free of the astute, watchful eyes of Thomas Chew.

He arrived early at the mill before the endless stream of drays appeared. For several minutes he studied prior production figures including the county's recently completed spring shipping records. In April of 1860 only about 1600 barrels of flour shipped from Dubuque. A year later consignments increased to 10,000. The past April the county exported over six times that amount including a fair share from the Chew Mill. This summer Thomas Chew profited not only from rising grain prices but also from the growing reputation of his recently-hired manager who fairly and efficiently expedited transactions. John utilized every opportunity to feel the pulse of the area while his subordinates weighed and unloaded grain. Today he chatted with one of the more prosperous farmers in the county. Thirty-five years ago Frederick Consear arrived in Michigan from Prussia as a teenaged immigrant. Twenty-five years later he liquidated his Michigan holdings to fund his venture to Iowa. To his fortune he arrived before the choicest tracts of land disappeared. His prosperity grew with the contributions of his hardworking sons.

"Mr. Consear, good to see you. A plentiful wheat harvest?"

"Ah yes, Mr. Yates, even better now with eastern markets paying more than we ever received from the south, although the railroads gouge us with unreasonable rates."

"With your acreage, Mr. Consear, I assume more grain waits for harvesting?"

"No, lad, unfortunately not," responded the man. He paused, shook his head, and stared despondently into the ground before his eyes met John's. Slowly, reverently, he continued, "When my boys Heinz, Bertram, and Siegfried worked the fields with me all of my fields produced. Hired help if found never works same as family," he complained before remorsefully continuing. "We lost my oldest, Siegfried, at Shiloh, or so they tell us. They recovered no remains. His final resting place is only in our minds. Mama believes he'll walk through the door one day but you and I know better. It would please me to see middle son Bert walk through the door on two legs but that will never be. Two months ago in Mississippi when clearing a path through the forest a damned city boy from Chicago lets the ax slip from his grasp. The sharp blade slices my boy below his knee. Dang green festered in wound. The surgeons, they cut off half his leg. Now one boy's dead, another's crippled, and Heinz, the headstrong one, he joins the cavalry the day after we receive word that Siegy's dead. Momma's favorite, my only remaining son, just goes kaput, doesn't think of Momma, or the homestead, just revenge. Mr. Yates, when I leave Germany I realize that's a no good reason to fight a war. Revenge, never revenge! Far worse than fighting to free Negroes hundreds of miles away!"

John sympathetically grasped the man's forearm. Words provided little comfort. Widows, children, or siblings continued with life's everyday demands while staring at the tintype on the table or the vacant chair, but war cast its cruelest shroud over the aged parent. The gray-haired farmer's future rested with his sons. His concern for his own economic future paled in comparison to the future now shattered which he had prepared for his sons. Somewhere in Tennessee a piece of Frederick's heart lay with Siegfried, covered with dirt on the somber Tennessee battlefield. Another piece lay severed in Mississippi. Only Heinz remained. Revenge-minded warriors become reckless men. John's thoughts raced to his mother, about Mr. Consear's age. Both struggled to manage acres of productive land which in years gone by effortlessly yielded a bounty for all. Were the North and South so different?

Consear continued speaking. "I joined the majority of voters in Iowa by siding with Lincoln. I believe in the Union, but preservation at all costs? Not if the price means our Heinz also. I apologize for the rhetoric from this long-winded old man, Mr. Yates. You and this mill are necessary. You stay away from the war," requested the worn farmer as he climbed onto his wagon and rolled away.

Hundreds of miles west of Virginia the war too spread its misery. The conflict apparently drained dedication from the staunchest of Union men. Did an opportunity truly present itself to wage war behind the lines? Beall emphatically believed yes as he yearned to hear from a Confederate contact.

23 – SEARCHING FOR PLAYERS

The lull in the procession of grain wagons coincided with the growling emptiness in John's stomach. He opted to take his noon meal of bread, meat, and fruit under the shade of a large elm tree. He also garnered more valuable knowledge pertaining to mill operation from his foreman, Timothy Murphy. The occasional pie Murphy's attractive red-headed wife McKaylah surprised the men with further enticed John to remain. As the two men's familiarity grew, Murphy's dissatisfaction with the war surfaced.

"They're rumors of Lincoln soon drafting men into the army. Hear tell America waged the second war with the bloody English over impressments of our citizens into the British navy. Now the blasted politicians speak of instituting a like practice. There will be hell to pay and not just with words mind you. We Irish, other then a fortunate few such as me, rest at the bottom of the ladder. Now they ask us to die to squeeze darkies onto that rung. Why in Mary's name would we do such a thing?"

"What else can a man do, Timothy, if the authorities say he shall go?" John asked, desiring more insight into the Irishman.

"What do I do, not a damn thing! But we," he paused deciding whether to trust this man he'd known less than a month. "Tell me, Mr. Yates, how did you come by that nasty wound in your chest?"

The unexpected question caught John off guard. Who said the Irish intellect superseded only that of the Negro? Collecting his thoughts he responded with a question of his own. Offering his vintage disarming smile he replied, "Why Tim Murphy, I didn't take you as the kind of person to spy on a man, especially one tending to a slow-healing injury."

"An injury instead of a wound, how did tha about?"

John spoke deliberately but with an air of confiden "A grinding gear at a mill in Indiana shattered last fall. Meta scattered throughout the air. Very fortunate I wasn't killed. One boy even lost an eye."

Timothy scowled, placed the remainder of his lunch in his cloth sack, and stood.

"Where you going?"

The foreman coldly stared and said, "To find a sincere man to engage in honest conversation."

"Timothy, what causes you to question my integrity?" challenged Beall with a tint of irritation.

"By total accident your office door hung open a crack the other day. As I raised my hand to rap I observed the seeping hole in your chest. I've treated enough such injuries, as you prefer to call them. The only flying metal that deeply rips a round hole into man's chest comes from a bullet. Excuse me sir, I need to tend to nature afore we commence the afternoon's work."

John surmised that either he provide the man with enough information to gain his confidence or risk Tim prying deeper into his past. "Sit for a moment, please." His pleading tone proved effective when the skeptical Irishman sat with a shrug of his shoulders. "You're correct. My injury's a wound, and I'm actually from Baltimore. My circle of friends and I, all strong Union Democrats, understood the southern dissatisfaction with the Republicans who also possessed the audacity to question our loyalty to the Union. They sequestered us to take the *Oath of Allegiance*. To say the least we grew indignant, for we desired to peacefully remain loyal to the Union, pursue our business activities, and allow the saber rattling to die down. But after the whipping administered at Bull Run any man not supporting Lincoln or not wearing the blue uniform aroused suspicion." John paused to gaze into the distance with a remorseful expression which only added credibility to his yarn.

ad of Massachusetts volunteers herded us together that afternoon to administer the oath. My close ... aniels, a short-tempered lad to say the least, ... ded revolver from his pocket and demanded ... nt name the charlatan who authorized the ... e. The officer, you know the type, a lifelong piss ant until someone gives him limited authority for kissing their ass, grabbed one of his men's carbines and pointed it at Luke, cocked the hammer, and snarled, 'from this.' The gun discharged when my friend pushed the muzzle away, wounding Luke in the left shoulder. By reflex he fired his colt, mortally wounding the aggressor, sad to say." John paused and frowned, portraying an event almost too painful to repeat. "More shots rang out instantly murdering Mr. Daniels. During this bedlam I received my injur…, wound. When I came to I found myself in the home of an influential businessman with Southern sympathies. Apparently another of our band carried me away from the fray when the Yankees scattered, leaving the two bodies on the bloodstained street. Before sunset they issued warrants for all of us. My newfound protector concealed and nursed me for a fortnight. Under the cloak of darkness my guardian angel booked steamer passage for me to New York from whence I traveled to Chicago where I planned to remain and fully recover, only to discover the city infested with Federal soldiers and spies. I concluded it best to head out here, partly because I possessed experience in the grain business. Wounds such as mine heal slowly. I harbor no burning desire to put on a Rebel uniform to fight against our Union, but I most assuredly will support any activity that returns our beloved Democracy to control of a righteous government."

"Mr. Yates," replied Tim, smiling warmly and extending a hand sealing their new relationship, "My apology and sympathy for the sufferings you've endured. In these times a man must know his friends.

"Timothy, over the past month I've tried to ascertain exactly where our benevolent employer stands. His comments lead me to believe he is a staunch Republican, but does he completely support their doctrine here?" John asked with his closed right fist over his heart.

"A fair question. The man's cut from the fabric of the true Yankee trader," answered the Irishman, rubbing his forefinger and middle finger back and forth across his thumb. "He follows the greenback. If there be profit in abolition, then an abolitionist he be. If there be profit in ignoring slavery, then so it be. But don't assume the man lacks principles. He's dedicated to the eventual return of the South to the Union. That being said he's probably a Republican for business convenience, so he holds no strong objection to their running of the government. I am cautious of what comes out of here," the Irishman said pointing to his mouth. "I'm sure he would report to the authorities any suspicion of what the Republicans refer to as treasonous acts. Powerful men such as Mr. Chew store favors whenever the opportunity arises. Rumor circulates though that within the breast of his wife does reside a soft spot for Southerners."

A wagon heaped with grain turned off the road. Beall stood and with a wink concluded their conversation. "We better grind some wheat or we'll be accused of hampering the war effort. At a more convenient time further conversation will be in order." He pointed to the dozen men sprawled by the stream and instructed his foreman, "Get your men to work, Timothy."

John turned and heartily greeted the teamster who just set the brake and jumped down. "Good day Mr. Koppelman. I see another full wagon. How goes the harvesting?"

Karl Koppelman, a short, frugal Dutchman known throughout the county for his keen business acumen, sighed deeply. "Very frustrating to plant all these acres and receive the blessing of ample rain, but then lack sufficient laborers for the harvest. Fortunately, despite low grain prices, I purchased a reaper last year before this unfortunate war commenced. I'll glean all my fields with another week of dry weather."

"Do you maintain such optimism for a cease of hostilities?"

"Mr. Yates, I respectfully decline to comment. Unfortunately even in Dubuque County officials twist the words of others to suit their needs. If I utter no words no one can misconstrue them. All I say is that I desire the Union's restoration as soon as possible. Shall we unload the grain?"

"That we can, Mr. Koppelman." John soon bid farewell to the gentleman as his empty wagon rattled down the road. A continuous procession of grain laden wagons forced the men to work well after six. Dry weather coupled with lengthy hours of daylight would result in many such days the remainder of July.

While Timothy disengaged the stone John climbed the steps to his office to reconcile the consignments written over the course of the day. He looked up from his desk when his foreman, coated with white dust, entered the office.

"Mr. Yates, a group of us with a common interest are meeting with a visitor of importance tomorrow after dark. Care to join us?"

"Timothy, under no condition share with anyone the events I divulged this afternoon. If knowledge of my past surfaces I shall find myself on a train to Maryland to suffer God only knows what consequences. Swear to silence on that subject."

"On the soul of my sainted mother," he promised, making the sign of the cross with his hand.

"Timothy, is your group associated with the Knights of the Golden Circle?"

"Do you believe in ghosts, Mr. Yates?"

"What kind of answer is that?" John impatiently asked.

"I apologize for the riddle. Early in the war rumors of a secret society with roots spreading throughout the South caused great anguish for our Republican friends. Recently the Lincolnites, in a manner revitalized the society, leading the good citizens into believing scores of armed traitors lurked in every county, itching to overthrow local governments at a predetermined signal. You might say the bloody bastards turned the tables. Authorities now fabricate just cause to arrest anyone, anytime. Do you understand now, sir?"

John glared with disgust, fully comprehending the underhanded tactic. "I'll attend. No strings attached, but I believe we share a common interest."

The group planned to gather after eight to allow darkness to extinguish the glowing prairie's sunlight. They rendezvoused several miles outside of town at a deserted farm a safe distance off the main road. Its former owner died of camp fever in Tennessee the past winter. The corporal's widow chose to return to Ohio with her two small children rather than attempt to operate the farm alone.

Fortunately John had resided in a boarding house for a week. He had clumsily fabricated a need for keeping odd hours at the mill and avoiding the disruption of the Chew household. Margaret strongly challenged his rationale as she had become quite fond of the mill manager. Mr. Chew wisely avoided becoming involved in the issue as John awkwardly pleaded his case with Margaret.

Since arriving in Cascade, John partook of leisurely evening rides and thus traveled about without creating curiosity. Tonight's outing proved anything but relaxing. The moon's gleaming beams lit the thoroughfare but also cast bizarre shadows into the vegetation along the path. He jerked the reins. Riders at the edge of the road? No, just a decaying cottonwood tree with fallen branches. He continued on, hesitating now and then when branches swayed to and fro in the balmy breeze. The chirp, chirp, chirp of crickets gradually sedated him as he neared the turnoff. A rustle in the brush to his left startled him. A threatening form darted towards him. His revolver almost cleared his holster when the buck leaped across the road and vanished from sight. His own spontaneous laughter calmed him. He veered to the left at the stone pyramid which the former owner constructed to mark the lane. John wondered how much farther, who would be present, and what would be discussed?

"Halt and be recognized!" commanded a sharp voice shattering the darkness. Beall instinctively gripped his revolver handle, ready to draw, to fire, and to retreat if necessary. An obscure image emerged from the shadows pointing a carbine directly at him. Beall's grip on his pistol instinctively tightened, even when he recognized Ezekiel Stein. Recalling his first encounter at the mill with the inept watchman, John's lips curled into a smile. Some choice for a gatekeeper, although he might be less dangerous outside than in the meeting.

"It's John Yates, Ezekiel. Tim Murphy invited me."

"He said you was coming, against our better judgment."

Who's we, John wondered? His first encounter at the mill did nothing to endear the trio to the newcomer. Had they tainted others present?

"Advance, slowly," the sentry ordered, relishing his position of perceived power.

"Thank you, sir," John mockingly replied, although his sarcastic innuendo flew past Stein's simple mind.

"You may pass," the sentinel allowed with his imagined air of authority.

A hundred yards down the lane a clearing appeared revealing a vacant house and several outbuildings. Light flickered through gaps in the barn's weathered siding. John dismounted slowly near six other horses which stood with their tails swaying contentedly.

A voice among the horses demanded, "Identify yourself."

"John Yates, I was invited by..."

"You're the last one on the list," the concealed individual interrupted. "Enter."

"And to whom do I have the pleasure of speaking."

"The man who keeps uninvited guests out."

Impressive. Those circumventing the dunce at the entrance relax and unexpectedly face a competent, concealed challenger at the meeting site. John entered the structure illuminated with three bright lanterns. His gaze drew him to a well-dressed man with knee high riding boots. Jet black locks of hair flowed beneath his gray narrow-brimmed hat. His mane glistened in the kerosene lamp's light. His immaculately trimmed moustache complemented his dark complexion. His intense black eyes locked onto John when he entered.

Timothy introduced them. "Mr. John Yates, meet Mr. Isaac Mathew White from the beautiful state of Kentucky."

The special visitor took three brisk strides and greeted John. "Pleasure to meet you. Mr. Murphy tells me you've managed the mill almost a month. You're positioned to interact with many prominent individuals. Prior to your arrival in Cascade you worked in southern Indiana. Where bouts, exactly?"

"Evansville, a thriving metropolis on the river."

"Having spent much of my life in Louisville, I identify with river communities. How goes things along the bend in Posey County?"

Fortunately Beall's purchase of a guidebook detailing towns along the Ohio River prepared him for such an inquisition. "I beg to correct you, sir. Evansville is the seat of Vanderburgh County. Posey's to the west."

"My error, it's been years since I traveled the river."

John recognized the clever ploy, which amplified his anticipation of the intriguing evening. He also acknowledged Smith and Swenson who maintained their distance from him.

Timothy formally introduced John to the other two. He greeted Captain Carlos McCall, who piloted the *Vicksburg Duchess* from New Orleans to St. Paul before war confined him only to the northern Mississippi and the Ohio. A jagged two-inch scar running diagonally above McCall's right eye appeared particularly menacing in the flickering light. If the muscular captain received that memento from an altercation Beall had no desire to view the other combatant.

Timothy turned to the last gentleman. "John, you've probably seen our livestock dealer Ezra Davis passing through town occasionally." The lean man tipped his hat and smiled, allowing Timothy to continue. "Due to his sometimes exuberant support for Buchanan, Ezra lost his beef contracts with the army when the Republicans won the election." With a nod Timothy turned the floor over to White.

"Thank you, Timothy, and fellow patriots, and contrary to Republican belief, we assemble tonight because we are patriots. You each must pledge your secrecy to never divulge anything I share with you beyond this group. I represent a grass roots network of Democrats desiring the reclamation of the *Constitution* our forefathers authored. Let me begin by analyzing our Union's successes, or lack thereof, in this unnecessary war well into its second year. In the west incompetent Confederate generalship lost Forts Henry and Donelson. The abolitionists claimed absolute Union victory also in the horrific battle of Shiloh that followed. In truth, the best that might be claimed is a draw only because Buell barely arrived to save the bungling alcoholic Grant from total disaster, even after the brilliant Southern commanding general died in the early stages of the battle. The Union controls New Orleans but the impenetrable fortress of Vicksburg prohibits navigation two hundred miles above the river's mouth. And in the east, Washington sacrifices thousands of lives and spends millions of dollars with nary a victory. Manassas served as the precursor to future battles in Virginia. A year later the South's greatest general falls seriously wounded as fighting rages on the outskirts of Richmond. Then Bobby Lee, a military genius in waiting, though outmanned, totally humiliates his better equipped foe who crawls away after another sound whipping."

"You sound like a recruiter for the damn Rebel army," interrupted Swenson.

The orator politely smiled and acknowledged the affront. "Quite to the contrary, Jonas. Actually we oppose all recruitment, whether in the North or South. Take this farm. It should be a hub of activity this time of year. Why isn't it? Because Lincoln called for troops to put down a rebellion that never truly existed, and many a patriotic but misinformed man such as the young farmer who labored in this very barn marched off to the first beat of war drums. Whether he died in battle or from disease which rampaged through the camps, his death was another unnecessary lost life."

Smith shook his head, thinking of his two sons.

White continued. "Discourage enlistments and the Union's reduced manpower no longer conducts an offensive war. A draft would only spread discontent. Although rumors abound, do not expect Lincoln to take that gamble. The shrinking army eventually shall lack sufficient troops to even protect Washington. An armistice followed by a reunification treaty shall again bring both sides together as one loving family. With our Democratic brethren to the south allied with the concerns of our western Democracy, the Republicans shall wither and die like the Whigs before them. Only the Republican Party's footnote in history shall be much shorter."

Enthused voices echoed approval.

White held up exposed palms to quiet the gathering. He slowly lowered them and continued. Passion burned from within his eyes as he softened his voice and gained absolute attention from his listeners who advanced several steps closer while they intently focused upon the speaker. "If we hesitate, a different vision is fulfilled. Instead of the vibrant country expanding westward with the opportunities Jackson visualized for all men we watch a feudal system develop. If the South sues for peace, the Republican government transforms Democratic strongholds into fiefdoms ruled by rich New England lords. Freed niggers receive the vote to keep their benefactors in office. Soon they commingle with the wives and daughters of former masters, or migrate north to pollute our white population."

Captain McCall stepped forward to challenge White. "With all respect, sir, I know the Southern people. They profess extreme loyalty to their state and their women. I doubt that in the unlikely event that the South experiences irreversible defeats that her chivalrous knights would allow such desecration even after hostilities halted."

"An astute observation, Captain, but only if the southern states maintain current boundaries. A fond acquaintance of mine who recently departed New Orleans overheard with his own ears a recommendation by the uncivilized pig, Ben Butler. He purposed that to truly subordinate the South after her defeat that Southern state boundary lines should be completely redrawn. New states composed of noncohesive counties would strip them of their once proud heritage which evolved since inception."

Beall uncontrollably blurted, "Absurd!"

"You believe such practices impossible, Mr. Yates?"

John jerked his head up and down emphatically.

"I too, Mr. Yates, skeptically listened to my friend's tale, politely acknowledged his comment, and returned the conversation to a more practical dialogue. Less than a month ago, several days after hearing of the farfetched premise, I met with a key member of our network, a man who has contacts inside the White House. As we speak, Lincoln and his court scheme to dissect Virginia." White noticed Yates's fierce stare but continued, "All of Virginia from Harpers Ferry to the west and north, plus all counties beyond the Allegany range, shall within the year form a new state, another Republican fiefdom." Looking directly into John's livid blue eyes which glared from his tensed, flushed face, White paused before innocently commenting, "Mr. Yates, you appear visibly upset."

John stoically responded, "What dedicated Democrat fails to view such vile practice with contempt?"

For a brief second the two men discreetly sized each other up, sensing more lay below the surface of the other than met the eye.

"Well said, sir," replied White. "Now to continue, we stated our first objective, that of discouraging enlistments. Each of you interacts with a number of able-bodied white men each day. But proceed with subtleness lest we arouse suspicion from the nigger lovers burrowed amongst us.

"We possess a second opportunity highly complex in nature, so much so that much of the concept exceeds this simple-minded Kentuckian's ability to comprehend. By the end of the first year the Republicans depleted the treasury while paying for the war. Lincoln's government now irresponsibly prints paper money without the backing of gold deposits. The opportunity exists to further devalue paper currency and economically bring Lincoln to his knees. The less gold in circulation, the more paper currency that circulates. Simply supply and demand identical to fluctuating grain prices. Members of our network shall purchase all the gold you accumulate with paper currency, but at a premium of 15% to as much as 25%. We transport the gold to Europe for safe keeping. Lincoln soon wages war with one eye on the battlefield and the other on his eastern banks. A bit far-fetched but economic geniuses within our network assure me such practice produces favorable results."

Swenson prepared to confront White for a second time. He stared uncomfortably at his feet before looking up and stammering, "Everything from eggs to flour to clothes cost twice what they did last year. If I understand correctly, my paper money becomes worth less and I'm the cause. Why place further hardship on myself?"

White transformed into a stern but supportive teacher. "First remember you receive a substantial premium for any gold you accumulate to reward your effort. You understand the broad concept, my friend. We must visualize the far-reaching results. We unite to end the rampant abuse of power. Each day the cornerstone of Jackson's Democracy, the individual, unknowingly relinquishes his freedom to the government centralizing power in Washington. We drive our southern Democratic friends away not by the slavery issue but by the growing despotism in Washington. You're a very astute man, Jonas." A self-conscious smile beamed across Swenson's face. White stepped forward and compassionately grasped the man's shoulders. "But like many of us, you, my dear friend, are short-sighted." Moving back and making eye contact with everyone, he continued. "With the irresponsible fiscal policies of this president, inflation continues without our interference. True, our involvement will further intensify inflation, but men," he slowed and boldly enunciated, "our short-term sacrifices shall most assuredly expedite the demise of Lincoln and his Republicans." White again singled out the most vocal individual within the group. "Jonas Swenson, are you willing to personally sacrifice several months of higher prices in exchange for the future years of rule by our Democracy, which governs by the people, not over the people?" White kept his eyes locked with Swenson's while his extended forearm and index finger swept the room. "Are you the kind of man, Jonas Swenson, whose friends and neighbors shall admire for journeying on this sacred crusade?"

The amber glow from the kerosene lamps radiated from the faces of the gathered saints awaiting Swenson's reply. "No man here or alive anywhere can ever say that I, Jonas Swenson, shirks from his duty when his country most needs him."

"Bravo, my friend. In times such as these a man chooses between right or wrong, cowardice or courage. Are we all willing to display the dedication of Jonas Swenson?"

"Aye!" echoed the chorus of the remaining five men.

John realized this charismatic man certainly was not the simple-minded Kentuckian who White attempted to portray. His well-planned, finely-tuned performance rivaled any oratory John ever witnessed from politician, preacher, attorney, or thespian.

"Gentlemen, we now disperse to avoid the misfortune of detection. Depart in groups no larger than threes, preferably ones or twos. Our network shall maintain contact. Good evening." Timothy departed first, followed by Swenson and Smith who lead Ezekiel's horse. John waved to Captain McCall and Ezra Davis as they started up the lane. As John mounted his mare he wondered where the guard disappeared, until he heard voices from inside the barn. He meandered alone up the lane. Gaps in the fast-moving clouds displayed bright moonlight while periodically extinguishing the illumination.

Moments later two horsemen atop steeds that would draw envy from within the soul of the most prosperous Kentucky horse breeder, paused before reaching the main road. A magnificent black mare and a gorgeous bay nervously swayed their tails in the moonlight while anxiously waiting for their riders to continue.

The horseman on the bay spoke first. "Major Carpenter, or shall I say Mr. White, did our naïve recruits accept all we conveyed? And above all, do they believe us to be dedicated citizens who oppose the Republicans but staunchly desire reunification of the Union?"

Carpenter answered his tall, slender companion who sported a ragged beard. "Experience teaches us, Lieutenant Ryan, that men such as Murphy and Davis follow with devotion. Captain McCall literally is captain of his own ship. Such men efficiently give orders but reluctantly receive them. We encounter men such as Yates who thoroughly scrutinizes all aspects before committing. We also need men such as our dear friend Jonas Swenson." A cynical smile crossed the major's face. "Sheep such as Smith and our outpost sentry, I believe Stein they called him, need a lead animal to follow. Hence, we develop our loud-mouthed, impulsive Mr. Swenson into our first staunch supporter. Alas, as the warmth of our revival gives way to the evening chill our fickle friend falls aimlessly from our tree, much like an autumn leaf, to an insignificant resting space. Could I depend upon our marionette to perform this evening?" With a sharp slap of his thigh and a hearty laugh Carpenter answered his own question, "Always, although without the dexterity of an accomplished puppeteer to pull the strings he soon becomes idle." Hesitantly he added as he rubbed his chin, "Better inactive and harmless than active and incompetently dangerous."

"What of Yates? I searched his horse and those of the others but discovered nothing contradictory with anyone's.

When I challenged him upon his arrival he seemed neither intimidated nor irritated. Highly unusual."

"Exactly my reaction, Lieutenant. The man hailing from southern Indiana seems all too composed in his new setting," commented Carpenter as his cynical smile resurfaced.

"Until you mentioned the dissection of Virginia."

"Precisely," replied Carpenter. He noticeably unraveled when I surprised him with Lincoln's plan to carve up Virginia. A Northern anti-Lincolnite would be irritated by such a despicable act, but I witnessed sincere uncontrolled rage from within, although blanketed by the man's poised exterior."

"Could the man actually be a Virginian, possibly even from that vicinity?"

"Valid assumption, but however remote, we must also consider the man may be a Yankee spy. He could be a valued asset or the Achilles heel that disrupts our entire body of work here. Unfortunately Richmond works with a network of agents from the east while our army in the west develops another. One hand never knows what the other does. I'll inform Tim Murphy to closely watch our friend. I'd place my life in Timothy's hands. They come no more faithful than that old Mic. Time to move. We'll travel south before making camp. Tomorrow evening we should reach Davenport. I'll travel to Chicago via rail to report to Mr. Sims while you ride south to Memphis to report to the colonel." The horses cantered away, stimulated by a light jab of spurs into their ribs.

Camouflaged in the nearby brush in the shadows of the tall trees, a solitary man unwrapped his coat which muffled his horse's muzzle, and cautiously led his animal to the lane. Beall pulled himself up onto the saddle and warily journeyed towards the road. He chuckled upon realizing Major Carpenter used the name Isaac Mathew White. How clever, I. M. White. His mind swarmed with the strategy presented in the barn. Were these men whose conversation John just overheard actually who they seemed? If so, how could his beloved Confederacy achieve anything but victory and independence? The South apparently already utilized dissident Union Democrats to unwittingly aid the South. He felt a tinge of guilt using Tim in that manner, but after the war citizens of both of countries would benefit from the demise of a short-lived Republican party. Beall's concern rested with talk of gold manipulation. Greed lurked throughout the North and the South. Did Carpenter actually manipulate Yankee currency or had he developed an elaborate scheme to line his own pockets? Communication from a contact could sort out many of the complexities.

Tonight's meeting opened many avenues upon which to travel. The mill operator's position provided opportunity to establish financial arrangements with regards to whom, where, and how to ship newly ground flour. If John's rationale for diversification seemed logical to Mr. Chew, random shipments completely bypassing eastern markets could be sent directly to the continent. With creative accounting, small quantities of European gold could discreetly be siphoned into Confederate accounts with the balance exchanged for paper currency and no one the wiser. He reached the livery after midnight. The stable hand, reeking of alcohol, snored loudly on a pile of straw. He unsaddled his mount, glanced at the passed out hand, and smiled, realizing no need to fabricate an explanation for his late return.

24 – THE GAME CONTINUES

Murphy was already hard at work when John arrived." Another roaster today, sir. Good for crop growth though. They say when it's hot enough for the old lady to kick the sheets off at night the corn grows by the hour."

"Aye," replied John before pulling his watch from his green plaid vest pocket. "Tis only half past seven and my body tells me its mid afternoon." He motioned his foreman to follow him out of earshot of the other preoccupied laborers. "Tim, what knowledge do you possess of last evening's illustrious guest?

"My first encounter, sir. Never heard an orator who could hold a candle to that man. Our people in Dubuque speak highly of him. I hear he's met several times with Charles Mason himself. That's a fine introduction in my book. Why? Do you hesitate to commit to us?"

Beall returned the forthright stare, placed a firm hand on his companion's shoulder, and without hesitation replied, "As you fondly say, for the love of Mary, no! The man's stated desire to discourage enlistments as a means of hampering the Republicans strikes a cord with my personal convictions. My uncertainty derives its roots from men with allegiance to the North or South who sing the patriotic tunes and wave either the stars and bars or the Union banner but scheme to build wealth to satisfy their own greed. Mention of gold causes a bit of discern to this soul."

"Mr. Yates, an incapability to comprehend high finance might be a hereditary trait inflicted upon us simple Irish," Murphy chuckled. "I sincerely confess such talk settles in the clouds far above me head. I restate me faith in the likes of men such as Charles Mason."

John sighed and smiled. "Unlike me, you're familiar with Mr. Mason. In times such as these selecting who to trust is crucial. You, I unquestionably trust, and if you trust Mason who in turn maintains a confidence in our Mr. White, than so do I."

"Gratified by the sentiments, sir," glowed the Irishman.

"While riding here this morning I realized once our Democracy regains control of Washington, the gold shall rebuild our reunified country which shall be burdened with unfathomable debt. Back to the grinding now." John then cautioned, "Remember subtle is the watch word. I suspect we would both find ourselves unemployed and facing charges if anyone suspected our activities."

"Without a doubt, Mr. Yates."

John would vigilantly proceed with his own agenda while portraying himself to Murphy as a willing participant in the Iowans' activities. Maintaining confidence of a trustworthy man such as Murphy would prove crucial in the coming days. He avoided visualizing the hurt inflicted upon Timothy if his confidant realized that John duped him into aiding a clandestine Confederate operation.

Later that day he overheard Murphy conversing with Horst Kochendorf, a struggling farmer of German descent. "Your brother Wolfgang considers joining the army? Very noble of him, although I thought you two left Germany to avoid military service?"

"Dat ve did," answered Horst shaking his head and momentarily staring east far over the horizon to Europe with its unpleasant memories. "Here ve have da right to chose if ve fight. In da old country da army comes and takes us away to become soldiers. Wolfgang says he fights because he has da choice. He believes dis war about keeping freedom to choose."

"Well put, Horst, but is Wolfgang's greatest contribution that of a soldier, something he knows nothing of, or in producing food to nourish our army. An army eats, yes?"

"Yah, you make good point Murphy."

"Folks understand. You and Wolfgang finally recovered from the rough times in'57. No offense, my friend, but it would be foolish to jeopardize your farm by allowing your younger brother to join the army. There's too much work for you alone and we've all experienced the high cost of laborers with so many able bodied men gone to fight. Who will tend the fields?"

"Good thoughts, Murphy. I put sense in Wolfgang's thick skull tonight, yes?"

"God be with you," Tim bid the German as he boarded his empty wagon.

In the coming days numerous occasions presented themselves to dissuade men from enlisting. To date neither Beall nor Murphy experienced ramifications from the activity. On several occasions John managed to obtain small amounts of gold for special concessions such as discounting flour 17% for specie payment from emigrants traveling west. He finally met his contact for the first time on the second Saturday in August in Dubuque. There he exchanged his gold for a 21% premium in greenbacks which more than offset the undetected dispensation. John, unbeknownst to Timothy, also accumulated his own stash of gold for any unexpected crisis.

On Friday the following week John sat alone in his boarding house room. Uncomfortable, humid, overcast weather epitomized his dreary mood. Seven years ago to the day his dear father passed away. Time healed all wounds? Apparently not the emotional hurt of losing one's father. The cynical throbbing in his chest reminded him that time also too slowly healed physical wounds. He reviewed his life. He thought longingly of Martha and his hollow commitment to her. He degraded himself for his deceit to Thomas Chew. John's blatant dishonesty with a naïve but trusting Tim Murphy further demoralized him. Would the South maintain God's favor if her people resorted to the same distasteful treachery practiced by the Yankees? He prayed for his merciful Lord's forgiveness of his sins motivated by his desire for an honorable victory for a just cause. On that pretext he slept soundly in preparation for another busy Saturday at the mill.

A pained expression lay heavily across Murphy's face when John entered. "Problems with the machinery?"

"May we talk in your office, Mr. Yates?" Sensing concern John warily ascended the stairs with Murphy trudging close behind. When the door closed the news emotionally spewed forth of events from the previous day in Dubuque. "Authorities arrested poor Dennis Mahony yesterday. No formal charges, just hauled him away. Our people say that devil Hoxie sent him east to Washington for trial. Who's next? Has word leaked of our activities? I never believed such tyranny existed in America."

"Compose yourself, Tim," calmly ordered John. "Bad luck for Mr. Mahony indeed, but also an indication of the dire straits the Republicans find themselves. In the east McClellan and Pope together cannot corral General Lee. Union forces face Indian uprisings to our north in Minnesota. To our south Missouri partisans captured Independence last week. The Republican empire crumbles. Lincoln's critics sit in prison waiting for charges that may never come. We must first experience the rain clouds before we enjoy the rainbow. But it may be best to lessen our activity for several days and especially avoid men with whom we lack familiarity."

Although he concealed his concern, Beall feared for the retribution Mahony might face. He met the editor on several occasions in Dubuque and grew genuinely fond of the man.

By the fourth week of August their crusade to inhibit enlistments escalated again. John also managed to consummate another gold transaction which increased his cache to over $1600. With fears of the growing presence of Federal spies, John's liaison recently suggested that he delicately prepare for departure to Canada. Beall also considered traveling to Pittsburgh or Baltimore where the network remained active. His disappointment lingered with his inability to detour more than minimal amounts of gold to Confederate accounts.

Early in August, on the pretext of reoccurring back pain, he had purchased a buggy to aid in a rapid evacuation if necessary. The mode of transportation would allow conveyance of his essential belongings and the gold, besides lessening aggravation to the dawdling healing of his chest. After initial chiding from numerous acquaintances referencing his age, the townsfolk thought nothing of the mill manager rattling by seated upon his new carriage lead by two beautiful matching roan horses.

On the eighth of September he relaxed with windows open as balmy air circulated throughout his room. Activity at the mill had reduced from a hectic gush to a steady flow. He poured over newspaper accounts of the bloody encounter in Virginia, now referred to as The Second Battle of Manassas. The estimated combined casualties of 24,000 men appalled him, almost fives times those of the first battle on the same site thirteen months earlier. He silently prayed for Will's safety, unaware the lad lay seriously wounded in a crude field hospital. He visualized the faces of his comrades remaining with the 2nd only to be interrupted by two sharp raps on the door. Strange, no one ever called on him here. He shoved his revolver into his side trouser pocket and guardedly opened the door. An expression of utter surprise covered his face. There stood the petite figure of redheaded McKaylah Murphy with a green cotton cloth tied around her hair. She held a woven basket covered with a large white napkin.

In an unusually loud voice for all within listening distance to hear she clearly said, "I hope 'tis not deemed improper for me to bring this special treat over. Tim's off socializing in the tavern but insisted I deliver to his kind overseer one of the first fresh apple pies of the season. I made three, and you know how my Tim likes to share my bake goods so that he may boast to all who listen of his wise selection of a wife." She quickly whispered, "You're in great danger. The authorities plan to question you tonight. Leave immediately. Message in the basket."

Responding in an articulate voice for anyone overhearing their conversation, John succinctly replied, "I've enjoyed your delicious cherry pie and tasty peach pie Mrs.

Murphy. I eagerly anticipate your apple pie. Tomorrow my kind words shall have that lovable husband of yours grinning ear to ear." In hushed tones he added, "I am forever indebted to you both. Give Tim my regrets that I could not give a proper farewell." He then exclaimed, "Excellent, Mrs. Murphy. Excuse my manners but I yearned to sample your treat before you departed." In a hushed voice he whispered, "God be with you both.

In like tone she replied with a melancholy expression, "And with you also John Yates."

In their final parting John again agonized over his deception of the Murphys. He shut the door and impatiently lifted the white linen napkin. He discovered a hundred dollars in greenbacks wrapped in another napkin adjacent to a worn leather purse holding a small quantity of gold coins. Beneath the pie tin protruded the corners of several sheets of brown paper. He hurriedly unfolded the message.

Upon my arrival home I received word of our good Marshall Hoxie's intent to interrogate you. I plan to spend the evening in Patrick O'Malley's with plenty of witnesses to vouch for my where bouts. I trust even the Republicans won't suspect my dear wife, as she occasionally makes deliveries to numerous townsfolk including the Chews. After your escape we'll claim ignorance as to the secretive meetings in your office with the dealer who never sold grain or purchased flour. May St. Michael travel with you.

While Beall impatiently waited for the sun to drop he hastily shoved his belongings into several carpetbags. He stuffed the pie, possibly his only nourishment for a while, into a cloth sack. He discretely carried his possessions from the boarding house to the livery where he concealed them in the shadows along the exterior wall. He entered the dimly lit structure and woke the napping stable hand. "Jimmy, ready my hack. I'm going for an evening ride."

"Mr. Yates, you missed the sunset, and what a beauty she was. Where you off to at this hour?"

"Ah lad, look at those sparkling stars," John replied, looking at the sky through the wide open barn doors. "In a fortnight the chill of autumn sets in for the duration. A man needs to pause and appreciate the beauty of God's creation. A mild evening provides occasion for a leisurely ride in the countryside. Here lad, I'll return late. Treat yourself to some refreshment." John flipped two bits to the stable hand, who fumbled the coin before reclaiming it from the dirt. In no time the lad hitched the two horses to the buggy. With a wide grin he raced down a side street to his favorite saloon and shouted something inaudible. John climbed on the seat, shook the reins, and rattled west to the outskirts of town. He doubled back, grabbed his things, and headed east to stop briefly at the mill before traveling northeast to Dubuque.

Near the mill entrance he tied his team and briskly strode to the building. He unlocked the door and ignited a lucifer. Inside his office he blew out the match after lighting the kerosene lamp on his desk. He quickly scribbled "Possible KGC Recruits" at the top of a list upon which he wrote the names of several men rumored to be members in neighboring counties to the south. Not personally knowing the men he felt no remorse in sending the authorities on a wild goose chase in their direction. He also listed Timothy's and Jonas's names. He drew a bold line through Murphy's name with a notation stating "undependable, a staunch Unionist", thus protecting his friend. He smiled silently after he wrote Swenson's name and crossed it off in like manner. He wrote, "Loudmouth, all talk, no action. Committed only to being center of attention. A Unionist at heart."

A shame he'd miss Jonas's discomfort when confronted with the notation. Next he scratched a short message to Tim, instructing him to allow the authorities to discover the list as soon as possible. He closed by wishing Murphy well, adding that God willing they might reunite in better times. Stepping onto the white, dusty landing outside his office he removed the stone concealing the cavity where he and his foreman stored secrets these past weeks. Inside the office John removed another stone exposing a nook he created for his own use. He removed the $1600 in gold and a loaded revolver. He extinguished the lamp, moved cautiously down the darkened stairs, and untied his team. He entered the highway when he heard horses clomping down the road. He pulled his rig into the tall grass opposite the mill. Once the horsemen entered the mill he sped around the bend away from the bridge traversing the north fork of the river.

"Marshal Hoxie, why we out here if the stable hand saw Yates ride west?" questioned one of the two riders accompanying the lawman.

"Deputy Wheeler," Hoxie replied with agitation in his voice, "these conniving traitors elude us because they're sly. Mr. Chew kindly accompanied us at this late hour when he could be sitting in the comfort of his home with his lovely wife. Through no fault of his own he unwittingly hired a traitor to manage his mill. Fortunately our astute detection of Yates prevented irreparable harm. Now, Mr. Chew, if you'll please show us his office we'll search for the vermin's droppings."

Five minutes later the three exited the mill. "Told you he wouldn't be here," gloated the deputy.

The marshal glared and shook his head in disgust. "The odor of kerosene smelled fresh. The lamp felt warm to the touch. Someone visited recently. We need to estimate the direction he traveled."

Deputy Wheeler, consistently slow of thought and fast of mouth, matter-of-factly said, "Obviously he's headed east since we didn't meet him on the road. That is," he hesitated before condescendingly saying, "if he really was here?"

Turning to Chew, Hoxie asked, "What do you think? You worked with the man for three months."

"That I did," he nodded, "but as I told you Marshal, the greater authority I conferred upon Yates the less I saw of him, especially once he moved out of our house. It seemed odd. I guess I assumed he only wished to be free of my wife's pampering, him being an eligible young man and all. His weekly summaries seemed in order. Receipts always balanced. We turned a handsome profit the months he worked. In hindsight I did take comments repeated to me about his attitude toward the war with a grain of salt, primarily delivered by jealous associates, repeating what they heard from the German farmers. We acknowledge foreigners easily confuse with their limited intelligence as it is. Yates and I never discussed politics amongst ourselves. He appeared a devout Christian man. He stated several weeks ago of his only concern being that of turning a profit for me. He seemed content to let the politicians and generals fight the war, trusting the Almighty with the final say. That being said, I have no inkling where he now travels."

"I believe he assumes we'd search here for evidence once we discovered his boarding room vacant. It puzzles me who tipped him off. If I knew I'd hang that son of a bitch for treason tonight myself. My gut tells me let's head west." Marshall Hoxie also smugly thought to himself that if his deputy suggested east then west would be the intelligent consideration. "We'll escort you home, Mr. Chew, before we send out telegrams to alert other authorities. We'll explore several hours longer. If we have no luck we'll return to the mill at daylight." After a fruitless search they decided to wait for morning.

The first rays of the rising sun brightened the eastern sky. They danced off the lazily moving Mississippi as John shielded his eyes to gaze across the river towards East Dubuque, Illinois. The steam powered ferry effortlessly slashed against the cross current on her first run of the day. His twenty-eight mile journey to the river took almost seven hours, slower than by horseback but John expected as much. He awakened his contact in Dubuque who instructed him to travel the twelve miles to Galena and take possession of another $500 in gold. At a bustling general store in Galena he casually purchased supplies in mid morning and departed as inconspicuously but as hastily as possible. He traveled an hour before he day-camped in a grove of cottonwoods a hundred yards off the road where he collapsed on his blanket and fell asleep. Five hours later he awoke startled by loud shrieks from a flock of crows roosting in nearby trees. He breathed a sigh of relief upon remembering where he was. He lay there reliving the past twenty-four hours. He eluded his pursuers, deflected suspicion from Tim Murphy, and escaped detection in Dubuque and Galena. Lying on his back he watched clouds float west in the late afternoon sky. His worn body refused to move. He begrudgingly admitted he'd never regain the stamina to maneuver through the rugged countryside Stonewall Jackson demanded of his troops. The irregular sharp jab within his aching chest served as the exclamation point for his assumption. Following his contact's suggestion he journeyed to join other Confederate agents to winter within the safe harbor of Canada.

25 – JANUARY 1863

January 1, 1835. Twenty-eight years today. How many more?

He turned his attentions to a long overdue letter to Martha.

My dearest Martha,

Twenty-four months ago, despite the gathering storm clouds, my beloved family celebrated my birthday before we journeyed to the annual Lucas New Years Day open house. All seemed optimistic war would be avoided. If not circumvented, the worst case scenario appeared to be a conflict of short duration, followed by acknowledgement of an independent Confederacy by a Yankee government with no stomach for war. Two years and tens-of-thousands of lives later the bloody conflict continues. Can freedom only be purchased with the priceless blood of so many noble Southern men willing to die so that we may live without tyranny?

A year ago as I recuperated with my gracious Mississippi friends on New Years Day, victory seemed so near. Today victory still eludes us while death and suffering locate us wherever our proud armies march.

By the grace of God I am now committed to you, the only soul who makes me whole. When shall we unite as husband and wife? When shall we even share the joy of each other's presence, if only briefly? Enough selfish complaining!

I shall summarize my past year's adventures since I wrote in June. I traveled to Iowa to visit my dear brother Hezekiah. I became involved with men, though Northerners, who were devoted Democrats as much so as I, to terminating the Republican reign. These men resided in Dubuque

County, an area long dependent upon Mississippi River commerce; hence these citizens held affinity for their oppressed brethren down the river. The vast numbers of people residing in states beyond the eastern mountains feel similar estrangement with eastern Yankee abolitionists as do we. I anticipate if the conflict continues throughout this new year without unforeseen progress by the Federals, Mr. Lincoln and his band shall very well face both southern and western foes. I visualize states north of the Ohio and beyond the upper Mississippi joining our Confederacy. Forgive my digression, my love.

In Iowa we succeeded in discouraging enlistments, condemning the forthcoming draft, and developing a format for eroding U.S. currency. I regret I must refrain from divulging full detail lest I innocently jeopardize the operation. Perhaps when we meet opportunity shall exist to share this business with you. Overall we achieved successes very detrimental to the Union. Local authorities scrutinized anyone suspected of participating. We believe Stanton demanded constant surveillance of alleged participants. Only by advance warning from a devoted friend did I narrowly escape catastrophe before my hasty departure from Iowa. A harrowing journey to Dubuque, a hazardous route of travel via Wisconsin to Chicago, followed by an adventure to Kalamazoo, led me to the border. I crossed into Canada above Detroit to avoid Federal authorities. In November, after guarded movement, I reached Dundas, Canada West, or as the Canadians abbreviate, C.W.

I pondered sailing to England to support our cause from the seas since I realize my erratic health resulting from my wound prevents me from ever marching again with the glorious 2nd. But alas, a competent Canadian physician in Hamilton advised against the arduous ocean voyage, counseling total relapse or worse would transpire. I plan within days to commence my return journey to Virginia so that I may volunteer my service in whatever capacity feasible. I have been assured this message shall circumvent the dishonorable eyes which intrude upon the most intimate thoughts shared between two affectionate people.

My dear Martha, do you remember that initial enchanting evening we enjoyed in the general's parlor as we began our journey toward our lifelong commitment. I have saved the verse from the sentimental tune you so beautifully sang, 'When you and I Were Young Maggie'. I often find myself singing the tune and thinking of you. I insert Martha for Maggie. I enclose my rendition for your eyes only.

It was only eight months ago, Martha
When you said you'd always be mine
At the bridge with the stream below, Martha
Rushing past the sweet scented pine.
Though the days were a precious few, Martha
In the tranquil land by the sea
I surrendered myself to you, Martha
For all of eternity.

26 – LOOKING FOR WORK

The dreary February afternoon epitomized John's mood as he ambled along the spacious wooden Main Street sidewalk in Richmond. Lines of wagons loaded with war materials and random carts carrying civilian goods clogged the adjacent street. Before he entered the Lucas law office John gazed at the former Virginia Statehouse resting proudly atop the hill several blocks beyond. Two springs ago the Confederacy selected the building for the new dwelling place for their nation's legislature. Against the background of a stark sky the stone structure boldly flew the Rebel flag, audaciously symbolic of her citizens' dedication to the daunting task of fighting a bloody war while forming a new nation. Few people outside the South expected the Confederacy to survive a year, let alone two. If brilliant military commanders continued victoriously leading outmanned but spirited troops against better equipped Union troops, a stalemate at the very least would continue. The Northern citizenry's dissatisfaction festered with the prolonged impasse. Republican election setbacks the previous fall confirmed the premise. John aspired to discuss the plans for spreading discontent which he'd been mulling over since his return.

After the two warmly embraced Dan initiated an update of events transpiring over the past eight months. "I regretted resigning my staff position with General Wise. I feel inadequate performing civilian tasks in Richmond while our comrades daily face danger from battle. Unfortunately the damage from my tumble years ago still inhibits my physical ability. A man's either an asset or a liability; I recognize to my disdain that in battle I become a liability. And you, my dear friend, what are your plans?"

Dan's awkward posture indicated he constantly coped with aggravating back pain. With compassion and frustration John said, "I for one identify with your discomfort and disappointment. Two years ago I held my own with any man in Jefferson County whether on horseback, dismounted, and most assuredly on the shooting range. Today I too would fail miserably on the battlefield. Guilt envelopes me whenever I think of Will lying wounded in a Manassas field hospital last summer without family to encourage his recovery. Unfortunately I contemplated my departure from Iowa unaware of his struggle for survival. I thank the Lord for watching over the fallen lad."

"You could always apply for the bar. In spite of the war I find more than enough cases to try," Dan interjected with a soft grin.

John's palms flashed upward in mild protest. With an expression of embellished fear he replied, "No occurrence in the past ten years has enticed me to enter that profession. Better possibilities surely exist. Unfortunately a Canadian physician dissuaded me from the arduous journey to England to invest in a blockade runner." Beall's disarming smile then appeared. "Opportunities to serve at sea on this side of the Atlantic abound. But financial recompense fails to motivate me, as I only desire to survive this horrid affair to spend the balance of my life with those I love."

Dan reached into his desk drawer and withdrew several envelopes. "Speaking of those dear to you I received several letters. John reached for them eagerly searching for the identity of the senders. Dan smiled. "They appear to be from your mother, Mary, and an M.O., whom I assume to be Miss O'Bryan."

Late in the summer John wrote Dan of his commitment to Martha. He stuffed the unopened correspondences into his coat pocket, rested his elbows on the desk, and clasped his raised hands together. His host prepared to attentively listen as he recognized all too well his guest's determined expression indicating that there would be devil to pay for anyone who might interfere with his goal.

"While traveling to Chicago via rail I encountered groups of prisoners being transported to prison camps in Ohio, Indiana, and Illinois." He frowned as he recalled the ridicule the incarcerated men behind the fence inside Camp Douglas absorbed. "I actually visited the Chicago camp, from outside of course. While in Dundas, Canada, I calculated the distance of about 170 miles to another prison, an officer's compound in southern Lake Erie, located only twenty miles below Canada's southernmost boundary. In Toronto I encountered men incarcerated at the compound. They called it Johnston's Island. They reconfirmed to me that our treaty with Britain following the second war permits only one armed U.S. ship upon the Great Lakes. Much of last summer that craft, *The Michigan*, docked in Chicago."

John's friend tilted back in his desk chair, raised his eyebrows, and bluntly asked, "What do you propose? Row to the prison, unlock the gates, and release the prisoners."

"Daniel Lucas, I've pondered the opportunity before me many times over. I've determined a daring band of men could commandeer civilian boats, seize the shore batteries, and train them upon the prison. Arms smuggled to our men beforehand could provide support from within when the assault commences. In an hour's time 2,000 badly needed Confederate officers would await transport to freedom."

"Well conceived, but how do several small vessels ferry two-thousand men to Canada?"

With an air of confidence John answered, "Excellent concern, counselor. I've gained an insight into the thousands of dedicated Democrats wishing to shed the bloody yoke Lincoln fastens around their necks. Our show of force in secure Northern cities shall draw the willing support of these men to demand an end to this unwanted war. The Union prepares to initiate its draft of hundreds of Northern men who detest this conflict and a subsequent mandate that they shed their blood for it. My scheme, if successful, evolves into a rapid deployment of released men to Camp Chase in Columbus and Camp Morton in Indianapolis, with intentions of release more prisoners. Within twenty-four hours we'll unleash an army of ten thousand veteran troops upon Ohio and Indiana." In a contemptuous tone foreign to Dan's ears, John seethed, "And God only knows the pent-up retribution these men shall wreak upon the homeland of their cruel captors."

Immersing himself in the complicated plot, Dan delicately replied. "My friend, if your design reaches fruition, I delight that I am the first to gain knowledge of the scheme in its embryonic stages. Graciously accept without offense the obstacles you must overcome for your brilliant plan to mature. Foremost is our government's approval which insures resources and logistical support. Government sanction also prevents you from becoming branded a renegade pirate outside of the laws of war, although the Yankees follow no such standard. Secondly we must evaluate whether such action adversely affects our relations with Britain." John stared into space pondering the last comment.

A bit of the gleam left Beall's eyes. His shoulders drooped as he dejectedly asked, "What course do you suggest I pursue?"

"We have several paths. Prior to discussing these I must ask if you possess alternative courses of action."

"I considered obtaining a small vessel to capture Yankee merchant vessels sailing along the Chesapeake coastline." John shook his head with the surreal thought. "Who'd believe three years ago that I'd consider selling goods which I stole? The Yankees do bring out an inner self once entirely foreign to our souls. If you please, your solution to my dilemma in Ohio?"

"The prerequisite for securing government approval requires connections to gain audience with men of influence." Dan removed his watch. "Fortunately by pure coincidence in forty-five minutes a man with such influence arrives for a visit. Perhaps Providence ordains your operation."

At 3:30 Colonel Edwin Lee entered the office. "Greetings, Cousin Dan, and also to you Johnny Beall, our vagabond comrade," The glint in Lee's eye indicated his fun loving spirit still thrived. "Our paths haven't crossed since, has it been the summer of '61?"

"Aye," he replied offering a polite salute. John had long known Dan's first cousin who was raised on the family's Maryland estate, Bedford, just across the Potomac from Shepherdstown. Edwin's father, Edmund Jennings Lee II, had the fortune of being General Robert E. Lee's first cousin. Prior to Robert's assent to the apex of the Confederate military hierarchy Edwin, of his own accord, advanced rapidly through the ranks. His membership in the gray-clad Hamtramack Guards, Shepherdstown's local militia, led to an appointment as adjutant to the 2nd Virginia during the formation of the unit in the spring of 1861. Brigadier General Thomas Jackson appointed young Edwin to the position of his own aide-de-camp. Edwin's progression coincided with the rise of Stonewall Jackson's star. By late 1862 as a new lieutenant colonel he commanded Jackson's old Stonewall Brigade.

"At ease, Mr. Beall. Unfortunately after receiving my commission to command the brigade, my deteriorating health forced my resignation. I now search for another opportunity to defend the honor of our state."

A broad smile jumped across John's face as he looked to the man one year his junior before he clarified his blissful expression. "I too covet such prospect. Your cousin Dan believes you possess the key to opening the door for my daring plan to shorten the war by months."

John captivated Lee with highlights of his bold operation.

"A war on three fronts. East, west, and now north. I doubt even the resources of the enemy avail him to cope with a triple threat." He nonchalantly commented, "I'll arrange a meeting with President Davis to advance your proposal. Such an interview might not occur for several days due to the president's compact agenda."

On February 10, John exited behind Edwin Lee from the ornate carriage Lee rented for their appointment at the

Confederate White House. The Greek revival structure sat on the southwest corner of Clay and Twelfth Streets. Lee climbed several steps to the entrance door while his companion paused to view the mansion. The rectangular building with walls of massive smooth cut stone served both as a residence for the first family and as an occasional meeting site with the president.

A light complexioned Negro doorman welcomed the pair into the spacious receiving hall with its bright yellow walls. He escorted them to the small library to the rear where several straight chairs set near a matching loveseat upholstered with deep pink fabric, accented with white marble topped tables. Floor to ceiling bookshelves filled with leather bound volumes lined one of the walls from corner to corner. The mulatto servant departed saying, "The president will be down shortly."

Minutes later a slender, immaculately dressed gentleman entered the room. Had the individual not been the leader of Confederate States of America one might use the term emaciated to describe the thin, raw-boned individual, with a reddened right eye and worn features from the never ending responsibilities his position demanded. He rigidly stepped forward with a soft smile. "Edwin Lee, how good to see you again." Turning to John he said, "You must be Mr. Beall. Very good to meet you." The chief executive's erect posture appeared statuesque.

"Very honored to meet you, Mr. President."

"Please be seated gentlemen and share your proposal. While my schedule is limited I insist upon learning of all the details." No one questioned Jefferson Davis's dedication to the cause. The position required the ability to delegate but unfortunately the man obsessed himself with micromanaging the executive department. His desire to study in minutia all that passed over his desk contributed in large part to his erratic health. In less than five minutes Beall outlined his grand design for President Davis. Only in passing did he mention an alternative option of raiding Union shipping along the Chesapeake coast.

"Ah, my friend, your bold plan exudes the confidence that in the end shall carry the day for the South. The intricacies of your scheme require that I confer with my cabinet. Although Britain sympathizes with our plight, Lincoln's unrealistic proclamation to free the slaves forces English leadership to proceed with delicacy. Your cousin's leadership, Edwin, gives Europe confidence our continued battlefield victories shall pave the way toward our ultimate goal of acceptance by the Yankee government. If Lincoln continues his oppressive tactics such as those of several days past with his suspension of publication of the *Times* in Chicago, the wrath of the northern citizenry shall soon boil over. I so desire to take to the field again where my military talent might be utilized, but we each relinquish our own ambitions for attainment of our ultimate objective." With that comment Jefferson Davis stiffly rose signifying the interview's termination. "If the plan on the Great Lakes exhibits overwhelming diplomatic drawbacks you shall have ample opportunity for an alternative adventure. Farewell, my loyal patriots. Secretary Mallory should meet with you by week's end." With that Lee and Beall exited to bide their time for a concrete response.

The pair received notification of their much anticipated meeting with the Secretary of the Navy Stephen Mallory for Friday at the War Department offices. Mallory, along with Secretary of the Treasury Christopher Memminger and Postmaster General John Reagan, remained as the only department heads from the six cabinet officers originally appointed in 1861. Prior to the war Floridians elected Mallory to the U.S. Senate where he served as Chairman of the Naval Affairs Committee which provided him experience for his Confederate cabinet post. Since Davis's prior areas of military expertise included only the army Mallory operated his department with minimal supervision. The secretary of his own initiative pushed into production the manufacture of ironclad warships. He also traveled to England to develop relationships with British ship builders for the construction of blockade runners. If any man would approve a blueprint to free the prisoners on Lake Erie it would most certainly be Mallory. Lee and Beall walked through the building, recognizing that the perception of opulent government offices greatly overstated the bureaucrat's stark workplace.

In the Naval Secretary's upper floor office the duo seated themselves across from the fifty-year-old Floridian as he spoke with a convincing air of confidence. The solidly built man with a full face and a bountiful head of wavy hair displayed a narrow band of whiskers growing from ear to ear below his jaw. His cheeks and upper chin remained clean shaven. After casually discussing everything from weather to inflationary prices Mallory enthusiastically delved into details of the proposal. "Gentlemen," began the secretary with his deep, thick, southern dialect, "your plan from a military perspective to say the least is brilliant. The havoc such a successful operation would spread throughout the Yankee's northern borderlands would, as you so astutely perceive, create a third front for our oppressor to face." He chuckled before adding, "I wonder which incompetent general they might select to futilely fend off that confrontation."

"However," Mallory continued, upon which some of the gleam left Beall's eyes with the utterance of the secretary's foreboding word, "damn diplomacy interferes with our most desirable pursuits. I totally, albeit remorsefully, concur with President Davis that any venture requiring our troops' departure from Canada seriously compromises our carefully constructed relationship with Great Britain. The hell of it is, such a triumphant operation most assuredly expedites victory." The secretary returned to his upbeat persona. "But I've been enthusiastically urged to encourage you to pursue an alternative operation of preying upon Union shipping along the Maryland and Virginia coasts. As you are aware all that you capture, inclusive of ships and cargo, becomes yours to dispose of as you see fit. Besides serving your country you shall also conclude this war with wealth beyond your wildest expectations."

Beall and Lee momentarily gazed at each other before nodding in agreement. Edwin asked "Where do we become equipped and when do we meet our crew and depart?"

Mallory apologized for several of the minor details he 'neglected' to convey. "Our resources are now directed to either naval warships or blockade runners. You are therefore responsible for procuring your own vessel and crew. Arms may be available, although if you procure your weapons you shall be at sea sooner." The former senator, a competent and crafty politician in his right, added, "Gentlemen, I spend hours attempting to navigate the bureaucracy all governments so effortlessly become. I pray you never contend with my frustrations. I must remember to add, you both shall become commissioned officers in the Confederate Navy which protects you by internationally accepted codes of warfare. Colonel Lee, on behalf of the Confederate Navy, welcome!" energetically exclaimed the secretary. Mallory enthusiastically added, "I've per your acceptance soon-to-be commissioned Acting Master Beall completed preliminary work for you to resign from the army."

Beall and Lee rattled through the Richmond streets in their carriage eagerly anticipating their forthcoming adventure. Despite anxiously awaiting his new assignment John Yates Beall felt a diminutive void acknowledging indeed his days of belonging to the 2nd Virginia would officially terminate. A renewed vitality injected him as a new chapter of his life lay just beyond the next tributary.

27 – THE NAVAL CAREER

The following Monday John Yates Beall resigned from the 2nd Virginia Infantry Regiment, attached to the Stonewall Brigade, in the II Corps of Army of Northern Virginia. In March he received his official commission as acting master in the Confederate States of America Navy.

The task of building a crew took center stage. In addition to placing ads in newspapers and posting signs in areas frequented by likely recruits, Lee and Beall searched the docks for veteran seamen with a desire to fight. Much to their chagrin they discovered the lion's share of veteran sailors long ago enlisted in the Confederate Navy while the truly adventuresome and ambitious men eyeing a slice of the lucrative contraband pie had signed on with the blockade runners. The Confederacy's draft, instituted in 1862, seized other potential crewmen, leaving primarily a pool of shirkers, draft dodgers, or physical misfits from which to select. Luck changed when John encountered two Scotsmen.

A stout, round-chested man with glistening blue eyes and a fair-skinned face void of facial hair, and his companion, approached Beall. "Are you sir the gentlemen in need of trustworthy souls willing to risk life and limb for the bounty from the merchant ships which the Yankees are about to unknowingly offer up to a handful of deserving lads in search of adventure?"

"Perhaps, my friend, had I so eloquently worded my notice, I might not be that man, but aye, I'm he," John answered while looking up to the other man. I certainly could use you both."

"Name's Maxwell, John Maxwell," replied the bearded giant of a man sporting a full head of thick, black hair. Maxwell nodded to his companion. "This be my friend and fellow adventurer Bennet Burley."

"I'm Acting Master John Beall. Welcome to our entourage."

"How many men are now committed to our band, Acting Master Beall?" asked Burley.

"With the commitment of you two we reach half the strength necessary for our foraging expedition."

"Mr. Beall, are you of Scotch descent?"

"My father's lineage goes to Rob Roy McGregor himself while my maternal grandfather, God rest his soul, was one hundred percent English."

"If you be a purebred bloody Englishman I would challenge your evasive answer but since you claim Rob Roy as your ancestor I submit to your tactful reply," concluded the Scot with a robust laugh.

Beall smiled. "You two make four. Captain Lee, who incidentally's second cousin to thee General Robert Lee, anticipates more additions by week's end." After a brief exchange of contact information Beall contentedly walked away.

Later that day Edwin Lee informed John that Ned McGuire, brother of Stonewall Jackson's surgeon, Dr. Hunter McGuire, had joined them. Several days later two other Virginians joined, Roy McDonald and James Phillips. Ezra Jones and Gabriel Edmondson brought the contingent's number to nine, an adequate number to commence operations.

The privateers scavenged the waterfront for a vessel while remaining ever mindful of the scarcity of small arms. The Union blockade successfully impeded the flow of imported muskets. The army retained priority for weapons manufactured domestically and also for guns which slipped through the Yankee barrier. Next in line stood the Confederate Navy. Independent units waiting at the end consisted of those officially sanctioned such as Beall's and Lee's but also the roving bands of partisans with their own agendas. Beall and Lee determined they must obtain weapons by their own means.

In early April the band departed for a quaint coastal town about seventy-five miles east of Richmond. Matthews Courthouse rested near the mouth of the Piankatank River on the Chesapeake Bay. The close proximity to vital shipping lanes, the unsettled miles of rugged terrain, and the area's friendly citizens combined to establish a perfect base for operations. Small subsistence farms, typically owned by hardcore secessionists, offered safe harbor from occasional Union patrols. Tall pines sprinkled with hardwoods towered above the tangled undergrowth which Yankee pursuers would unexpectedly be obliged to circumvent. An official naval contingent had previously operated in the vicinity. Former U.S. President Zachary Taylor's grandson, John Taylor Wood, who formerly served on the ironclad *Virginia* before her demise, utilized the area as a base the prior year.

Lee remained at Matthew's Courthouse optimistic that the healthy sea air might serve as an anecdote for his weakened physical state. Meanwhile Beall, restless for action, led the balance of their men on an expedition in search of arms and supplies. Only twenty-five miles to the south beyond the Mojack Bay and across the York River stood Fortress Monroe. Although the North abandoned the nearby Norfolk shipyards two years earlier it managed to maintain a foothold in the area with its occupation of the fort. Surely the opportunity would present itself to capture needed supplies and weapons from small Yankee patrols or Union sympathizers.

After crossing the bay the band roved cautiously south, traversing the small streams and large rivers periodically impeding their march. Along the Black River, Beall silently signaled a halt. The scent of burning wood in the mild, humid, late afternoon air alerted the raiders to the presence of an unknown force. "Follow my directions closely until we determine whether they be friend or foe. Burley and Maxwell, ready your revolvers and each take a flank," Beall whispered, pointing to the left and right. He looked to McGuire. "Remain near in the event I become incapacitated." John reassuringly made eye contact with the others before saying, "The rest of you spread out with knives in hand. If we attack scream like a pack of wild Indians but we only attack on my orders."

Trees and small shrubs concealed their movements as they slowly advanced over ground gleaned bare of firewood. Distant voices froze their movement. Beall's left hand shot up halting the group while his other held a revolver itching for action.

"No sign of sentinels," he whispered to McGuire. "Have to be civilians. Whose?" The raiders crouched and began creeping forward. Voices became more discernable.

"Sounds like niggers," mumbled someone loud enough for all to hear. Beall jerked his head around, touched his fingers to his closed lips, and cast a cold, silencing glance toward the noisy offender. Several more inching moments brought the camp into view and confirmed they happened upon Negroes.

Beall concealed himself behind a cluster of bushes and motioned for Burley and Maxwell to move closer. In hushed tones he directed, "Only two appear armed with muskets. You two focus on the one sitting in the rear. Ned and I will take out the one near the fire. Watch for concealed pistols. All probably carry knives. We'll take them on my command. Avoid shooting if practicable."

The Rebels snaked to within thirty yards of the clearing to view the entire entourage. A barefoot adolescent girl wearing a dingy blue cotton dress entertained a young boy clothed only in oversized ragged trousers. A woman sat at the far edge of the encampment breastfeeding an infant. Three others prepared the evening meal on one side of the open fire while a man with a long branch stoked it. Idle male chatter occupied five more, oblivious to the nearby intruders.

The tranquil setting evaporated the instant Beall and his seven companions sprang to their feet. "We reclaim you as property of the Confederate States of America."

"We ain't going back," vehemently responded the muscular ebony man nearest the fire. He grabbed his musket, cocked it, and swung it up to aim. Two shots seconds apart reverberated from Beall's and McGuire's revolvers. The target's left shoulder jerked. His brief shriek abruptly ended an instant later when the second round tore into his chest. Crimson stains on his yellow shirt disappeared from view as he fell forward on top of his unfired weapon. He lay motionless except for a futile attempt to continue his labored breathing. Simultaneously Burley and Maxwell screamed a demand for surrender to the slender mulatto armed with the other musket. Being of slight build he threw down his cumbersome weapon and raced away from the clearing with errant revolver shots resounding through the heavy air. Beall's other four men dutifully brandished gleaming knives and erupted with bloodcurdling, high-pitched yells perceptually doubling their number as they sprang to capture the remaining victims. Instinctively the females fled to safety with the children in tow through the rear perimeter.

Two middle-aged black men sprinted to aid the women in their rush from danger. The other two assumed the role of rear guard. One dove for the unfired weapon below his mortally wounded comrade. The other wrapped his hands around the four-foot oak branch smoldering in the cooking fire. He yanked it from the flames and began wildly flaying the club. Glowing embers scattering through the air created a weapon all the more menacing while disrupting Confederate pursuit of the women and children. Rebels wielding knives cautiously circled the man swinging the fiery club. Burley and Maxwell moved to position themselves for unobstructed shots while their adversary held the frustrated foursome at bay. Beall and McGuire concentrated on the man reaching for the bloodstained musket beneath his dying comrade. He grasped the firearm and momentarily stared remorsefully into the dying warrior's glassy eyes. The unfortunate hesitation allowed Beall and McGuire to fire two rounds. The Negro yelped with pain when one round splatted his right forearm. While his wounded arm went limp, he wrapped his left hand around the muzzle of the unfired musket and flung it towards Beall and McGuire. The two Rebels dove to the sand to escape the musket spinning erratically toward them. They regained their feet only to realize their agile target vanished. Everyone's attention turned to the remaining Negro. Enraged shouts from the ever-tightening pack encircling the prey added to the confusion as curses and threats flew from all directions in the pandemonium.

"Save me a slice of the uppity nigger."

"Hang him first, then we'll carve him up."

"Let the captain shoot the black bastard so we can get out of here."

The wild-eyed center of attention's irrational expression kept the Rebels at bay. Uncontrolled rage faded to subdued anger when Beall ordered, "Back away men. They'll be no hanging or disfigurement of this boy." Looking directly at the surrounded black man, Beall commanded, "Drop your club immediately or I shall leave the boys to finish you in any manner they see fit." The crew responded by backing away from the terror-stricken prey who understood his only chance for survival rested with Beall.

The glowing club dropped on the sand. Jimmy Phillips bound the prisoner's wrists and slipped a crude hemp leash around his neck. Defiantly the captive shouted, "I be free again. Next time forever. The Union gonna free us all. Massa Lincoln promised."

A heavy boot thudded into the slave's groin. He crumpled to the ground rolling back and forth in agonizing pain. Phillips tugged on the coarse rope, forcing the choking prisoner to regain his feet. "Boy, your only hope for freedom forever comes if I toss the end of this rope over that tree, hoist you up, and let the buzzards have at you when your feet quit dancing. But seeing how the captain ordered no such thing you'll have to continue with God's preordained station for you. Now be a good darkie and move along." The raiders gathered the two muskets and departed for Mathews Courthouse.

Although he possessed captured weapons and income from the slave's sale Beall continued roaming Richmond in mid May in search of additional crew members, weapons, and the elusive vessel. All were shortly forthcoming.

The name Lee, even that of Edwin, provided influence to garner uniforms, side arms, and nautical instruments. Before the summer equinox arrived half the crew returned to Mathews County in advance of the others.

On the morning of June 25th Beall and four crewmen sat inside a small, two-room clapboard house built along the meandering Pepper Creek, a narrow, lazily flowing stream draining into Mojack Bay. "Mrs. Gale, our crew by no means avoids the Union forces without the generosity and protection of loyal Virginians such as you," said John, casually sliding his chair away from the table. "Besides endangering yourselves, you and your neighbors without fail supply food to nourish us before we embark on our crusade to drive the invaders from our land."

The feisty hostess sharply replied, "Damn Yankees can't blockade the fish. Lived here twenty years and the good Lord's always provided a bountiful harvest to fill an empty belly. Never without rice. Flour's still plentiful, though a bit pricey. And the garden keeps producing tators, greens, and other such victuals. Only lack good male company from time to time since my boys joined the army."

John gazed through the doorway beyond the quaint pine-planked porch shaded by a sloping wood-shingled roof. Thick, hazy air hung heavily over the surrounding landscape. Dense, green vegetation covered the river bank. Honey suckle, with dangling trumpet-shaped white blossoms, dotted the low lying thicket on a patch of ground the late Mr. Gale once cultivated. The canopy of the trees covered the carpet of uninviting, thorny underbrush which separated one homestead from another except for the narrow worn footpaths which connected them. Strands of riverside vegetation gradually transformed into a dense inner peninsular jungle offering refuge for Rebel fugitives.

This morning the combined chirping of the various bird species produced a harmonious melody synchronizing with the occasional flopping of a chunky catfish along the river's surface. A soldier in this setting could effortlessly forget a lethal war ripped the country apart. The tranquility vanished with the muffled drone of a distant steamship. Alerted Rebels sprang to their feet, grabbed their weapons, raced out the door, and dashed into the safety of the thicket before the source of alarm drifted into view. Two landing barges appeared, each packed with a force of over a dozen blue-clad troops. Off shore drifted the *USS Crusader.* Soon a junior officer stood in the shade of the porch roof, wiping perspiration from his brow while his sweat-soaked men endured the beastly heat emitted through the haze from the early morning sun. "Ma'm, I'm Lieutenant Daniel Cook, attached to the United States Ship *Crusader*, assigned to search your premises for Rebel pirates rumored to be in the area and sheltered by you. If you please, we shall enter and search your home."

"And if I don't please you'll still bring your hoard traipsing through my simple dwelling," retorted the spry, petite woman.

"With all due respect, Mrs. Lucy Gale, these are my orders," mundanely replied Cook.

Despite no formal introductions the gray-haired woman understood the seriousness of the situation since the Yankee knew her name. She stepped aside but not without mockingly bowing down and motioning for the king's men to enter.

Before he crossed the threshold the lieutenant ordered, "Privates Kelsey, Schmitt, and Jones, accompany me with weapons ready. Sergeant Adkins, station the other men around the perimeter." In a louder voice he added, "Open fire if you detect Rebels." Cook and his trio disappeared inside the home. In a matter of moments the men looked under the bed, poked their heads into the hot attic, and rummaged through the bureau drawers searching for secesh evidence.

As Cook prepared to exit the house he turned and pointedly demanded, "Mrs. Gale, how does a woman living alone manage to accumulate a wash basin of dirty dishes?"

Undaunted, she smirked condescendingly before barking, "This frail old widow ain't been well lately. Hoping the smothering heat disappears before I make the effort to commence with my chores."

For several seconds Cook's penetrating glare challenged the lady. Before him stood a healthy old woman in a clean beige and red checkered cotton dress, with well-brushed hair drawn back from her face into a tight bun. Despite poor health or excessive heat, not the type of house keeper to allow unclean dishes to accumulate after meals. He walked onto the small porch and indignantly shouted to his sergeant, "Nobody in this rundown little shack. Fan out. Somebody was here recently."

While Cook hunted for evidence inside, Beall's crew crawled carefully on their bellies through the thicket away from the Yankees and toward the obscurity of the forest. The Rebels retreated three-quarters of the distance with fifteen yards remaining when the Union lieutenant advanced randomly into the brush in Beall's direction. Yankee musket barrels and attached bayonets glistened in the sunlight. In less than a minute they would stumble upon Beall. Out numbered five-to-one the Confederate's only asset remained the element of surprise. The twenty-seven sparsely distributed enemy soldiers either guarded the barges or tramped over the property. The Yankees uttered curses as the thorny brambles punctured their skin. The lieutenant with his revolver in one hand and sword in the other erroneously lead his men directly to the prone enemy.

A quintet of Rebel yells shattered the peaceful landscape. Beall's men rose to one knee and simultaneously unleashed a hail of lead thundering from their revolvers. Nesting birds flapped their wings fleeing into the safe haven of the skies beyond. Widow Gale peered through the lower corner of her window as Cook's saber dropped from his grasp. He awkwardly attempted to shove his unfired revolver into his belt with one hand while he reached for his upper chest with the other. A split-second later another round splattered his lower cheek, splintering slivers of bone and spatters of blood away from his imploded face. A nearby soldier caught his staggering commander before the lieutenant fell. Cook's blood soaked into the assisting man's blue coat as he dragged the mortally wounded officer behind the fleeing Union soldiers. One brave Yankee turned and fired an errant shot. He screeched when return fire shattered his upper arm. Another yelped the instant a ball scraped the flesh from the edge of his hip. Once the Yankees exited the thicket the remaining U.S. soldiers emptied their firearms towards Beall's position. The Southerner's already flattened themselves on the ground and continued snaking toward the overgrown forest refuge. One more volley belched from Union rifles in the enemy's direction. The barges quickly loaded to transport them to the safety of the steamer. Artillery shells from the *Crusader* tore into the thicket in the fruitless attempt to inflict damage upon a departed enemy.

Mrs. Gale softly smiled from behind her window at the sight of the three wounded Yankees transferring onto the steamer, one being the uppity lieutenant now near death. Fifteen minutes later two barges loaded with troops returned to repay the sympathizer and her neighbors for their transgression of harboring partisans. They doused Mrs. Gale's porch with kerosene and restrained her as she begged to remove several keepsakes such as the tintype of her deceased husband.

The soldier holding the match vehemently snarled as he dropped the lucifer onto the fuel-soaked porch, "Your request is approved only if Lieutenant Cook so orders." Flickering flames of hatred reflected in the man's eyes whose thoughts returned to his dead commander and long time friend. Seven suspected collaborators, including John Kirwin and Ralph Davis, stood in horror witnessing their homes burning to the ground. The Yankees carried the aged and blind Captain Boswell Kirwin from his bed and laid him unceremoniously outside. The greasy smell of kerosene fumes prior to the acrid stench of burning lumber reached his nostrils before the crackling sounds of the destructive inferno resounded in his ears. The enraged Confederates, withdrawn several thousand yards into the wilderness, observed the distant black plumes of smoke. The men returned after dark to reconnoiter the site. To their chagrin only eight eerily smoldering heaps remained where inviting shelters sat early that morning.

Beall commiserated over his utter lack of success during the past three months. One dead and one captured Negro along with several small arms. One dead Yankee lieutenant, at the expense of hardship inflicted upon eight innocent civilians. The recently confirmed news that the northwestern counties of Virginia officially became part of the new Yankee state of West Virginia further darkened the shroud of melancholy over him. To hell with the self-righteous counties bordering Ohio and Pennsylvania but he seethed with the knowledge that Lincoln stole Jefferson and Berkley Counties in a farce of a free election where men filled ballots under the vindictive eyes of Yankees with threatening bayonets! The blatant hypocrisy of Yankees! Free the slaves because slavery is evil but only in the Confederate states, not in the four northern states where it existed. The dictator without conscience dispatched armies south into states possessing the constitutional right to secede; states forming a nation Lincoln refused to recognize because each still belonged to his Union. If true, how could he amputate a portion of one state to graft the formation of another? Beall restlessly looked ahead for his opportunity to avenge all Yankee sins.

On July 5th Edwin Lee, still convalescing, placed Beall temporarily in charge. John detailed Ned McGuire with four men to set sail on their recently acquired canoe and to capture the northern merchant ship *George W. Rodgers* which supplied Fort Monroe. They returned reporting only mild success. The merchant vessel departed an hour prior to the Rebel's arrival. However, the men managed to cut the important cable between Cherrystone and Old Comfort Point. After this excursion everyone returned to Richmond where Beall presented his official report to Secretary Mallory along with the souvenir of a sliced section of cable.

Edwin Lee, frustrated with his lack of a full recovery from his illness, tendered his resignation effective July 21st. Though in sole command Beall's commission remained that of acting master, more an official recognition within the CSA military for protection rather than a rank which would allow further promotion. Though referred to by subordinates, Confederate officials, and Union foe alike as Captain Beall he never advanced beyond acting master.

With August on the horizon the new commander prepared to aggressively inflict serious damage upon his ruthless foe. He inventoried his resources of men, vessels and equipment. A full contingent of dedicated men accompanied him to the coast. Although Maxwell, Burley, and Phillips disappeared from the first group of recruits a second wave brought the number to over twenty. This second group volunteered for a variety of reasons. George Stedman, editor of the *Richmond Enquirer,* enticed his apprentice William Baker to enlist by feeding him tales of an expedition to China to interrupt U.S. shipping. Thomas McFarland of the *Richmond Whig* also joined. Stedman and McFarland yearned to provide firsthand accounts similar to those from the mysterious *Richmond Dispatch* correspondent rumored to be traveling with John Taylor Wood. The exploits of Wood garnered dramatic headlines in newspapers all along the Atlantic seaboard. The lure of riches certainly lured some men to Beall. Others accustomed to life on the seas longed for an opportunity to serve their country while living in an environment reminiscent of their prewar vocation. Several dedicated souls even volunteered solely out of sense of duty although they selected this option to avoid the arduous regimen of the traditional army or navy. Another lad threw in his lot with the privateers as much from dedication to the cause as allegiance to his brother. Captain Beall readily welcomed William Beall along with newcomers Robert Annan and Mel Stratton from Richmond, Michael Fitzgerald from Norfolk, plus Severn Churn and Robert Thomas from across the Chesapeake in Accomack

County. Paul Crouch, Robert Etter, and Ralph Rankin along with several others completed the force.

Beall finally obtained two vessels in early July. They christened the white twenty-eight foot sail canoe the *Swan*. The twenty-two foot yawl with a black hull they appropriately named the *Raven*. Both vessels could be manhandled from the water into the camouflaging brush fringing the coast although a more common and expedient practice persisted in selecting a protected inlet, filling the boats with sand bags, and sinking them in shallow water. Oars and wrapped sails could be easily concealed in the dense vegetation near the shore. Beall never employed Wood's practice of hauling sets of wheels to support and transport boats overland from one water route to another.

Scavenging, begging, honest purchasing, and fraudulent requisitioning insured each man carried at least one revolver and a knife. Assorted rifles, muskets, swords, hatchets, and ample shot and powder added to the crew's arsenal.

On August 1, the *Raven* and *Swan* crossed twenty-five miles of open Chesapeake Bay waters toward the southern tip of the peninsula that jutted to the fifteen mile channel linking the Atlantic Ocean and the Chesapeake Bay. Just east of the peninsula, Smith Island's towering light house guided ships along the treacherous coast. Only a skeleton Union garrison protected the sparsely populated island. On August 3, the crew beached their boats and managed to avoid the lackadaisical Smith Island guards.

About 10 a.m. Beall and McGuire approached the light house. Waves slapped rhythmically on the beach while squawking seagulls hopped along the shore. Partly cloudy skies and coastal breezes provided a pleasant setting.

A gruff voice interrupted the tranquil scene. "What are two able-bodied boys such as you doing snooping around my lighthouse?" A short, portly individual, with a weathered face, shaggy gray hair, and three days growth of white stubble covering his face stood before them.

Beall casually answered, “Just two honest men taking a break from the toil of fishing. Nothing biting so we decided to get a closer look at this fine light house.”

Peering from under the bill of his faded brown cap the ornery lighthouse keeper curtly retorted, “If you two were worth anything you’d been out a lot earlier and already had your catch. You look like the type that spends more time in the tavern than in your fishing boat. Where is she by the way?”

Pointing back towards the west shore John answered, “Over there.”

The light house keeper sized up Ned while continuing with the interrogation. “What’s the matter boy? The cat got your tongue, or don’t he allow you to talk son?”

“Apologies, sir. Always been the bashful sort. Ma says I’ll never get me a wife with my quietness. Pa just laughs and says that if I’d get me a wife it wouldn’t matter anyways as she‘d be doing all the talking.”

A slight smile broke across the man’s face. “Your pa seems a pretty knowledgeable fellow in the ways of woman.” Glancing from Ned to John the smile departed when he pointedly asked, “What’s your all knowing pa say about the likes of you and your companion lounging about while good men are fighting to save this grand country of ours?”

John calmly answered, “While serving I received a severe chest wound, as of yet insufficiently healed for me to return to the field. My cousin here wants to enlist but his ma says her other three boys already serve and she needs someone to tend to the chores as his pa’s getting up in years.” Breaking the stalemate, John introduced himself. “Private John Yates, on leave from the 1st Maryland. This here’s my cousin from my ma’s side, Ned Stewart. You sir are?”

“Jonah Mills.”

“Mr. Mills, we would immensely appreciate a closer examination of your incredible lighthouse. The mechanics of these always intrigue me,” he said before softly smiling.

"I'm sure an experienced gentleman such as you could fill the empty minds of these inquiring souls."

The trio entered the doorway into the limited living area containing a cramped kitchen consisting of a stove, a table, two chairs, a small pantry, and a wash basin. A narrow undersized bed occupied the space below the window providing a view of the Atlantic and allowing ventilation from offshore winds. Behind the door leaned an ancient flintlock rifle with powder horn and shot pouch. The two guests trudged up the winding stairs behind their slow-moving host. At the top of the tower they inspected an enormous oil lamp surrounded by several strategically placed mirrors which reflected the flames bright glow.

"Mighty sophisticated setup you have here, Mr. Mills. Must require years of experience to learn to operate this," John said in a most complementary tone while thinking even a field hand could haul fuel up here, fill the oil reservoir, and light a match.

With an index finger and thumb rubbing his neglected chin, Mills stood erectly with puffed out chest and boasted, "Lads, years of experience and a keen mind are of necessity for keeping this complicated equipment operational."

Ned McGuire innocently said, "Must take a great deal of fuel to keep this light burning, especially during the long winter nights."

"With this damn war, oil is always a concern for me. Before the war I got regular shipments to maintain at least a month's supply. Early on in the conflict I got resupplied only when I got below 100 gallons. The military tired of my pestering. Now I got 300 gallons stored out in the supply shed. Our navy's finally keeping the coast clear of the dirty Rebs, so irregular transport is no longer much of a problem," concluded the simple lighthouse keeper with a satisfied grin. The trio descended the stairs and walked outside.

"You boys get back to work now," admonished Mills.

"One more thing Mr. Mills," Beall said before hesitantly pausing.

"Spit it out boy," replied the older man, regaining his crotchetiness.

"In the name the Confederate States this pair of dirty Rebs, as you refer to us, along with twenty men soon to appear over those dunes claim your oil and equipment. After which we shall make your lighthouse inoperable," added Beall in a very businesslike manner. Turning he waved toward his concealed men to advance.

"Thieving bastards! You traitors can all burn in hell."

Ned unemotionally replied, "That oil of yours should keep it burning mighty hot, wouldn't you say?"

Veins raised on the neck of the red-faced man. With clenched fists he muttered, "One on one I'll whip every one of you slimy pirates."

Etter and Baker escorted the fuming Mills a safe distance away while part of the crew set to removing oil from the storage shed and loading it on a nearby yawl. The others entered the lighthouse. Simple enjoyment seems to overtake a man in busting things up, especially property belonging to an enemy's government. The crew transformed into demons intent upon totally destroying the lighthouse's interior. At the sound of shattering dishes Beall shouted, "Leave the man's personal property alone."

"Aw, Cap," responded an unidentified voice.

Another anonymous one sharply replied, "Yes, sir."

From the top of the tower echoed the sounds of shattering mirrors while hammers and metal bars clanked against machinery. By noon the *Raven* and *Swan* sailed into view to escort the island's transport yawl onto the sea. Beall paroled Mills for twenty-four hours, secluded his vessels in an inlet between Smith Island and the peninsula's eastern shore, and waited for sufficient wind to navigate across the Chesapeake after dark.

A week after their lighthouse raid Beall's satisfied crew roamed the streets of Richmond spending freely of their share of the sale of the yawl and premium sperm oil. Another man's nautical escapade soon overshadowed Beall's first successful venture.

John arrived slightly ahead of his friend, and had just seated himself in the Lucas law office when the barrister entered full of excitement. "Johnny, what do think of John Taylor Wood's latest venture?"

"Haven't heard. What did he do now, capture Washington City?" questioned John sarcastically.

"He captured two Federal gunboats, the *Reliance* and the *Satellite*. With them he captured the *Golden Rod*, laden with valuable coal. Then he turned his guns on two anchor sweepers, the *Coquette* and *Two Brothers*, carrying a combined total of over 43,000 pounds of anchors and chains. He burned all five ships but retained the cargos and anchors." Grinning ear to ear Lucas chuckled. "How are the Yankees ever going to protect their merchant ships if they can't even protect their own battleships?"

Beall irksomely retorted, "Captain Wood may well find others entering his little foray."

"Why Captain Beall, do I sense a bit of jealously?" jested Dan.

"Not jealously, only a commitment to fulfill my duty to the utmost."

28 – SUCCESS IN SEPTEMBER

The York River Railroad locomotive chugged away from the station in Richmond. As the momentum increased Beall and his followers gently swayed in synchronized motion with the passenger cars. Soon the dull mechanical humming of steel wheels grinding over iron rails lulled John into a reflective trance. September first already. Almost two years since his wounding at Bolivar Heights. Two-and-a-half years since war commenced. Recent official reports from the Gettysburg battle confirmed Lee's army incurred horrendous casualties. Fortunately the Rebels inflicted sufficient damage to Mead's army to prevent him from invading Virginia. For the first time since 1860 Virginia farmers planted, nurtured, and harvested crops. Their land had been free of invaders since Chancellorsville in early May.

His thoughts flowed to Martha, whom he'd last seen seventeen months ago. Love was cruel with the unbearable pain of separation, but love was also kind with its soothing memory of her which provided him the incentive to continue.

His thoughts gravitated to the optimism of the future. Over two years of dreadful fighting, yes, but a stalemate existed and a deadlock meant the Confederacy still survived. Just as General Washington's determination outlasted the British the Confederacy's resolve would outlast the Yankees. His lips slowly curled into a smile with acknowledgement that this generation's George Washington, Robert E. Lee, continued outlasting his opponent with only the loss at Gettysburg to blemish an illustrious record.

His yearning for the sea coupled with the excitement for the coming venture rejuvenated his spirits and refortified his flesh. Marginal successes the past five months didn't minimize the valuable experience his crew gained although they sailed without Burley, Maxwell, and Phillips. While in Richmond he learned Burley had been captured and faced trial. Unfortunately the Yankees brutally hung Phillips where they captured him. Maxwell's fate remained unknown. Beall's thoughts returned to the future, to his cohesive unit of men working in unison, willing to die for their cause, and for each other. They would unsheathe the swords bringing retribution to an enemy who brutalized innocent citizens from Virginia to Iowa. With that final reassuring thought his chin slowly dropped against his chest as he dozed into a deep slumber. Two hours later metal wheels screeched to a halt, jerking John awake as the rail car lurched forward. Forty miles completed by rail; twenty miles remained by ferry.

Over the next two weeks Beall's crew on occasion visited with Sands Smith, Thomas Smith, and Colonel Tabb along with Mr. Ransom and Mr. Brooks. Their casual acquaintances had matured into warm friendships. John objected to their outward display of hospitality, remembering all too well the barbaric burnings which destroyed the dwellings of Mrs. Gale and her neighbors. Rumors circulated Yankee retaliation became the rule rather than the exception. The elder spokesman for the group adamantly squashed Beall's reluctance to accept civilian aid. "Any Yankee soldiers telling Sands Smith who he can feed and who he can shelter on his property riles a hornet's nest they'll wish they never stirred."

Daylight faded into night on September 18, signaling their departure. Beall skippered the larger *Swan* while McGuire commanded the smaller *Raven* as the two parties shoved off into dark waters and headed southeasterly across the Chesapeake. They reached the southwestern edge of Virginia's eastern peninsula at daybreak. The band remained secluded until they mobilized for another nocturnal voyage. Early morning sunshine and mild seas greeted the men sailing the inner channel between the peninsula and Atlantic coastal islands. To their starboard towered the Smith Island lighthouse. Although a second visit with Jonah Mills seemed enticing the crew sought larger prizes. The decision proved prudent since unbeknownst to them three artillery pieces strengthened the force of blue-clad soldiers protecting the refurbished lighthouse. Farther up the coast distant sails appeared below a fluttering Union flag. Following Beall's orders the *Raven* lagged behind the *Swan*. Beall assisted three men in struggling with the oars while five crewmen secluded themselves under a canvas. Within ten minutes Beall's innocent looking vessel pulled aside the *Mary Anne*. All color drained from the sloop captain's ruddy face the instant he stared down the barrel of Beall's cocked revolver. The *Mary Anne's* small docile crew obligingly joined their ship's master imprisoned below deck. The trio of boats sailed northward. Within the hour two prisoners from a pair of small fishing skiffs unwillingly joined the *Mary Anne's* crew after the Rebels set the pair of craft adrift. The journey continued with Beall absorbing the tranquility of the addicting sea as the late September afternoon sun soothed the aching, sleep-deprived bodies of the men.

The sailors readily followed their leader who willingly took a turn at the oars or prepared a meal while his party attended to other duties or indulged in much needed rest. This afternoon Beall seized advantage of an opportunity to display appreciation for his men. Before the Rebels cast the two scows adrift they removed the fishing gear. Beall allowed his men to alternately fish along the sandy shoals of Cobb Island as the journey continued. Sunset found the crew and prisoners alike gathering on the beach around aromatic cooking fires and gorging themselves on a feast of freshly roasted fish. John shook his head in amazement while reviewing the surreal day. A sleepless night preceded the capture of three enemy ships, or at least vessels, considering the size of the two fishing craft. Festive hours of fishing and eating became interspersed with crewmen playfully splashing water towards each other while bragging of their unparalleled fishing prowess. With full bellies and several hours of uninterrupted sleep Beall's men could challenge half the Union Navy.

They awoke to overcast clouds ushering in the first day of fall with its decreasing daylight and lower temperatures. Where to now? The *Mary Anne* possessed moderate value. Capture of the small fishing scows served as little more than a practice drill. He desired the prize yielding the riches he promised when he enticed his crew to join. The flotilla glided northward with the skies growing ever more ominous. White caps sprouted on the surf. By the late morning of September 21st strong winds fiercely slapped water against wooden hulls and soaked everyone with chilling saltwater. Wool clothing protected the men better than cotton but Beall knew once the storm subsided drying clothing would be a priority.

"Stand fast men," he shouted above the roar of the sea. "We've endured worse."

An hour before dusk Beall stared into the horizon at a distant shape. Another ship ripe for the picking, or a small island with several trees transformed into an imaginary prize? Cautiously the *Swan* advanced. A wide smile crossed his stoic face. Before him, on the Atlantic side of Wachapreague Island, lay a large rigged schooner in anchor waiting out the howling storm. Too high a profile for a blockade runner. Had to be a Yankee vessel!

"Row back to the *Raven*!" Beall ordered.

Twenty minutes later his vessels nestled between a small island and the mainland, receiving protection from the full fury of the weather while Beall conferred with McGuire. "We'll board the ship an hour before midnight while the Yankee crew sleeps. This tempest may leave their deck unguarded although we cannot assume such," continued Beall, pulling his second-in-command nearer to speak directly into McGuire's ear. "You'll board on the starboard side with the *Raven* while I assail the port side. Caution your men that in these damp conditions their pistols might not fire, but draw them for effect. Be ready with the knife or hatchet. Demand the men bend low while rowing and above all, maintain silence. Noise eliminates our greatest ally, the element of surprise."

At 10:15 Beall's white vessel slashed through the waves with McGuire's black boat closely following. Two guards remained with the captured sloop. Three-quarters of a mile beyond their bows the *Alliance* bobbed up and down in rough waters. In the dry warmth of the *Alliance's* head cabin her captain passed the miserable evening winning his third game of dominoes from first mate Ira Greene. Not much of a challenge, thought Ireland, as his opponent scratched his shaggy head, looked at his pieces, and stared at the table, searching for the discovery of a grand Napoleonic strategy for obtaining victory. Five frustrating minutes later Greene examined his new pieces in preparation of another match.

"When do you think this squall'ill die down, Captain?"

"Maybe tomorrow, surely the day after. These autumn storms tend to hang on longer than others. No worry though. We've traveled twenty hours from Philly. Two days of good weather and we'll be unloading our goods in South Carolina to sutlers eager to gouge the poor fighting lads," concluded Ireland before returning his attention to the noncompetitive contest before him. Never let the crew think they're smarter than you, even in a simple game of dominoes.

The war had been profitable for David Ireland. He owned a comfortable two-story white frame house with a wraparound porch overlooking Raritan Bay from Staten Island. He enjoyed the benefits of living near but not in New York City. He relished toiling in the vocation he loved while contributing to the defeat of the rebellious traitors. Another year or two of this war would allow him to retire by age sixty and partake of a relaxing, comfortable lifestyle.

The raiders reached the *Alliance* on schedule. The downpour continued hampering visibility. Harsh, unfriendly seas interfered with the detailed plan of assault. Beall veered to the left of the *Alliance* while McGuire steered to the right. Large swells lifted and dropped the *Raven*. The black yawl's crew fought to avoid smashing into the *Alliance*. Beall squinted into the darkness for any shape resembling a sentinel guarding the deck. Unless well-hidden, no form appeared. Mother Nature, who concealed the Rebels' advance, became their fiercest enemy. Beall piloted the *Swan* to the port side of the schooner while struggling to attach a rope to the *Alliance* which rose and fell with each passing swell. Successive waves now seemed determined to pull Beall's boat away from the *Alliance*.

On the other side of the big ship McGuire faced a converse predicament. His crew fought to avoid smashing into the schooner. A never ending progression of rolling seas seemed obsessed with shattering the black yawl against the towering hull of the adjacent craft. One such swell wrestled control of the *Raven* from McGuire and slammed it against the schooner. The crackling splintering of the wooden rudder foreshadowed looming disaster as wrecked pieces floated from the *Raven*. McGuire feared they might be sucked completely away without their steering mechanism. Swells carried the *Raven* beyond the *Alliance*. Fatigue transformed into searing muscle pain while drenched, chilled crewman fought the sea and rowed back to the *Alliance*.

A muffled crash reverberated through the *Swan* and the *Raven*. Miraculously the black vessel narrowly avoided smashing atop her sister although her hull crashed against the *Swan*. Shouts of "man overboard" drew everyone's attention to Ned McGuire flailing helplessly in the black water. Beall's accurately cast rope pulled McGuire to the *Swan*. Hearts raced with the anxiety of deadly flashes of gunfire exploding from the deck at any instant. Mother Nature chose again to become an ally. The overwhelming force of her fury muted the echoes of the commotion outside of the unsuspecting schooner. In moments a dozen Rebels controlled the uncontested deck of the *Alliance*.

Beall motioned McGuire to secure the aft area below while he moved down the passage to the front. He drew his revolver, trusting the well-greased lead balls sealed the front of the cylinder cavity while the percussion caps protected the narrow passage to the rear of the powder charge despite the drenching just endured. With his left hand he touched the reassuring presence of his knife handle protruding from his boot top. He subconsciously rested his hand on the cold, hard head of the hatchet shoved into his belt. His squad wobbled behind him as the schooner continued rolling side to side. Pistol muzzles pointed upwards. Three fingers firmly grasped wooden grips, index fingers rested against trigger guards, and thumbs nervously waited to draw back hammers prior to leveling and firing. Leaning against the right side of the passageway to maintain his footing he drew his hatchet from his belt with his left hand, grasping the wooden handle just below the lethal head. He turned his eyes toward the cabin's entrance. He motioned for Will to prepare to fling the door open. Calm but barely audible voices indicated the occupants remained clueless of the Confederate boarding.

The door banged open against the passage wall. Two startled men stared awestruck at the intruders. The young, skinny sailor froze in his chair waiting for orders from his captain. The older, portly man wearing a blue woolen jacket moved with surprising agility toward the desk against the far wall. A set of .36 caliber Navy Colts lay in clear view on the dark mahogany desk.

"Stop or you're a dead man!" ordered Beall.

Ireland immediately but reluctantly froze in his tracks and faced his captor. He glared at the group of devil-may-care men with salt water dripping from their soaked clothing. Their leader's indifferent blue eyes implied he preferred shooting Ireland to debating the issue. Beall calmly demanded, "What's your cargo and where are you headed?"

Not easily intimidated, Ireland brazenly replied, "Who are you pirates and what are your intentions?"

John concealed his admiration for his unwavering adversary. "I am Acting Master John Beall. I seize this ship and make you my prisoner in the name of the Confederate States of America."

Contemptuously Ireland replied, "Military men, even traitors, wear uniforms. Pirates prefer civilian clothing," he concluded as his eyes roved up and down perusing Beall's nonmilitary apparel.

Admiration turned to aggravation. Ireland nervously observed his enemy's thumb drop to the revolver hammer. The tightness in Beall's gun hand indicated patience wore thin. With an irritated voice Beall said, "Your ship is mine, Captain. Your life remains in your hands. If you intend to retain it I suggest you respond with direct answers. For the last time, what is your cargo and to where is it destined?"

Ireland accepted his responsibility to remain alive to provide leadership for his crew. The audacity of these pirates plundering private vessels for their own financial gain under the guise of a sanctioned military force, especially that of a renegade government, galled him to no end but he swallowed his pride. "Mr. Beall," began the schooner's deposed commander purposely omitting John's military rank, "I'm Captain David Ireland of the schooner *Alliance* for these past seven years. When you ravage through my goods you shall find my ship carries a cargo of sutler's stores designated for our brave Union men fighting to the south. After you rummage through the ship's papers, if you can read, you'll discover our port of departure was Philadelphia. Our destination is Port Royal, South Carolina."

"Captain Ireland, I don't believe our good Lord shall provide you and I the years necessary to list the outrages committed against Virginia and the South by your despicable government. Stay clear of the weapons on your desk but take a blanket with you to your new quarters in the aft. We'll speak in the morning.

The balance of the crew, except for those guarding the prisoners, remained above deck while Beall and McGuire ventured below with lanterns to examine the cargo. There eyes gazed across barrels of oysters, smoked fish, hams, sugar, syrup and other edible delicacies. Cases of wine and liquor, obviously intended for officers and bureaucrats, along with crates labeled *Havana Cigars* caught their attention. Wooden boxes containing watches, pens, pencils, papers, and an assortment of clothing not issued by the military also filled the hold. "My word, Johnny, there's got be tens of thousands, maybe hundreds of thousands of dollars of

Yankee goods here, all waiting to be sold in Richmond! Might grow fond of this line of work."

"Ned, help me carry some of this bounty up to the men. They earned it. Food, a cigar for everyone, and dry clothes. Leave the spirits here. That will only come to no good." The men gorged themselves on delicacies many forgot existed. The slackening storm allowed the men to change into new, dry clothes. The aroma of tobacco smoke and the laughter of a happy crew filled the air. John divided the men into groups of three so each man received five or six hours of sleep. John joined the first watch. Before retiring, the men heard a short dissertation similar to that which God gave Adam and Eve relative to the dangers of eating the forbidden fruit. The captain sternly forbade anyone to venture below into the cargo hold upon the threat of severe punishment.

After his three-hour watch John headed toward Ireland's cabin, stopping to awaken Churn and Baker for the next watch. That placed Ned in charge of the final watch as dawn arrived. Beall assumed the choppy seas kept Yankee gunboats docked or in shallow waters. His head no sooner hit the bed than Ned awakened him from a sound sleep. Soft light flowing through the small cabin window indicated John slept for six uninterrupted hours. He stretched and walked up on the deck where the aroma of fresh coffee greeted him. He settled on one of the empty cargo crates littering the deck. The hot brew he sipped warmed him as it sharpened his senses. He suddenly sprang to his feet and shouted for Ned. The two disappeared below into the cargo hold.

"Ned, I don't remember bringing up any coffee, do you?"

His embarrassed second-in-command who already drank several cups winced. "Damn, Johnny, we didn't."

Slapping his comrade's shoulder, Beall consoled his friend. "Almost got by me too." The former farmer scanned the area. Over the years he developed a keen eye for storehouse shortages resulting from the pilfering of irresponsible slaves. He recognized the missing goods which created the void he now observed.

Seething with anger no one witnessed prior to this morning the fuming commander loudly ordered, "All hands on deck, now!" The multitude quickly assembled. Beall stood beside McGuire and ordered the second watch men to line up in front of him by the rail. "Gentlemen, after so generously offering you a sampling of our spoils last evening I find some of you against orders slithered below and absconded with some of our goods. Besides disobeying orders you display the morals of a common field hand. Step forward if you committed the deed so the innocent may not suffer." No one came forward; instead everyone nervously inched back toward the rail.

"Very well. Lieutenant McGuire, search them." Ned's careful examination produced no contraband.

"Be warned gentlemen, besides disobeying my orders, you stole from the rest of us. Discipline will be maintained. Had I discovered contraband with anyone he would have been shot and had his thieving carcass thrown overboard. Dismissed!" Turning to Ned, John requested a conference in Ireland's cabin to plan the day's activities.

After the door closed McGuire asked, "John, did you really intend to shoot those boys?"

A sheepish grin replaced Beall's cold scowl. "Of course not, but do they believe I would?"

"Johnny, I believe you would so they most certainly do. I confess, as I searched them I noticed several dozen cigars floating atop the water below the rail where they stood." Beall's blue eyes glistened. "You devil," Ned laughed. "You ordered them near the rail so they might empty their pockets." John nodded his head affirmatively, confident that henceforth his orders would be followed. The two men turned their attention to their next course of action, cognizant of the need to man their two assault craft and the two captured schooners. They decided to anchor the *Alliance*, leave six trustworthy crewmen to guard her, and venture out with the *Swan* and *Raven* to continue their streak of luck.

Less than twenty-four hours later a Confederate lookout on the *Alliance* shouted in alarm, "Three unidentified ships on the horizon." Rebels quickly congregated below the lookout. Without the presence of either Beall or McGuire, differing opinions digressed into heated arguments. The watchman's voice from above abruptly terminated all debate. "Dang it boys, shut up and listen. The *Swan* and the *Raven* sail along side them. Cap'n Beall got us three more prizes."

Within the hour the *J.J. Houseman*, which they commandeered before noon the previous day, and the *Samuel Pearsall* and the *Alexandria*, both of which they captured after dark, lay anchored along side the *Alliance* and *Mary Anne*. The three Yankee schooners brought the total number of enemy vessels, counting the two small fishing scows, to seven. John and Ned faced the dilemma of selecting the most prudent course of action. They captured more vessels than they could man.

Mel Stratton felt obliged to throw in his two cents worth. "Captain Beall, excluding the cargo, we captured five valuable ships. If we dispose of them for even ten cents on the dollar we shall generate a small fortune to divide."

"With all due respect," John calmly replied to the uninvited speaker, "we have eighteen men, forcing us to depend upon each captured ship's crew to pilot her back to Virginia with only a small guard. We could easily be over powered, and don't think for a moment that men such as Captain Ireland would not jump at the advantage to reclaim his vessel."

"Mr. Beall," continued the irritated crewman, foregoing recognition of John's military title, "we have four guards per vessel."

"Sir, you evidently forget the S*wan* and the *Raven*!" McGuire interjected in an aggravated tone.

"Huh?" mumbled Stratton with an indignant shrug of his shoulders. "Sell just one of the schooners and you'd have enough to buy a dozen of your little rowboats."

"Mr.Stratton, when you signed on you knew our primary function was interruption of Yankee shipping. We accomplished this with my little rowboats, the *Raven* and the *Swan*," Beall angrily retorted. "To navigate these waters we need these craft. Remember sir," Beall admonished, "we operate to defeat the Yankees. Any riches that befall us we gladly take but I jeopardize neither our crew nor our assault craft. Am I understood, sir?"

"Clearly," responded Stratton, who walked away and mumbled something about the inefficiencies of a short-sighted military.

"What shall we do, John?" questioned Ned. "Gut the vessels we don't want and burn them?"

"Ideally yes, but smoke brings unwanted visitors. We'll strip them and set them afloat unmanned. The good Lord may dispose of them as He wishes."

By noon the crew cut loose the *Mary Anne, J.J. Houseman*, *Alexandria*, and *Samuel Pearsall*. Beall brought David Ireland up on the deck of the *Alliance*. "Captain Ireland," John began in a businesslike manner, "you freely conveyed to me your vast experience, particularly in this area along the coast. You and your crew shall now safely lead us through these shoals and islands into the Atlantic toward the Chesapeake." Beall pulled his revolver, pointed it directly at the Yankee sea captain, and calmly added, "If by intention or even if purely by accident you run us aground it shall be my distasteful duty to shoot you where you stand."

John's thumb pulled the hammer back for effect. In Ireland's eyes Beall witnessed the bitter glare reminiscent of surly Negroes, eyes conveying helplessness to resist now but searching for later opportunity to retaliate. The *Alliance* soon glided across calm waters with the sun glistening off the serene, glassy sea. Beall remained within several paces of Ireland but allowed him room to function without hovering over him. Besides guarding the skipper John used the brief thirty mile voyage to glean nautical knowledge from an unsuspecting, experienced mentor. Favorable winds carried the fleet to their familiar stop on Cobb Island where the Rebels encouraged their captives to accept a parole conditional with three days of silence. Since John located an experienced Canadian ship's captain familiar with the Chesapeake Bay he offered Ireland the opportunity to accept a parole also.

Inwardly John respected his foe who gruffly retorted, "In no way shall I accept a parole from a pack of thieves claiming to represent a country that does not exist." With that Ireland walked down the boarding plank to join twelve other prisoners dispersed between the *Raven* and the *Swan*. Beall remained on the *Alliance* with a skeleton crew while McGuire assigned the balance to the two smaller craft. In the Chesapeake Bay off Cherrystone Lighthouse, Beall parted from the *Raven* and the *Swan*. Ned headed for Mathews County to transport the prisoners and conceal the two boats while John planned to navigate far up the Piankatank River to sell the cargo and dispose of the *Alliance* before reuniting with the others in Richmond.

McGuire, Baker, and Stedman took Ireland, his first mate, his purser, and three other prisoners while three Rebels including Edmonds voyaged with seven other prisoners. Unpredictable fall storms reared again that night. The *Raven* and *Swan* survived the treacherous journey only with the ferocious bailing of all aboard. The *Alliance* proved her seaworthiness as she navigated under the guidance of the experienced Canadian pilot. Beall's vessel sighted the Piankatank's mouth a good hour before Ned's crew's safely reached harbor in Cape Horn. A smile crossed Beall's lips as he neared land.

On the eastern horizon smoke appeared. Visible smoke in these waters usually preceded Yankee gunfire. "Get us into the river channel!" Beall shouted to his pilot who navigated toward the river's mouth. Two minutes later John and his crew slammed to the deck. "What the...?" he exclaimed regaining his feet.

In haste to reach the river the Canadian ran the ship aground. He missed the channel by less than twelve feet. No time to waste. The distant black plume rose from a smokestack atop the unidentified vessel. Beall calmly ordered instructions for the cargo's removal. "Rescue the nautical instruments first. Then get items of value that won't be broken or be damaged in the water." In disgust he screamed at one of his men, "Damn it, Eli, leave the cigars. Get the silk cloth and canned goods. Any weapons you find remove. Then …" The roar of gunfire followed by a geyser of sea water fifty yards to the starboard side confirmed the presence of a Yankee gunboat. Sorting of goods below abruptly stopped. The four men below hastily carried merchandise up through the hatch to four others who hurriedly dumped it over the edge into the water. Beall detailed two men and the Canadian skipper to guide the floating boxes and crates to shore. A minute later another shot splashed in the water thirty yards away.

Beall shouted into the hold for two of the men to keep hoisting up goods and also yelled, "Will and James, find the several barrels of oil I saw down there!"

"Johnny," Will screamed, "no way can we lift up those barrels. They weigh a ton!"

"Find them and roll them below the hatch. We're burning the ship. The Yankees have our range. We've got several minutes to fire her and get off." The *U.S.S. Thomas Freeborn* sped to salvage the balance of the cargo. Beall jumped into the hold and ordered everyone but Will off the ship. His hatchet splintered the tops of two fifty gallon oil barrels before he and Will tipped them over. Greasy, clear liquid splashed and flowed across the hold floor. The brothers scampered up the steps to the deck. Will quickly lit two lanterns and handed them to John, who momentarily held the two flickering lamps and glanced into the dark area beneath the hatch. Water from another round sprayed the two brothers.

"My Lord Johnny! That one landed fifteen feet away."

"Compose yourself Will, they're only using solid shot, not explosive shells." He handed Will one of the lamps. "Turn up the wick and throw it down." Each grasped a lantern with both hands and slammed it into the hold. The crashing shatter of glass followed a loud phooph preceding a bright flash of jagged light dancing through the hold. In seconds spiraling smoke billowed from the hatch followed by ravaging flames reaching above for oxygen.

A short time later Beall, his men, and the Canadian stood soaked and shivering on the shore beside the salvaged cargo, warmed only by the sight of offshore flames encompassing the schooner above the waterline. The voyage's immense success faded with the realization that at best ten per cent of their goods reached safety. They turned their attentions to collection of their beached goods. Beall only derived solace from his awareness that the Yankees shared the same empty feeling of loss from failing to salvage the balance of the *Alliance*'s rich cargo.

29 – PENDING DANGER

On the last Friday in September, John reclined on his bed and reread of his recent exploits in the *Richmond Enquirer*.

With less than twenty men in two small boats, and facing the dual threats of stormy seas and Yankee gunboats, the brave band of Confederate patriots in less than a week captured seven Yankee ships. The prize vessel, the schooner the Alliance, brimmed with sutler's goods destined for enemy troops occupying South Carolinian soil. The Alliance carried a cargo valued in excess of $200,000, although a small portion of the goods was destroyed when a Yankee gunboat stumbled upon the schooner after she inconveniently became grounded near the mouth of the Piankatank River. As the Federals struggle to contain John Wood they now contend with the twin threat of the Mosby of the Sea, Captain John Beall.

He didn't need the headlines although he acknowledged publicity increased the men's moral. His contented smile indicated that he reveled being mentioned in the same sentence with John Taylor Wood. He prayed details gleaned from the article in no way aided Yankee agents operating in Richmond. The paper accompanied him to the dining room where he joined Ned. Together the two would plot their next foray into enemy waters. John also remembered that he owed Martha a long overdue letter, especially with departure imminent.

The clatter of dishes, the chatter of voices, and an occasional hearty laugh encouraged by the flow of spirits greeted John when he walked to the table where McGuire awaited him. "Days are getting shorter, Ned. What do we have, maybe two good months before winter does us in?"

"If that John," Ned said before jokingly adding with a facetious smirk, "unless you want to remain in Richmond spending your share of the $200,000 and basking in the fame George pours upon you."

"If we only salvaged half of that, but I guess the $10,000 we netted for a week's work is tolerable. It simplifies attracting recruits. Stratton's replacement found us. Nonetheless our men have had sufficient rest and recreation although I prefer not to hear details of their exploits," John laughed with a twinkle in his eye. "I do believe its time to capture a Yankee gunboat."

John waited patiently for McGuire's forthcoming response. A good natured grin appeared before he replied, "Well Mr. Mosby of the Seas, are we competing with John Wood?"

"You know me better than that, Ned! Capturing a U.S. gunboat with our ragtag band of pirates, as Captain Ireland referred to us, would significantly boost moral. It would emphasize Yankee military ineptness, plus further legitimize us."

Ned broke out with a deep laugh as John realized that he swallowed the bait without hesitation. The two finished a fine cod dinner with boiled potatoes and greens, topped off with fresh apple pie, after which John excused himself. "I have several reports to complete. Good evening, Ned."

"Johnny, before I retire I'll stop by the jail." Ned patted his breast pocket and mischievously added, "I must drop off several of these fine cigars Captain Ireland provided us. He's soon to be paroled and the generous man deserves a show of our appreciation for his benevolence."

John entered his room, sat at his desk, and began writing.

My Dearest Martha,

Words cannot describe the cold void within me that only your warm presence fills. Eighteen months have passed since we promised ourselves to each other. I once read the phrase "time and distance makes the heart grow weaker." That quote could only have come from a cold-blooded Yankee. Every night my final thoughts are of your image. Every morning your love lifts me from my bed so that I might continue the mission of freeing ourselves from the oppressive bondage of the barbaric invaders.

If only you could see the dedication, sacrifice, and commitment of my men, which is characteristic of so many of our brave soldiers, you too would realize our crusade shall only end in victory. I hesitate to share with you specific details of the operations I conduct. We must always be cognizant of the potential for the Yankees intercepting our correspondence. Trust that I experience great success doing all within my power to inflict damage upon our callous foe while with great enthusiasm I continue to serve our country. Yours forever,

With immeasurable love,
John

That same evening one hundred miles to the south a cluster of Union officers met in the parlor of Major General John G. Foster's home. The dwelling set amidst the buildings protected by the massive stone walls forming the pentagon shaped perimeter of Fort Monroe. The forty year old host, a career army engineer who served in the Mexican War, possessed a full head of wavy dark hair complemented with a full beard. Foster witnessed firsthand the beginning of the current war. As a captain he aided Major Robert Anderson in the nighttime evacuation from Fort Moultrie to Fort Sumter, where he remained until the Federal capitulation on April 14, 1861. Late that year the army assigned him to the department encompassing North Carolina and southeastern Virginia.

Another officer in the parlor was cantankerous fifty-one year old Rear Admiral Samuel P. Lee, a distant cousin of the renowned Confederate general. The troublesome peacetime officer killed a passenger on a Mississippi steamboat in one of the two documented duels in which he participated twenty years earlier. His innate aggressiveness served him well in the wartime Navy while now commanding the North Atlantic Blockading Squadron of over sixty vessels.

Brigadier General Isaac J. Wistar, a former attorney, attended per Foster's request. Upon the outbreak of the war he raised a company of men. After Edward Baker's death at the Battle of Ball's Bluff, Wistar advanced to the rank of colonel. His competent leadership led to a promotion of brigadier general, not without some members of the army brass questioning the thirty-six year old's ability to command a brigade.

A forty-eight year old Mexican War veteran and former Indian fighter also attended. Samuel P. Spear rejoined the regular army in 1860 as a private in a Pennsylvania cavalry unit despite being a native of Massachusetts. When hostilities erupted he advanced quickly through the ranks.

Junior and staff officers comprised the remainder of the sixteen men gathered. General Foster ended the small talk by formally requesting Admiral Lee to speak. The fiery Virginian with his face flushed with emotion wasted no time responding. His ruddy complexion accentuated his white sideburns, flowing moustache, and receding hairline.

"Gentlemen, Secretary of the Navy Welles recently contacted me concerning the recent rash of brazen assaults upon our shipping. Washington demands we locate the parties involved and terminate their activities. Until recently we suspected, with the exception of John Wood, only random bands loyal to neither side waylaid our vessels, disposed God only knows how of the crews, and pillaged the ships of valuables before casting them adrift. We recently confirmed one well-organized band of Rebel partisans, referred to by disloyal locals as the Confederate Volunteer Coast Guard, seized five schooners within a week's time. Crew members from the captured ships confirmed that less than twenty men," the naval officer's voice quivered as he paused and emotionally said, "less than twenty damned Rebels in two small boats inflicted the damage. A Captain

Beall leads them. He holds a token Confederate Naval commission only to save his neck from the noose when we capture him, and gentlemen, we shall capture him!" concluded Lee viciously slamming his hand into his fist.

General Foster took the floor. "Gentlemen, I am pleased Admiral Lee and I jointly received orders to support each other to hunt down and destroy this band of traitors. Look here." His gloved finger pointed to the lower right corner of a map where he traced the route upward.

Foster looked to his slender, clean shaven brigadier. "General Wistar, this Sunday evening you shall gather your forces at Yorktown in preparation for departure several hours before daybreak on the 5th. Do not assemble your men until after dark." Foster looked directly at Wistar before he returned his attention to the map covering the white marble table top and added in disgust for all to hear, "Their cursed agents sometimes know our targets before our company officers. Keep the operation's details to yourselves. General, by daybreak you shall reach the York River. By mid morning you shall be across the river and begin your advance to the eastern neck of the peninsula where your troops shall spread out before dark to prevent the Rebel's escape. We understand passable roads lead from Gloucester Court House to your evening destination twenty miles away, though the path traverses forested terrain interrupted by swampland. I emphasize, send experienced scouts ahead to prevent bushwhacking or advance warning to the Rebels. How many effectives do you command, General?"

Wistar nodded to the stocky cavalry officer to his right, looked back to Foster, and answered with precise detail. "Colonel Spear's detachment from the 11th Pennsylvania Cavalry consists of nearly 450 horsemen." Wistar's dark, narrow eyes sparkled as he continued rattling off numbers. "The 1st New York Mounted Rifles under Captain Poor number 50. Colonel Duncan commands over 700 troops with his 4th U.S. Colored Infantry." Wistar, a resident of pro-abolitionist Philadelphia, looked directly at native Virginian Admiral Lee and smugly said, "I must add that these troops perform commendably."

"Continue General Wistar!" Foster barked while glaring at his subordinate. The timely rebuke prevented Lee from making a blistering trademark response. The admiral, not eager to disrupt the planning, bit down on his lip and nodded in appreciation to Foster.

Wistar continued, oblivious to the chasm he nearly created within a mission requiring cohesion between land and naval forces. "One section of Battery E from the 1st Pennsylvania Light Artillery manned by 27 men along with one section of the 8th New York Battery manned by 24 men are commanded by Captain Orwig, greatly complementing our infantry and cavalry."

"Thank you General," said Foster, relieved his subordinate ended without further incident. "Major Stevenson, unable to be with us this evening, commands a flotilla of army gunboats in conjunction with Admiral Lee's naval gunboats. If the rats burrow in Mathews County our navy shall encircle them on the waters while our army prepares a snare on land. Questions?"

One staff officer commented, "Seems like an awful lot of men to catch a couple dozen Rebs."

Foster briskly retorted, "Stanton himself told Secretary Welles to do whatever's necessary to rid us of the vermin. He specifically stated that civilian interference shall be considered guerrilla activity and dealt with accordingly. Those discovered aiding this rabble, if fortunate enough to avoid hanging, shall find their property confiscated or destroyed. We enter a stage in this war where we must realize that taking the fight out of the civilian population becomes as critical as whipping the Rebel military."

"Be aware gentlemen that our forces in Tennessee attained a great deal of success by controlling the waterways with gunboats while working in unison with land forces. Washington shall watch closely with the expectation that we in the east too perform with similar results. Good evening," concluded Foster, "and successful hunting."

The following morning in Richmond, Beall and McGuire completed arrangements for their departure. Ned gathered foodstuffs including salt pork, flour, and molasses while John begged shot, powder, and caps from an army storehouse. Neither relished the task of rounding up the crew. The first men they encountered they detailed to the brothels. Ned and John took upon themselves the unenviable assignment of prying others away from sweethearts or family.

By early afternoon with all present and accounted for, the train pulled away from the station. Ned and John chatted briefly before pulling their hats over their eyes to steal a few more hours of sleep which would become in short supply once they entered the sea. The passenger cars gently rocked them to sleep amidst tales the men swapped of their brief sabbatical in Richmond.

"Shoot me if I ever again sit down to a card game with my prize money," Severn Churn commented to Baker. "I thought our luck on the water would continue in Richmond. Guess I was wrong."

Baker only smiled to his comrade before a voice from the seat behind said, "My gosh Vern, I bought my own luck. Most of my earnings is gone but partook of good food, ample spirits, and three turns with that red-headed Cindy Lu, with her pretty smile, wide green eyes, and big, soft tits. I'm ready for us to have another good run at sea so I can do it all again. If we do really good I just might retire and marry her."

"Bobby," Rankin quipped, "whores don't never give it away, so what makes you think she'd marry you and let you have it for free?" Laughter broke out in the rear of the passenger compartment where the entire crew sprawled in the sparsely populated coach.

Will, facing George Stedman, asked in a serious tone, "Mr. Stedman, I know what the papers say, but how do you think the war's going. Folks talk like loosing Vicksburg ties down a large force of Yankees just to occupy the land they've captured, so despite us losing 10,000 troops, it isn't a totally bad thing." Before the answer he turned his attention to the eastern theater. "I know many a good man who never returned from Gettysburg. Some fellas say the fight's gone out of Lee's army. We're going on three months, right in the middle of prime fighting season, and nary a shot's been fired by the Army of Northern Virginia," concluded the younger Beall, somberly shaking his head.

The former newspaper editor thought it better not to tell Will that Pemberton actually surrendered 30,000 men at Vicksburg. "I don't know much more about the west than do you, my boy," replied Stedman in a mentoring tone. "But my sources in Richmond bestow this simple Bohemian with a great deal of firsthand information. True, General Lee invaded Pennsylvania primarily to draw the Yankees onto a battlefield of his choosing, whip the bluecoats, and waltz into Washington with old Abe a waiting there with peace settlement in hand." Steadman paused to chuckle. "I don't suspect Bobby Lee actually believed it would be quite that simple. Even though the general didn't choose Gettysburg for the fight, he'd still have added George Meade to his collection of Union trophies had our corps commanders not bungled so badly, but you'll never hear that because General Lee takes pride in never casting blame upon his men if things don't proceed as planned. That's one reason his men follow him anywhere." Stedman frowned momentarily and mumbled something about, "if only we had Jackson."

He promptly shook the thought free and continued, "My apologies for deviating. Those close to President Davis believe as I do. Although we failed in our ultimate goal, by just relocating the fighting from Virginia our farmers could plant and harvest crops uninterrupted for one season, a victory in itself. Never forget, William, the longer this war continues, the more Yankee commitment weakens and Southern resolve strengthens. Don't forget either that Lee sent Longstreet west to bring some eastern generalship to that struggling army, which played a key role in the Yankees' humiliating defeat at Chickamauga. Rosecrans reached Chattanooga with his tail between his legs and nearly lost his army. We'd have captured it all had that damn traitor George Thomas, from our very own Virginia, not performed so admirably." Stedman reached across to grasp the shoulder of the young soldier and confidently concluded, "Remember lad, our first war for independence commenced horrifically and lasted eight years. We've only been fighting this one for two years. Freedom from the Yankees is nearer than we suspect. Think of it Will, you'll be in your prime, building your life as we build our nation."

Etter piped up from the other side of the aisle, "Better not take eight years. My oldest boy'ill be a man. My little girl'ill be married. The farm'ill be a weed patch. And the wife'ill forget me."

Sweeny couldn't resist ribbing his companion. "You think just maybe she might be downright happy with the arrangement as it now stands?"

Everyone broke into laughter before Edmondson added, "I keep telling you single fellers all marriage does is complicate a man's life. When you can depart and take your heart with you instead of leaving it behind life is much simpler and more pleasurable."

Partially awakened, John thought to himself, simpler, yes; more pleasurable, no. He slowly nodded off with the pristine image of Martha O'Bryan filling his mind while the train rolled toward the destination where the Rebel band camped for the evening.

They awoke the next morning to the splendor of a beautiful fall day. Autumn's paintbrush highlighted the upper fringes of the taller trees with brilliant yellows and oranges. Today's bright warm sunshine and balmy dry breeze outshined the harsh weather anxiously waiting to appear later in the month to sweep the loveliness from the landscape. The relaxing ferry journey ended in Mathews Courthouse where Mr. Ransom, Mr. Brooks, and Colonel Tabb transported the men six miles to Sands Smith's home.

A sinewy, dark complexioned fifty-five year old man of average height opened the door and trotted down the steps to greet the men with whom he'd become so fond of the past six months. Above his graying beard spread his hospitable smile. On occasion John observed the man's coal-black eyes transform into cold, deadly spheres whenever Yankee atrocities came to light. Today they radiated with the affectionate warmth evident whenever surrounded by his loving daughters. Beall marveled at the physical prowess a man that age possessed. The life of farming, lumbering, and fishing contributed in part to Sands Smith's vitality.

Before greeting the newcomers Smith looked over his shoulder to the young ladies crowding the doorway. "Looks like we'll have a pleasant dinner this evening with plenty of good company. Get to cooking girls."

A chorus of, "yes, Papa," echoed as the women scattered to begin preparations.

The gentlemen who transported the Rebels politely begged off, desiring to return home before nightfall. Beall spoke for his men and also politely declined. "Mr. Smith, no way could we impose upon you this late in the afternoon, especially with food being so difficult to come by."

Sands Smith abruptly cut off the young man. "Nonsense! The least we can do to show our appreciation for your dedication in ridding the area of the blight that plagues our land. Besides," the man winked under furrowed eyebrows, "when you departed after your last foray, a bolt of cloth and a dozen fine cigars mysteriously appeared on the porch. Assorted editable delicacies we seldom enjoyed even before the damn Yankees began all this foolishness appeared inexplicably in our storehouse, which contains sufficient provisions to share I might add. And quit calling me Mr. Smith, you earned the right to call me Sands."

"Yes Mist…, err Sands." John replied and nodded affirmatively. He'd yet to witness the strong-willed man ever failing to get his way.

About the time the glowing orange ball in the blue western sky touched the distant pines across the inlet seventeen hungry men seated themselves on wide benches around two long tables. Their host occupied his familiar seat at the head of the table in a sturdy cane-backed chair with heavy oak arms and legs. He insisted upon like seating to his immediate right for John, who tranquilly scanned the panorama's peaceful setting.

A dozen yards to Sands's left stood a well-maintained, white clapboard two-story dwelling, ventilated by numerous long windows, and accentuated by green shutters. To the right, beyond two large oaks, a spacious lawn rolled to the northern edge of Horn Harbor which led to an inlet draining into the Chesapeake Bay. Smith's girls, each blessed with their father's slender figure, busied themselves with the tasks inherent in feeding a small army. Several stirred the large, steaming black kettle suspended over the crackling fire. An aroma of fish, chicken, potatoes, onions, carrots, and a secretive blend of garden herbs drifted to the hungry men's nostrils. Other sisters distributed tin bowls and wooden spoons. John politely sampled Smith's potent wine but insisted his men receive only the weaker beer in their metal cups. Soon loaves of fresh warm bread and crocks of mouth-watering apple butter arrived while two girls commenced ladling bubbling soup from the large kettle into four well-worn pots.

Mr. Smith motioned his daughters to be seated among the men. All bowed their heads in preparation for the patriarch's blessing. "Dear Lord, bless this abundant food which you mercifully continue to provide us. May it nourish these young men who prepare for another crusade against the infidels who threaten your Christian servants. We beseech you to offer them the protection you provided Moses as he journeyed toward freedom from a heartless pharaoh. Continue to protect the girls' brothers, Zeb and Zach, as they kill Yankees. Remember also my sons-in-law, Elizabeth's, Katherine's, and Mary's men, doing the same. If you find it in your heart to select from this noble band of warriors here tonight a husband for Eve, Ruth, Esther, or Lillian, I'd be most appreciative. Harriet and Julia are a bit young yet. Bless this food to our needs. Amen."

The four older single girls blushed and rolled their eyes at their father for his unsolicited petition. The younger two glared as only adolescent girls could. Soon conversation and laughter erupted around the table.

"Shame you're no longer eligible, Johnny. Eve would make you a fine woman," whispered the proud father with loving radiance emitting from his face. He glanced to Eve, who was thoroughly engrossed in conversation with Ruth. All of Smith's unspoken-for-daughters were prizes in their own right but John recognized Eve possessed an abounding wholesome beauty complementing her caring personality, similar to his Martha's. John's strong bond with Sands allowed him to share his intentions for his Tennessee sweetheart, albeit with a stipulation that the secret be revealed to no one else.

Sands changed the subject, and as was his nature, bluntly asked, "What you planning to do to the Yankees this time, Johnny? Pretty tough to top the last escapade."

John basked in Sands Smith's excitement whenever John shared his plans. Such disclosure further drove the privateer to achieve his objectives. "Word reached us a Federal gunboat occasionally stops in Mojack Bay for supplies. Richmond could surely use the vessel after we utilize it to capture a few more prizes."

Conversation switched to lighter topics the next two hours. Beall finally broke up the gathering. "Time to turn in men. Yankee prizes await us tomorrow." Thirty minutes later contented snoring resounded from blanketed forms spread on the ground near the fire, atop the tables, and sprawled about the house.

John, Will, Ned, Edmondson, and McFarland awoke before daybreak. Illumination from their bright lanterns cast flickering light over the submerged scow and canoe, which they raised and readied for departure. After consuming freshly baked bread and piping hot coffee they bid farewell and rowed east toward the first glistening rays of morning's light. Beall confidently watched the men's oars propel the *Swan* and *Raven* effortlessly across the glassy surface of the inlet. Perhaps wind might soon billow the sails and ease the arduous task of rowing. They glided past fishing yawls whose friendly operators waved. John softly smiled, pleased with the flawless beginning of the beautiful day.

A frown would have displaced his pleasant expression had he realized that to his south, congregated on the far bank of the York River, a Union force of over 1,300 waited to cross, committed to hunting down and exterminating Beall's tiny band.

Brigadier General Wistar gloried in his role of commander of the land expedition. He yearned for a second star on his shoulder straps and the capture of a renowned band of pirates might add that star. Wistar, Spear, and Duncan watched the second transfer of cavalry reach the north bank, with three cavalry crossings remaining. Wistar turned to Duncan who sat atop a dapple gray mount to the general's right. "Colonel, begin forming your regiment. I expected a larger transport, which now necessitates a forced march to reach our assigned position by nightfall." Wistar guided his black stallion several quick steps back and looked to Colonel Samuel Spear. From beneath the colonel's forage cap protruded locks of wavy brown hair, tinged with gray strands which touched his ears. Spear's broad, thick forehead occupied the expanse between his cap and his brown eyebrows. A dark moustache rested upon his upper lip while a graying goatee grew on his chin. The man's muscular physique coupled with his no nonsense façade depicted the demeanor of a man preferring to settle issues with a revolver rather than a debate. Rumors abounded one such argumentative and now deceased sergeant under his command unfortunately confirmed as much.

Although Wistar felt compelled to firmly establish his command position he possessed no burning desire to cross the cavalryman. "Colonel Spear, when you and the remainder of your men reach the other side, wait for Duncan's infantry to ferry across. Then proceed to your destination."

Spear saluted and trotted to await the oncoming boat. Wistar turned his attention to Colonel Duncan. "When you reach the other side, order your troops from the first crossing to form a protective perimeter beyond our landing area. Position the second element beyond the dock. I'll send the artillery units across and follow with the balance of your troops. Captain Poor's mounted rifles cross last to protect our rear." Duncan saluted and rejoined his men.

Almost ninety minutes passed before Wistar crossed with the 4th U.S. Colored Troops. Being a progressive minded northerner, he maintained full confidence in the Negro troops who received additional training and instruction required to transform men of their race into effective soldiers. He gloated at the visions of disdainful expressions exuding from civilian faces whenever Black soldiers marched through their towns and villages.

When the final blue contingent rambled out of sight the local ferry operator shouted for his son. He sent the mop-haired, freckled-faced boy of fourteen on a mission to notify the local populace in Mathews Courthouse. The ferry operator knew partisans used the area as a base to enter the sea.

At the time Wistar impatiently waited to complete the crossing Beall observed two plumes of smoke on the horizon. Fearing the presence of Yankee gunboats, he reversed course much to the disappointment of his men. Along the way they encountered a local fisherman rowing to meet them with word that a large Yankee force of infantry and cavalry, supported with artillery, advanced to form a barrier across the county's narrow neck of land. Beall opted to elude the Union gunboat by escaping into the Chesapeake. Silhouettes of numerous gunboats filling the horizon dashed that plan. He shouted to Ned, "Row to Sands's and hide your boat. We'll rendezvous at the house." Besides developing into a dear friend Ned had grown into a reliable second-in-command who encouraged John to focus beyond the immediate situation at hand.

The band congregated on the very spot that twenty hours earlier served as the site for a casual evening of food and fellowship. With a distraught expression John grasped Smith's hand firmly within his and apologized. "Mis…,

Sands I fear we placed you in extreme peril. If the Yankees discover our boats, or equipment, or realize you harbored us you shall face cruel retribution."

Smith placed his free hand over Beall's and nonchalantly laughed. "You concealed everything. No one in these parts has an inclination to tell the Yankees about you. And on the remote chance they discover the boats, what will they do to a harmless, half-senile old man surrounded by a brood of cackling hens?" The anything but helpless old man sternly ordered, "Now get your legs moving before they discover you and we do have a sure-fire calamity on our hands."

John squeezed the man's hand tightly several seconds longer, released his grip, waved to the girls, motioned his men to move, and trotted to catch them.

"Travel a good fifty yards off the road!" Smith shouted. He turned to witness tears of concern streaming down the cheeks of several of his daughters who had become quite attached to the boys. As Beall evaporated into the vegetation Sands Smith's gut knotted with an uneasy feeling. Eighteen men against an enemy force estimated to number over 1,000? Tough odds, even for these boys. Deep within his soul he feared he would never again see the dear lads facing such insurmountable odds.

30 – TRAGEDY

John motioned Ned to join him. "I don't know what we'll face. Spread out with the *Raven's* crew while I travel on the other side of the road with my men. We'll meet at Tom Smith's and march together to Colonel Tabb's. God's speed. See you within the hour."

Beall arrived first. While his men stayed in the brush at the edge of Tabb's property he moved cautiously from shadow to shadow toward the house. Livestock grazed calmly in the nearby pasture, oblivious to the human drama playing upon Mathews County's stage. Smith happened to step outside when Beall reached the back porch.

"Johnny, get in here. Yankee cavalry and foot soldiers are everywhere. They posted guards at the end of the lane by our gatepost." In the spacious dining room John peered around the heavy, green, faded drapes. No sign of Yankees.

"How'd you leave Sands?"

Beall apprehensively shook his head. "I sunk my boats on his property and hid our gear nearby. I fear I placed your brother in jeopardy."

"Nonsense! That old coot, though feisty at times, is cautious. Behaves tolerably around the Yankees, especially with the girls there. Won't offer them cake and lemonade but won't pick a fight either. You've observed him turning on the charm. You're the one for whom we're concerned. Bring all your men with you?"

"Eight, Ned's bringing the rest." John paused with the sound of footsteps gliding down the stairway followed by the entrance of Tom's twenty year old daughter Lizzie.

"Johnny Beall, delighted to see you again," she said as she ran over and gave him more than a sisterly hug. The well-portioned woman with wavy brown curls bouncing on her shoulders secretly hoped he might become more than just a cherished acquaintance. John yearned to inform Tom and his daughter of Martha but the proper setting never presented itself. As always, Lizzie bubbled with her efflorescent personality. The scourge of the Chesapeake Bay plainly lacked the courage to speak of his engagement with Martha, and this certainly was not the time.

"How many for dinner, Papa?"

Before Tom answered John interrupted. "We have the full crew but must regretfully decline, especially with the enemy camped at your gate."

With blue eyes twinkling and a wide grin spreading across her face Lizzie playfully replied, "Well gosh almighty, Mr. Beall, I really hadn't planned to invite the Yankees too."

Tom interjected, "And you really shouldn't venture further until after dark. Call your boys in. Place one on guard duty if you deem necessary."

On the back porch John touched several fingers from one hand to his lips while he waved his men in with the other. A smile of relief crossed his face when Ned stepped from the brush also.

Once inside John informed them, "Miss Lizzie kindly requests our presence for dinner, which as true southern gentlemen we cannot refuse. I'll conceal a guard by the lane and also need a volunteer to reconnoiter our route to Colonel Tabb's."

Edmondson eagerly stepped forward for the recon duty. After a minute's instruction he trotted out the door and vanished into the vegetation. An obscured Rebel guard crouched near the lane. John settled in the dining room with the remainder of his men, with the exception of the wide-eyed few chosen by the attractive hostess to help prepare dinner. Will, never zealous to hone his culinary skills either at home or in camp, managed to wrangle his way into the kitchen. John chuckled, wondering if Lizzie failed to snare one Beall that she might settle for the other.

Darkness enveloped the landscape when Tom Smith bowed his head. His prayer concluded with, "And bless this food as it nourishes the bodies of these young men facing a foe who desires to smite your Christian servants seeking to reestablish the God-fearing country you guided into creation eighty years ago. Amen."

Plates filled with sweet potatoes and ham. Cups of cider quenched thirsts. Small baskets filled with ripe, red apples beckoned from the center of the table. Periodically gentle laughter erupted, but without the spirited joyousness of the meal twenty-four hours earlier. Tonight a more serious tone hovered over the gathering. During the casual conversation John noticed Baker seemed unusually quiet.

Looking across the table he asked, "Billy, you alright? You don't act well?"

Baker softly whispered, "With all due respect Captain, there's a squad of Yanks five minutes up the lane and God only knows how many more scour the countryside for us. Shouldn't we be leaving?"

Baker's futile attempt at subtleness instead drew the attention of his comrades.

Fitzgerald jested, "Billy, relax, there's only a thousand of 'em. The way we fight, and the way they fight, should provide a fairly even match. And when it's even you know we always whip 'em."

Hearty laughter from all but Baker broke the tension. John endeavored to put the lad at ease. "Billy, we can whip the whole Yankee army, and navy if necessary, but we won't face those odds. That's why Edmondson's out scouting." He paused, wondering as to the whereabouts of the scout now absent three hours. "We'll get through this. Trust me, lad."

Forty-five minutes later Beall apprehensively looked over to Ned whose uneasy eyes met John's. Both harbored feelings of concern for their missing scout. John prepared to leave without him when Edmondson walked in the back door with the sentry. His dirty rumpled clothing gave pretense of a tall tale about to unfold.

"Where have you been?" grilled Beall, in a manner not unlike a father interrogating a young suitor belatedly returning from an evening buggy ride with the man's daughter.

"Captain!" exclaimed Edmondson, plopping down in a chair. He poured a tall, cool glass of cider and dramatically recounted his adventure with a performance rivaling that of the most accomplished orator. "There was Yanks all over. Hundreds, maybe thousands, mostly on foot, though I observed some mounted too. Anyhow, I finally get near Colonel Tabb's. Moved cautiously because I didn't want to bring the whole damn Yankee army to his doorstep." Edmondson paused, looked to Miss Lizzie and bowed his head momentarily in a show of repentance before he said, "I apologize for the use of vulgar language." Realizing he had the undivided attention of a score of attentive listeners he added, "I'll try to refrain from saying 'Yankee' again."

While his peers, Lizzie, and Tom roared with laughter, Beall impatiently awaited relevant information. Abruptly and without a trace of humor he ordered, "Continue."

"As I was saying, Yank..., I mean enemy troops swarmed all around. I crawled to a boat near the bank and dove inside just afore a dozen of the meanest looking Federals you ever seen marched past. I covered myself with my coat, hoping to conceal myself if one of 'em per chance looked into the craft. They must have marched back and forth for an hour, sometimes in pairs, sometimes by the dozen, once maybe even a company of a hundred of 'em."

Later Edmondson confessed to his comrades he actually fell asleep for an hour and when he awoke the enemy had disappeared. When he darted from the boat to begin his return he unfortunately left his coat behind. His rendition continued, "Following the direction of the road but staying at least fifty yards off, I began my perilous journey back. On this side of Tabb's a line of infantry with cannon blocks the road. And pickets spread adjacent to the road every couple hundred feet or so. I hugged the ground while swinging wide around their lines. Until we cross that first line, sir, we should be able to travel on the road, though cautiously I might add. I suspect another line waits beyond Tabb's, as I heard voices and saw clusters of men up the road. Captain, I know if we move now we'll get through before daylight," Edmondson concluded with an air of confidence much to his leader's approval,

John stood and squeezed his scout's shoulder several times before laying out instructions. He looked to the end of the table where the scrawny McFarland sat, with long greasy hair hanging to his shoulders and moustache ends drooping to his boney chin. "Tom, were those tales you spun about traveling unscathed through Indian country fact or fiction?"

McFarland smiled but quickly dropped his head as if deeply offended by Beall's challenge to his credibility. The good natured Irishman lifted his head to reply, "My dear Captain, only words as pure as the new fallen snow ever flow from these lips. Thomas McFarland's spent many an anxious night crossing hostile Indian territory. Creek, Chickasaw, Choctaw, and even Comanch." Holding up his stringy locks he added, "And still have my hair. I'd rather face ten Yankees any day than one of those red devils."

Beall's men thanked the Smiths, and cautiously commenced their treacherous journey. They wove single file along the road, with McFarland, Beall, and Edmondson in the lead while McGuire brought up the rear. Although John admired the crew's confidence he feared they underestimated their foe. Only he and Will had faced fire from organized Federal forces. He carried the reminder in his chest while Will retained a scar on his thigh. An ominous premonition that he would fail to lead all his men to safety gnawed from within.

McFarland's hand shot up to signal a halt when the procession neared the first Yankee line. Following their pathfinder the column slithered around enemy pickets. Gaps in the slow moving clouds intermittently revealed the moon. The sporadic light both guided and exposed them. Near Tabb's the clouds separated, forcing the Southerners to dive into a deep ditch to avoid detection. Blue soldiers marched along the thoroughfare perilously close to the men hugging the side of the trench only yards away. The Rebels heard little talking from the exhausted, sleep-deprived troops marching past. Their lack of alertness significantly benefited the secluded Southerners.

After the third large U.S. contingent passed Edmondson requested, “Captain, just yonder beyond the wood lot sets the boat where I left my coat. Seeings how it seems we’ll hold up here a spell, how about if I scamper over and get it?”

“And jeopardize the seventeen of us left here?”

“Captain,” began the soldier, whining as a child commencing to wear down a fatigued parent.

Beall held up his hand, shrugged his shoulders, and emphasized, “Go carefully; return quickly.” As Edmondson moved down the trench Beall whispered, “If you’re captured I’ll hang you myself when I get hold of you.”

The cocky Marylander returned fifteen minutes later wearing his newly recovered coat. With no more enemy soldiers in sight the procession crawled from the ditch. McFarland skillfully led them around the second line beyond Tabb’s. The wiry scout whispered, “Damn, Captain, they must have the whole Union Army hunting us down. Hope this is the last line.”

Beall waved him on hoping there would be no more obstacles. To everyone’s relief shortly before sunrise they wove around the third and final enemy line. Slits of mid morning sunlight sliced through the dense pine forest when they reached their refuge within the Dragon Swamp. Exhausted men scrambled to claim precious patches of dry ground. John watched the land grab unfold but advised that a two man watch would be detailed to guard the perimeter.

“Captain,” complained Thomas, “the whole dang Union army’s behind us. Why do we need sentinels?”

“Not all of their army, Thomas, maybe only half,” Beall curtly responded. “Besides I’m more troubled by their cavalry. There’ve been reports of several hundred horsemen roaming about. On this soft ground they’ll be upon us before we know it. Will and I shall assume first watch. Ned, you and Annan relieve us. Assign a pair to replace you. We'll rotate every two hours. Sixteen men stretched over the ground for much needed sleep while the Bealls assumed their positions.

Will yawned and mumbled something about, "The privileges accompanying those knowing men in high places."

Four miles away a squadron of cavalrymen from the large force that filled Beall with uneasiness cantered up to a two-story white house with green shutters. Outside the door a young lady swayed back and forth in a rocking chair while mending a shirt. A short lieutenant, with a nasty scar above his eyebrows, ordered four men to search the grounds while he and his corporal remained. He looked from high atop his horse and squirted a stream of tobacco juice to the ground. Drips of the brown liquid dribbled down the three days growth of stubble on his chin. He spoke in the condescending tone an overseer imparts to a field hand. "Girl, any men folks here about, or for that matter any more pretty young dishes such as you inside?"

The stout corporal chuckled and said, "Herman, you certainly has a way with the ladies, specially the secesh persuasion."

The woman looked up and then continued sewing. Prodded by the corporal's remark the lieutenant snarled, "Cat got your tongue missy?" He indignantly ordered, "You answer when an officer of the United States Army questions you."

The front door flew open. Controlled anger simmered within the coal black eyes of the lean man who briskly leaped over the several stairs to the ground. He stared fiercely into the eyes of the mounted officer towering above him. "When you're on my property you will speak with respect to my daughter."

The door creaked. Four more girls crowded the home's entryway. Three others peered through the window.

The lieutenant's eyes roved rapidly past the ladies and then returned to lecherously focus again upon each one. When he finished gawking he said, "Girls lucky they don't take after you, Mister…?"

"Smith, Sanders Smith."

"As I assumed. Rumor has it you're the feller running the bordello for Rebel partisans. You got yourself a nice harem here, Smith," chided the lieutenant. His amused corporal slapped his thigh in response to the crude humor. The anger simmering within Sands Smith transformed into a boiling rage as he raced into the house.

"Don't you turn away from me, old man," screamed the irate lieutenant before he taunted, "unless you're bringing one of your whores for me. I prefer red-haired wenches if you please."

The corporal mockingly added with a licentious sneer, "As long as the bitch is tight and white I don't care what color her head be."

"Papa!" gasped Eve, jumping from her rocker the instant her father emerged from the house.

The insults exorcised all self-control from Sands Smith. His rage spewed forth in unstrained fury when lightening thundered from one barrel of his 10-gauge shotgun with a deadly, deafening roar. The instant the gun's muzzle hurled the heavy buckshot, shreds of crimson flesh flew from the lieutenant's neck while holes tore into his dark blue blouse spattering a bloody mist over the uniform's yellow trim. His upper torso jerked back. His horse reared and toppled the slain rider to the ground. The terror stricken corporal froze as Smith advanced. A sudden adrenalin rush revived the trooper. He instinctively shielded himself from the wrath of his assailant by cowering behind his horse's neck. Smith threw down his shotgun, grasped the bridle with one hand, reached up with the other, and heaved the struggling rider to the ground. Smith slapped the horse's flank to send the stead galloping away. The ashen-faced soldier fumbled with the flap covering his revolver. Smith retrieved his shotgun. His thumb drew back the hammer behind the other barrel when a cavalry saber ripped painfully into his left shoulder. An instant later another blade tore into his right forearm before a stunning blow from a rifle butt crashed into his skull. Dazed and staggering, he dropped his weapon and slumped to his knees. Two troopers dismounted and pounced on the groggy man.

Only Sergeant Elwood Hazard's shrill command prevented a savage beating. "Away from him now! Schmidt, pick up his weapon." The sergeant's eyes carried past the corporal sitting on the ground. He stared at his martyred commander, motionlessly prone on his back, with his left cheek resting in a gooey pool of crimson mud. The corpse's right eye stared motionlessly at the empty kepi resting several inches from his face. Long, blonde strands of hair absorbed blood from the widening puddle. A partially chawed plug of tobacco protruded between his teeth.

The sergeant returned his gaze to the shaken corporal. "Newman, what the hell happened?"

The girls rushed to tend to their father while the distraught corporal stood erectly, dusted himself, and remorsefully commenced with his rendition of events. "The lieutenant and I rode peaceably up to the house to question the civilians while you and the other men searched the grounds." He pointed to Eve as she cleaned her father's wounds, unaware of the blood soaking into her dress sleeves and congealing in her hair. "We politely asked that one if any men folk were inside or on the grounds. That bastard, excuse my language ladies." The trooper paused and patronizingly tipped his cap. "That citizen came a storming out of the house spoiling for a fight."

"Liar!" screamed Julia, now kneeling beside her father. "You know..."

Hazard sharply cut her off and glared at the Smiths, "If any of you or the old man interrupt us again we'll confine you ladies inside and lock the murderer in the barn. Continue Corporal."

Staring arrogantly towards Smith and his daughters, Corporal Sidney Newman continued, confident his account would be recorded as the official version. "Lieutenant, God rest his soul, told the man we was only doing our duty and asked if he knew of any Rebel partisans in the vicinity. He flew into a tirade, ran into the house, and came out with both hammers cocked, fingers on the trigger, told us to get the hell off his property, and called us names I wouldn't use in the presence of respectable women, especially if they was my daughters. The lieutenant of course showed concern for the safety of the ladies and hoped to avoid violence, God rest his soul." Julia's eyes rolled with the repetition of the overused phrase. The lieutenant calmly asked Mr. Smith to lay down his weapon so we could complete our mission peacefully. Peacefully. That word just crossed his lips when the cowardly bushwhacker coldly pulled the trigger, with a smirk on his face I might add. I charged the culprit but my horse stumbled throwing me to the ground. He was preparing to send me to kingdom come when you boys arrived just in the nick of time. I guess that's it." As he concluded with a sympathetic glance toward his fallen comrade, Corporal Newman wondered if the sergeant would now be promoted to lieutenant and he would become Sergeant Newman

A chorus of accusations flowed vehemently from the outraged women. Sands Smith glared proudly, consigned to whatever fate his actions precipitated. In grand Southern tradition he chivalrously defended his family's honor from the ruthless invaders. The dead Yankee spread across the ground served as his vindication.

Sergeant Hazard ordered, "Private, escort the ladies inside, regretfully by force if necessary, while we prepare the bushwhacker for transport."

"Where you taking him?" demanded Eve, hesitating at the stairs. A fair-skinned private, with the two month's growth of hair barely visible on his upper lip, grabbed her at the elbow and futilely endeavored to herd her inside. Twisting free, she again insisted, "Sergeant, what are doing with him?"

"A Federal officer has been murdered in cold blood by a civilian. We'll give your father a fair trial and act in accordance with our verdict." Looking at another dismounted trooper to his right the sergeant ordered, "Private Gerard, assist Private Weems in escorting Miss Smith inside." Eve again shook free of Weems, pivoted to climb up the stairs, and sauntered over the threshold into the house.

Newman rambled toward the prisoner in an open buggy pulled by a black gilding with white splotches. Two privates roughly forced Sands Smith onto the rear of the vehicle. They bound his ankles to the front seat support after which they tied his wrists together with a long strand of course, thick rope before wrapping it through the bottom of the rear luggage rack. Secured near Smith lay the lifeless form of the charlatan who sparked the lethal chain of events. Smith's daughters' final opportunity to bid their beloved father an eternal farewell faded when the buggy rattled down the lane. Julia screamed from the door, begging for just one precious moment with him.

Hazard motioned the entourage forward and vindictively shouted, "He'll receive the same opportunity to bid his family farewell that he gave our lieutenant." Smith's daughters painfully watched the cavalrymen and the buggy, with a pair of riderless horses trailing behind, vanish from sight. The remaining guards mounted and galloped to join the procession.

The subdued prisoner assumed the humiliating kneeling position the entire three mile journey. He endured leg cramps. He suffered sharp pain whenever the wheels hit ruts and slammed his knees against the hard wooden floor. Several times his head cracked against the storage bench when the carriage lurched high and crashed down upon hitting a large pothole. Newman looked back and cynically consoled his prisoner, "Cheer up Reb, soon you'll be feeling no pain just like your companion aside you."

Outside the Smith home Lillian admonished Eve to immediately wash her blood stained dress, if not dispose of it. Eve emphatically replied, "This dress remains with me until every murdering Yankees is driven from our land. Until the day we vanquish our foe and the entire civilized world recognizes us, this dress, soaked with the blood of my father which today spilled upon sacred Virginia soil, shall remind all who falter of the brutality of the barbarians sworn to destroy us. The day freedom arrives I shall purge the blood from this dress and wear it proudly. This cloth shall remain forever with our family, a dear symbol of the cost of freedom."

The entourage arrived at Federal headquarters and halted directly in front of General Wistar's headquarters tent amid gathering curious onlookers. A staff officer exited the tent to investigate the commotion. He spun, lowered his head, opened the flap, and communicated to his superior a summarization of the events. Five minutes later Brigadier General Isaac Wister, immaculately dressed, preceded his staff officer outside.

"What shall we do with the prisoner, General?" questioned Corporal Newman, ignorantly bypassing the chain of command.

"Hang him after we provide him a just trial." Wistar requested three chairs be carried from the tent. He occupied the center seat, ordered his staff captain to sit to his right, and motioned for Sergeant Hazard to sit to his left. The general looked to several dismounted cavalrymen. "Place the remains of our murdered comrade over there." Two privates gently lifted the slain officer from the buggy, carried him five paces, and delicately laid him on a soft, green bed of clover. Weems drew one of the corpse's arms tightly against its side while positioning a forearm and hand over its belt. The private respectfully placed the officer's forage cap over his face. The ugly coagulated hole in the neck continued glaring from the white lifeless skin. Corporal Newman started to untie Smith from the buggy when Wistar bluntly ordered, "Leave him as he is. His penitent posture seems appropriate. Corporal, I understand you are our only witness. Proceed."

In several minutes Newman recounted his earlier testimony.

"Guilty as charged," Wistar unemotionally declared, leaning back in a highly relaxed posture. In an afterthought, as he headed for his tent, he ordered, "Hang the bush-whacker."

"When sir?" queried a staff officer rapidly scribbling notes.

"Its four hours until sundown. Swift punishment is just punishment. Captain, as my witness accompany the lieutenant's squad. Execute him fifty yards from the camp entrance on the road leading into Mathew's Courthouse. Leave him dangling for these traitors to witness the repercussions for defying the United States government."

"We gonna stand him in the buggy and slap the team away?" asked Private Gerard when they arrived at the execution site.

Oblivious to the chain of command Newman smiled. "That's too easy." In frustration Sergeant Hazard looked on, realizing the privates had become mesmerized by the vindictive corporal. Newman untied the prisoner's feet, loosened the rope wound around the luggage rack, and escorted Smith directly below a sturdy maple branch fifteen feet above the ground. Instead of tying the man's hands behind his back, Newman simply grasped the excess rope dangling from the victim's wrists, pulled it taunt down near the feet, and wrapped it securely around only one ankle. Smith stood erectly and defiantly stared at Newman while the corporal formed a simple noose with the coil of rope sent from headquarters. On the second toss the loop dropped from the limb, dangling in front of the condemned. When Newman tightened the noose around Smith's neck the fiery Southerner bravely snarled, "Vengeance is mine sayeth the Lord."

The crude corporal responded by spitting a mouthful of foul smelling saliva into Smith's face before he yelled for two men to join him in the "heave-ho." He sadistically smiled in anticipation of swinging legs and a twisting torso, flailing to survive a few extra scant seconds.

When Sands Smith's feet left the ground his weight constricted the rope tightly around his windpipe. His hoarse cough digressed into ghastly choking. The Yankees drew his body and soul upward while his fleeting thoughts floated to the cloudy recollection of the insults hurled at his innocent daughters. He ordered his body to freeze. These barbarians would not rejoice with humiliating entertainment from the spectacle of his death. Newman enjoyed only subdued guttural sounds emanating from the prisoner. Within minutes the chest expanded one last time prior to the final retraction.

The lifeless body hung motionlessly below the heavens. The frustrated corporal fired a round into the lifeless form. For the next hour shots echoed whenever the swaying of the body ceased. In the morning troops and citizens alike passed the bullet-riddled body.

31 – THE CREW DWINDLES

The late afternoon sun beamed through a gap in the tree's canopy where a mammoth pine once proudly stood. The tree now lay on the forest floor, decaying and returning to the earth from whence it came. The tranquil light from above offered rays of hope. Only the occasional slap of a sentinel's hand followed by a muffled oath broke the camp's silence. Sweeney and Etter envied their sleeping comrades, completely shrouded with blankets for protection from the obnoxious insects. Etter pulled his timepiece from his vest pocket. Fifteen minutes until his watch ended. He looked across to Sweeney, held up an open hand, and thrice formed a clenched fist. The guard's growling stomach reminded him that his hadn't been filled since last evening. Beall requested to be awakened after the fourth watch. Sweeney hoped this deeply inside the wilderness Beall would allow cooking fires but acknowledged that the captain preferred caution to comfort. Within half an hour an active camp sprang to life as the dormant embryos shed blankets and sprouted to life. Their leader informed the men their leftover meal consisting of ham and sweet potatoes would be washed down without hot coffee. Campfire smoke would assuredly draw the enemy's attention. Hungry men craving food of any sort ambled about camp. The mild dry air compensated for the lack of the warming fires.

John and Ned conferred apart from the main body when the newly assigned picket Rankin shouted, "Strangers in the forest." A handful of men reached for their weapons and raced for protection behind stout pines. Others flattened themselves on the ground and loaded muskets. With revolvers in hand the Rebel leaders dove into the brush.

"I'll investigate, Ned. If we face a small force, I'll lead the attack. If it's too large you direct the withdrawal."

"Johnny, what if the visitor's a friend?"

"We'll meet in the middle and praise the Lord," he replied before zigzagging towards the impending danger, winding his way to Rankin who concealed himself by the fallen evergreen. A single image emerging from the dense forest walked innocently toward them.

Beall jumped from cover. "Silas Greene! What are doing sneaking about besides almost getting yourself shot?"

The lad's eyes widened as eighteen marksmen stood and dropped the sights of their weapons away from him. Everyone knew the fourteen year old orphan who frequently stayed with Thomas Smith. Greene's pa tragically died while serving in Lee's army fourteen months ago when a runaway team pulling a heavy wagon trampled a trio of unsuspecting soldiers. Corporal Greene died immediately. Another companion passed on the following day while a third man returned to duty a week after the accident. The fortunes of war. The lad's mother collapsed with the dire news, deteriorated for six weeks, and finally joined her husband, leaving Silas without family.

The round-faced teenager's engaging smile was ominously absent today. He removed his weathered gray slouch hat, subconsciously crumpled it in his large hands, and blurted out, "Captain Beall, sir, they hung Mr. Smith!"

"The Yankees? Tom Smith. Why?"

Tears uncontrollably rolled down the boy's face. The crew gathered closer to decipher short, choppy sentences spewed between emotional sobs. "No sir, Mr. Sands, Mr. Sands Smith. They come this morning. He kilt one with his ten gauge. About to do another in when the rest of the Yankee cavalry cut him with sabers. Hog-tied him and hauled him away in his own wagon. Hung him outside their camp on the road to town. Heard they used him for target practice." He shook convulsively and screamed, "Why Captain, why? Such a good man, and his poor daughters." Several men stepped forward to comfort the lad so overwhelmed with grief that he could no longer speak.

A sharp crack splintered the silence. Startled men instinctively tightened the grips on their weapons until they realized the source. Irrepressible rage claimed the soul of John Yates Beall. The unnerving sound resonated from an eight foot oak limb he'd grasped and broke across a nearby tree trunk. Several more vicious swings and the piece again snapped in half. John continued slamming the club against the trunk until Will grabbed his brother's shoulders from behind, took the chunk of wood, and tossed it on the ground. The two distanced themselves from the group.

Tears streamed down John's cheeks as he repeated, "My fault, all my fault. God forgive me for leaving the boats there." He stared at his throbbing, reddened palms and swore for all to hear, "I'll strangle every one of the cowardly sons of bitches when I get my hands on them." Both hands clenched into tight, threatening fists.

Embarrassment replaced aggressive emotion. He'd showed vulnerability to his men and his brother, none of whom had ever witnessed such weakness. He'd cast off the mantle of leadership with his disturbing outburst when his men most sorely needed his leadership. In his tirade he'd uncovered the naked persona of his tightly wrapped inner being. He'd allowed them a glimpse into another feature of his character. He never comprehended that instead of eroding his crew's respect he solidified their desire to courageously follow him.

Ned allowed the Bealls five minutes together before joining them. He repeated the remainder of the lad's account. The slain lieutenant vulgarly insulted Smith's daughters until the Yankee forced Sands to defend their honor. A corporal blatantly lied. Silas told how amid jeers and laughter the Yankees heartlessly carted Smith away for execution without a minute's interlude to bid his daughters a final farewell. John's guilt lessened when Ned informed him the *Raven* and *Swan* remained submerged off Smith's beach. No detection of his boats precipitated the ruthless act.

After he composed himself Beall called his men together. "Gentlemen, I apologize for my unacceptable outburst. We did not ask for this war the Yankees thrust upon us, but as soldiers in the Confederacy we willing accept the danger we face as we perform our duty. We reluctantly acknowledge the deaths of our comrades in arms, such as James Philips, but know that we must move forward. I ask that as we mourn the atrocious murder of our dear friend, Sands Smith, who freely welcomed, fed, and sheltered us at every opportunity, and that we keep the memory of the loving father and his grieving daughters burned into our souls as we fight for freedom. I beseech each of us to recommit ourselves to the unfinished task remaining before us. One final comment. We are civilized Virginians and Marylanders, not ill-bred Yankees. Henceforth, as your commander, I shall conduct myself as such, and I also expect such from each of you. Tomorrow morning Lieutenant McGuire and I shall inform you of our upcoming plans." John looked directly into the devoted eyes of seventeen riled Rebels envisioning the havoc about to descend upon their cruel enemy. They unwound together while sharing their evening meal. The tranquility would have transformed into apprehension had John foreseen the tragic shrinking of his circle of followers before their return to Richmond.

The next day Ned and John agreed it best for everyone to remain close to camp. Silas had brought sufficient provisions to feed the men another day. After Beall reluctantly sent the lad back with instructions to travel cautiously, he dispatched several men to reconnoiter a half mile radius of the camp. Early the following day they scouted a radius extending a full mile. It seemed prudent to send Ned and two others farther out to determine the exact location of the Yankees and to also replenish their sparse food supply. The trio reached the road barely a mile beyond camp when the vibrating earth and the thundering sound of galloping horses forced McGuire to dive into thick vegetation behind his companions. He almost flattened himself when he heard a Union cavalryman scream, "There goes one, over there in the brush."

A sprint to flee from a dozen horsemen would be foolish. The men hugged the ground praying for divine intervention. Seconds later the Rebels heard the sickening command to stand with hands raised or be trampled and shot. A mounted officer towering above them with a raised revolver, accompanied by a detachment of soldiers itching to discharge their carbines, convinced Ned surrender to be their only hope. All three slowly stood with hands raised.

"You Beall's men, or maybe one of you is the pirate himself?"

"Just three men making our way to the coast to sign on as shipmates," answered Ned.

"That's a shame," replied the lieutenant, causing a puzzled expression to appear across the prisoners' faces. Sensing their confusion he continued, "If you're military men we take you prisoner. Shucks, you'd get paroled in a matter of weeks. You'd be commingling with your slave wenches by Christmas. I know a secesh spy when I see one. Since you're not military we'll just have to visit the official hanging tree we christened two days back." Looking over to his sergeant he asked, "Porterfield, you think that limb will hold three kicking Rebs about to piss their pants?"

The scrawny horseman glanced at the captives, shook his head sympathetically, shrugged his shoulders, and looked back to his superior. "If the limb breaks after they're hoisted up, and if the fall don't kill'em, we'll keep a heavin' them up on a new branches until they gasp their last," he answered displaying a malicious grin while staring at the youngest captive.

Rankin's knees weakened. Acid crept into his throat. He suddenly screeched, "Lieutenant, sir, we're all Confederate sailors."

"That's good son," replied the Union commander compassionately. "Where is the remainder of your comrades?"

Ned quickly interceded. "They left yesterday for Richmond to report to our government the cold-blooded murder of the civilian Smith two days ago. Richmond will respond with appropriate retribution. Three of us remained in the vicinity to garner more facts before we depart."

"Well, boy," continued the officer with a condescending grin, "for simple laborers out of work you're very familiar with the Rebels' whereabouts." He smiled cynically, smirked at Rankin, and looked to his sergeant. "Porterfield, do you think our astute laborers turned Rebel know what happens to enemy soldiers out of uniform participating in guerrilla activities?"

The sergeant grasped his throat with both hands, forced out a grizzly choking sound, and winced.

"You lying Yank," Rankin screamed. "You got no right, you said…"

"Shut up you miserable piece of white trash. The day you became a traitor you surrendered your rights. Our murdered lieutenant never saw it coming when your people bushwhacked him. Least you'll have the walk back to camp to make your peace with your maker before we send you to the devil. Even when you watch our boys throw the rope over the tree you'll have a minute. Hell, when they secure the noose around your filthy neck you'll have more time than our man had." Vomit splattered from Rankin's mouth. The lieutenant turned to his men and laughed. "This is a valid example of the ferocious foe we face once we drag him from his den into the open."

The captors bound the prisoners' wrists and tied them to a ten-foot lead rope looped around saddle pummels. They would either run behind the horses in the choking dust for two miles or be dragged the distance.

Beall impatiently opened his pocket watch for the fourth time in fifty minutes. Half past four already. If anything McGuire consistently demonstrated the uncanny talent of returning to camp within an hour of his estimated time. At the latest he said one o'clock. Two hours until dark. Maybe night would provide cover for his return. He longed to search for his missing comrade. He only shared a tighter relationship with his brother Will. He feared Ned encountered the blue hoards roaming about the countryside. If the enemy captured McGuire, Beall acknowledged any attempt to extricate him from a heavily manned Yankee garrison would be foolhardy. Instead he comforted himself envisioning Ned concealed within a stone's throw of unsuspecting Union soldiers. Smiling, he remembered McGuire's ability to masterfully spin a yarn. The tales that will grow from this incident. Darkness gradually encapsulated the camp. John bedded down for a restless, unsettling sleep. Eagerness for and yet dread of daylight intertwined his two contradictory emotions throughout the night. Mid morning arrived and still no sign of Ned or word of his demise.

John spoke with Edmondson who served as surrogate second in command. "We need to withdraw to Richmond this evening even if Ned doesn't reappear. If he's captured the Yankees are closing in; if he's only delayed he'll find his way to Richmond." They bided their time, waiting for the slow-moving day to bring darkness to cover their departure. In late afternoon Silas Greene appeared from the shadows.

"Damn boy," admonished the sentry, "you got a death wish?"

"No sir," replied the jovial lad whose pleasant personality returned. "Just wanted to determine how quiet a scout I could be." Looking at the picket he chuckled. "Pretty damn good, aren't I?"

Laughter erupted from the good-natured crowd gathered around.

"Not good enough to cuss like that," reprimanded Beall. When the adolescent turned red with embarrassment John realized the harshness of his rebuke. He placed his hand on the lad's shoulder and smiled. "We are indebted to you for passing through enemy lines to bring us provisions."

Uplifted by the compliment, Silas reported, "Yanks left today, the whole filthy, plundering pack of 'em. Wanted to visit yesterday but Mr. Tom wouldn't allow it with so many Federals still about. I debated the issue but the hardheaded old man refused to listen."

A grin spread across young Greene's face when John softly said, "Whether you know it or not that hardheaded old man cares deeply for you. Any word about Ned?"

"Mr. McGuire, no. What happened?"

"He left camp yesterday and hasn't returned." John delicately asked, "No word of prisoners or executions?"

"No sir." A melancholy demeanor replaced the lad's jovial manner.

John encouraged Silas with a slap on the back and some hollow reassurance. "No news is good news." Within the hour the boy returned to Tom Smith's while Beall's crew headed for Richmond.

Across Mojack Bay at his Yorktown base Isaac Wistar promptly completed his writing of what would become a permanent report in the *Official Records.* In part his summary to Major General J.G. Foster read:

"*About 150 boats and sloops destroyed, some 80 head of cattle out of a drove of 150 belonging to the Confederate Government and en route to Richmond, were captured and brought in. A few horses and arms were taken, and about 100 prisoners more or less connected with illicit trade were arrested, but I deemed it best to discharge all except those whom I forward to-day with descriptive rolls.*

Sixteen of my men were brought back sick in the gunboats. One man was murdered by a bushwhacker named Smith, who was promptly hung, being taken in the act.

The country is full of forage, plenty of corn and fodder, and some oats. Sheep, poultry, and poor cattle abound. I am sure our visit has produced the best effect on the population. No marauding or pilfering whatever was allowed, and no house inclosure was entered by officers or non commissioned officers. To this I regret to say there was, however, an exception on the part of the navy gunboats, whose crews were sometimes landed without authority by me, and acted shamefully and disgracefully. In at least one case an officer was present consenting."

After commending Colonel Spear's force, Wistar complimented,

"The Negro infantry marched better than old troops I ever saw. Not a fence rail was burned or a chicken stolen by them. They seem to be well controlled and their discipline, obedience, and cheerfulness, for new troops, is surprising, and has dispelled many of my prejudices."[5]

Foster forwarded Wistar's report which mentioned the capture of four rebel officers, but noted their inability to capture the boats on wheels.

32 – RETRIBUTION

On a dreary, overcast November 9th morning Beall's band of privateers, now reduced to fifteen, departed Richmond's rail station. The high spirits they exuded five short weeks ago had dissipated and now mirrored the dismal fall sky. Their mindset coincided with the Confederacy's somber mood as the pivotal year of 1863 ebbed away. Thirty-one months of blood letting dampened enthusiasm in the North and the South. The unknown fate of three missing comrades further suppressed morale; yet fire still smoldered within the Rebel leader who awaited his opportunity to punish the enemy for Sands Smith's murder. First he would endure the highly emotional encounter of paying his respects to Smith's daughters.

Twenty-four hours later he reluctantly strode alone up several steps to the front door of the white house. Black bunting billowing in the cool breeze fluttered above the entry. While John dealt with his unenviable task his men faced the unwelcome assignment of wading into the cold water to locate the submerged *Swan* and *Raven*, scoop out the wet sand, and pull the boats ashore.

Eve greeted the handsome captain at the door. Totally uninhibited she said nothing but wrapped her arms snugly around him and tightly drew him near. She sobbed profusely while he silently fought back his own tears. Lillian and Julia, the only other ones at home, entered the hallway. John tenderly broke free of Eve's embrace when the other two reached for him.

"I shall sorely miss your father. His character often reminded me of my father. In fact I often thought of him as my…" Emotion overwhelmed him. He sobbed bitterly. His shoulders heaved up and down. He struggled to regain his composure to no avail. Ironically at George Beall's passing eight years ago he stoically shed nary a tear. Perhaps the years of suppressed emotion belatedly spewed forth with his grief for another father. He lingered longer than intended but finally forced himself to rise and join his crew in preparation for their evening departure. "I'm sure my men also wish to pay their respects before we depart."

Eve accompanied him on his walk to his crew. Ten yards beyond the porch she paused, looked up to him, and slipped her hands into his. "Johnny, I've so dreamed things would be different, but this war does complicate one's life doesn't it."

He stared into her soothing, dark, warm eyes. How could he break her heart at this time? But how in good conscience could he mislead her? He awkwardly stood in silence unable to properly arrange the words. He finally cleared his throat to say something, anything.

Eve smiled and emitted an amorous "shush" before she pursed her lips and stood on her toes. He closed his eyes, labeling himself a lecherous opportunist in anticipation of her soft lips pressing against his. The sensation of her planting a sisterly kiss upon his cheek completely stunned him. Her humorous giggle further disarmed him. "Johnny, a man like you needs the proper mate to tend to you after this war's over. Because of my affection for you I've long distressed that even if that woman stood directly before you, you wouldn't possess the common sense to recognize her." She paused and forced him to squirm for several seconds. "The evening you fled, the day before Papa…" She hesitated, attempted to complete the sentence, but couldn't say the word. She stammered, "You know," and continued. "I confided my worry to Papa. He swore me to secrecy but with him gone I feel compelled to address the issue." Her eyes sparkled when she said, "Papa told me of your engagement to the Tennessee woman. While not a Virginia belle," she teased before saying with complete sincerity, "I'm relieved and very happy for you."

The amazed man grasped her hands and discovered himself compulsively kissing her forehead before releasing her. "Eve Victoria Smith, you're an exceptional woman who shall forever hold a special place in my heart."

When he reluctantly turned away to depart, she softly said, "God's speed, Johnny Beall. My prayers for your safety shall ascend to the heavens every evening."

After a night spent crossing the Chesapeake Bay, John stared through the glassy waters into the depths of the sea off Accomack County. He looked deeply below the surface in search of his soul to understand himself and to perhaps comprehend the sacrifices demanded by this endless war. October's disaster supplanted September's grand success. No captured vessels. No pain inflicted upon the enemy, only misery dispensed by ruthless Yankees. Three crewmen lost including Ned McGuire. Their fates unknown. And Sands Smith. A horrible, horrible tragedy.

His concern switched to the crew. Would the drought without a captured prize deteriorate morale significantly and bring gross resignations if the men returned to Richmond empty handed? Would petty squabbling surface? How would the men react to Edmondson filling McGuire's vacancy? Always difficult to abruptly place a man in command of his peers. Edmondson reacted on impulse too. His devil-may-care persona served him well when under the leadership of a cool-headed superior, but Edmondson's recklessness could invite disaster for himself and his subordinates.

John evaluated his own abilities. He acknowledged his unwavering urge to follow the path dictated by duty. At times his narrow vision almost led to catastrophe, prevented only by Ned's profound ability to view the wider picture. Ned always mentioned the word "ramifications" whenever the two discussed a course of action. John recognized his own weariness. Physical demands in this line of work sucked energy from the most physically fit. His two year old chest wound, though long scarred over and healed externally, throbbed incessantly whenever he became fatigued. A part of him would forever lie on the battlefield at Bolivar Heights. He feared the loss of his men's focus which so brilliantly spread havoc in September. He recognized his sharp edge which confidently knifed through obstacles dulled significantly with Sands Smith's death. He prayed a careless decision of his would not result in deadly consequences for his men.

His head cleared when one of his watchmen shouted, "Schooner on the horizon flying a Union flag." An hour later they controlled the decks of their first prize.

"What next, Captain?" confidently shouted Baker. "We going to break September's record?"

Each month since Beall's band formed the presence of Federal gunboats on the Chesapeake increased. Time to hunt the hunters. "We'll use this vessel to set a trap for a Yankee gunboat."

"You serious?" questioned Baker.

The challenge rekindled the glimmer in Beall's eye. "Certainly. John Wood used the ploy effectively. If our gunboat accompanied the *Alliance* we would have escaped unscathed." Such rationale returned the men's thoughts to September's lucrative rewards.

The sun dipped below the western horizon before Beall finished inspecting the vessel, inventorying the cargo, and securing the prisoners below. He instructed Edmondson, "The size of the *Swan* and the *Raven* prevent them from serving as this schooner's tenders without causing suspicion. Take half a dozen men and conceal our craft in an isolated inlet along the shore. Remain until we capture a gunboat or until I signal you to return."

The moonless but clear starlit sky adequately illuminated the coastline for Edmondson to locate an inlet in which to seclude the craft. Upon reaching shore he ordered Baker and Fitzgerald to sleep on the boats, while he, Thomas, Churn, and Crouch located a safe, comfortable location to nap.

Bright sunlight glowing radiantly from a deep-blue cloudless sky finally awakened Baker. He crawled out of the *Raven*, yawned, and stretched. He smiled at the deep snoring of Fitzgerald, who peacefully rocked back and forth inside the *Swan* with the ebb and flow of the surf. Baker looked out to sea.

"Damn. Fitz, wake up! Now!"

Fitzgerald shot to his feet with a revolver in each hand. He gazed at the schooner and then back over his shoulder. "What is so all fired important to wake a man from much needed sleep for," he looked around again, "nothing?"

"Fitz, don't you see?" asked Baker nervously.

"See what!"

"See where Edmondson hid the boats."

Fitzgerald glanced at the *Swan* sitting in the water's edge and at the beached *Raven,* before he stared into the bay. "Damn, Billy, for once in your life you are right. I'll get Edmondson since he's in charge." Fitzgerald rolled his eyes as he did whenever he used "Edmondson" and "in charge" in the same sentence.

Ten minutes later Edmondson, still noticeably drowsy, begrudgingly accompanied Fitzgerald. He peered at the two boats, glanced out to sea, shrugged his shoulders, and asked with a trace of irritation, "So, what do you want me to do?"

"Tell us what to do, where to move the boats?" replied Baker.

Edmondson took off his hat, ran his fingers through his stringy, unwashed hair, and complacently said, "Let 'em rest where they are. If anyone comes nosing around tell 'em the fishing's been poor so we decided to rest a couple hours since we been out before three this morning. I'm going back to sleep. Call me if you need me." He walked away leaving Baker and Fitzgerald to deal with the poorly secluded boats.

"Well partner, looks like all of sudden we're in charge," said Fitzgerald. "We should take turns with the watch, though don't know how much sleeping we'll do at this time of day.

About noon a lone fishing boat floated into the inlet manned by a single angler. Fitzgerald casually stood and stretched to greet the stranger.

"You boys won't be catching any fish in here, especially with no lines in the water," the visitor chided with a dry laugh.

Fitzgerald looked over to Baker seated on the bow of the *Swan* with a cocked revolver concealed at his side. Fitz's eyes and a subtle shake of the head communicated no guns. He realized the echo of a '44 would draw any Union gunboat in the vicinity to them quicker than a shark to blood. "Well, sir," Fitzgerald began with the intention of following Edmondson's instructions to weave the fishing yarn, until he realized the absence of any fishing gear might raise eyebrows. "As I was saying, six of us are down for a little hunting expedition. Understand the navy got the area pretty well protected so we figured we could enjoy one good hunt before winter sets in. Planning to eat supper on shore and then anchor near the safety of our gunboats for the evening."

"Good luck, gents. Nothing like the aroma of fresh game over a campfire on a clear fall night," the stranger replied as he rowed away.

Anxiously Baker mumbled, "Should a let me shoot him. Areas overrun with Union sympathizers. What if he hightails it to the Yankee army?"

"And what if he's one of our'n, maybe with kin fighting for the South? You can't go shooting a man just because you don't know his politics. You sound like a damn Yankee sometimes, you scardy cat," Fitzgerald admonished disdainfully.

The pair stood side by side watching the intruder glide lazily into the school of fishing boats floating peacefully in the distance. "Told you there's nothing to worry about, Baker. The old boy just probably got bored, noticed us, and decided to break up the day by jawing with a few strangers."

Three-quarters of a mile off shore John Beall nervously paced the deck of the captured schooner. He questioned how a man could responsibly believe he concealed the boats, in that location! First time at sea without McGuire and already an impending disaster. Why did that little boat enter the inlet? Informant for the Yankees? Hopefully his boys possessed the common sense to move after dark. Nothing to do but wait. He paced uneasily throughout the afternoon, pausing to stare through his binoculars every five or ten minutes. His chest ached. His back stiffened. The continuous glare off the water spawned a dull, nauseous headache. His queasiness intensified in the middle of the afternoon when he lifted his glasses and observed two barges filled with blue clad men. They hugged the coast while advancing toward the inlet. Beall hoped Edmondson stationed sentinels at the mouth of inlet to sound an alarm of any incoming threat. Helplessly he watched them float undetected toward the *Swan* and *Raven*.

On shore Baker napped in the *Swan* while Fitzgerald relaxed on the sun-warmed sand with his back resting against the hull of the *Raven*. Lulled by four hours of tranquility since the fishing smack disappeared, Fitzgerald's thoughts focused on his home far away from the imminent danger. His memories of Thanksgivings and Christmases past abruptly ended in the present. He'd allowed two barges loaded with Yankees to migrate half way up the small inlet. He knew he was a sitting duck. His mind raced to decide how to alert Baker without causing his edgy companion to panic.

Lieutenant John W. Conner of the 1st Regiment Eastern Shore Maryland Volunteers, flanked by scores of soldiers with Springfield rifles trained on Fitzgerald, aimed his threatening revolver and demanded, "Arise very slowly with hands visible. If you attempt to escape you shall immediately die."

Rising slowly as instructed, Fitzgerald glanced toward his stirring companion. Any spontaneous reaction by Baker would bring forth a hail of bullets from the trigger-happy Yankees. Humbling himself, and praying he addressed the Union officer by proper rank, the vulnerable Rebel calmly said, "Lieutenant, sir, my companion is asleep in the other boat. If you'll allow, I shall turn my head to verbally awaken him and caution him not to flee."

"Very well. Any tricks and you'll be the first to die."

Fitzgerald turned his head while cringing at the thought of scores of minie balls shredding his flesh. He calmly called, “Baker, lie still. Don’t move Billy. Are you awake? Do you hear me? Lie still.”

A frightened high pitched voice squeaked, “What’s, what’s wrong?”

“Hundreds of Yanks are training their guns on us. Lay still and listen.” He turned his head to the captors and spoke deliberately to the officer. “I’ll ask him to show his hands first, then slowly stand keeping his hands fully visible.”

Per instructions Baker rose and joined his companion. The company of U.S. volunteers disembarked from the barges and sloshed through ten yards of knee deep salt water.

The sandy-haired lieutenant, with a trim, graying moustache, demanded, “Where’s the rest of your pirate friends?”

Fitzgerald chuckled and coolly said, “Lieutenant, we’re loyal citizens from Baltimore on a hunting excursion.”

“And after tonight’s meal you’ll anchor in the safety of our gunboats.” Conner advanced several feet, lifted his revolver, and pointed the muzzle ten inches from Baker’s nose. His thumb clicked the hammer back into firing position. “Sonny, where’s the rest of your pirate friends and who’s your leader?”

Beads of sweat rolled down Baker’s forehead. An uncomfortable need to relieve himself overcame him. He stared at the lead projectiles visible in the revolver’s cylinders begging to be fired. He oddly thought, damn, even if the first round misfires there’s more to do the job.

Conner’s hand tensely shook the pistol. “Sonny, I’m losing my patience!”

The staged intimidation forced a rapid response. “Ain’t pirates, we’re Confederate seaman assigned to Captain Beall. All our men’s hiding yonder,” answered Baker with a sideways glance over his shoulder, pleased he didn’t reveal Beall’s location.

Baker's relief turned to terror when the cold steel of the lieutenant's gun barrel pressed firmly against the bridge of the seaman's nose. "Where's Beall?"

Wholly unnerved Baker pointed to the schooner on the horizon. His life flashed before him as the lieutenant pulled the trigged but slowly released the hammer with his thumb. Utterly unraveled, Baker dropped to his knees emotionally castrated.

The Union column advanced into the underbrush but after five minutes detected nothing. Conner's stout sergeant, with a bushy gray beard, spit a stream of amber tobacco juice into the absorbing sand. "Not a sign of 'em, sir. The boy's lying."

"Sergeant, you see his face? When my revolver pressed against his forehead if I'd a told him to stand on his head and sing 'John Brown's Body' he'd a asked which verses? You ever hunt rabbits, Sergeant?"

"In my younger days, sir," answered the noncom inquisitively scratching the exposed back of his head below his forage cap.

"You remember how you scare out the critters when you know they're present but can't find 'em."

A comprehending grin crossed the sergeant's face. He called together the squad leaders. Rifles exploded in random directions peppering the underbrush. Four skittish Rebels as if on cue popped up and ran in unison.

The nine men on the schooner observing the drama on shore winced at the crackle of rifle fire.

Color drained from Will's face. He forced out words choked through the lump in his throat. "Johnny, you think they lined them up and shot them? Would they do that?"

Beall's mind flashed to the ghastly account of Sands Smith's bullet-riddled body swaying above the ground. "Nothing Yankees do surprises me." His mind reverted to grotesque Union remains stretched out on Bolivar Heights. Seemed like eons ago. Reluctantly John accepted nothing war did to mankind surprised him, whether by Yankee or Reb.

Under the cover of darkness the Federal barges snuck out of the inlet. Connor's heart pounded with excitement as he envisioned announcing to headquarters that the notorious John Beall lay in anchor off the Potomac Sound of the Chesapeake. If their luck held the pirate would be theirs in the morning.

Beall antagonized over his course of action throughout the night. He never appreciated the loneliness of command until he lacked McGuire's counsel. The decision weighed solely upon his shoulders. If they lifted anchor tonight and reached Mathews County undetected they could unload their cargo and arrive in Richmond with a pocket full of money to spend throughout the winter. If the Yankees executed Edmondson's men chances remained good that Beall floated undetected. In the early morning hours he leaned on the assumption that he remained unnoticed. The fact no party attempted to capture them added credence to the theory. He assumed the Yankees immediately would have launched an assault upon him if they knew of his presence, plus his curious nature yearned to visit the inlet to determine what happened, and to locate the bodies of his comrades if necessary. After weighing his options he decided to allow the morning sun to shed the necessary light on his dilemma.

His jittery crew stood apprehensively on the schooner's deck with the morning sunlight warming their backs. They anxiously awaited the next course of action. While each man possessed the instinct to flee to safety he also accepted his captain's obsession with duty. Beall, fraught with a mental tug of a war, struggled until he fell back to his comfort zone. He pursued his natural instinct to follow duty. He never considered how Ned might advise him before he addressed the crew. "Men, our mission remains unfulfilled. First though, we owe it to our comrades and their loved ones to determine their fate. The remote possibility also exists that the *Swan* and *Raven* might be salvaged. Our objective two days ago was to draw near a Yankee gunboat and capture it. I believe our diminished crew still possesses the determination to succeed in such a venture. We'll obtain a fishing scow to expedite a landing on shore after which we'll plan our trap to draw in a Yankee gunboat. If we don't accomplish our task by tomorrow night we'll head back to Mathews County and dispose of our prize.

Beall's plan to attract a Yankee gunboat unfolded beyond his wildest expectation. In less than thirty minutes an armada of Yankee gunboats churned from all directions toward the schooner. Realizing the dire confrontation about to unfold, Stedman walked up to Beall and broke the tension by quipping, "Brilliant strategy, Captain, which gunboat shall we commandeer?"

Hours of stressful anxiety exploded into uncontrolled laughter. Beall ordered, "To the cargo hold men. Dump the goods before the Yankees arrive. Eleven heavy crates remained when Sergeant Robert R. Christopher's heavily armed escort boarded the schooner. The Rebels concealed a dozen revolvers below deck in the event Beall's crew might be restrained there. Six lay conspicuously by the center mast. Seven rested on the bottom of the bay. The nine captives, with infantry rifles trained upon them, leaped onto a gunboat where Yankee soldiers securely bound them for transport to an unidentified destination for a fate unknown.

33 – ANOTHER PRISONER

One hundred thirty miles to the northwest, far across the Chesapeake Bay, Second Lieutenant Charlie Pierce sat staring at the ground. Almost 700 of his fellow Louisiana Tigers from Harry Hays's brigade joined him on the open field, surrounded by Union guards ominously sporting muskets with fixed bayonets. Pierce wondered if some of those bayonets showed traces of Southern blood from the Yankee night assault several days back. Rumors circulated that over half of Hays's brigade became casualties. Apparently no deaths occurred in his 7th Louisiana Regiment. In fact no one endured an injury more serious than a minor flesh wound. Charlie guessed 175 or maybe even 200 of his regiment joined him as prisoners. He accurately presumed that of the five regiments involved in the action most of the prisoners came from the ranks of the 7th. Unbeknownst to Pierce, only two men from the entire brigade died while sixteen suffered wounds. At the Rappahannock bridge, in the battle later known as Rappahannock Station, 683 men from the brigade officially became prisoners.

The athletic looking young man with a determined face and dark features stood to stretch his legs in the forty degree weather under partly cloudy skies. He stared out at the guards, envious of his captors' heavy woolen powder blue overcoats. A little firewood would be appreciated too. The scent of bacon drifted from the fires that warmed the Yankees and cooked their breakfasts. Charlie yearned for a hot meal but settled for hardtack and tough, uncooked salt pork washed down with river water.

Lieutenant Wallace Talbot, with a threadbare blanket wrapped around his shoulders, sat dejectedly on a cold rock. He gazed intently toward the south. Talbot's normally clean shaven face displayed rough, red stubble. His kepi tilted to the left to shield his eyes from the intermittent sun. Only Charlie's slap on his comrade's back broke the man's trance.

"Dang it all, Charlie!" Talbot bellowed, "Bad enough the Yanks poking and prodding me with their ugly bayonets. Now I got to beware of you too."

Corporal George Hoefer, Private William Nesbitt, and Private Julius Zork roared with laughter. Like Pierce, these three men enlisted as privates in New Orleans when units formed in the spring of '61. Pierce instantly ingratiated himself with the others. His fun loving personality served as a magnet. His unique blend of ferocity and coolness in battle caught the eyes of his superiors. In less than two years he advanced to Second Lieutenant Pierce with a bright future before him. Never overly impressed by rank, Charlie accepted the promotion but retained his down-home personality. His soft brown eyes would sparkle when he prepared to offer some of his homespun wisdom. He'd stroke the two-inch wide growth of dark brown hair which grew below his mustached lips down to the top of his throat. He'd often say, "Don't care what rank they give me, as long as it gets this damn war over quickly. I fear the unattached flowers of New Orleans shall all wilt while anxiously awaiting my return." Catcalls from listeners usually followed before an enticing smile split across his face.

He squatted down by Lieutenant Talbot. "Wallace, what you so intently looking at?"

"Home, Charlie, home." His eyes gazed away from his friend to the southern sky. "Suspect we wouldn't need blankets or overcoats down south yet, would we? This dang Virgini weather is sure cold enough. Wonder where we're headed next? Know it won't be south."

"Where we rumored to be off to Charlie?" asked Zork, assuming that if information existed Pierce knew of it.

"Afraid the scuttlebutts avoided my ears. We could find our new home anywhere from Baltimore to New York, or even in Ohio, Indiana, or Chicago. Not choice locations to winter in any case." Charlie looked over to Talbot and jested, "Course the Yanks graciously offer special accommodations to Confederate officers."

As Charlie facetiously puffed out his chest, quick-witted Billy Nesbitt, eager to collaborate with Charlie in such ruses, pulled off his slouch hat, pushed his long black hair away from his forehead, and innocently inquired, "Ain't that place somewhere up on the Canadian border, Charlie?"

"Damn you anyhow, Nesbitt," snapped Talbot.

Another chorus of laughter erupted. Hoefer's grin exposed a gap adjacent to several jagged teeth partially concealed by discolored, swollen lips courtesy of a Union musket stock the night of the assault.

In a serious tone Talbot looked up and asked, "Charlie, how you going to cope? My temperament allows me to accept the cards as dealt and to go with the flow. You're a different sort. The doctors still talk about how you begged to return to duty last spring well before you was healed. They say when we headed toward Pennsylvania in June that the matron responsible for your ward took your britches to keep you from running away and joining us. Fact is, they say everyone in the tent was told to keep his trousers on so you wouldn't steal 'em."

"Lieutenant," began Charlie with his all too familiar sheepish grin, "do you really believe a gentleman such as I would entertain the despicable act of stealing from convalescing comrades?"

"Yes!" echoed four voices.

"Especially if it meant getting back to killing Yankees any sooner," Zork said, before adding with a smile, "particularly since some of those petals now drop from the flowers of the large feminine bouquet in New Orleans who you keep jawing about in your fantasies."

Pierce's arms bent upwards with open palms signifying he surrendered to his friends despite his adamant refusal to ever capitulate so passively to the enemy. "You men have a pleasant stay in the Yankee prison. After I free myself I'll take in a few northern sights since I haven't been up there in four years. If I'm not back in Dixie by Christmas I'll assuredly be in route."

"Or die trying," Talbot ominously warned.

Later that day the Yankees marched the prisoners to the train station and herded them into boxcars for the cramped four hour journey fifty miles up the Orange & Alexandria tracks to the Old Capitol Prison in Washington City. Although the train stopped five times, the guards only allowed the captives in two of the ten cars to exit at each stop, where civilians filled the inadequate buckets with drinking water while prisoners dumped the waste basins. At the Washington train station the Louisianans marched three-quarters of a mile to confinement while subjected to verbal abuses hurled by local citizens.

A young lady with an encouraging smile shouted, "You'll be out soon boys," which filtered through the predominant insults from most onlookers.

Inside the gates blue uniformed clerks frequently hindered by missing or nonfunctional limbs registered and searched the Southerners. Negative responses or vulgar retorts echoed to the question, "You ready to swear off your secesh ways and sign the *Oath of Allegiance* to your rightful government. It'll mean better food, earlier parole, and separation from malcontents who started this conflict."

The first man brazen enough to spit on the document instantly doubled over in agony when a heavy walnut rifle butt smashed sharply into his abdomen. He became the last Rebel in the group to vehemently display such disdain.

The Yankees directed Pierce and Talbot away from the enlisted men. Both returned to the train station to begin their journey to the northern Ohio prison camp less than twenty miles from Canada. On the forty-eight hour ride to Sandusky, Pierce recalled the ploys he'd heard escaped prisoners implement to gain their freedom. His smiled at the challenge before him. Christmas in less than six weeks.

Far to the east another incarcerated Confederate soldier pondered his future. Little did Pierce know that if his independent attempt for freedom failed that John Beall might become a welcome ally in a quest for escape.

34 – NAVAL OFFICER OR PIRATE?

Hind sight, the nemesis of all leaders. Beall pondered how he could have been so irresponsible. He'd carelessly allowed the capture of himself and his crew. Glancing toward his fellow prisoners he especially anguished over the fate of his younger brother. Thoughts returned to Mother and his sisters, and the sorrow they would endure if his foolishness brought harm to Will. Would Ned have steered him clear of his rash decision? As he stood deeply in thought, comforting hands rested upon his shoulder.

Stedman offered a consoling smile. "Chin up lad. You did what your heart deemed proper. No one argues your choice. Let this play out."

"George, thank you for the reassuring words, but the Yankees cheerfully emphasized we are marauders, not Confederate soldiers."

"And they dare call Bobby Lee a despicable traitor too. You're in good company. We accept the consequences of our venture but we also acknowledge the swift retaliation with which our government shall respond if we are dealt with too harshly. Remember that the international community's perception does influence the Yankees. Go to your men and give them some encouraging words from their leader."

Moments later Beall cast a grateful smile to Stedman. He'd found proper words to buoy his crew's spirits as the former newspaperman did for him. Their conversation continued until the gunboats docked in Onancock. The prisoners knew of the existence of the excellent harbor although they never visited the port. The presence of numerous Unionist inhabitants and the routine appearances of Federal gunboats, coupled with the army garrison stationed five miles inland, deterred such a visit.

The prisoners disembarked flanked by a squad of soldiers eager for justification to use their bayoneted muskets. One of the escort, a short, heavyset private, looked to his superior and asked, "Sergeant Christopher, do we hang 'em here or we got to march 'em all the way to Drummondtown and shoot 'em?"

"Private Quartermain, enough!" admonished the sergeant. "You know we always give their kind a fair trial before their execution."

The crew's recently infused optimism seeped away. Late that afternoon three freight wagons transporting the infamous prisoners creaked to a halt near the jail. Guards escorted them into the outer room of the structure where Brigadier General Henry Lockwood waited. The forty-nine year old West Pointer from Delaware curtly acknowledged his prisoners. He slowly eyed each man from head to toe before condescendingly saying, "So this is the remainder of the secesh rabble referred to as the Confederate Volunteer Coast Guard. Not much to look at." He stared at John and snarled, "You Beall?"

With an air of Virginian arrogance, the band's leader stiffened his posture and stared squarely into his opponent eyes. "I am Acting Master John Beall of the Confederate States of America Navy."

Deep furrows appeared on Lockwood's wide forehead below his abundant curls of brown hair. Sour lines crept downward from the general's lips to his thick muttonchops. He scowled before replying, "Come, come, Mr. Beall, we know you're nothing more than a common pirate." He smiled and added, "Even your band calls you captain. Do they even know of your alleged military rank?"

"Richmond shall provide proper documentation."

The Union officer's amused expression evaporated. His face reddened. In a stern tone he sarcastically refuted Beall's threat. "A bastard government fabricates papers to sanctify an illegitimate commander and his band of shiftless criminals operating illegally in U. S. waters? You Mr. Beall, with your Southern haughtiness insult me and the United

States government." His closed fist crashed hard atop his desk. "Expect no mercy from me, sir!" he screamed. He turned to the squad of guards. "Corporal Appleton, I'm becoming nauseous. Dispatch these men as we did the others."

Lockwood watched color drain from the prisoner's faces as they visualized the expediency of the firing squad. After they departed the general shook his head in disbelief and commented to Sergeant Christopher, "You ever see boys so fearful of a night in jail? Guess without their slaves they're helpless."

Through the heavy rear door of the jail's office the prisoners walked into a hallway lined with small cells. When they reached the next door, their legs weakened in anticipation of the dreadful end they were about to face. Instead they found themselves in a large, dingy cell. Shouts of jubilation echoed as Baker, Fitzgerald, Edmondson, Churn, Thomas, and Crouch jumped to their feet to greet them.

Amid hugs and handshakes Will exclaimed, "We thought the Yankees shot you dead!"

"And we figured you got away," commiserated Edmondson.

For an hour the men exchanged accounts of the past two days' events. Guards carried in several buckets of fresh water but nothing arrived to subdue their hunger. They slept restlessly that evening hoping for a better tomorrow.

The next morning the captives meandered about the large cabin on the main deck of a steamer departing for the nine hour journey to Baltimore. They observed the open deck where two guards marched dutifully to and fro. Just beyond the sentinels rested two tripods of bayoneted rifles stacked near lounging relief guards.

Beall nonchalantly whispered, "Men, if we overpower the sentinels, secure their weapons, and seize the two stacks of rifles, this ship shall be ours. A prize for our efforts, but we must act quickly. In several hours we'll enter hostile waters. I need four men to subdue the guards while six of us race to the unattended rifles. You other five wait for our volley. I counted twelve soldiers, plus an officer, and a ship's crew of six. Do not assume any seamen are unarmed. Are we ready?"

Dead silence. Annan spoke first. "Captain, if the others are well positioned we could be sitting ducks even if we get off a volley."

Several other dissenters voiced their views. While the objections aired Will gradually inched his way to the rear. Though he too feared tragic results he certainly did not relish opposing the officer in charge.

"Boys, if we don't try now we're in for a cold, miserable winter in some disease-infested Yankee prison. I say if we perish we do so like men rather than withering away in some Yankee dungeon."

Edmondson stepped forward in a show of support for the plan. The others solemnly remained where they stood. John searched for Will's face. His brother avoided eye contact while staring at the deck. That in itself served as a statement of no support. Overcome with frustration Beall resigned himself to his men's cowardly decision. "The day shall come when you shall look back at this moment and," he paused, "and you painfully realize you ignored the opportunity to strike a blow for your own freedom, not to mention our greater cause." With a statement reeking of sarcasm he concluded, "Live with that thought noble gentlemen of the South."

The remainder of the voyage the somber Rebels spoke little preferring not to suffer another tongue lashing. Guards gathered the prisoners together when the ship entered Baltimore harbor. Much to Beall's chagrin he overheard one guard say to another, "I'd a bet a month's wages they'd take the bait. Those rifles couldn't of been stacked much closer to 'em. Guess the papers are right. The fight's going out of the Rebs. Damn, Oscar, instead of unloading fifteen corpses and hitting the taverns we got to spend half the night taking these boys to Fort McHenry."

Before they crossed the fort's drawbridge the men received Beall's heartfelt apology. The gates securing the star shaped fortress clanged shut behind as they trudged to the former stable for the evening.

After a Spartan breakfast of stale bread and diluted coffee the men marched to headquarters. This offered them a daylight view of Fort McHenry. Construction on the structure began just before the turn of the century. The thick twenty feet high brick walls protected Francis Scott Key while he penned "The Star Spangled Banner" during England's failed attempt to capture the bastion. Federal use for a prison commenced in early May of 1861 with the sole purpose of holding political prisoners. The massive walls surrounded five large buildings. Healthy Southern prisoners lived on the upper floor of one of two 120' by 30' brick rectangular buildings. The prison hospital occupied the second floor of the other building. Whenever the prison population exceeded the ideal capacity of 400 the overflow settled in other structures such as the converted stable where Beall spent the previous night, a location usually accommodating Union deserters.

The "fresh fish," as veteran prisoners referred to new arrivals, entered a large office for registration and orientation. A neatly dressed corporal, his wooden crutches propped against the wall behind him, sat with pen in hand ready to document essential data relevant to each man. The clerk rolled his eyes when each prisoner preceded his name with a Confederate Navy rank.

Edmondson boldly demanded, "What of my possessions confiscated in Drummondtown?"

In a high pitched New England dialect the corporal shot back, "Not my problem. Your funds and watch, if you owned one, came along for safe keeping." He smugly smiled and added, "We're not a pack of thieving pirates you know."

Beall irritably interjected, "Those of us who own watches should have them returned immediately."

"There's been talk of you receiving the jewelry," replied the corporal before he winked to the guards standing by the wall to his right.

"Wonder what that's all about?" whispered Will inquisitively to Fitzgerald who haplessly shrugged his shoulders.

"March the prisoners to their next stop," ordered the corporal upon completing his paperwork. In another room the commandant reviewed prison rules before releasing the men to their barracks.

They effortlessly acclimated themselves for several days until guards accompanied them to headquarters. Fifteen uneasy men stood in ranks two lines deep waiting for the Union colonel to address them. "Gentlemen, it is my duty to inform you that you are officially designated marauding pirates and as such it is my responsibility to have you clasped in irons for the duration of your confinement."

Beall aggressively stepped forward and emphatically protested, "I object to such unjust treatment!" The guards sprang forward and thrust their bayonets against his stomach.

He coolly stepped back in line but promised, "There shall be retribution."

"We shall see, Mr. Beall, we shall see," answered the colonel with a confident smile.

By the end of the day all prisoners received their new iron jewelry. A month later the prisoners still wore the dehumanizing manacles. Wrist irons connected by a length of chain hampered every daily activity from shaving to eating. Wherever they walked leg irons impeded their movements. Over time bits of flesh rubbed away, creating painful, bloody, open sores. The metal's extra weight also increased fatigue. Exercise on the large parade ground lost its appeal. Reactions from guards varied.

"Now you endure the suffering you've imposed on your Negroes," jeered a New England abolitionist.

Several soldiers, especially those with crippling war injuries, gloried in their enemies' misery. Most though seemed indifferent. For them the prisoner's punishment only complicated their duties. The Rebs moved slower and on occasion needed special considerations.

One evening a young private from Ohio with a noticeable limp offered to remove Beall's irons at the start of his watch with the intention of replacing them before his shift ended.

"Why?" asked John with a skeptical look of suspicion.

The simple Northern lad tapped his leg. "Before this war I assumed a great deal. Knew I wouldn't be encumbered by frail limbs 'til my hair turned gray. Terrible sights my eyes have witnessed in this gory conflict. Ever see your best pard fighting along side you one minute, then be laying shot to pieces the next, with them baby blue eyes staring right at you but not seeing a dang thing?" He paused while a tear rolled down his youthful cheek. Beall's mind reluctantly reproduced the image of Seth Hendersen.

The Northerner continued, "I'm only twenty-one but I'm surprised my hair ain't white by now. I sure have the leg of an old man. You ask why I offered to loosen your irons, Mister? You remember how this fracas commenced as a grand expedition like we all was a going to a county fair in some far off state. You Southerns was going to whip us in four weeks. We was going to whip you in a month. I truly believe after the first blood spilled it became all about revenge. Just maybe one act of kindness will lead to another, and soon we'll all decide to quit this fight and go home."

John softly smiled and humbly replied, "Private, I do appreciate your expression of kindness but for this war to end the compassion must flow from governments. Yours ordered these irons placed on me. I shall wear them as a symbol of oppression until your government removes them. We all have our cross to bear. These chains are mine."

"Every time Ma started in with the cross to bear speech Pa would say, 'don't make it any heavier than it need be, Mother.' I suspect there's truth in that. There's just a great deal about you folks I don't understand."

"I must admit your people puzzle me too, especially the God-fearing Christian ones."

"Mister, answer me one question. You pray to the same God I do. Which side is He on?"

Beall slowly shook his head pondering the depth of the question posed by the simple westerner. He thought of savage acts committed by both sides before he solemnly said, "Many days, probably neither. Thank you for your thoughtfulness. Good night."

The lad bid John a good evening and in uneven steps limped down the corridor.

Several days later the prisoner sat at a simple wooden table in the barracks staring at paper and pen. He struggled to compose positive thoughts for his second annual New Years Day letter to Martha. The damp, stark room mirrored the gray winter sky along the waterfront which emulated his inner soul. He sighed, glanced at the paper, picked up the pen, and hesitated again before he finally began.

Dear Martha,

I do pray this message finds you, Miss Fanny, and your brothers safe and well. I hope that my friend has informed you of our recent misfortune and new accommodations here in Baltimore. My entire crew arrived with nary a scratch. I do have a few encumbrances but I do believe our government shall soon eliminate them.

I yearn so to see you, to hear you, to hold you. My fondest hope is the termination of the war by this year's end when you and I shall be together as one. I have witnessed so much suffering on each side but I have also witnessed random acts of compassion. As I did last year I have composed another verse for the ballad of which I spoke.

Two years since I held you near, Martha
When cruel war again beckoned me
The loss of my comrades so dear, Martha
In our struggle to be free.
I sit tightly bound in chains, Martha

So that I cannot fight
My devotion for you remains, Martha
My one sustaining light.

Love,
John

By early January retaliatory threats from Richmond freed the captives of their irons which in turn led to their transfer to another site. In mid February John stood on the confined exercise grounds of Fortress Monroe. Placing his hands on Will's shoulders and looking up into his eyes he said, "Brother, I regret leaving you but they say I'm to be paroled from Point Lookout in several weeks, and they indicat you'll soon be free also. I do regret bringing you into this sordid affair. I just thank our Lord you escaped injury. I…"

Will interrupted him with a rough bear hug. "Johnny, would never trade these past several months with you, least wise until the capture," he replied with a grin. "The tales we'll tell our grandchildren, that is if you ever find a woman to tolerate you."

They chatted several moments longer before guards escorted John away. He pragmatically anticipated the war would continue at least until November. He so hoped Will would escape injury, if only so Martha could meet his younger brother. Then he silently prayed that God's will be done.

On March 3rd John signed his parole papers and left the confines of Point Lookout in Maryland. Unlike Fort McHenry and Fortress Monroe, this camp only offered protection from the elements with its village of worn tents during both summer's heat and winter's chill. The overcrowded facility transformed into an unsanitary quagmire whenever moderate rain passed over. The ground never dried the two weeks he resided there. Once freed he set off for Richmond. Ten days later he sat at dinner with Daniel Lucas.

"Johnny, you do look well considering you just survived four months in Yankee prisons, manacled like a belligerent Negro."

"The exterior may appear fit, my friend, but the interior's worn emotionally and physically."

"What's your next course of action? I trust you won't be content sitting idly in Richmond, or have you experienced enough of this war? Perhaps a visit to Miss O'Bryan?"

John leaned back in his chair, placed his hands behind his head, flexed his elbows, and smiled contentedly. "Yes on all counts."

Dan's head jerked in surprise.

John placed his elbows on the table, leaned forward, and continued, "I've had more than enough of this war. The fresh graves. The maimed bodies. The stark columns of names listed in newspapers. Yes, I've had enough. The harsh treatment of civilians by Yankees. The barbaric murder of a dear friend for simply defending his daughters. Perhaps I had enough after all I witnessed on Bolivar Heights, although my wounding seems insignificant when judged against other tragedies!"

"John, forgive me for dredging up such memories."

"Dan, you did mention Martha, a fond memory of course." He cynically smiled and bitterly continued, "The fortunes of war keep us apart." Then in childlike wonderment he shook his head comprehending the ambiguity of fate. "But the fortunes of war also brought us together. I'll visit Martha soon. I must hold her, look into her warm loving eyes, and know she is real and our love for each other is true. I need to believe once more that our life together can only be fulfilling without the bonds of Northern tyranny. I've had more than enough of this war, but nothing diminishes my desire to serve Virginia until she's free."

For several moments the room remained quiet. Each man savored the profound calming influence offered by the other. Dan broke the silence. "Shall you attempt to return to the army or does the Chesapeake still call?"

"Much of my strength returned over the past year but I lack the stamina for the days of forced march so common in the army. I reluctantly admit the Yankees control much of Virginia's coast but I question how much of their coast they really control."

"I now understand the feeling of helplessness from incarceration. My thoughts return often to my interview with President Davis and my desire to free our prisoners held captive near the Yankee's northern border. Perhaps," he hesitated and peered momentarily to the corner of the ceiling. "Perhaps with our military reversals on the field the past eight months our government shall become more open to my proposal." A broad smile crept across his face. Imagine Lincoln in the coming election canvas attempting to convince Northern citizens they must steadfastly continue their invasion of the South when their northern boundary is not even secure."

Lucas emitted a soft chuckle while envisioning the scenario. "Speaking of Old Abe, you hear he booted Halleck and pulled Grant off the jug to become lieutenant general over the entire Yankee army? Kind of feel sorry for the man. John Pemberton is certainly no Robert E. Lee, which Grant shall soon discover. We must allocate funds to construct a larger display case for Bobby Lee's next trophy. Mighty crowded in there with McDowell, McClellan, Pope, Burnside, Hooker, and Meade."

Small talk continued until John excused himself for a good nights sleep in a soft, warm bed. He decided to rejuvenate himself for a week in Richmond before traveling south to locate Martha.

35 – PLANNING FOR 1864

On March 24th two men, the physical antithesis of each other, met in Washington City to plan the end of the war. The tall lean man motioned the short dumpy soldier to be seated.

"General Grant, please share your plans for the spring offensive."

Grant detested the capital city's environment with its vicious, scheming, political web. At every turn a politician with an agenda for climbing farther up the ladder to more power was followed by an army of job seeking loyalists whose government position depended on their patrons' continued hold on an office. Those close to Grant warned him Lincoln might be the shrewdest official in Washington. Beneath the country bumpkin façade dwelt a cunning politician. Despite the cautions the general instantly felt at ease with the president. Both men shared modest western roots. Only the Ohio River separated Kentucky and Ohio, their respective states of birth. Illinois proved the last stop for each before the call to duty. More than roots though—Grant just plain trusted the man. He believed Lincoln would gladly relinquish the presidency if the act reunited the divided Union. Grant also realized the Union's survival paralleled Lincoln's political survival. In turn Lincoln understood Grant's western assignments had prevented him from becoming contaminated with the Washington power spheres. The president gambled the eastern army would develop the qualities the general bred into his western troops—persistence and a winning attitude.

"Mr. President, with our implementation of the draft and the large numbers of new enlistments complementing our reenlistments, we possess the manpower to continually refill our ranks. We need to utilize our numeric advantage, sir. Southern ranks deplete with every battle yet we willingly exchange prisoners to offer them relief." The general paused before rhetorically asking, "Why we allow the exchange I do not know?" Excusing himself for digressing Grant continued, "I shall engage Lee from the north. If we capture Richmond, fine, but our objective must be the Rebel army. The perception exists that Richmond is the head of the serpent. That head, with all due respect, is Lee's Army." With a comprehending smile Lincoln encouraged Grant to elaborate. "Sherman shall advance south into Georgia and engage Johnston. Our trans-Mississippi forces shall in the very least occupy General Forrest. I hope to maintain a force in the Valley to protect my rear, and to also land a force on the peninsula to stretch Lee from below."

Lincoln startled Grant when he let out a loud whoop and slapped his knee. "All the foxes headed to the hen house and not enough hounds to guard every door. Excellent General!" exuberantly exclaimed the president standing to shake his new general-in-chief's hand. The euphoria soon dissipated when he added, "General, I have total confidence in you and your plan but realize, understand, you cannot hesitate, for if the work's not completed by November I fear the South wins by default."

"Sir, if I don't succeed by then we'll both be out of work with poor prospects for new employment."

Lincoln admired the man's ability to analyze the complex and reduce it to the simple. Before they parted Lincoln lowered his voice. "The issue of prisoner exchange, let us keep that between us. When events occur to prudently act, we shall."

Less than three weeks later a headlining event from the west crossed the wires providing Lincoln with the catalyst to address the exchange issue. In Tennessee rumors abounded that following Fort Pillow's capitulation hot-blooded Confederates slaughtered scores of Black Union soldiers. Lincoln and Stanton concurred that either the South agree to include Negro soldiers in all exchanges or all exchanges would cease. Although the Davis government claimed that none of the Union soldiers killed at Fort Pillow had surrendered, the Union stipulation, if accepted, forced the Confederates to acknowledge Black U.S. soldiers should receive equal treatment to Confederate POW's. More to the point, the Southerner's could expect reciprocity for their actions. After a week of nonproductive discussion between U.S. and Confederate emissaries, the South as Lincoln expected, firmly refused to exchange Negro prisoners. Ulysses Grant, with Lincoln's blessing, announced on April 17, 1864 that all prisoner exchanges would cease.

As the active military campaigning season began to unfold, attention within Richmond's inner circle of leadership focused, as it had in 1862, on complex operations behind enemy lines to offset the imbalance of Northern manpower, war materials, and transportation systems. On the last day of April, Jefferson Davis prepared to meet with his secretary of state and several Confederate agents concerning a risky operation the South prepared to launch. If successful it would seal Lincoln's fate in the upcoming election.

In the first floor library of the Confederate White House, President Davis sat erectly in an arm chair beside Secretary of State Judah P. Benjamin. The rotund Louisianan, with an oval face and reddish brown hair, peered over his spectacles as the two men engaged in small talk while awaiting the arrival of their guests. Warm, heavy air blew through the windows, lifted the curtains, and effortlessly dropped them. The fragrant scent of blooming azaleas migrated throughout the room.

Benjamin deeply inhaled the scented air, looked outside, and smiled. "Mr. President, spring most certainly abounds."

A forlorn look crossed Davis's gaunt, pale face while he aimlessly glanced through the open window. "Our fourth spring of war. The commitment of the Southern people continues to astound me. If only the price were not so terrible," he said with a sigh.

Suddenly the president's expression changed from that of an overworked, solemn chief executive burdened with the survival of the Confederacy, to a vibrant, resilient, confident leader dedicated to the permanency of his government. The source of the immediate transformation stood in the doorway.

"Morning Papa," said the little boy, with an innocent grin. His light blue linen night gown hung loosely at his knees above his bare feet.

"My le man," smiled Davis, permitting his posture to relax. "How nice of you to visit. Papa's tightly held his good morning hug for you since I awoke this morning. Come grab it before it flies out the window."

No second invitation needed. The child leaped onto his father's lap and wrapped his small arms around Davis's neck. After a thirty second embrace the chief executive said, "Joseph, as a Southern gentleman, you must remember to greet our guest."

"Sowy, Papa," responded young Joe. He hopped from the cozy lap to the floor, stood rigidly, leaned forward in a cursory bow, reached out his hand, and greeted the secretary. "Good mowning, Mista Benzaman. How nice to see you gin."

The personable secretary chuckled, stood, and with an exaggerated bow that allowed his eyes to look directly into the child's, gently shook hands and responded, "I assure you, Master Davis, sir, the pleasure is all mine."

The lad beamed with joy until he heard the feminine voice from upstairs. "Joseph, Joseph Evan Davis! Come up here immediately to get dressed."

Joe instantly darted towards the hallway, but then halted his rapid departure. He turned and seriously said, "Good day, zentleman," before the sounds of little bare feet slapping over the carpet faded away.

"Jefferson," said Benjamin, who rarely addressed the president with such informality, "you and Mrs. Davis have a wonderful son. He lightens my world as I am sure he does yours."

"Thank you, Judah. We only receive a finite number of days to leave our mark from the moment we enter this life until the Lord calls us. Providing civilization with future leaders like Joseph insures such contribution. I pray this war for independence shall leave the world with our blueprint to build future governments. For the sake of unborn generations we must succeed. As you recall, the Lord inexplicably called my Samuel to heaven ten long years ago. Had my dear Varina not consoled me, and had my country not so needed me, I might have allowed my health to deteriorate and join him. A faith in the future blessed me with another son. Joe shall never be Sam but he fills the void left by the child's death." Davis added despondently, "If only voids in our army could be so replenished." A slight smile crossed his lips while his right eye sparkled. "A triumphant mission in the North may just bring us such accomplishment."

Benjamin reseated himself and shifted the conversation to a serious note. "Mr. President, you seem committed to appointing Mr. Thompson as chief commissioner in Canada, with even military personnel reporting to him." The secretary paused and slowly preceded treading cautiously so as to avoid releasing the president's hair trigger temper. "With all due respect, I know of his past disloyalty to you."

Benjamin referred to the ongoing conflict between the two one-time friends after the paths of Davis's and Thompson's political aspirations intersected. For nearly twenty years the men battled each other in Mississippi politics. To add fuel to the fire Davis's most hated political enemy, Henry Foote, allied himself with Jacob Thompson. Throughout his public life Davis handicapped himself by evaluating people, actions, and events in his black and white world. Gray did not exist. If an acquaintance achieved Davis's blessing the man could commit no wrong unless he transgressed with a grievously disloyal act. If a man associated with a charlatan such as Foote, then he too became unequivocally branded as such. Benjamin's question might have incurred the infamous Davis wrath had it been asked by other men, but Davis viewed Benjamin in a bright, positive light. The astute Jewish gentleman, with an admirable job performance, unquestioned loyalty to Davis, and a network of influential supporters, skillfully ingratiated himself within the tiny inner circle of Confederate leadership.

Davis stroked the three inches of hair hanging below his chin on an otherwise cleanly shaven face. He shook his head, expressing wonderment at his own decision. "I often ask myself that same question." He paused, almost embarrassed by his choice, but quickly defended it. "For this action to succeed we must involve unscrupulous men without conscience to direct men who maintain conscience. I reluctantly acknowledge we may be in league with Satan himself. If so, we require the services of one of his most adept lieutenants." He hesitated a moment while searching for proper words. He continued with language dripping with venom. "The Yankees chose to descend into the bowels of hell and return with conduct unacceptable in civilized warfare. I regret we must fight fire with fire."

"Sir, you are referring to Colonel Dahlgren's futile attempt?"

Blood rushed through the president's pale face. He slapped his thighs and leaned forward. The secretary inadvertently had ground salt into a raw wound. Davis stood and paced about as anger spewed forth. "That, sir, was the crowning blow. We prohibited destruction of Union property during our campaigns into Maryland and Pennsylvania even after the Yankees burned homes and stole property throughout the South. General Lee still demands Yankee civilians—women, children, and even men be treated with respect. Our chivalry is repaid in territories occupied by Yankees with hangings of innocent men, starvation of blameless children, and who knows of what dastardly acts forced upon our women. I have hundreds of documents describing such deeds. And now, now," he stood and strode to the window to momentarily compose himself. Uncontrolled rage reignited the tirade. He pointed outside to the busy streets and ranted, "Now they consort to send mounted hoards into Richmond, led by barbarians such as Dahlgren, to enter my home and those of my cabinet with orders to slaughter us in the presence of our families, and inflict God only knows what sort of degradation upon our women and children. If that were not sufficient, Lincoln instructed his mercenaries to storm the prisons and to unleash Yankee prisoners to burn, rape, and pillage our lovely city." He slowly turned to Benjamin and allowed his emotion to dissipate. "Excuse my outburst, Judah. I sometimes feel so helpless. In essence the Yankee's challenged me to a duel but also selected the location and weapons. I now accept their challenge and shall battle the vermin to the death within their rules of warfare." Davis just seated himself when he heard his doorman greeting visitors.

Jacob Thompson entered first. The fifty-three year old, who long ago migrated from North Carolina to Mississippi, showed signs of a receding hairline. His bushy oversized goatee and hair maintained most of its original deep brown color. His thin eyes, set closely together on his dark complexioned face, stereotyped a man lacking integrity. The tall gentleman politely extended his hand and superficially said, "Very good to see you again, President Davis." He acknowledged Benjamin and likewise insincerely added, "And you as well Mr. Secretary."

Davis and Benjamin nodded politely before greeting the other arrival. A more heartfelt exchange transpired with Clement Clay. The middle age Alabama planter and one-time U.S. Senator looked directly into each man's eyes while warmly shaking their hands. His healthy head of hair and thick full beard framed his honest face.

President Davis motioned for all to be seated. "Gentlemen, because of the numerous sacrifices of our brave soldiers and loyal citizens, we now commence our fourth year in our noble struggle. I proudly state the civilized world never expected us to survive for such a period. If so, many countries would have recognized us as the independent, sovereign nation which we are. I further advance that much of the Yankee population, particularly in the west, longs for this conflict to cease. As I said during my inauguration, all we ask is to be left alone. I believe many of our former fellow citizens in the North wish the same for us."

"Let us review our deficiencies. Our transportation system suffers with our weak rail system and the loss of the Mississippi River. Growing and transporting agricultural products to fuel our army and feed our nation presents a constant challenge, but the ingenuity and dedication of our Southern people continues to meet our trials. However, our greatest shortage is manpower. We acknowledge one Southern boy can whip three Yankee men. After all, their army is primarily composed of urban riffraff, newly arrived foreigners, and yes, even Negroes. We only possess a fixed number of warriors to send into battle. Incompetent Yankee generals continue sending their sheep to slaughter knowing immigrant mercenaries and stolen slaves refill their ranks. We shall not stoop to such practices. Our enemy recently demanded that we acquiesce to accept the exchange of one Negro prisoner for one Southern man. Imagine!" Davis slapped his hands together. "A nigger acknowledged the equal of a white man. Of course honor dictates we refuse the obscene request. Shortly thereafter, Grant, Lincoln's new excuse for a general, suspended all prisoner exchanges. I assure you after this so-called western military genius meets General Lee he too shall join the other Yankee castoffs."

"Now, for our advantages," continued the president exuding an air of confidence. "Since the commencement of hostilities our manufacturing steadily increased. Adequate weapons arm our troops. Shot and powder seem ample. Shoes and blankets remain in short supply though after each victory, shall I say, we requisition many from our foe no longer in need of them. Funds continue to flow to us from patriotic Southerners, friendly Europeans, and even from sympathetic Northerners, not to mention the occasional Yankee payroll. Of larger concern is proper utilization of these funds. Perhaps our greatest assets are time and disenchanted Northern citizens."

Thompson and Clay focused on Davis with increased attentiveness. After momentarily absorbing the men's expressions Jeff Davis explained, “Lincoln’s newspapers last summer all but promised the Northern people victory by year’s end after our withdrawal from Vicksburg and our redeployment of troops from Pennsylvania. Two months later the Federal army barely escaped annihilation at Chickamauga. Only the actions of a Union general who turned his back on his native Virginia saved the Union army in Tennessee from extermination. Bloodied and intimidated by Lee in Pennsylvania, Meade respectfully followed orders and probed into Virginia but wisely avoided a second confrontation with our army. Now we enjoy the prospect of a new Yankee general becoming acquainted with Lee. Remember, General Lee has never retreated from a field of battle on Southern soil. The war weary North eagerly anticipates this fall’s election when its dictator and his fellow usurpers are deposed. We must maintain our current military lines in Virginia, but we must also encourage discontent in the North. One of those objectives is our purpose for finalizing plans today with you gentlemen before you depart in several days. Commissioner Thompson, for the benefit of Mr. Clay and Secretary Benjamin, please repeat your orders, as you and I discussed.”

Jacob Thompson so enjoyed his placement on center stage that he failed to realize Davis only wanted Thompson to repeat his instructions before two of the president’s most trusted associates. “My, or should I say our assignment,” began the Mississippian with a nod toward Clement Clay, “appears on the surface to head the peace delegation meeting in Canada to discuss cessation of hostilities. If successful we shall return to Richmond with documents granting our independence to be acknowledged or revised by our government. The prospect of such accomplishment suffers from Lincoln’s absolute refusal to acknowledge the Confederate States of America. Thus, while negotiating with Northern peace delegates, we shall also plan for the execution of well-timed operations in the nonabolitionist western states. Our goal is to spread discontent among the Northern populace who in turn shall force Lincoln to sue for peace. Our worst case scenario would be waiting for Lincoln's defeat in November rather than obtaining peace this summer. In either case the war terminates by year's end."

Clement Clay immediately voiced a concern to the secretary of state. "Mr. Benjamin, I've always assumed military activity initiated by us from Canada most certainly would damage the prospects of an alignment with Britain."

Benjamin emitted a deep, gregarious laugh. "Though caution is essential, our Yankee foe blundered diplomatically once again." He politely smiled and continued. "You, Mr. Clay, have not enjoyed my confidential conversations with British and French representatives following Dahlgren's aborted raid into Richmond. True, officially the Europeans perceive us a prodigal child nearing our return to our Yankee father. Elected Republican leaders not only condoned the assassination of the head of a government, albeit an unrecognized one in their eyes, but they actually conceived the deed. Removal of heads of state by assassination greatly concerns our friends on the continent. Acceptance of such acts could spread chaos throughout the civilized world if this Pandora's Box remains open." Staring at Thompson, and then Clay, and pointing his index finger upward, Benjamin reiterated, "You are correct Mr. Clay when you say we must proceed vigilantly lest we lose the important card our foe so recklessly dealt us."

Davis requested Thompson to "recite the military aspects of our operation."

"Surely, Mr. President," answered Thompson happy to regain the floor. "Our desire, without jeopardizing relations with Britain," added the commissioner with a glance toward the secretary of war, "is to secure the freedom of thousands of Southern soldiers held captive in Ohio, Indiana, and Illinois. Our coordinated efforts shall thrust a new theater of operations upon the unsuspecting Yankees. While our manpower generates from this untapped source, the enemy must draw existing troops from either the eastern, western, or trans-Mississippi areas. I suspect maybe from all three. Our agents inform us that vast unnumbered legions of discontented Democrats, organized as the Sons of Liberty by the Knights of the Golden Circle, await the opportunity to rise up with the desire for separation from Lincoln's government. I repeat for all present," continued Thompson, as his eyes moved from the president's to the secretary's, "that while planning may occur within Canada, all missions must initiate from Yankee soil."

With the ringing of church bells through the open window signaling noon's arrival, President Davis stood. "Gentlemen, another morning's vanished but may it be part of a very productive day which brings forth fruit from the seeds we planted three springs ago. Thank you for your attention and dedication. God's speed to you both."

As the three began their exit Davis called out, "a word with you please Mr. Secretary." After the other two disappeared the president asked for, "your thoughts, Mr. Benjamin?"

"I am optimistic for our prospects." Always eager to acquiesce to the president's want of positive feedback he added, "Although Thompson and Mr. Clay shall doubtfully function together, your decision to send our Alabama friend to chaperone our commissioner and the two million dollars appropriated for the operation shall in the least keep Mr. Thompson an honest man. Brilliant, if I may say so, sir."

Davis smiled, relishing a confidant who always saw eye to eye with him on such matters. "Clement Clay is a rare breed indeed. Most men assign their allegiance to either one faction or another. Those who don't, alienate both parties. Mr. Clay possesses the integrity to tactfully dissent when necessary but maintain respect from all. I understand both his detractors and benefactors still hold the man in high esteem. If we have no more to discuss, I bid you good day,"

The president climbed the back stairs to his second floor office. An hour later Varina arrived per her daily schedule with a basket containing the midday meal. She covered a white plate with red berries, bread, and fish, set it before him, and handed him a knife and fork. The first morsel of cod reached his mouth when a shrill shriek followed by the rapid thumping of footsteps echoed up the rear staircase. The children's nurse Catherine appeared, hysterically informing them little Joe fell from the stone balcony rail to the brick drive on the south side of the house. His fork clattered on the china. Joseph's father and mother sped down the stairs and raced outside. The horrific yet touching sight of seven year old Jeff Jr. kneeling with lips moving in prayer over his younger brother rattled the parents who advanced for closer observation.

Jefferson and Varina gasped in terror. The left side of Joe's battered, contorted face, with blood dripping from the mouth, rested motionlessly on the bricks. His small shoulder pushed grotesquely against his neck. His thin left arm extended out with a misshapen bend between the elbow and wrist. His right arm lay beneath his slender torso which erratically rose and fell as the child struggled to breathe. His distraught father delicately scooped the shattered form and carried it inside. Varina's emotions poured out as she sobbed uncontrollably and followed behind. During the brief interlude from the time they summoned the physician until he arrived the child expired.

For the second time the man who bore the burden of the deaths of thousands of sons of the Confederacy suffered a loss of his own boy. The following day, instead of attending church for a joyous service of worship on the first Sunday in May, the Davis family, joined by friends, dignitaries, and numerous well-wishers, laid young Joseph Davis to rest.

36 – TOGETHER AGAIN

While he stood on the station platform in Columbus, Georgia, John gazed over to the curling smoke escaping from the stacks of the iron foundry operating along the banks of the Chattahoochee River. After confirming Martha still resided in the bustling industrial city near the Alabama state line John endured another inconvenient journey via the Southern rail system. Rail travel proved even more disrupted and inefficient than it had two years ago. At the station a fellow passenger directed him up toward 10th Street. He eagerly yet apprehensively ascended the hill. Barely two months together; over two years apart. Time changes people. War transforms them rapidly. He prayed during their separation that they grew closer, not farther apart. His pace reduced the trek to ten minutes. He paused to gaze at the white brick two-story home with red shutters before he opened the black wrought iron gate, climbed the steps to the spacious porch, and took a deep breath. Three short raps with the brass door knocker. The tall, narrow door creaked open after which a skinny teenaged Negro girl greeted the guest.

"Who may I announce has arrived, sir?" the servant politely asked.

"I'm John Beall from Virginia here to …"

"Lord Almighty," she shouted, "you is all Miss Martha said you'd be and then some." In her exuberance she left the visitor standing on the porch with the door wide-open while she raced through the house shouting, "Miss Martha, Miss Martha! He's here! Your Massa Beall's arrived!" Suddenly remembering protocol she scampered to the entryway. "Massa Beall, forgive this rude girl. Right this way sir."

As she escorted him inside, Martha, Fanny, and an unfamiliar man appeared from the rear. The moment their eyes locked John knew the fire from two years past now blazed even more intently. He opened his arms as she wrapped hers around him. The feel of her warm, supple body pressing against his fit more naturally then during her farewell embrace in Mississippi. The well-mannered Southern lady pulled away, embarrassed by her unbecoming display of public affection, all to the good natured laughter of her audience.

Fanny advanced to greet John. "Since my sister is distracted with other thoughts I would like to introduce you to our gracious host. Colonel Ambrose Chambers, this is, Captain now, I believe Mr. Lucas informed us? Captain John Beall. And you left us a mere private, though Lord knows we still need plenty of them." A heavyset elderly gentleman leaning on his cane limped forward. "Mister or should as I say Captain Beall, I am pleased to meet the man of whom Martha speaks so highly."

Instead of deviating into the complexities of his rank John simply replied, "Honored to meet you sir, and for the next two weeks we can dispense with the military title." Acknowledging the older woman who just appeared John said, "You must be Mrs. Chambers."

A tall, slender lady stepped forward and softly offered, "I now understand how our Martha is so smitten with you, sir." The last statement forced a crimson flush over both of the young lovers' faces.

Colonel Chambers saved John by saying, "Ladies, please allow me the indulgence of a brief time with our guest to divulge current war news which so slowly filters to us from Richmond."

The newcomer's smile communicated his deep appreciation for the rescue.

That evening, John and Martha's conversation remained casual even after the others retired. The exhaustion of the trip caught up with John while the excitement of his arrival drained Martha. They sat side by side, hands entwined, with Martha's head resting softly against John's shoulder. Each thankfully learned the other's immediate family remained safe and sound although John expressed concern for Hezekiah, who no one had heard from for almost two years. He avoided accounts of his varied experiences, especially the tragic events the previous October. The next day he'd reveal those details.

The following morning Martha accompanied John on the short walk to the livery to rent a carriage. A storm front had moved through prior to sunup. The previous day's hazy mugginess had blown off to the east. Clear blue skies overhead, mild temperatures, low humidity, his sweetheart on his right arm, and a picnic basket on his left. What more could he ask for? His head shook as if to clear his mind. Just an end to the war, Confederate independence for Virginia, and Martha as his wife.

She patted his upper arm with her right hand as they walked, and asked, "Something troubling you this fine day, my love?"

"Nothing really."

Martha abruptly halted and stared directly into his eyes with her admonishing schoolmarm glare. "One day, God willing in the not too distant future, all your concerns and cares shall be mine, and all of mine shall be yours. This should be our relationship now."

Not ready to reveal all his thoughts to anyone quite yet, he attempted to sidestep the issue as they resumed their stroll. "My apologies, Miss Martha. I'm somewhat inexperienced with the engagement business. I shall attempt to be more open in the future. Where shall we ride today?"

"Where shall we ride today?" she sarcastically laughed. "The better response is thank you for being so concerned, my dear. These are the thoughts I wish to share."

Another frustrated shake of his head followed. Trapped by a war; trapped by a woman. Guess I'll take the woman. He paused, looked directly into her sparkling hazel eyes, and promised, "Thank you for being so concerned, my dear. The thoughts I wish to share shall be disclosed once we ride into the country."

Outside the livery John clasped her hand and assisted her up onto the buggy seat all the while staring longingly at the appealing feminine shape poured into the simple green cotton dress. Their carriage soon rattled behind the ancient beige mare ambling down Front Street.

Fragrant red roses draped over white picket fences and trellises. Blue hydrangeas accented homes. Long spirea branches, laden with white blossoms, bowed down to touch lush green lawns. Chirping of birds filled the air with shrill melodies. "When I left Richmond spring was fully descending upon Virginia." Taking a deep breath of aromatic Georgia air he stretched, smiled, and added, "I see spring arrives here far earlier."

"Yes it does," she replied impatiently. "Well?"

"Well?"

"John, we're in the country. What troubles you?'

"I'll tell all Martha, with the proviso that you demand as much from our children as you do from me."

"If I love them as deeply as you, which I assure you I will, I shall require more."

Spontaneously he wrapped his right arm around her and drew her close. John understood a delay would only initiate another lecture. "Martha, as we walked to the livery I realized my only desire for happiness beyond being here with you is having you as my wife."

"John, if …"

"Please listen my dear. This war traps us so. We agreed marriage shall wait until after the war. Until then the years of our lives drift away. Three years ago I entered the war with a healthy, twenty-six year old body. Some days I believe I live in a forty year old shell. I fear if I inherit my father's physical flaws my years with you shall be numbered. I resent being placed in such a predicament. My sanity returns only when I pray, 'thy will be done,' for we must maintain trust in the Lord."

Her enchanting round eyes peered from below her pale yellow sunbonnet's large folds. "John, since the day we promised ourselves to each other I've yearned to join you in marriage anytime."

"Aye, Martha, and that knowledge tortures me. Remember when we agreed a man cannot serve two masters? A self-serving man choosing between a kind, loving wife or a cruel, heartless war chooses the former. But the man who chooses the wife while he forsakes his country is alas, no man at all. Perhaps my expectations are too lofty. I desire the perfect wife," he said while squeezing her tightly, "but I also long to live in the perfect world which I'm fighting to obtain."

Tears trickled down her cheeks as the mare trudged onward. To their left appeared a lane bisecting a small, flat meadow terminating at an embankment overlooking the river.

"I'm developing a powerful hunger, Miss O'Bryan. Care to join me for a midday meal?"

"I'd be most delighted sir. I assume you are taking me to the overlook?"

"As you wish my dear."

White flowering heads randomly sprouted from rich clover. Orange day lilies swayed majestically along the distant fence row. Queen Anne's lace and blue corn flower dotted the meadow's predominantly green carpet. John set the wagon's brake as they halted beneath a mature oak tree.

He hopped down to assist her. When her arm stretched out he extended his hands and boldly placed them firmly on her narrow sides. With a lunge she fell into his arms. As he drew her tightly to him he could feel the excited beating of her heart thumping through her light summer dress and vibrating against his chest. The contour of her sensuous body filled the voids of his strong masculine frame. Soon their lips parted with moist, warm tongues rubbing together. She slowly broke away.

"Is it sinful to crave all of the passions of marriage?" she piously asked.

"I do believe your desire, and mine, are only natural. Is it sinful to long for that which is natural? No. Is it sinful to submit to such yearning before God's ordained time? Yes. One of our common bonds is our dedication to living our Christian lives as directed by our Lord. By devaluing our respect for Him we cheapen the bond we share."

She initiated another embrace. "John, I love you so. Our visions for our future, our values, our souls, all one. If you could hold me forever I would never ask for anything else. Is that possible?"

"Only after this cursed war."

Following a satisfying meal and light conversation the couple boarded the carriage. Martha reluctantly asked, "How much longer shall the war continue?"

"I suspect the war as we know it shall cease by year's end." He knew her furrowed forehead and wide-eyed expression asked for clarification. "A Republican defeat in November, or of course an overwhelming victory by General Lee in the field gives us our freedom. If the highly improbable reelection of Lincoln occurs the war continues for years in some form. Yankee manpower and industrial output continue to replenish their voids. We would continue shrinking with more of our territory becoming occupied. I fear eventually our soldiers would fade into the countryside only to periodically reappear as partisan fighters for years to come." With a shrug of his shoulders he haplessly added, "Maybe such activity would eventually bankrupt the Yankees."

A gloomy frown twisted Martha's appealing lips downward. She despondently replied, "Then we may well expect the killing and misery to continue much of our lives."

Gripping her hand firmly he buoyantly replied, "Martha O'Bryan, I refuse to wait that long. I've recommended a plan to Mr. Davis for an operation deep into Yankee territory to bring this conflict to a satisfactory conclusion by November."

She jerked away from his shoulder and with a flabbergasted expression of wonderment could only say, "President Jefferson Davis?" When he nodded affirmatively she challenged, "You never wrote that you interviewed with the President of the Confederacy!"

"And for good reason. The mails are unreliable. Yankee cavalry raids rampage deeper south. Inefficient transportation allows bags of correspondence to be set aside and forgotten. Cowardly Yankee agents ingratiate themselves into positions to read our mails. I regret, my dear, that in this case my master, the military, receives the nod."

"I understand, but share what you've done and what you're planning."

The buggy reached the livery by late afternoon, but prior to their return John shared a great deal including details of his seafaring adventures. While he romanticized segments of his escapades for her enjoyment, tragic events such as the unknown demise of Ned McGuire and the murder of Sands Smith visibly pained the narrator. "Damn Yankees" spewed from Martha's lips when told of Sands Smith's horrendous treatment. After swearing Martha to secrecy, he divulged his dream of freeing prisoners from the Lake Erie prison camp and of spreading havoc across the North. She gasped with excitement while he painted the image of a successful attack on the prison, followed by the chaotic retribution visiting the secure citizens of targeted Northern cities. When they reached the colonel's home euphoric optimism engulfed the couple. They trusted within the year war would reside only as an ugly memory, existing neither on the battlefields nor in the mountains.

Their remaining days in Georgia disappeared faster than a shooting star. When the departure day arrived, Amelia Chambers and Fannie remained at the house while the colonel drove Martha and John to the station. The gentleman shook John's hand, wished him well, and wandered away, "to tend to some very pressing business matters that need my immediate attention."

Avoiding the pain of farewell John mumbled something about her remarkable relatives. "First General Williams and now Colonel Chambers."

Disregarding all propriety Martha begged, "Johnny hold me. Hold me until eternity comes or the train departs."

With every piece of new artillery secured atop a flat car, or every freight car door that banged shut, John realized the end of their time together drew nearer. Finally a loud "all aboard" officially terminated the visit, the two-week period he later referred to as the happiest time of his life.

He broke loose from her tightly pressing body and gave her a quick kiss. "I love you, Martha O'Bryan."

She managed a choked, "Love you, John Beall."

The train's departure flooded Martha's cheeks with tears. Three years ago such a show of weakness would have embarrassed her. Now her visible demonstration of love comforted her. She smiled believing deeply within her soul the war's end neared.

37 – LET THE GAMES BEGIN

A small wiry man descended the grand stairway and commenced pacing to and fro in the busy Montréal hotel lobby. He glanced at the clock behind the desk, shrugged his shoulders, and seated himself on a plush red upholstered chair. Three minutes later he reached into his vest pocket, removed his watch, shook his head in disgust, and impatiently rose. He strode to the window, stared onto the street in both directions, and again commenced walking back and forth. He softly muttered, "Damn bureaucrats, always set the schedule but still arrive late.

From a distance the annoyed slightly-built twenty-three year old with delicate features appeared effeminate. His slender frame blended with natural dexterity to create the skilled horseman and the deadly combatant who rode with John Hunt Morgan into Indiana and Ohio. Unfortunately his elusive talents failed to prevent his capture during the July raid a year ago. Nervous energy and confinement had been known to suck the spirit from incarcerated men. Not Thomas Henry Hines—the caged Kentuckian designed the daring escape plan from the Ohio Penitentiary in November that same year.

On March 16, 1864, Secretary of War Seddon assigned Captain Hines the lead military role in a vague assignment to work with discontented Northerners to intensify dissatisfaction with the Lincoln government. Hines arrived in Canada almost two months prior to the Confederate peace commissioners. His enthusiasm for the mission escalated as he conversed with numerous escaped Confederate prisoners and Union draft dodgers. Their dialogue confirmed all Richmond led him to believe. He dutifully accepted his subordination to the newly arrived chief commissioner and his entourage, although he became impatient with every wasted moment as the grains of sand drained from the Confederacy's hour glass. Where were they, wondered Hines? Whether it be a week, a day, or just fifteen minutes, in these crucial times unproductive movements by civilians irritated him. Hell, he didn't even know what the emissaries looked like. Just three well-attired Southerner civilians, a description fitting half the men in Montreal.

Jacob Thompson, accompanied by two other gentlemen, entered the lobby. A skinny fellow near the far wall who pivoted and paced over the carpet caught Thompson's attention. Richmond authorities told the commissioner his contact bore a striking resemblance to the renowned actor, John Wilkes Booth. Jet-black head of wavy hair, trim moustache, high cheek bones, deep skin hue, piercing eyes, slight build. Should be his man. Hines's eyes met Thompson's. Both walked instinctively forward for introductions.

Rumors relevant to Thompson abounded. Some positive—the rest? Hines wondered why Davis trusted the man. Other men refusing the assignment possibly limited the president's choices. Hines turned his attentions to the next man. Although everyone held Clement Clay in the highest esteem, concern existed for the lack of stamina in a man not quite forty-six who tired easily. Hines then met James Holcombe. Insiders told Hines not to expect Holcombe to contribute more than a congenial southern intellectual personality which could ingratiate acquaintances crucial to the operation's success. Beyond that Holcombe's usefulness appeared limited.

Thompson suggested they become better acquainted over dinner. After seating themselves in the elegant dining room Hines spoke. "The papers morbidly refer to the spring battlefields as killing grounds. Papers regularly exaggerate statistics. Are causalities actually that horrendous?"

Thompson set his partially emptied wine glass down and answered somberly, "Unfortunately, yes."

Clay added, "Without remorse Grant casually trades Northern blood for Southern blood. The Yankee general apparently desires to bleed the Confederacy to death even if his army expires in the process. Simple genocide," concluded Clay with a grimace.

Holcombe interjected, "One easily concludes the black Republicans goal is to eradicate all white men in the North and South so the niggers inherit the entire land."

Hines hoped to avoid unproductive political ranting and focus on crucial matters at hand. Ignoring the mild-mannered Holcombe, he looked to the chief commissioner. "I imagine the Northern citizenry is as appalled at the slaughter as are we. While tragic, Providence places us here at an opportune time, wouldn't you agree?"

"Very astute, Captain Hines," replied Thompson. "What do you advise my boy, now that you've resided in Canada for several months?"

Typical slippery politician, thought Hines, though the captain didn't permit his outward demeanor to betray his inner cynicism. I propose the recommendation and he obtains the credit if we succeed, while I receive the blame if we fail. "My last instructions from Richmond were to communicate with anyone here who would listen that our presence portrays our aspiration for a negotiated peace." Hines paused, leaned back and reflected before saying, "Believe me, there is no shortage of attentive ears. Some belong to petty men with self-serving motives. Others to poorly disguised Yankee agents. A few to important men of value with noble character desiring to end the bloodshed. In fact Commissioner Thompson, I've arranged an interview with one such man next Thursday in Windsor. I took the liberty to arrange the initial discussion alone with Clement Vallandigham knowing you gentlemen require time to travel the 400 miles to Toronto. If potential for productive conversation with Mr. Vallandigham presents itself I shall wire you. Otherwise you shall not waste valuable time."

"Excellent, Captain." Looking for approval from his companions Thompson asked, "Agreeable with you gentlemen?"

"Jacob," Clay curtly snapped, "you understood James and I believe we shall perform more effectively in Montreal rather than in Toronto. Was I not direct on this issue?"

A delicate operation led by men with visible animosity toward each other. How did Davis select this group, Hines wondered?

"Certainly you expressed yourself, my dear friend," answered the unflappable commissioner. Smiling, he placed his hand on Clay's shoulder and patronizingly continued. "I only wished to extend the courtesy to you to rearrange your plans if you so desired." Holcombe received no similar courtesy as Thompson correctly assumed Holcombe's path followed Clay's.

Unimpressed, Clay brusquely questioned, "And the funds assigned to me to operate shall also be deposited prior to your departure?"

Thompson pulled his hand back and feigned injury to delicate feelings. "Of course, my dear Clement. Have you ever known me not to be a man of my word?"

Clay declined to answer while Hines silently questioned the value of that word.

"You shall have $90,000 credited in your name Mr. Clay." Turning to Hines, Thompson casually said, "That still leaves me $800,000 with which to operate."

The bread riots ignited by hungry housewives in Richmond flashed through Hines's mind while he absorbed the nonchalant decision of trusting a man like Thompson with almost a million dollars, while rumors circulated that the Confederate treasury neared depletion. Hines returned to the business at hand interrupted by the spat between the envoys.

"Mr. Thompson," Hines interjected before the conversation deviated onto another unproductive course, "I trust you gentlemen wish me to continue my outline of our operations?"

"Definitely," replied Clay, relieved to listen to anyone but Thompson.

"I've been instructed with your continued approval and under your supervision to sow seeds of discord wherever the opportunity arises. Our schemes may include joining forces with sympathetic Northerners or freeing a number of our lads incarcerated in Yankee prisons."

The trio uncharacteristically nodded in agreement.

Hines stood to conclude the meeting. "I'm sure you gentlemen are tired. Mr. Clay, Mr. Holcombe, you shall find Montreal a hospitable and pleasant city. Mr. Thompson, we shall maintain contact through channels by which you shall become very familiar. I pray my interview with Mr. Vallandigham brings you to Windsor."

The following Thursday, Hines stood on the broad planked walkway outside the Hirons House in Windsor observing active commerce on Pitt Street. Business appeared brisk with shoppers entering and leaving McMichenson's dry goods store to his left. Drays brimming with goods from the docks filled the thoroughfare. Other than the appearance of an occasional Southerner dressed in the remnants of a butternut uniform or the passing of a suspected Yankee draft dodger, one would never suspect Canada's neighbor across the Detroit River struggled in the throes of a four year civil war. Hines's head told him the draft dodgers might become valuable allies. His heart told him if a man chose to run from a fight he would be of little value when events called for action. The Confederate agent inhaled a deep breath of the warm June air and entered the hotel. The desk clerk directed him to Vallandigham's comfortably furnished room.

"Mr. Hines, please come in," welcomed the former U.S. Representative from Ohio, who offered a sincere handshake but a cautious expression. "Meet my associate, Mr. Edgar Shelby, who is just preparing to depart."

"My pleasure, Mr. Shelby. Enjoy this beautiful day, sir," he added as Shelby disappeared through the doorway.

Vallandigham motioned for Hines to sit in one of the dark wooden arm chairs on either side of the round white marble-topped table. The renowned Copperhead opened the upper-story balcony door, glanced to the left, closed the door, and sat down. “Preferred a room without the veranda, but no other vacancies existed on the second floor. Prying Republican spies infest this fair city. But forgive my ranting. Commence so that we may determine if we share common ground with which to work for a common goal.”

Though youthful, Hines‘s experiences these past several years taught him politicians fell into two categories. The former crowd championed a specific agenda with eyes focused on individual gain. The latter faction consisted of highly principled men whose integrity demanded uncompromising dedication for their ideals. Clement Vallandigham fell into the second group who sacrificed wealth, physical well-being, and family. Hines familiarized himself with Vallandigham’s arrest in Ohio the previous year and the subsequent exile to the South. Hines looked into the former attorney’s eyes and trusted he faced an honest, well-intentioned, but inflexible person.

“Mr. Vallandigham, I assume you also cringe at the appalling casualties thrust upon us after only one month of the spring campaign. Yankee, excuse me sir, Union casualties are estimated at 55,000. That’s half Grant’s eastern army!” Hines dramatically covered his downcast eyes, shook his head, and sighed. “Our sources tell us the Army of the Potomac only, and I shudder to use the term ‘only’, suffered 100,000 casualties during the first three years of the war. The same sources inform us Lee’s lost over 20,000 men since the first of May. At this rate who shall populate this country a year from now? Lincoln must be stopped. Our…”

“On that issue we don’t share common ground, we own it!” the emotionally charged peace Democrat forcefully interrupted. “The fiend destroyed more of the *Constitution* in three years than prior generations have since the document’s inception eighty years ago. Keep in mind, the man, though ruthless as a grizzly bear, is also cunning as a fox. Last year the imbecile Burnside proved himself capable of neither commanding troops on the battlefield nor garrisons in occupied territories. The fool arrested me and figuratively speaking dumped me on Lincoln's door step. Had the president incarcerated me, loyal Democrats in Ohio and other western states might have openly rebelled, but my release would have undermined military authority. Lincoln instead shipped me to President Davis's door step. He created the perception of me as a conspirator returning to my compatriots. Poppycock! I no longer would aid the Confederacy in her rebellion than I would the Republicans with their injustices."

Interesting comment, thought Hines, before Vallandigham presented his closing argument. "At all cost this country as we know it shall be destroyed forever with another four years of a Lincoln presidency. Freedom of speech and freedom of press no longer remain guaranteed rights. What liberties shall next be usurped?"

"Unfortunately, as you know, Mr. Vallandigham, on Tuesday Lincoln became the official Republican nominee for president. Do you anticipate Fremont's nomination by the radical contingent of their party, which splintered and held a separate convention in Cleveland hampers Lincoln?"

"Hampers? Yes. Stops? No. That responsibility rests solely with our Democracy. We cannot fracture as we did in '60. May I ask who you supported in that election?"

"Breckinridge hailed from near my home in Kentucky."

Vallandigham countered, "I canvassed tirelessly for my good friend, God rest his soul, Stephen Douglas. You and I both share responsibility for this current slaughter. Either gentleman running unopposed would have appealed to the masses and been elected president." Placing his hand firmly on Hines's, he solemnly stated, "We must not allow such shortsightedness to interfere this November."

Build the bridge, Hines thought. No value in stating Douglas's northern ties would have brought the same result, although his death in June of 1861 would have elevated Douglas's running mate, Georgian Herschel Johnson, to the presidency.

“Mr. Vallandigham, you elegantly state you and I possess common ground on the issue before us. While total agreement on all matters remains unlikely I believe another conference in several days, with Commissioner Thompson, shall assuredly draw us to deeper commonality. With your permission, may I arrange a meeting this Saturday?”

The Ohioan stroked his chin whiskers thoughtfully and locked into Hines’s eyes. “I often feel the Confederacy and the Lincoln administration both perceive my greatest value as a pawn in this despicable chess game. Forgive my hesitancy, Mr. Hines. You present yourself as an honorable man and on this basis only shall I acquiesce to continued dialogue. I shall see you here Saturday at, say one o’clock?”

“Perfect sir,” answered Hines. He rose, bid Vallandigham farewell, and headed for the telegraph office.

38 – ANOTHER MEETING

The following Saturday, Thompson conversed with his subordinate in Hines's room at the Royal Victorian Hotel in Windsor. Hines reiterated, "If Mr. Vallandigham believes we solicit his aid to achieve Confederate independence we forfeit all opportunity for his cooperation."

A somewhat irritated senior commissioner asked his know-it-all subordinate, "How then do you recommend we proceed?"

Hines unflappably answered, "We first convince the man our role in Canada, should we fail to initiate a peace conference, reluctantly becomes a plan of operations in the northwest to capitalize upon the disenchantment of Northern citizens. Emphasize the funds available for dissenting newspapers. Discuss currency manipulation. If the session progresses satisfactorily we must tread toward the prison camp objective."

"Is it prudent to discuss gold purchases?"

"Probably not, Commissioner. The fewer men aware of that activity the better but we must superficially introduce the concept of liberating prisoners to gauge his reaction."

"Very well," agreed Thompson. "Since Mr. Vallandigham seems comfortable with you, initiate the dialogue. I'll intercede to gain his confidence when the opportunity arises," concluded the lifelong politician in a condescending tone.

Two light raps outside room 27 and the dark oak paneled door opened. Edgar Shelby invited them in and excused himself. The Confederate agents approached Vallandigham who warmly smiled as he shook the younger agent's hand. "How very good to see you again, Mr. Hines." With noticeably less cordiality he turned to greet the commissioner. "And you, sir, I assume are Mr. Thompson."

"Mr. Vallandigham, I've so anticipated this meeting. Mr. Hines communicated much of your sentiment."

Back off Jake, thought Hines as the men seated themselves. Don't steer the conversation. Let it flow to us.

As if intuitively reading Hines's mind, Thompson questioned in a disarming manner, "Before we begin, I seem to recollect you interviewed John Brown shortly after the insurrection?" Vallandigham nodded affirmatively to which the commissioner asked, "What was your opinion of the man?"

"A very interesting person. In his own misguided mind he believed himself to be an instrument of God, ordained to fulfill a destiny at Harpers Ferry. While I abhorred the man's motives and loathed his abolitionist actions I truly admired his self-sacrificing commitment. Enough of the past. Our focus must remain the present, specifically the November election. Our good Mr. Hines implied financial support is available."

Thompson smiled and bobbed his head affirmatively. "Despite limited resources within the Confederacy our congress recognizes no reconciliation shall occur with the current administration. Funds are allocated to allow Northern publications promoting peace to continue. I trust you sir may offer recommendations for worthy recipients."

Vallandigham smiled as a handful of deserving beneficiaries crossed his mind.

The commissioner moved swiftly to capitalize upon his newfound momentum. "Although we strive to avoid violence our adversary occasionally drives us to forceful measures. In the past citizens of the South and Democrats of the North united to keep the abolitionists at bay. Currently we may be forced to encourage civil unrest in select Northern cities. Many unfortunate Southern boys now rot in Ohio, Indiana, and Illinois prisons. Coincidently these states desire to sever relations with the New England radicals."

Vallandigham interrupted and emotionally decried, "Mr. Thompson, at no time have I approved of the formation of the Confederacy! I certainly harbor no designs to further shatter our beloved Union!" Looking to Hines he admonished, "Did I not make myself clear to you on that premise?"

"Absolutely clear, sir. Forgive my inability to better communicate such to the commissioner."

Realizing his misstep Thompson quickly withdrew his foot and delicately danced past the irksome issue. "My sincere apologies, Mr. Vallandigham, I must elucidate myself."

Hines winced and waited for the commissioner's fabricated explanation. The soldier detested the deceit necessary to operate behind lines. Men such as Thompson lacked conscience. For a straightforward man like Hines fabricated explanations were simply lies. To the commissioner such responses merely perfected the truth.

Thompson cautiously began, "Nor do I desire a further fracture of our beloved Union. I reluctantly agreed to the temporary separation three years ago hoping our brief absence would arouse the true Northern population into demanding reconciliation. Lincoln manipulated the first shots on Sumter confident he could mobilize an army and place himself on the throne as commander-in-chief. I fear even his defeat in November might fail to remove the power-crazed monarch from his lofty seat. For this reason we must reluctantly stir the embers of unrest."

Vallandigham glared at Thompson. His fiery eyes locked into Hines, who prayed Thompson avoided recklessly sabotaging their undertaking. To Hines's relief Vallandigham reached across the table and firmly grasped a hand of each Southerner. "Gentleman, my only objective remains toppling the traitor who divides our Union by trampling over our *Constitution*. But violence must be kept to a minimum."

Thompson asked, "Mr. Vallandigham, how many men are at your disposal? I understand the Sons of Liberty number in the tens, maybe hundreds of thousands."

Vallandigham leaned back. He asked his guests if they cared for a glass of wine or brandy to momentarily divert the conversation while he gathered his thoughts.

Thompson enjoyed brandy while Hines politely sipped mellow concord. The leader of the Sons of Liberty replied, "Gentlemen, though I respect your integrity I must decline to answer only because I received the knowledge through my pledge of secrecy. If I release such information I shall no longer be the man of honor with whom you desire to collaborate. True?" he asked, subtlety nodding his head affirmatively.

Thompson concurred. The term 'touché' flashed through Hines's mind as he recognized both politicians adeptly played this game.

Vallandigham offered, "Of the Knights I possess no firsthand knowledge. I suspect you Southerners embellished their strength to intimidate the Republicans. They turned the worm by exaggerating your numbers to strike fear in the hearts of Northern citizens in order to more easily bypass the *Constitution*. I'll provide sufficient men from the Sons of Liberty to spread the chaos you desire only if necessary. May I assume funds for this venture shall also be promptly forthcoming?"

"Of course," replied Thompson. "Greenbacks, or even gold if necessary. What is your next course of action sir?"

"On an undecided date, maybe July Fourth, I shall return to Ohio."

Hines quickly protested, "But you shall be arrested again."

A sly grin crossed the man's face. "Precisely. I humbly anticipate a second outrageous arrest shall incite the civil unrest you so covet."

"But what of our plans together, Mr. Vallandigham?" objected Thompson, visibly upset.

"My dear friend Jacob, if I may take the liberty to speak with familiarity?" A large organization such as the Sons operates within sufficient structure for subordinates to competently grasp the reins when need arises. Lack of such structure is suicidal, is it not?"

Thompson reached across to grasp Vallandigham's hand between his. Responding to the Northerner's lack of formality the commissioner responded, "Clement, I truly underestimate you and your organization. Lifting his glass he toasted, "To the Union as it was; to the *Constitution* as it is."

"Hear, hear," resounded the echo throughout the room.

Shortly thereafter the Southerners strode through the lobby and acknowledged Edgar Shelby sitting in a wingback chair reading the *New York Herald*.

During the evening meal with Thompson, Hines asked, "Do we consider Mr. Vallandigham a useful ally?"

"As November draws nearer our friend must recognize the value in joining us. His Sons of Liberty are a spirited group of men committed to a common cause or so it seems. Despite his adamant belief that his arrest shall ignite flames of discontent in Ohio and elsewhere, and that the Sons of Liberty shall be guided effectively by officials within their established hierarchy, our people tell me Vallandigham is without exception their only leader. Our people suggest some of the Sons actually follow the man more than his cause. In any event, without our expertise to lead them in the field I fear little of consequence shall occur."

"I assume we shall continue to plan independent of him. Often large numbers impede rather than assist an operation," Hines added.

"True, but realize ours in no small undertaking. If successful we'll release upwards of 30,000 men simultaneously from five prisons. Rumors persist the Sons membership rolls exceed a quarter of a million. Unleash Vallandigham's men with ours and even the Yankees lack the manpower to stop us."

"Commissioner Thompson, I respectfully suggest membership of the Sons remains entirely speculation. I acknowledge the accuracy of the prisoner count but I hesitate to risk all on a far reaching alliance with men whose stated position is reestablishment of the Union, not independence for the South."

"Thomas," replied Thompson reaching across the table and condescendingly patting the captain's arm, "among the inner circle of men in Richmond responsible for conducting this war exists a nucleus who understands the proper blend of military force with diplomacy to achieve one's end."

Diplomacy or politics wondered Hines?

Thompson continued, "With the utmost appreciation for all the burdens of state thrust upon Mr. Davis, I recognize his comfort level lies with the military. His noted inflexibility in matters of state indicates he continues operating with the mindset of a disciplined army officer. The Confederacy needs to augment its deficiencies by capitalizing upon all opportunities presented to us. If we achieve freedom by defeating Lincoln in the ballot box rather than on the battlefield independence is ours just the same, is it not? Our dedicated President Davis dreams of a last grand victory on the field of battle reminiscent of Yorktown where we humiliated the British. Proper manipulation, excuse me, proper handling of Vallandigham's forces combined with extraction of our prisoners all but removes Lincoln and his cronies from Washington with or without military victory. But our military shall not be forgotten. General Longstreet, imagine Longstreet the defensive genius, proposed an offensive operation into Kentucky this spring to capitalize upon the unrest in the Ohio Valley. I persist in communicating with Secretary of War Seddon in hopes of initiating activity in Kentucky and Missouri coinciding with our activities."

"When shall we precede, sir, since the Democrats postponed their convention from July 4th to the end of August?"

"Probably in the latter part of July. Remember the necessity of flexibility. Favorable situations may arise in the North, or on the battlefield, or even relish the thought," smiled Thompson, "from intervention by our European friends."

"Our work begins in earnest, doesn't it?"

"That it does, son. That it does."

Several blocks away at a corner table in the Hirons House, Shelby dined with Vallandigham. The former inquired as to the specifics of his associate's interview with the Confederates.

"As I expected Edgar, our organization could be useful for their operation to instigate unrest in the northwest. Mr. Hines appears to conduct himself in a transparent manner. Mr. Thompson," Vallandigham smiled before he continued, "let us suffice it to say Mr. Thompson obviously spent a great deal of time in Washington before the war and now seems well-versed in Richmond politics. His position drifts like the tall grass in a gentle summer breeze."

"You shall avoid collaborating with the likes of him I assume?"

"On the contrary, my good friend. I'm reminded of the story of the two roosters that schemed to rule the hen house. Just as one prepared to wrest control the fox stole a hen. The roosters realized the fox might eventually abscond with the entire female population while the males battled one another. Together the two gents laid a successful trap and disposed of the predator. Mr. Shelby, do you know which one ruled the roost after they eliminated the fox?"

Shelby shrugged his shoulders allowing Vallandigham to finish. "Nor do I, but they eradicated the nastiest threat leaving the victors to settle the issue for the greatest advantage of the chicken coup. If we utilize Mr. Thompson to depose Lincoln our next objective shall be easier to obtain provided we avoid becoming the bait to draw in the predator. I informed the Confederates we plan to depart on Independence Day. I assume you've freely spread the same in casual conversation?"

Shelby nodded affirmatively.

"Good. Time is on our side. Lincoln appears set on Grant. Davis contends with advances from North Carolinians and Georgians wishing to negotiate a separate peace. It is an ideal setting to separate, but not divorce ourselves from our Southern friends. We'll inconspicuously cross into Detroit in three days rather than the three weeks we've led everyone to believe. Then on to Dayton for my arrest.

Wine glasses clanged in a unified toast, "To success."

39 – JULY 1864

Commissioners Clay and Holcombe stormed from Thompson's Toronto hotel room, leaving Hines standing awkwardly alone with the chief commissioner. Thompson seemed unaffected by Clay's latest verbal barrage.

"St. Catherine's provides an excellent setting for the peace conference, don't you agree Captain Hines?"

"Beyond its proximity to the border, Niagara Falls appears a pleasant site to conduct business of this nature. I am surprised you declined attending."

"Captain Hines, we both realize our current circumstances preclude any settlement with the Yankees. Lincoln simply quieted Horace Greeley by thrusting him into the situation after the newsman proclaimed peace might appear just for the asking. True, Sherman stumbled in Georgia at Kennesaw and Grant now faces General Lee across the trenches at Petersburg. On the other hand Lee encounters a different foe, one who stubbornly stands and fights after victory or defeat. Lincoln maintains hope the Yankees shall achieve victory in the east before the election while Mr. Davis believes General Lee shall defeat Grant when the Union general errs. Under the shadow of uncertainty neither president shall accept a concession with such high stakes on the table. Our time shall be better put to better use nurturing our plans to break this stalemate. Let Mr. Clay and Mr. Holcombe attend and discover the futility of the conference."

"Old Jubal Early put a scare into Washington City," interjected the usually sedate Kentuckian with a chuckle. Hines always thrilled at the word of another lightning quick raid.

Thompson replied, "We've consigned ourselves to the fact that Maryland is a Union state. Early's raid played well in Southern papers but meaningless raids into Northern territory accomplish nothing of military consequence except to encourage Northern citizens to support Lincoln against a perceived aggressive Southern foe."

"I now understand and agree with your view, Commissioner." Hines gradually developed an appreciation that politics and propaganda indeed influenced the war. "What now?"

"Our web of intrigue becomes highly complex. I'm meeting with Godfrey Hyams tomorrow."

"Hyams? Don't recall his name. What's his assignment?"

"You don't really want to know," curtly replied Thompson to his puzzled subordinate, abruptly closing the Hyams discussion. "Our primary task remains coordinating our Chicago activities. We postponed our July 20th date to mid August, I believe the 16th. We must widen our channels of communication with Mr. Vallandigham since his forces remain essential for a successful operation to liberate our men from Camp Douglas."

"You continue to trust the man? He deceived us on June 11 when he told us he would depart on the Fourth of July, but then crossed the border on June 14?"

"Captain, you must understand Mr. Vallandigham is a willing ally in our quest to evict Mr. Lincoln. He operates with a given degree of autonomy to protect his organization. While he complicates the coordination of our forces I understand his motives for a discrete return to Ohio. He assumed his arrest in his home town of Dayton would stir embers of unrest far more vigorously than would his apprehension at the border in Detroit; however, he miscalculated Lincoln's decision to all but ignore the homecoming. Our dynamic leader of the Copperhead movement still remains free for us to delicately utilize in our operation."

As Hines's anxiety lessened he remembered an issue requiring both men's attention. "The $70,000 draft is deposited in a Toronto bank for the cotton we shipped to

New York. We now have additional funds to meet our ever increasing expenses."

"Yes, perhaps more should be spread to our operatives in key positions," responded the commissioner. "Did I mention I scheduled an interview with a former member of Forrest's command who recently escaped prison and arrived in Toronto? His message indicated an interest in Ohio. We've focused so on Camp Douglas, while Johnson's Island, only forty miles across Lake Erie, holds over 2,500 officers. His scheme offers unique insights. I paid Mr. McDonald handsomely for few results. Perhaps this Cole may allow me a competent replacement. I do require your attendance when I meet with him. I've come to respect your consul Thomas. As our strategies leave the drawing board and are implemented in the field your input is critical since you are solely responsible for the military operations."

"I'm flattered, sir. I must say I've become restless with all these plans, but no action."

"Ah, to be young again, Thomas."

Casual conversation continued until two sharp raps reverberated from Thompson's hotel door. Waiting in the hallway stood a dapperly dressed man with neatly groomed light brown hair, fierce blue eyes, well-trimmed goatee, and a congenial smile. His freckled hands held a new black top hat. "Mr. Jacob Thompson, I have the pleasure to assume?"

"Yes," replied Thompson. The man's firm grip and competent manner impressed the commissioner. "And you are Mr. Cole?"

"Charles C. Cole, at your service gentlemen," answered the arrival with a sweeping, ostentatious bow.

"Mr. Cole, meet Captain Thomas H. Hines, our military liaison in Canada."

A great deal of information to a total stranger, Jake, thought Hines. "Honored to meet to you, Mr. Cole," responded the soldier with a pleasant smile. During the past six weeks Hines adjusted to masking his inner feelings with his external expressions.

"We eagerly await your presentation Mr. Cole. Please be seated," said the commissioner with a gesture toward the small sofa. "Care for refreshment? Brandy or some fine local wine perhaps?"

"Wine would be delightful. I avoid strong spirits while conducting business." Thompson poured a glass of dry white Niagara. Cole quickly drained his glass and extended it for a refill. Replenished, he seated himself.

Having observed his superior's penchant for gullibility, Hines asked in a very disarming tone, "What paths have this conflict lead you upon, Mr. Cole?"

The newcomer casually leaned back, dropped his right leg over his thigh, and smiled. "Raised in Tennessee and lusted for adventure. Joined General Forrest in '62 and rode with him until they captured me in January of '63 on a raid in West Tennessee."

"A rather late entry into the conflict," delicately challenged Hines.

"Very much so to my regret," answered Cole with his disarming smile. "Like most of us, I assumed we'd whip the Yankees in short order. Then I presumed since we failed to defeat them by the end of '61 that a settlement would occur the following spring." The speaker frowned, sighed, and stared momentarily down to the carpet before saying softly, "Shiloh changed everything. Duty called and I pried myself from my business responsibilities." He solemnly continued, "After my capture I found myself a prisoner in Sandusky."

"I thought that prison held only officers. You became an officer in only eight months?" grilled the suspicious captain while Thompson impatiently but respectfully permitted his young charge to purge his skepticism.

"Not exactly," grinned the relaxed visitor. "I'd heard officers fared better than enlisted men. Let us say I borrowed a lieutenant's jacket from a fallen comrade. Felt good to pull one over on the Yankees. After five months, just as the weather on the lake turned real fine, I got paroled." Hines detected a touch of disappointment in Cole's remark. The visitor continued, "My parole papers said lieutenant, so courtesy of the Yankees I became an officer in the Confederate Army. No telling where Forrest might be, so I migrated to Richmond and tried my hand in the Navy. Had some wild times on the high seas until our ship ran aground and we scuttled her earlier this year. While waiting for a new assignment, I overheard talk of an adventure in Canada. I humbly say that while in business I could sell spectacles to a blind man." You don't need any Jake unless they help you see through this character, thought Hines as Cole continued. "I sincerely believe you could utilize a man of my talents with the ability to ingratiate myself with people in positions of authority."

"And what experi…."

"Captain Hines," interrupted Thompson, growing weary of the interrogation. "I'm sure at a later date we can listen to more of our guest's exciting adventures but we must move forward. Your message spoke of a plan to gain control of the lakes?"

Cole placed both feet on the floor, stiffened his posture, rested his hands on his thighs, and tilted slightly forward. His excited eyes and confident expression grasped his audience's attention. "Tis common knowledge that Johnson's Island, without the protection of the warship *Michigan*, might indeed fall prey to us. If we commanded the *Michigan* the task would be all but accomplished. I propose gentlemen," continued Cole drawing both Confederates closer, "that with ample funds we shall purchase the vessel."

Hines's skeptical laugh proceeded Thompson's admonishing glare. The commissioner nodded for Cole to continue.

"Captain Hines," said Cole in an apologetic tone, "I do not insult the intelligence of either of you astute gentlemen. I desire the opportunity to curry favor with crewmen of the vessel and with sympathetic citizens in Sandusky. While I limit my intake of spirits I find providing such refreshment to new acquaintances hastens the opening to their innermost soul. I find a notable percentage of Northern seamen enlisted to avoid the draft. This breed of man's service is for sale. I merely determine his price and more importantly his reliability."

Thompson slowly replied, "I've experienced a constant line of men at my door since my arrival in Canada, all soliciting investment in an array of proposals. All held promise but to date none have born fruit." He added with a smile, "Ample funds remain to authorize several major operations, after of course I scrutinize all details. I must say, Mr. Cole, after this in-depth analysis of your design I concede we must move ahead. Do you have an idea of financial requirements?"

"I anticipate the common Yankee seaman's loyalty can be purchased for three years wages. Five hundred a man in greenbacks suffices. Naturally, the higher an officer's rank the greater the expense. I must also present myself as an affluent businessman. I must lodge in the finest establishments and dine in the most eloquent eateries in order to mingle with local citizens of interest. I recommend adding to my credibility by depositing a significant draft in a local bank. This generally spreads news of the well-to-do newcomer throughout a thriving city such as Sandusky." Without blinking Cole nonchalantly said, "To establish myself $5000, to open a bank account another $5000, expenses of maybe $500 to $600 per week, plus traveling funds of course." Of course, Tom Hines skeptically thought. He was becoming concerned perhaps this man possessed too much expertise with such schemes.

Cole rambled on. "Purchase of the *Michigan*, if I may use the term, may range from $30,000 to $60,000. I have no idea of your plans for the freed prisoners or captured vessel, Commissioner Thompson. I leave those decisions to you."

Thompson stood with a wide grin covering his face. "Mr. Cole, I look forward to this operation with great anticipation as does Captain Hines, don't you Thomas."

"Yes, sir," Hines unemotionally but obediently replied.

"You two won't be disappointed by the performance of Charlie Cole," the cocky newcomer confidently added.

"Mr. Cole, Thomas and I have unfinished details to attend, financial arrangements to conclude, and an array of other issues to address. Can we meet next week?"

"Excellent," said Cole, who apparently missed Thompson's cue for dismissal.

"Anything else?" asked the commissioner.

"Commissioner Thompson, I'm embarrassed to admit I'm short of funds. The journey exhausted my meager resources."

"Charles, Charles, you offend me by not being more forthright in your needs. I apologize for not realizing such." Thompson walked over to his desk, opened the top drawer, and removed a handful of bills from an envelope. With cash in hand the visitor happily departed.

Thompson flowed with exuberance. He gleefully boasted, "Finally, Thomas, a man who shall bring us results. Imagine, control of the lakes and 2,500 freed Confederate officers roaming northern Ohio, all for less than $100,000. We must coordinate this good fortune with our activity in Chicago. We'll then review our possibilities with the other three prison camps."

Hines feared his superior's over confidence would only provide the Confederacy with a depleted treasury and unfulfilled promises. General Morgan's raid proved that a small number of men of action far exceeded the empty words and the spending of money by shallow men. Hines's objection to Thompson would be fruitless, so he bid the commissioner farewell.

The following week only Cole and Thompson met to finalize the initial stages of the operation. "You're in charge of the operation in Sandusky, answering only to Captain Hines and myself. I've reassigned McDonald to a different position where his talents may be better utilized. Your first assignment, Mr. Cole, shall be to travel along the U.S. shore visiting Buffalo, Cleveland, Sandusky, Toledo, Detroit, Chicago, and possibly Milwaukee. Report to me the fortifications and manpower in these port cities." Thompson briefly outlined plans to simultaneously free prisoners in other locations.

At the conclusion of their meeting Cole mentioned his fiancé would join him in Sandusky. “Miss Brown, who by then shall be my wife, possesses the exquisite fusion of beauty and charm which draws conversation from the tightest lipped gentleman. She may be our strongest asset. I assume you approve of her involvement, sir?”

“Certainly, Charles.” Thompson firmly rested his hand upon the shoulder of the man standing aside him. “I trust you to be as astute a judge of character as I. Now proceed. The day of retribution for the Yankees nears.”

Little did Thompson realize that before the end of the month the Yankees would visit his elegant Oxford, Mississippi mansion to unleash their own form of reprisal upon the traitor. The acrid smell would fill the air from the smoldering ruins after the blue clad troops marched away from another devastated estate.

Cole walked down the plush red carpeted hallway away from Thompson’s suite toward the wide stairway. He imagined the pleasured look on Annie Brown’s face when he told her of their extravagant adventure funded courtesy of the Confederate States of America.

While Cole anticipated his rendezvous with Annie the last week of July, John Beall filled his lungs with fresh salt air on the deck of the *Canadian Empress*. After he exited the killing fields near Richmond, Beall traveled to Mathews County and visited his dear friends for several days before crossing the Chesapeake to Baltimore and then traveling north. While in New York for two weeks he listened to the locals’ disgust of the Union government’s handling of the war. He enjoyed a brief stop in Halifax before sailing around Cape Breton Island and docking in Quebec City. He floated down the St. Lawrence River to Montreal and into Lake Ontario before reaching Toronto.

His mind drifted to his time in Georgia with Martha. Afterwards, when John had returned to Richmond, Grant’s lines continued sliding south hoping to lasso the Confederate capital. He took up arms until the Yankee debacle at Cold Harbor. With that Union disaster, he migrated in good conscience toward Toronto to meet with Thompson by early August. He optimistically read of the Union's inability to toss the loop of blue clad soldiers around Richmond. A contingent circled south to capture Petersburg, hesitated, and inexplicably fell back, leaving Richmond in possession of critical supply lines to Petersburg. If Lee withstood the siege through November, Lincoln would face difficult odds for reelection.

The Yankee's shallow character had again incurred the ire of honorable men like John with the Union's insincere peace charade at St. Catherines in mid June. Clement Clay, James Holcombe, and other Confederate emissaries met with Horace Greeley and several Yankee diplomats including Lincoln's Secretary John Hay. The Republican government balked at the credentials of the Southerners. They stated due to the Confederate emissaries' lack of authority to negotiate, any discussions would be futile. Beall smiled, recalling the Yankee newspaper accounts of the conference detailing Lincoln's gracious offer to welcome the rebellious states back into the Union with the institution of slavery dissolved. Holcombe and Clay eloquently replied, "If peace could be restored only after submission to such terms of conquest, the generation is yet unborn which will witness its restoration."[6] Beall's sentiments exactly.

He sighed contentedly and walked onto the Toronto dock with his worn, battered body rejuvenated by his maritime journey. His blood flowed with excitement in anticipation of his new assignment. Finally he might debut his two year plan to release Confederate officers from Johnson's Island, spread Southern vengeance throughout Yankee cities far from the front lines, and provide the impetus to dispose the Republican President in November. Tonight would be his first meeting with Commissioner Thompson.

That evening Beall declined liquid refreshment as he seated himself by the small table separating him from the commissioner. Heavy midsummer air mingled with the bustling noise from the city street below, and circulated through the second story windows. Secretary Seddon cautioned Beall that Thompson's agenda might differ somewhat from President Davis's. Having heard nothing but positive comments referencing Clement Clay, John experienced disappointment that no opportunity existed to meet him.

"Mr. Beall," began Thompson, "I understand after your interview several months ago with Secretary Seddon that you refused the opportunity to join our newly formed secret service. I assume you would have even had a voice in the architecture of such an organization. You refused. Why?"

"The covert nature of that service could result in orders being issued by men I might not know. I function best within a framework such as this which allows me independent operation with prior instructions from a man I trust. I feared a request, no matter how unlikely, might be issued to perform an act bringing dishonor to our cause and me. I understand you're a Southern gentleman of highest integrity so I harbor no reservations in answering to you, sir." Beall correctly assumed flattery indeed would confirm the assignment he desired.

"Captain Beall, beneath me our command structure places Captain Thomas Hines, a famed member of Morgan's Raiders, at the head of military activities in the northwest. He currently reconnoiters Chicago for our operation at Camp Douglas which coincides with our business at Johnson's Island. Charles Cole, late of Forrest's Calvary and a veteran of our navy, bears responsibility for activities in Sandusky. Your cooperation with him is imperative. I'll arrange a meeting in Sandusky."

"Sandusky? Might that be risky? Two strangers meeting in a small city brimming with Federal troops?"

"I appreciate your caution, Captain. Remember only half the men of military age in the North serve in the army. You'll blend inconspicuously with other civilians. Mr. Cole's cover of an affluent oil investor from Pennsylvania creates the perception that you're just another traveler conducting business with him."

A slight grin crossed John's weathered face. "Commissioner Thompson, that's precisely what I'm doing, conducting deadly business, but business just the same. Do we possess a schedule for the operation?"

Several weeks ago we pointed to August 16, two weeks prior to the Democratic Convention. Unfortunately the leadership of our Democratic allies in the North seems preoccupied with choosing a nominee and identifying planks of their platform rather than supporting our efforts to embarrass Lincoln. I fear they're getting their cart before their horse. Clement Vallandigham desperately seeks his party's nomination. Captain Hines fears we may again be forced to delay the action, this time to coincide with the actual convention. The August 16 or the 29 dates could prevent concurrent action in Sandusky due to time constrains. Unrest in Chicago could draw the *Michigan* to that city, which would aid our cause in Sandusky. We shall see. I'll arrange the meeting with Mr. Cole to detail the entire plan for you. You'll need to recruit men and determine your means to secure a vessel with which to transport your men." The conspirators stood, and Thompson concluded by sternly cautioning, "We must do nothing to jeopardize the neutrality of our host nation. At times I fear England searches for an excuse to wash her hands completely of us."

"Message received, sir," acknowledged Beall. He exited the suite, wove his way through the mire of visitors in the lobby, and stepped outside to the boardwalk.

His mind buzzed with the complexity of the details. He'd only walked ten paces when he looked up, stopped, and froze. At that instant a ghost's eyes penetrated his. A man he long presumed dead lunged toward him. "Johnny Beall, last I heard my you enjoyed the fine hospitality of the Yankee government in Fort McHenry."

The two hugged one another while slapping each other's backs before separating and staring at each other. "Aye, Burley, and then to Fort Monroe, and eventually to

City Point. But Benny, you have the advantage. I feared a Yankee noose stretched your neck, or that a Federal bullet ended your life."

Bennett Burley recounted his unfortunate capture on a Virginia beach where he stopped two Yankee bullets. He disdainfully described the hanging of young Philips, only a bridegroom for two weeks. "Laughed as they strung him up. Sad to say if the lad received the wounds that I did he might be alive today. I feigned severe injury. Got carted off to Fort Delaware to heal myself before my proper hanging. Of course, once they initiated the paperwork the benevolent Yankees said that they would give this guilty bastard a trial before they hung him. God bless me dear father who tossed me in the water at a young age and made me a strong swimmer. Another lad and I entered the prison drainpipe leading into the river. Don't know of his success but I surfaced, swam to near fatal exhaustion, and by good fortune reached a Dutch ship which rescued me from the sea." He winked as he said, "Twas my good fortune the kindhearted ship's captain saw fit to provide dry clothes and a small stipend to this wayward son who fell from the vessel from which he stowed away, so that he could make his way home across the ocean to his distraught mother."

"You always could spin a yarn my friend."

"Aye, only wish Ned McGuire's pa had dumped him in the water at a young age so he could've joined me on my adventure."

For the second time John froze with the resurrection of another dead man. "Ned McGuire? Alive?"

"Johnny, when 'ave you ever known this man to lie. Ned's only discomfort appeared to be acknowledging he would enjoy the fine fare and accommodations from our gracious Northern host while I fended for myself as a freed man. No rumors of hanging or the like either. Any word of our friend, John Maxwell?"

"While in Richmond his name surfaced. Suffice it to say the big man has big plans for a big explosion. Are you currently employed?"

“Just visiting kinfolk and awaiting new prospects.”

“Bennett Burley, you have the rare fortune to again become the first member of a new crew which I am recruiting, with designs to throw Lincoln out on the street come November unless General Lee first performs the good work.”

The two walked down the planked sidewalk toward an upscale saloon while Beall reiterated his conversation with Thompson. Before they entered the tavern Burley paused, looked up into the bright blue sky, and envisioned the gasping young Philips struggling for his last breathes. The Scotsman simply said, “I’m in.”

40 – MR. COLE

A bright sliver of sunlight slicing through the room permeated Charles Cole's eyelids. He turned his head to the left, blinked several times, and focused upon the soft, slumbering form nestled warmly against him. He carefully drew back the blanket. The sharp crack as his hand slapping her bare rump resonated through the room. The purring feline's eyes flashed open as she prepared to bare claws across the stinging source of pain.

As her eyes met his, she transformed into a love starved puppy. Pressing her warm breasts against his chest she whispered enticingly, "Charlie, is this the manner to awaken your new wife? Won't be noon for another two hours. Why'd you wake me so early?"

"Remember my dear you officially become Mrs. Cole only when my mission takes us to Ohio. Here in Buffalo you're who you've always been, Miss Annie Brown. I must now depart, alone, to proceed with that mission. I reiterate this assignment provides us an opportunity to enjoy a very comfortable lifestyle the next several months. If I play our cards masterfully we may even exit this damn war with a substantial purse."

Instead of sulking with his rebuff Annie, began plying the skills of vocation. She forced her sensuous body tightly to his, nibbled at his ear, and ran her slender fingers tantalizingly down his torso. He jumped from the bed, grabbed his robe, and in a fit of frustration complained, "Curse the man who said business before pleasure."

The young woman's long brown curls spread across her pillow. With her magnetic eyes drawing him near, she smiled with her appetizing ruby lips, and patted the empty sheets aside her naked body. "For that reason, my dear Charlie, my business is pleasure."

After a hurried breakfast he returned to the room to gather his luggage. After he pulled away from Annie's passionate farewell kisses he departed for the docks only accompanied by her appealing fragrance. He already anticipated their reunion in several weeks with her as his surrogate wife. He pondered his future with her. Charming, witty, intelligent, beautiful, and a real joy when the lamp turned down, although she astutely possessed the ability to assess his ulterior motives.

As the steam powered side-wheeler departed the wharf Cole reviewed his itinerary. First stop Erie, followed by stops in Cleveland, Sandusky, and Toledo, then cross into Michigan for a stay in Detroit, followed by a journey via rail to Chicago, unless time afforded travel north through the Great Lakes. He returned to Buffalo upon completing his whirlwind tour in less than two weeks. Excerpts from his report to Jacob Thompson read:

Buffalo is poorly protected; one regiment and a battalion of invalids. There is a large amount of government stores there, a large quantity of ammunition in the United States arsenal, and also some cannon mortars, and small arms. I left for Cleveland and met on the passage a gentleman who will benefit our cause in Chicago. He assisted me materially in Cleveland, and took me around the government works, and introduced me to the foreman of the cannon shops, who told me there were about two hundred and fifty men employed there, and that they were shipping large cannon to Sandusky, Milwaukee, and Chicago, with one hundred rounds of ammunition to each gun. I learned the bearings of the lake around Cleveland. I met the engineer of the Pacific, who I think, money can influence. I concluded my information from him and left for Detroit with him. From Detroit I went to Chicago, meeting with Mr. Charles Walsh.

I ascertained there the water needed for crossing the bars, and the amount of tonnage of the tugs, which would be most serviceable in time of need. The new tugs are of say one hundred and seventy-five tons, one screw engine, and are capable of carrying coal for thirty-six hours' run; will mount two guns, one large gun at the stern and a small fieldpiece at the bow; are easily managed, and will make ten knots an hour even in the severest weather. There is little difficulty in bringing guns to bear on the camp. There is an immense amount of shipping, and among the first thing would be to destroy the different draw-bridges, and then the whole city is accessible by water.

Milwaukee is an easy place to take possession of. They have no fort, and twelve feet of water up to the first draw bridge. The Milwaukee and Detroit steamers are below the first draw-bridge; there is a large amount of grain shipment and quantities of coal. Sheboygan supplies all the country from Fond du Lac; sends grain and produce there for shipment. Port Washington is a small settlement with little advantage, but its people are strong friends, and determined in their resistance to the draft. Mackinaw has a natural fortification, and mounted at the observatory are three guns bearing on the straits. Lake Erie furnishes a splendid field for operations. Erie is a difficult place to get at, more so than any city on the lakes. I have formed the acquaintance of Captain Carter, commanding United States steamer Michigan.

He is an unpolished man, whose pride seems to be touched for the reason that, having been an old United States naval officer, he is not allowed now a more extensive field of operation. I do not think that he can be bought. [7]

Charlie reread his report, folded it, placed it in an envelope, and laid it on the desk to for the morning courier. He grinned as he advanced to Annie in anticipation of their active night of farewells before they separated. Tomorrow he would travel to Sandusky to ingratiate himself with civilian and military men of prominence. He opted to travel by train to familiarize himself with northern Ohio's rail network.

41 – MR. COLE, MT. HOPE OIL CO.

As Charlie boarded the 6:00 a.m. westbound train, he smiled visualizing Annie ever attempting to function at this hour. When he awoke at the first whistle stop in route to Erie he mulled over his recent correspondence from Mr. Thompson. Complexities in Chicago might force the Sandusky operation to the rear. If Chicago had proceeded on August 16, Sandusky could not develop to coincide. Captain Hines was becoming increasingly disenchanted with the support from his peace Democrats in Illinois. He cynically commented to Cole during their meeting in Chicago that politicians seemed extremely adept at starting wars but proved highly inept at ending them. The northwestern Democrats proved no exception. Hines therefore rescheduled the operation for the end of August in conjunction with the Democratic convention on the 29th. Selfishly Cole embraced the delay. The Johnson's Island operation might then proceed concurrently with the freeing of Camp Douglas's prisoners. The confusion of simultaneous chaos at two sites three hundred miles apart undoubtedly would complicate a Yankee response.

At Erie, Cole disembarked to stretch his legs and followed the herd of male passengers to a nearby saloon. He dropped five cents on the bar when the saloon keeper handed him a hefty foam-topped mug of beer. Charlie piled several pieces of orange cheddar on a slab of dark rye before adding a portion of pink ham and a second slice of bread. He drained the mug and ordered another to wash down his sandwich before he meandered toward the train. A gentle breeze momentarily refreshed the passengers before they boarded for the stuffy ride to Cleveland.

Cole noticed an empty seat across from two attractive young women. He located himself there beside a simpleton wearing frayed clothing and a slouch hat. After properly introducing himself to the man, Charlie all but ignored him as he turned his attention to the pleasant, fair-haired creatures facing him. Enlightening conversation ensued until the sound of hissing steam and screeching brakes announced their arrival in Cleveland.

He transferred to a different train where he boarded a less congested coach. He even obtained a window seat. A broad faced man with a thick graying beard seated himself across from Charlie. “Afternoon sir, I’m Charles Cole of the Mount Hope Oil Company from Harrisburg.”

“Rush Sloane, returning for a short visit to attend to affairs in Sandusky before journeying back to Washington City, to continue assisting the president in terminating this bloody conflict the slave holders initiated.” He paused and stared intently at his listener. “I assume being from Pennsylvania you firmly back the Union.”

Man assumes a great deal, thought Cole. “Sir, I would be insulted if you concluded otherwise.”

The newly minted Pennsylvanian acquired a great deal of information concerning Sloane and the political landscape in Sandusky. It seemed the city actually served as an active terminus for the Underground Railroad, rather than just a city drawn at random in Mrs. Stowe’s despicable *Uncle Tom’s Cabin.* Sloane’s intriguing involvement with the Underground Railroad gradually surfaced. During the prior decade the one-time attorney faced charges for breaking the Fugitive Slave Law by aiding escaped Negroes. More astoundingly, the man arrogantly acknowledged the act to authorities, thus simplifying his conviction for the prosecution. He paid the $3000 judgment, $330 court costs, and $1000 attorney’s fees, offset only by contributions nearing $400 donated by scores of local citizens. Apparently quite a den of abolitionists resided in Sandusky, which further justified sacking the city.

The rays from the lowering sun glistened across Sandusky Bay when the passengers disembarked. “Thank you Mr. Sloane for the informative conversation. I appreciate your insight and long to become better acquainted with your community.”

“The pleasure’s all mine. Always enjoy conversing with a good Union man. When I speak with Mr. Moss I’ll mention your need for a depository for your funds. I trust you’ll enjoy your accommodations in the finest hotel between Chicago and New York.”

From the Cleveland & Toledo Railroad platform Cole hailed a hack. The Negro baggage handler grinned when the traveler flipped him two bits. After traveling all day in confined coaches he enjoyed the four block ride in the open carriage down Water Street’s cobblestone thoroughfare. A gentle westerly breeze followed Charlie and filled his nostrils with the agreeable aroma from the Bay City Brewer, located behind him. He observed a combination of business enterprises such as Norcross & Upp’s Sash, Door & Blind manufacturing facility between Lawrence and Fulton across from the rail station. On the northwest corner of Fulton he noticed the U.S. Express Office. As they neared the looming West House the businesses transitioned from lumber yards and blacksmith’s shops to furniture, clothing, and hardware stores, and then eateries. The saloons and restaurants on the block appeared to cater to respectable clientele. To the east beyond the massive hotel Charlie observed a combination of soldiers, seaman, and laborers entering the less appealing drinking establishments.

The elegant five-story West House towered above the city’s other buildings. The ornamental cupola setting atop the northeast roof corner accentuated the building and served as a beacon for the main entrance below. A freshly lit gas light flickered near the doors, adding an inviting hue to welcome guests into the elegant hotel. The large clock on the nearby post read half past seven. Cole tossed the driver four bits and strode inside to register. Numerous gentlemen, occasionally accompanied by splendidly attired woman with sparkling jewelry, filled the spacious lobby. Men in blue uniforms also dotted the foyer. Cole turned the page in the guest book on the front desk to add his name to the top of a new page for August 11 entries. He returned the pen to the ink well and requested a room on the north side.

The skinny head desk clerk peered over his spectacles while he craned his neck to read the guest book. In a high pitched monotone he bluntly retorted, "Sorry Mr. Cole, but with the summer heat everyone wants that side of the building. We have pleasant rooms on the west side which provide ample ventilation."

"And the afternoon sun," Charles curtly replied.

"Well yes," he squeaked, "but with so many visitors to the Rebel prison, we..." The clerk gasped as the stranger's hand shot into his pocket. To the man's relief instead of a weapon the visitor opened his palm with a handful of coins. A five dollar gold piece clanked on the oak counter. A relieved smile crossed the clerk's face. "As I was saying, with so many visitors to Johnson's Island we shall," he paused and stared at the shining coin, "we shall need a few extra moments to locate accommodations to your liking. For your convenience, we offer ample seating in our hotel restaurant for 300 people. We offer liquid refreshments in our facility also, although patrons sometimes enjoy George Stahl's saloon and eatery which you may enter from the street or through those interior doors."

"Thank you, Mister?"

"Huntington, sir, Harold Huntington, at your service, Mr. Cole." The clerk quickly snatched the gold coin and secured it in his vest pocket. "Hope your stay is long and pleasant. Call on me anytime for anything."

Damn mercenary Yankees, thought Cole as he walked toward the saloon. Upon his return Huntington directed him to a spacious room on the north side of the second floor. He seemed to have just fallen asleep when shrieks of squawking seagulls awakened him to the dazzling morning sunlight. He reached for his pocket watch on the lace-covered night stand. Seven-thirty already? Traveling does tend to tire a man. Was it only yesterday he'd left his warm, sweetly-scented Annie? He lay in bed and turned his thoughts to organizing the day's activities. In less than three weeks the fuse would ignite in Chicago. Charlie needed to meet select citizens, renew his acquaintance with Captain Carter, explore the city, ascertain the true convictions of the numerous yet unidentified men whom Mr. Thompson claimed sympathetic to their cause, and somehow make contact with a General Trimble supposedly held on Johnson's Island. The commissioner's military operative, Mr. Beall, would also arrive any day. Annie too, with her pleasing distractions, would reach Sandusky within the week. Cole glanced at the vacant space by his side, and for a fleeting moment longed for her soothing diversion.

After enjoying a leisurely breakfast in the West House he walked outside to the busy intersection. Another hot, humid one. His dark clothing instantly absorbed the heat from the morning sun peering over the buildings across the street. He glanced to his left toward Sandusky Bay and inhaled the heavy air with its unique waterfront odor. The *Island Queen* bobbed up and down with the ebb and flow of the sea slapping her against the pier where she moored. The vessel made occasional runs to Cleveland and numerous trips to the islands. Docked near the *Island Queen* floated the *Little Eastern*. In the hazy distance beyond the harbor numerous ships glided over calm waters.

On the street corner a bearded man with a weathered face engaged in a friendly conversation with a naval officer paused, and turned to Cole. "Another beautiful morning on the water, isn't it?"

"That it is but business keeps me ashore this fine day, Mister?"

"Actually it's Captain, Captain J.C. Monk, and the vessel beyond the second buoy," smiled the seaman with the beaming face of a new father, "is my newest addition to the waters. She's the *General Grant*, 140 feet long, 158 ton, with double Klotz and Kromer engines built in this city precisely to my specifications. Launched her a week ago. Hoped the other General Grant would have plowed through Richmond before my *General Grant* plowed through the bay but suspect the Rebs will soon enough be in his wake.

"She stop at the secesh prison, does she?" Charlie asked.

"Only if I can convince Ensign Hunter here to persuade Captain Carter or Colonel Hill to provide me the opportunity to service the island. An interesting question for a stranger?"

"Forgive my manners. This relaxing setting swept all courtesy away. I'm Charles Cole, Secretary of the Mount Hope Oil Company, desiring to enhance my company's position by gaining new investors and also purchasing additional oil rights in Ohio." Looking to the naval officer he said, "Ensign, although military men yearn for action, I imagine on days such as this you appreciate the peaceful setting to which you're assigned."

"Peaceful on the surface, but vigilance is the watchword twenty-four hours a day. Rumors circulate that in desperation the Rebels might attempt to free the prisoners, although with the *Michigan's* firepower that would be suicidal. I read several days ago in the *Commercial Register* of rumors that the Rebs might instead launch an attack against Buffalo from Canada. Whenever, wherever, the United States Navy shall repulse any such ill-conceived operations."

"You gentlemen spoke of Captain Carter. I had the fortune of meeting him earlier this summer. I look forward to visiting the congenial gentleman again."

Hear Carter called many things, thought Hunter, and congenial isn't one of them. With a slight nod of his head the officer broke away. "Captain Monk, Mr. Cole, good day."

As Monk walked away Cole asked, "Captain Monk, where does your newest ship dock? I must examine her more closely."

Pointing down Water Street he said, "Along the shore beyond the depot. Make yourself known and I'll personally escort you aboard."

The men parted with Cole crossing Columbus Avenue. He chuckled at the irony of commandeering the *General Grant* to free prisoners to lay waste to a staunch Yankee city. The aroma from D. Block & Company's cigar and tobacco shop reached his nose. A necessary stop later in the morning to replace his dwindling supply of stogies. He continued south past a tailor shop before pausing to gaze into Textor & Lerch's jewelry store. Annie definitely will requisition funds for a visit here. He strolled by Gagan's Grocery, Washington Dewey's Stoves & Tinware, and a shoe store before he reached his destination, the Moss Brothers Bank.

After he presented his card Charlie eyed an empty lobby chair, but before he sat a clerk led him through the bank's inner sanctum into the office nearest the vault. Cole exchanged greetings with the bank executive and seated himself in a plush chair across from A. H. Moss's rich mahogany desk. The impeccably dressed banker's finely tailored clothing most certainly originated in New York. A glittering watch fob hanging from his vest pocket further spoke of his success.

With a grating eastern accent he spoke. "Good to meet you, Mr. Cole. I visited with Mr. Sloane last evening. He mentioned you might be calling. In the city for the oil business, I hear. A necessary commodity, especially with the war. Once we whip Jeff Davis and his pack of traitors we'll require vast quantities of crude. Think of the strength of our nation after we stop the destruction and commence the building." He winked while saying, "With an added cheap labor supply our northern economy will boom. My circle of associates certainly believes victory nears."

Leaning back in a relaxed posture Charlie said, "I enjoyed hearing Mr. Sloane's rendition of the accusations from the slave catchers. I deciphered a rather strong contingent of influential gentleman supported him."

"Even five years ago we spoke of such actions with guarded caution. Today, with Richmond on her knees about to bow to submission, and Lincoln's *Emancipation Proclamation* the law of the land, we may properly recognize the courage of those devoted men." Moss proudly proclaimed intimate friendship with eight such individuals. He spoke especially flatteringly of Oran Follett, president of the Sandusky, Dayton, & Columbus Railroad. While Follet discreetly loaned support to abolitionist activities his wife Eliza participated openly. Whenever he reminded her of the illegality she replied that she answered to, "a higher law than man's."

After a pleasant and informative conversation with Moss, Cole deposited $70,000 and departed. Outside he removed a pencil from his coat and scratched the names of the men the banker mentioned. After his noon meal he searched for a rental horse to allow him better familiarity with his base of operations. He discovered the city operated fewer liveries than he estimated. Perhaps residents living near the water opted for pleasant boat excursions rather than relaxing horse or buggy rides through the countryside on Sunday afternoons. He also learned a fire earlier in the year raised the Townsend House Hotel and an adjoining stable. He selected a docile mare from one of the two stables located in the same block as the West House. After his three hour ride he was comfortably acquainted with the vicinity.

That night, following a delicious meal featuring roast pheasant, Cole sat in his room and stared at the open log book on his desk. He added the name A. H. Moss below those identified to his previous entries under "Men of Influence". He also reviewed his newly established "Prominent Businesses" page. This category included four waterfront lumberyards, two banks, the boatyards, the marine engine factory, three dry goods stores, and numerous hotels. An untitled page indicated the train depots, telegraph office, and arsenal, followed by notations of the city's two largest liveries, plus a handful of smaller one's scattered about. He listed local drug stores, logical sources for turpentine. He smiled at the thought of Sandusky's commercial waterfront transforming into a blazing inferno. Instead of sending these abolitionists to hell he would bring the devil's firestorm to Sandusky. So much the sweeter if freedom crazed Confederate officers inflicted just retribution while aggressively confronting anything or anyone blocking their path.

He reached for his coat and hat, and exited for a brief stroll along the waterfront to be capped with a tall drink at the hotel bar. Outside the streets bustled with activity although the sun vanished an hour earlier. He crossed Water Street and strode past the Hubbard Building which housed among other establishments the Cosmopolitan Art and Literary Association. He stopped at the dock where the *Philo Parsons* arrived earlier that evening. He stared across the shimmering moonlit bay to the island incarcerating over 2500 Southerners. Really need to reacquaint myself with Captain Carter, Cole thought, maybe even tomorrow. This Beall fellow might arrive any day. Familiarity with the prison's interior would prove essential in formulating their plans. No messages from Mr. Thompson. Apparently the Chicago operation remained scheduled for the 29th. Could the Sandusky scheme actually proceed in less than three weeks to coincide with Hines's operation? Cole hoped Beall possessed abilities comparable with his own.

The concern momentarily evaporated when cheap heavy perfume infiltrated Charlie's nostrils. A middle aged woman clung tightly to a blue clad soldier. The pair headed down Water Street toward the rumored pleasure houses several blocks to the east. The woman's low neckline revealed ample exposure of her alluring cleavage. Charlie stared as she shamelessly groped her companion to insure her catch would not escape. The action beckoned Charlie to follow their path for a sensuous interlude to temporarily release the mental strain of his demanding assignment. He sighed with disappointment as he thought better. Small town. No use offending the self-righteous citizens. Annie's soft image reentered his mind. He sighed and smiled. He would wait. He gazed intently to Johnson's Island and meandered back to enjoy his nightcap.

Since the trains and passenger boats arrived before dark he found the West House lobby vacant. Loud voices obliterated by occasional boisterous laughter echoed from the room beyond the large dining facility. Charlie pulled a Havana from his breast pocket and entered the smoky bar. Out of habit he selected a table near the wall to observe the entrance. After striking a match against the round oak table he lit his expensive cigar, inhaled deeply, and exhaled a bluish gray plume which floated to the murky haze above. Tilting back in his chair he surveyed the room. Numerous men with drinks in hand lined the long mahogany bar. Eight chandeliers illuminated the saloon. The large ornate mirror behind the bar further amplified the radiance. Two or more men each occupied most of the twenty some tables. Charlie proceeded to the bar to mingle with the patrons and to order a julep.

Just as the sugar-coated rim touched his lips and the fresh fragrance of mint reached his nose, a large man to his left obnoxiously bellowed, “Any son of a secesh who orders a damn Rebel drink is nothing but a yellow traitor.”

Charlie instinctively turned with clenched fist to confront the insufferable oaf until he remembered his role. Forcing his tenseness to dissipate he smiled and tipped his hat. “Sir, this drink originates from the noble state of Kentucky which contributes many a fine son in our courageous struggle to reunite the Union. Fact is, I’m fortunate to say I’m friends with many such brave Kentuckians.” He paused, caste his eyes toward the wooden floor, and remorsefully added, “And sad to say I have a fair number of former misguided acquaintances who selected the alternative path which shall prevent me from ever referring to them as friend again.” Charlie reached for his drink, held the glass high, stared into the glazed eyes of his adversary, and boldly stated for all interested onlookers absorbed in the confrontation, “To that brave Kentuckian who first defied Rebel cannon fire. To Major, now General Robert Anderson, who courageously refused to surrender until all hope vanished.”

The inebriated man advanced and fell into Charlie while attempting to slap his back. “My apologies. Oscar

Reese had you figured wrong. For a minute though feared you was bout to toast abolition too. I'm here to tell you I'm a Union man tried and true." Then where's your damn blue uniform, the Southerner wondered, while Reese continued. "Whatever it takes to whip the traitors I'm for except freeing a pack of darkies which'ill find their way up here." Gazing around the room he added, "And I'm not the only one, am I boys?"

A few nearby cronies replied with a resonant, "Aye!"

Most of the audience chuckled and returned their attention to other interests.

Charlie reached into his pocket, pulled out a ten dollar gold piece, flipped it on the bar, and loudly ordered a round of drinks for everyone, finally extricating himself from his awkward predicament. While the hoard scrambled for free liquor he glided through the oncoming surge and settled at his empty table in the rear. He started to seat himself when he glanced to his right, hesitated, and stared in disbelief.

"Captain Carter?"

The officer cocked his head inquisitively before replying, "Forgive me. Do I know...?" An expression of recognition crossed Jonathan Carter's face. "You're the gentleman I encountered in Cleveland?"

"Cole, Charles Cole. You graciously invited me to make my presence known upon my arrival in Sandusky. I feared with my consuming responsibilities as Secretary of the Mount Hope Oil Company that our paths would fail to cross. May I order you refreshment sir?"

Carter chuckled but refused. "I notice you were placed in circumstances already requiring the purchase of a good many drinks. Besides, I must return to my ship."

Charlie's charismatic eyes met Carter's. "Come, come, Captain. I purchased those drinks from necessity. Please join me for a brief interlude of pleasure and conversation before I too retire for the evening. What may I order for you sir?"

"A nice glass of Madeira certainly completes an evening in fine fashion."

A waiter holding two glasses and an expensive bottle of wine returned.

"Mr. Cole, I believe I said a glass," the naval officer casually admonished while subtly implying he enjoyed the hospitality. "But your generosity is appreciated."

As Charlie began to pour, a distinguished gentleman approached the table. "Evening Captain, good to see you again. And who might your companion be?"

"Allow me to introduce Mr. Charles Cole of the Mount Hope Oil Company. Mr. Cole, meet Mr. W. T. West."

"May I assume," said Charlie standing to acknowledge West, "that you are the proprietor of this fine hotel?"

"One in the same, and may I assume you are staying with us and find your accommodations acceptable?"

"Exceptional, Mr. West". Charlie motioned to an empty chair. "Please join us."

"Yes, please," encouraged Captain Carter. "Mr. Cole generously ordered more refreshment than I can consume and your pleasant company is always appreciated."

"If you insist but only if you gentleman allow the West House the pleasure of furnishing the beverage."

"Unnecessary but appreciated," responded Cole.

West seated himself and commented, "I understand the oil business can be very lucrative, but also by nature very speculative."

"Correct on both counts Mr. West. Fortunately I am an officer in a financially sound company refusing to overextend itself by foolish speculation. Our philosophy mandates that we harvest a thousand barrels of oil from a site before we record it as a producing well. For every two wells that produce we purchase another lease. We are not averse to subleasing our wells either. As we say in business, everyone has their price; everything that can be bought can be sold." Turning to Carter, Charlie said, "At least in the navy you don't deal with speculation."

Carter shook his head in disgust. "Unfortunately as we fill our manpower needs we face a similar sort of guesswork. Scores of incompetent men join us believing they avoid danger. With the first sounds of battle they cower as the spineless creatures that they are. At least we don't contend with the blasted bounty system with which our brothers in the army contend. There a charlatan collects as much as $1000 for an enlistment bonus, skedaddles with a purse full of greenbacks, and relocates only to repeat the shameful act."

"Mr. West, do you encounter such distasteful corruption in the hotel business?" asked Cole.

"Very limited, but much more so in the construction business."

"Construction? I had no idea."

"Yes, one of my other enterprises."

"Don't be so humble," interjected Carter. Turning to Cole the captain clarified, "W.T. West and Company, and Feick Brothers, are arguably the area's finest and most successful builders. This fine building and the military complex on Johnson's Island represent two of Mr. West's more notable accomplishments."

Smiling broadly, West proudly acknowledged, "This building offers me great satisfaction. My hotel announces to all visitors that our community offers elegance far exceeding that of the other stops along Lake Erie's waterfront." His enthusiasm evaporated when he added, "The compound across the bay resembles anything but a masterpiece. When General Hoffman visited in the late fall of '61 he had two prerequisites for his bidders—cheap and fast. Those two words are not conducive to fine architecture, however at the time we toiled under depressed economic conditions. We gladly accepted any work coming our way. Once the Union war machine swung into full gear conditions improved for everyone except the poor lads courageously sacrificing life and limb to win this bloody conflict Jeff Davis instigated."

Keep nodding in agreement, Charlie told himself. Only a matter of time before the hotel and prison both become heaps of smoldering rubbish. With a mask of uneasy fear covering his face he asked, "How secure is the prison Mr. West? I shudder at the image of a hoard of vengeful mercenaries escaping confinement and ravaging this fair city and its noble citizens."

West took a leisurely sip of wine and smiled confidently. "I claim no architectural masterpiece in the stockade which we started in November of '61 and completed by February of '62. But aside from its common appearance, we constructed a practical facility, one which functions effectively today although everyone believed it would be vacated long before with a Union victory. Colonel Hill, who competently commands both the prison and the fort, recently extended the west fence to increase security. He constantly strengthens the earthworks surrounding the big guns on the southern side near the wharf." West looked to Carter. "If the fools bypass those emissaries of death they'll face the capably manned *Michigan*."

"I believe I read somewhere an outdated but valid treaty permits us only a sole armed vessel to guard the lakes?" Cole questioned.

Carter diplomatically replied, "Correct, but Britain secretly acknowledges our vessel posses no threat to them. They realize the *Michigan* actually dissuades Rebels from launching operations from Canada which certainly would complicate our complex relationship."

West laughed inoffensively. "What I believe the captain would say if protocol allowed is that the Europeans accept the Confederacy lacks the ability to win this war. The countries on the continent certainly have no desire to confront the power of our American juggernaut. We whipped the redcoats when we were an infant and again as a child; now we're a strapping young man capable of whipping all comers."

Arrogant bastard, thought Cole. I'll light the match to this place myself. He seized the opportunity before him. "Never viewed a prison. I hope to board one of the pleasure craft which draws near to allow passengers a close observation."

"Mr. Cole, you offend me," jested the captain showing a warm smile. "I share your company and drink your wine," he added, before he nodded to West and said, "or Mr. West's as the case may be this evening." Turning his attention back to Charlie, he said, "I occasionally arrange with Colonel Hill for prominent men to tour the prison and even mingle with the Rebel rabble if their curiosity warrants. Inform me of an opportune date and I shall accommodate you."

"Probably the sooner the better. As my business activities progress my flexibility lessens. Though not on a strict time table my assignment may be completed by month's end."

West interjected, "Don't hesitate to tour the *Michigan*. Our captain would be offended if the army received all your attention."

"Yes, yes, by all means," insisted the captain who glanced at his watch, rose, and departed saying, "Duty really does call. Good night gentleman."

Before Cole left West confided, "I hold great sympathy for our Captain Carter. Neither a more dedicated nor competent officer serves our navy. Unfortunately the navy and the army both headquarter in Washington. The enemy to one's rear often proves more deadly then the one to the front. When officers indulge in politics they lose focus on the mission at hand."

"Captain Carter offended a bureaucrat?"

"No, not really. An ambitious young officer cognizant of Carter's qualities spread lies tying him to a drinking problem in order to leap ahead of our good captain on the promotion list. A petty clerk working in the office of a man of prominence managed to influence his patron to encourage the navy to press charges. Though an innocent verdict resulted, such accusations, no matter how ridiculous, follow a military man throughout his career. I trust, Mr. Cole, this last bit of information remains between us?"

"Most assuredly," answered Charlie as he bid West a good evening.

Upon entering his room Cole realized his log lay visible on his desk. No problem; it remained closed as he left it. Besides, the simple people of this self-righteous little city welcomed Mr. Charles Cole into their midst with open arms. He crawled into bed with the feeling of contentment resulting from a productive day. His accomplishments satisfied him even more than a night with his dear, sweet Annie. Well, almost.

42 – JOHNSON'S ISLAND PRISON

Captain Carter expressed remorse that unexpected circumstances prevented him from personally accompanying Cole to Johnson's Island. Perhaps Annie's arrival might entice the captain to at least more expediently schedule a tour of the *Michigan*.

From the Sandusky dock Charlie stared across the bay into a vast field of glittering jewels emanating from the sun's rays. The *Little Eastern* departed for the twenty minute journey. She effortlessly rolled over the two feet whitecaps although Charlie's stomach churned with the repetition of the vessel breaking over the choppy waves. How a man could yearn for the sea escaped the alleged sailor. Midway through the voyage his focus switched from his queasy stomach to the blurry white and green image of Johnson's Island. With each passing moment the distorted panorama sharpened. The irregular green pattern transformed into a canopy of mature maple, elm, chestnut, and oak beyond the northern edge of the compound. Light reflected from the surfaces of three year old buildings. Fresh whitewash coated everything. Offices, barracks, warehouses, barns, workshops, and stockade walls glistened.

As the *Little Eastern* neared the wharf Cole studied the distinct detail of the prison compound. Fourteen foot vertical boards enclosed the stockade. Guards marched along the wooden catwalk ten feet above the ground while shielded from the prisoners by the top of the exterior wall. Sturdy posts supported the three foot wide walk surrounding the perimeter of the stockade. Far to Charlie's right, on the northeast corner, protruded a large blockhouse. A matching structure above the massive southern gates protected the entrance. Captain Carter mentioned that Hill's men positioned small artillery pieces capable of spewing a deadly spray of canister from the fortifications across the prison yard. Sentry boxes scattered along the catwalk at regular intervals offered refuge during foul weather.

The passengers just regained their balance from the engine reversing gears when the vessel thudded into the wharf, causing the voyagers to grab the ship's rail to steady themselves. Two dozen civilian men crowded behind two ladies waiting for the exit ramp to drop. After they disembarked blue clad soldiers slowly exited. No use returning to duty before necessary. Beyond the pier stretched a wide, heavily-used road visible for at least 300 yards before it veered to the left and disappeared. A narrower but still highly-traveled street ran diagonally to the right before vanishing behind some buildings. The thoroughfares eventually joined another road to form the trapezoid which surrounded the barracks, post commander's dwelling, and headquarters in addition to other numerous buildings. To the right of the lesser path stretched the parade ground, vacant except for the towering wooden staff topped by the fluttering stars and stripes. The ladies walked along the narrower conduit leading directly to the prison gates.

Cole strutted along the larger path so as to absorb more of the complex. He inhaled the appetizing scent of fresh bread drifting from the open bakery windows. The building occupied land beyond the intersecting roads. To his left he observed the active quartermaster's headquarters, strategically located adjacent to the wharf. Loaded wagons, rattling by with drivers oblivious to civilian pedestrians, forced him off the path. He reached the last structure on the right. Before entering he paused on the porch to wipe dripping perspiration from his brow with a fresh white handkerchief. He stomped his feet, vigorously brushed away the fine dust coating his clothing, and entered.

A slender captain peered over the shoulder of a corporal seated at a desk examining some papers. Mr. Cole confidently strode forward. "Morning, gentleman. The weather tells us it is certainly August."

Seeing the visitor's engaging smile the officer stepped forward with a reciprocating smile. "Captain Scoville, at your service."

"I'm Charles Cole, visiting Sandusky from Harrisburg on business. My good friend Captain Jonathan Carter encouraged me to visit this incarceration compound for our misguided former brethren before my duties in Sandusky totally absorb me. I further desire to visit with captives of a more penitent disposition, of course only at Colonel Hill's bidding."

"Unfortunately the colonel traveled across the bay. He prefers to authorize deviation in standard protocol."

Charlie sighed, smiled, and patted Captain Scoville on the shoulder. "Time is limited but I realize that you sir have tremendous responsibility with 1000 prisoners and 100 men to oversee."

"Actually, with the termination of the prisoner exchange, and Grant and Sherman sending us new prisoners several times a week, our population swells to over 2500. And over 1000 Union soldiers in various capacities comprise the 128th OVI, including the Hoffman Battalion"

Cole feigned an expression of astonishment. "Huge burden my good man. The public in northern Ohio absorbs itself with headlines from battles in Virginia and Georgia while a massive pit of vipers slithers ominously within easy striking distance. Captain, I must in some small manner express my gratitude for the unrecognized service you so nobly perform for your country. Are you a man who indulges in spirits?"

Cole surmised the answer when he observed the corporal's smirk. Scoville replied, "I do enjoy on occasion, and only in moderation, a glass of fine brandy."

The Rebel agent turned and innocently reached for the latch. "I must return to Sandusky. I'll send a case of the finest brandy to your attention to disperse as you see fit."

The captain halted Charlie before he opened the door. "Without visiting the prison. Nonsense! If Captain Carter vouches for you the colonel would surely acquiesce to your request. Those two officers form a compatible, efficient tandem."

Not good to hear, thought Charlie, who still smiled at the opportunity before him.

"Corporal," barked Scoville, "fetch Lieutenant Benson immediately to staff headquarters so Mr. Cole and I may begin our tour. Our guest has many pressing issues awaiting him on the mainland."

Moments later Cole and Scoville trudged toward Johnson's Island's massive twenty-five foot stockade gates. The faint odor permeating the air increased to a nauseating stench as the gates opened. Recognizing his companion's pale expression Scoville nonchalantly commented, "Fortunately, or unfortunately, your nostrils adjust."

Before them six two-story buildings lined each side of a fifty yard wide exercise area. Several sets of stairs descended from the second floor of each building. Each dormitory, measuring 120 feet by 30, received a block number, with even numerals to the left opposite the odd numbered row to the east. Behind each block uninviting 12 feet by 8 latrines had been dug 2 to 5 feet deep. Structures 14 feet by 10 enclosed the excavations commonly referred to as sinks. Charlie observed the west row of blocks had been constructed nearer the stockade wall while a vast open expanse spread between the east blocks and the barrier.

Cole's host added relevant detail. "To our right behind the blocks the three pumps draw fresh water from the bay. To the west you may have noticed our new wall. Some Rebs tunneled from the latrines to the outside of the old fence. No wonder the stinking bastards smell. We moved the barrier back last month." Scoville pointed to a row of stakes forty feet inside the fence. "The drainage ditch now rests totally exposed within the deadline." Intrusion beyond the boundary invited fatal shots from trigger happy Yankee guards.

Charlie learned when the camp opened that Union planners assumed the compound would be vacated by the end of 1862. Upon Johnson's Island's opening several lower numbered blocks contained twenty-two partitioned rooms to accommodate officers while the remaining blocks divided into six rooms to hold enlisted men. By mid '62 the Yankees decided to house only officers on the island plus a smattering of political prisoners or spies. Block 6, with four wards, served as the hospital while block 1 housed prisoners isolated from the general population. Scoville referred to the men in that block as, "the realistic men who astutely took the *Oath of Allegiance* to the Union rather than suffer until the inevitable."

At the end of the exercise area they faced the gable end of block 13, setting symmetrically between blocks 12 and 11. Worn footpaths crisscrossed the grassy area before them. Numerous clusters of prisoners gathered in the shade of the buildings. As Cole and Scoville strolled about they overheard segments of various conversations, discussions, and arguments.

"The Bible says he that first believeth and then is baptized shall be saved," quoted a graying lieutenant.

"Says nothing about needing to be totally dunked," countered another.

In a different gathering they overheard a captain adamantly state, "I heard from a reliable source once McClellan's nominated, not elected mind you, that exchanges begin again." Several companions listened attentively while three others grinned and rolled their eyes.

Laughter erupted from several other men Cole passed. Not to be outdone by a friend's humor a Virginia lieutenant said, "Hear things are so tough in Richmond that it takes a cord of Confederate currency to buy a cord of firewood."

One-upmanship followed when another prisoner replied, "I hear things are so bad in Richmond that the army's enlisting men up to two weeks dead."

At the end of the boulevard bits of a debate as to which state contributed the most to the Confederate war effort filled the air. One captain said to another, "Dagnabbit Bufe, I'm so tired of hearing about you and your Bama boys.

Next thing you'll tell us is if your regiment was split down the center with half of yous at Gettysburg and the other half in Vicksburg we'd of whipped the Yankees in both battles." With that Buford's companion stood up, shook his head, and walked away.

"I do imagine in these close quarters men have a tendency to wear upon each other".

"Only about ten acres for twenty-five hundred men to avoid each other if that be their desire," replied the captain. "Winter's more confining. Remember too, the animosity between the men in block 1 with the balance of the population. Mr. Cole, you ever meet a bonafide Reb general?"

"Never. You board one here?"

"One, we have a number of them. I've got a crusty old bastard I'd like you meet. Epitome of Southern arrogance. Acts like Colonel Hill reports to him. Name's Isaac Trimble. One of the stupid sons of bitches who tried to take the crest at Gettysburg. He's been our guest since."

The same type of assault your blue troops attempted at Fredericksburg thought Charlie. "Captain Scoville, may I have your permission to record a few observations to include in my correspondence with my friends in Harrisburg?" Assuming permission Charlie reached into his pocket and removed paper.

"By all means, Mr. Cole," answered the officer as they trekked to block 4.

The Southern agent inconspicuously studied the surroundings inside the barrack. A Florida colonel with pen in hand sat on a bench with a tintype, paper, and inkwell before him. Cole correctly assumed thoughts of home constantly occupied prisoners' idle minds. At another table a foursome engaged in a game of poker. At an adjacent location a twosome contemplated the next chess move. Dominoes lay scattered atop an unoccupied table in the corner.

Scoville interrupted the card game and brusquely demanded, "Where's Trimble?"

"General Trimble?" replied a major with deep scar on his left cheek. He accentuated the general's rank which the Yankee captain failed to acknowledge. The major continued with repeated emphasis, "General Trimble's in the next room resting. Tripped the other day and the leg's been bothering him a bit."

They entered the adjacent room where a thin man with a sour expression occupied the lower level on a three tiered bunk. His eyes gazed toward the intruders while he rose on his elbows, reached down, and slowly grasped his wooden leg with both hands. He flung it to the floor and swung his good leg along side. "Here to tell me you're doing something about the starvation diet you put us on, Captain?" he asked as he grasped a bedpost and pulled himself to his feet.

"General Trimble, Colonel Hill stated he sympathizes with your plight but Washington dictates policy for our prisons just as Richmond does for yours."

"All fine and good Captain but sympathy doesn't fill a man's belly any more than the half pound of fatty bacon or boney pork and the 10 ounce loaf of bread you daily allow. I won't mention we barely receive adequate wood to cook one meal a day."

"Better than the rations our boys receive from your people, General."

"Poor debate. Your cruel blockade's placing hardship on your own besides our women and children." Trimble turned his head and stared at Cole. Noticing the pencil and paper in the visitor's hand the general asked, "You one of those damned abolitionist newspapermen who brought on this conflict?"

Charlie smiled at the old man's directness. "I may be many things, General, including one who believes more out of necessity than morality your peculiar institution must be abolished, but I'm no journalist. I temporarily reside in Sandusky at least until the end of the month when my business concludes."

"Business, what business?"

“Oil, General Trimble. When this bloody conflict ends the nation will need oil to keep the wheels of industry turning.”

“Yankee subjugation of the working class you mean.”

“General, with all due respect, you are an opinionated gentleman. Shall we contemplate a more amiable topic over which to converse? Your military background perhaps?”

Soon the former railroad engineer, now sixty-two, told Charlie of his ten year military career after West Point during which he served as an artillery officer. He departed long before the war with Mexico to pursue railroad ambitions. He eventually gravitated to Maryland until hostilities with the North beckoned his return to his native Virginia.

At the end of the dialogue Cole tore several sheets from his pad and stuffed them into his pocket. When Scoville turned and walked toward the door the Southern agent extended his right hand to the prisoner. Cole placed his left hand over their clasped hands. An inquisitive fleeting expression crossed Isaac Trimble’s face. After Cole and Scoville departed the general unfolded the paper which read,

Richmond remembers you. Freedom is near. Details coming. Your friend, CC.

Charlie spoke after the pair stepped outside. “Though secesh, a very interesting gentleman. Receiving the opportunity to gather information and refute his views would prove most enjoyable.” He glanced to his companion. “But I never will attempt to abuse this one-time visit, Captain.” Charlie glanced away as they continued walking.

“Nonsense, Mr. Cole, your visit offers a pleasant diversion from our mundane routine, and Colonel Hill most assuredly shall enjoy meeting you. Are you familiar with the new sport of baseball?”

“Some call it rounders, I believe?”

"Some have, yes. It's a modification of the British game of cricket. The Rebels, with need to occupy their time, developed an affinity for it. Before the end of the month a challenge match amongst them is scheduled for the enjoyment of the prisoners, my men, and special invited guests such as yourself although I hope you grace us with your presence before that day."

"It shall be my pleasure, and I do hope to visit prior to the event if my demanding schedule permits." The huge gate swung open. Charlie bid his new friend adieu. Aboard the *Little General,* he deeply inhaled the refreshing southwestern breeze carrying the repugnant stench away.

43 – LEARNING MORE OF SANDUSKY

Thirty minutes after departing Johnson's Island, Charlie visited George Hart's liquor emporium located several storefronts west of his hotel's corner entrance. "May I presume you are Mr. Hart?" he asked the bespectacled man with thinning hair who stood behind the counter.

"No sir, I'm his associate, Emanuel Blatt. How may I service you, a bottle of French port perhaps?"

"No, but I do desire a sample of your finest brandy.

The merchant shuffled to retrieve an open bottle from which he poured two fingers of the amber beverage into a clear glass. "To your satisfaction, sir?" Blatt smiled anticipating a positive response.

Charlie took a moderate swig and swished the brandy inside his mouth allowing his tongue to bathe in the liquid. He stared at the remainder, illuminated by the light flowing through the front window. Satisfied with taste and clarity he drained the glass and approvingly answered, "Emmm, excellent. Send a case of two-pint bottles to Captain Scoville, the second ranking officer on Johnson's Island. Are you familiar with him?"

Blatt's smile vanished. "Yes, on rare occasion he stops, but only to purchase a bottle of local Concord." Realizing he may have offended his new customer he extricated himself by adding somewhat insincerely, "I trust he shall most certainly appreciate your generosity. Unfortunately Mr. Scoville's position demands that he entertain like a colonel on his captain's wages. I'll ship your order on the evening boat."

"What do I owe you, my good man?"

"Eight dollars including the shipping, Mr. Cole. Do you desire to open an account with us?"

Charlie laid a ten dollar greenback on the counter. "No, I may be called away at any time and I wish to remain current with all the fine merchants in your fair city."

The liquor dealer reached into the drawer to remove the change but Charlie Cole, always generous with his government's funds, casually requested, "Keep the balance for your efforts." With a tip of his derby he departed anticipating a goblet of bourbon on ice in the West House saloon.

The clock near the entrance chimed half past four. Inside Charlie noticed a gentleman seated alone at a rear table. Walking past the bar he headed for an adjacent table. He seated himself, looked over, tipped his hat, and initiated conversation. "Sparse gathering today."

"Only for a brief period. The *Philo Parsons* docks in another hour followed shortly thereafter by the trains arrivals. A handful of local citizens also partake of their evening meal here. With all due respect, I assume you're a stranger to Sandusky?" Cole nodded affirmatively. With a welcoming gesture the stranger beckoned Charlie to join him. The man extended his delicate hand and introduced himself as "Joshua Merrick, architect from across the way." He pointed to the three-story stone building with narrow archtop windows on floors two and three.

Charlie introduced himself and offered details of his position and the purpose of his visit to the area.

"How do you find our peaceful little city Mr. Cole?"

"Pleasant, although after touring the prison camp with Captain Scoville I find myself harboring fears of an uprising any hour of the day or night."

"A concern to us all, Democrat or Republican, or Unionist as Lincoln now refers to his party."

"Do I judge correctly that you belong to the Democracy?"

"You assume correctly and your politics sir?"

Careful, thought Charlie, don't want to alienate anyone, especially a potential ally. He cautiously replied, "I remain a Whig at heart yearning for the days before this deadly business commenced. I now try to better myself for the day bloodshed ends so I may be of most service when rebuilding begins."

Tenseness evaporated from the architect. He leaned back, relaxed his stiff posture, and said with sincere congeniality, "If more men expounded that view four years ago we might well have avoided this unnecessary war."

"From all I've ascertained during my three days here, Sandusky seems to be a Republican community, albeit not totally pro Lincoln. I imagine men with your convictions may be somewhat ostracized."

"At times, but I resided here long before Fort Sumter. My acquaintances understand I have as much distain for the so-called Copperheads as I do for the Black Republicans. Each side of the spectrum consists of self-serving individuals dedicated to enhancing their position rather than building the great nation I envision in the future. Perhaps by nature an architect longs to build rather than destroy," added Merrick, while visualizing the beautiful but functional bridges he'd designed and built.

Cole tactfully commented, "Yet you most certainly must endure lonely and isolated days."

"Yes, but I am fortunate to posess likeminded friends for consolation."

"Really? Professional men I assume."

Merrick freely responded to his pleasant companion, "As a matter of fact, yes. John Williams is in partnership with William Scudder. They own the hardware store across the way not quite to Jackson Street. His views and mine coincide. Another friend, John Brown, gets a burr under his saddle occasionally, but only because his position as post master, a patronage office he held under the Buchanan administration, transferred to a loyal Republican with Lincoln's election. John's real estate activities have improved over the past several years with better economic conditions. At one time Dr. Ellwood Stanley regularly shared our company. We've distanced ourselves from him." Merrick's face grimaced. "The doctor's biting comments do neither himself nor his acquaintances any favors. While I detest Lincoln I lack the bitter hatred Ellwood espouses. I heartily believe he would revel in the Union's dissolution if Lincoln, Stanton, and the likes of our own Senator Ben Wade, along with that damn abolitionist Senator Charles Sumner, perished with it. His bitterness transcends all imagination. But enough of the war, Mr. Cole. Enlighten me as to the future of oil. I hear enticing stories of huge financial gains with a like number of terrifying accounts of financial ruin."

The men talked oil and assorted topics during the meal they shared after migrating to the dining hall. Back in his room Charlie removed his logbook from his valise and penned a new page under the heading, "Men to Watch". Beneath it he wrote the names of Joshua Merrick, John M. Brown, John H. Williams, and Dr. Elwood Stanley. Charlie wondered what the morrow would bring after the successes of this day.

Several days later he relaxed in the West House lobby while reading the *Commercial Register*. Gold prices up again, perhaps the most accurate indictor of the public's perception of the war. A smile crossed Charlie's face as he read of the Union army's difficulties. Sherman appeared fearful of confronting the Confederacy's newly appointed general in Georgia. Aggressive John B. Hood replaced passive Joe Johnston, while in Virginia Grant discovered Bobby Lee was no ordinary adversary. Yankee setbacks initiated rumors of Secretary of War Stanton's imminent dismissal from his post. Add to that reports of more Indian attacks in Minnesota. Timing for Hines's operation, if coordinated with the extrication of other Confederate prisoners throughout Illinois, Indiana, Ohio, Kentucky, and Missouri, appeared ideal.

Charlie meandered to the saloon to bide his time until Annie's arrival. He had returned late that morning from a fact finding trip to the west. He reflected upon his brief two day excursion to Toledo and Detroit. He convinced himself of the necessity to investigate potential escape routes. In actuality, Mr. Cole, abstaining far too long, craved an opportunity to solicit the female companionship readily available in larger cities, away from the self-righteous eyes of Sandusky's pious citizens. If he waited until Annie arrived his self deprivation would reach six nights, totally unrealistic for the vivacious Charlie Cole. Although passionate nights with Annie remained unsurpassed the occasional variety reaffirmed that she continued as his favorite.

Charlie gulped down his second bourbon and returned to the lobby for her imminent grand entrance. Within minutes she sashayed in leading the flood of new arrivals. When she reached out to embrace him he smoothly grasped her gloved hands and loudly said, "Mrs. Cole, how good see you safe and sound. I trust your trip was uneventful." He softly whispered, "You're a wife now, Annie, proper decorum!"

The couple directed the luggage handler to carry her baggage to the second floor room where he deposited numerous trunks and boxes, and exited with a generous tip. Charlie shook his head in amazement. "Mrs. Cole, you're visiting, not relocating."

"My dear Charles, to present myself appropriately within the social circles which you intend integrating us, I require a sufficient wardrobe."

Staring through the layers of clothing below her appetizing low neck line he smiled and said, "My dear Mrs. Cole, your most pleasing wardrobe for me is none at all."

She spontaneously wrapped her arms around his neck and squeezed her sweetly scented body tightly against his. Charlie's hands actively massaged her hips. She pulled away and teased, "Mr. Cole, you may partake of your matrimonial privileges only after your famished wife satisfies her appetite."

The two seated themselves in the elegant dining room. Mr. Cole selected a chicken salad a la mayonnaise, venison steak stewed in wine, with sides of oysters, cucumbers, and tomatoes. Mrs. Cole selected lobster salad a la ravigatte but debated between spring lamb with green peas and roast goose with applesauce. Side dish options of sugar corn, peaches, and cheese inhibited her decision making, although she decided her meal would conclude with English plum pudding smothered in brandy sauce.

Upon the waiter's second visit Charlie sent him to fetch another bottle of Claret, before he admonished, "Mrs. Cole, I realize the menus in eateries offer a wide variety from which to select. However, a lady must select one and stay committed to that choice."

Ruffled by his impatience after her exhausting day of travel she sharply recoiled, "Mr. Cole, I realize the numerous women of the world offer a wide variety from which to select. However, a man must select one and stay committed to that choice."

Wounded by her rebuke he sat silently sipping his wine until she ordered. Their conversion revolved around small talk, common acquaintances, and superficial talk of the war. At the conclusion of their meal Charlie informed her of an important telegram he received that morning upon returning from his brief but vital tour of Toledo and Detroit. He patted his breast pocket which held a telegram from Henry Thomas Heinzelman of the Northwestern Oil Company stating that the acquisition scheduled for August 29th in Chicago would proceed as scheduled.

Wobbling up the stairs from the affects of plentiful wine Charlie hoped one turn would satisfy her. He desired to represent himself well during his first meeting with John Beall, tentatively scheduled for the following day.

44 – ENTER MR. BEALL

Rather than travel to Windsor and book steamer passage to Sandusky, John crossed into Buffalo and traveled via Erie and Cleveland by train over tracks that occasionally stretched along the lake. When he looked intently into the aimlessly passing sea, symbolic of his life since war commenced, he visualized his dear Martha, the one constant in his life. He imagined the touch of her compassionate moist lips against his. "When This Cruel War Is Over," the title of the song resounding from every parlor, hall, and saloon throughout the North and the South, echoed his sentiments exactly. How much longer? Ever? His heart beat intensely as he envisioned his vital participation in dealing the culminating death blow deep behind enemy lines.

Meeting a new superior created the predictable anxiety although Commissioner Thompson audaciously claimed the head of the Sandusky operation exhibited the dedication and character to initiate the crucial steps of the bold plan. Fresh lake air rejuvenated John's spirits. How he'd grown to love the sea. When this deadly business ended he yearned to return to his beloved Walnut Grove, but he also anticipated voyages to Europe with Martha and their children.

After registering at the Colton House, he meandered toward the mammoth West House. Beautiful city, he thought. What better location to bring the horrors of war than to this bustling but secure setting with its 25,000 inhabitants. At the West House desk he requested Mr. Cole's room number.

"Room 134, but Mr. Cole awaits you in our saloon, as Mrs. Cole has yet to rise. Strenuous rail trip yesterday you know," offered the young clerk with an impish smirk. Harold Huntington irritably glared at the boy's lack of propriety. In a sharp tone he snapped, "August, you're keeping our important visitor from his meeting with Mr. Cole. Notify him immediately." When the adolescent disappeared John envisioned a lad that age in Virginia manning the trenches around Richmond while this unpolished Ohio boy only concerned himself with carrying a message from one room to another. The North deserved an awakening.

"Are you staying with us, Mr. Yates?" asked Huntington.

"No sir, unfortunately my company only authorized stipend sufficient for the Colton House."

"I'm sure you'll find those accommodations suitable, although simple, nonetheless adequate," he responded in a condescending tone.

As John turned away to await Charles Cole he longed to reply that in a matter of days the West House's ash heap may be larger than the Colton's but the stench would be equal. Cole appeared through the door, tossed the lad two bits, and greeted Beall. A rather liberal tip, John thought, before his mind returned to the business at hand.

Cole motioned him to follow. "We'll seclude ourselves in a corner of the dining room. The afternoon clientele is significantly smaller than the evening crowd. If my wife vacates our room we'll relocate there, or perhaps we may even rent a hack or horses and tour the countryside. You're preference," stated the agreeable agent.

Following their meal the conspirators rode on horseback to the outskirts of town over the Columbus Plank Road. After reviewing the strategy for Sandusky, Cole concluded by saying, "And of course Mr. Beall, I mean Mr. Yates, I must synchronize my actions to simultaneously converge with yours for a successful mission."

Beall's sparkling blue eyes contrasted his worn face. The corner of his lips curled upward ever so lightly. This could really bring the end, maybe not in September, or even October, but most certainly by November as the Northern people deposed their ruler by election or whatever means. He could marry Martha, perhaps by Christmas, the Lord willing.

"You've accomplished a great deal in a limited time, Major Cole. My compliments."

"Thank you, Mr. Yates. However, I am highly disappointed that I have yet to tour the *Michigan*. Details too of our support forces are vague at best, although I realize Mr. Thompson's burdened with the enormous complexities of the Chicago operation. Before you depart we must devise a means to communicate with each other as our date with destiny nears," Cole added with a confident smile. "What are your primary concerns?"

"I need to locate a vessel to transport my crew to the *Michigan*. More critical, I must first recruit a crew and arm them. I fear I may not discover who I may rely upon and who shall falter until we face the heat of battle. I only have one man committed, but he is the most fearless and trustworthy man with whom I have ever fought."

"John," began Cole dispensing with all formality, "Canada abounds with many a brave man desiring to bring retribution to these pious Yankees. Finding two or three dozen committed Southerners should provide no challenge. Besides, once I execute my intricate plan to incapacitate the *Michigan's* officers, a dozen boys and old men could overpower the vessel."

Overconfidence or arrogance? Neither desirable. "How do you plan to disable them?"

"After I gain their confidence I'll host a banquet for them and drug their champagne, allowing the ship to be yours for the taking."

Beall concealed his apprehension for a plan that appeared long on optimistic generalities and short on concrete details. "Very interesting, Mr. Cole," was all he managed to reply as the duo began their return through town.

That evening John joined Charles and his wife at the West House. He discovered Cole's spouse to be a pleasant dinner companion. Most women possessing her beauty lacked the depth to comprehend the complex events contributing to current conditions. She exuded a survivalist mentality indicating her social sophistication may have developed later in life rather than being inbred upon inception. Both the Coles masterfully played their roles of affluent Northerners. Each also effortlessly utilized allocated Confederate funds to the maximum.

Annie shielded her modest disappointment when John mentioned his commitment to his "friend in Georgia," as he referred to Martha. This man exuded the wholesome integrity so lacking in the circles within which she socialized and the environment in which she worked at her chosen profession. Men such as John Yates really did exist. Her eyes wandered to Charlie—always only one step away from unbridled success. However, to date no better prospects appeared on the horizon.

When they separated Charlie informed John he hoped to visit the *Michigan* tomorrow before John departed.

45 – ABOARD THE *MICHIGAN*

Ensign Hunter's small color guard stood at attention on the Columbus Avenue wharf. Captain Carter immediately welcomed Cole aboard. Once underway the 163 foot long ship with a 27 foot beam glided peacefully toward the channel linking Sandusky Bay with Lake Erie. The *Michigan's* pair of paddle wheels with diameters of 21 feet effortlessly churned through the water.

"We shall tour below decks during our return," said Captain Carter as they stood in the wheelhouse. Due to the size and weight of the warship Charlie avoided even the slightest queasiness which habitually accompanied him on the water. Carter offered a brief history of the vessel. "They built her in Pittsburgh during the last half of 1842, disassembled her, shipped her overland to Erie, reassembled her, and launched her late in '43. We officially commissioned her the following September as the U.S. Navy's first iron hulled ship. Due to our treaty with Britain she's the only warship permitted on the Great Lakes."

"I'm amazed that the Canadians accept a ship so heavily armed," commented Charlie.

"We're limited to only an 18 pounder on the forward pivot." When Charlie inquisitively glanced at the numerous guns mounted about the ship Carter winked and explained. "Politicians conjure up these documents and thirty years later completely different threats exist. No one could have foreseen that by 1861 our severest menace would lay within our own borders rather than beyond them. With our victory so near, England certainly harbors no desire to jeopardize her neutrality with us. That being said, rest assured that if the Rebels held the upper hand the Brits would cuddle with the Confederates despite the ramification that action might create. We man our vessel with over 100 efficient and dedicated seamen prepared to utilize our 30 pound rifled Parrot, the five 20 pound Parrots, the six 24 pound smoothbores, and our pair of 12 pound boat howitzers."

"Fourteen cannon, a very strong deterrent for any foolhardy party confronting you, Captain."

"Rumors continue circulating of a reckless attempt by the Rebels to free the prisoners," Carter said, pointing to the prison camp off their port side. Such an attempt would be suicidal. With my firepower and those guns mounted in the stockade blockhouses a ghastly massacre would ensue. Even the arrogant secesh are not that rash."

"Enough of the armaments, of which there certainly are enough," Charlie said, as he smiled with his witty play on words. "What of the rest of the ship? The engine and area below deck intrigues me."

"Our engine drives two cylinders, each with a thirty-six inch bore and eight foot stroke, powered by two boilers capable of 330 horsepower. When we cruise the lake we utilize the sails rigged to our three masts."

"Which sufficiently reduces coal consumption, I imagine?"

"Affirmative, Mr. Cole, although we carry 120 tons of the fuel. Use of our sails in conjunction with our engines allows cruising at sustained rates between ten and fifteen knots without taxing the boilers in the least."

After the vessel entered the open waters of Lake Erie the ship's captain ordered his pilot to make a wide, gentle arc to reverse course and return to Sandusky at a reduced, leisurely speed. Charlie followed his host below. Above the gun deck hung dozens of unoccupied hammocks. Stairs descended to yet another deck."

"I assume the powder magazine is safely situated in the center of the ship below the waterline, Captain Carter?"

"Yes, and with reinforced walls," shouted the Captain above the deafening roar reverberating from the aft section housing the boilers and engines.

To Charlie's relief the captain strode to the stairs leading back to the gun deck. With the engine's roar again muffled the captain spoke in a normal tone. “The shear power of the rotating engine arms is a sight to behold. However, the heat in that compartment, especially this time of year, is suffocating so I took the liberty to avoid that area.”

Becoming familiar with that portion of the ship would have proved beneficial for the upcoming operation. However the stale air trapped throughout the claustrophobic lower deck unsettled his stomach. Fresh air circulating through open gun ports flushed color into Charlie’s ashen face. They passed the galley and the officer’s cabins before reaching the spacious quarters of the ship’s master. Glistening dark mahogany paneling and woodwork complimented the oak bunk, armoire, table, desk, and chairs.”

“Beautiful accommodations,” Cole said admiring the reddish brown wood grain. “This serves as a sleeping room, chief executive’s quarters, planning center, and entertainment site?”

“To a degree, although the ship’s dining room capable of accommodating over two dozen people has remained unused for the past three years.”

After the two left Carter’s cabin they walked past a door labeled *Ship’s Armory*.

“I imagine you maintain a sufficient number of small arms and weapons. With your big guns though I assume you would keep an enemy at a distance to all but eliminate the need for sidearms.”

“Perhaps, although desperate men perform foolish deeds. Every damn Rebel on the high seas imagines himself to be John Taylor Wood, the only man to ever successfully board and commandeer a small Union gunboat. Others have tried only to meet repulsion or capture. Several squads of proficient marksman armed with Springfield rifles further strengthen our ship’s defenses. In the unlikely event of an enemy boarding attempt our arsenal contains carbines, revolvers, and cutlasses. Two officers remain on board at all times with keys to access the weaponry.” Charlie shook his head, frowned, and wiped his brow as he began to understand the daunting task facing him. "You appear troubled, Mr. Cole."

Charlie laughed in his usual good natured manner and patted Captain Carter's shoulder. "I visualized the carnage resulting from any irrational attempt to confront you. Forgive my reaction. Slaughter of one's enemy, though essential in time of war, is nothing to savor."

"Spoken like a warrior already familiar with the true face of battle."

"Thank you, Captain, but allow me to reaffirm that in the event of such action I trust the Confederates shall receive all they deserve."

The *Michigan's* commander shook his head in agreement without realizing what he just acknowledged.

Upon disembarking the *Michigan,* Cole headed to the West House lobby where Beall left a message reminding Charlie he planned to depart on the six p.m. train. Cole immediately walked to the Colton House to meet with Beall.

"Eventful morning, Mr. Cole?"

"Very much so. I just completed a first rate tour of the *Michigan* with Captain Carter. I visited all crucial areas of the ship. Engine room, powder magazine, coal bins, gun decks, crew's and officer's quarters, including the captain's. The *Michigan's* fire power is fearsome, twenty guns in all. I also entered the room holding arms for several hundred men. Imagine those weapons in the hands of our liberated officers."

"Gaining control of the vessel shall prove a challenge indeed, Mr. Cole."

Charlie stiffened his posture, cocked his head, smiled, and replied, "The execution of my detailed plans and the timely assault of your handpicked crew shall overcome any obstacle. By daybreak the following morning our liberated prisoners shall be miles away from the smoldering ashes of Sandusky. Shortly thereafter our names shall be spoken with reverence from the lips of citizens throughout the South."

"Certainly a spectacle to behold," Beall responded unemotionally as he bid the Sandusky chief of local operations adieu. "May we meet in eleven days on the deck of the *Michigan*, Major."

Beall relaxed in his seat until his coach lurched forward simultaneously with the sound of escaping steam and grinding wheels over iron rails. His two days in Sandusky proved exceedingly informative. Familiarity with the prison's location, the waterfront's landscape, and the city's unusual street layout encapsulating the Masonic emblem all proved beneficial. Disconcerting was the chief operative. Men with inflated egos took too much for granted and oversimplified the task at hand. He feared Cole was prone to focus on broad generalities and ignore specific details, a fatal trait conducive to inviting error. He dissected their dialogue and became concerned with the inconsistencies in the facts presented. His skepticism grew as he recalled the liberal use of government funds, perhaps necessary to play the part of the oil executive, but certainly not to that degree. And Charlie's wife? Something seemed amiss. Diplomatically expressing his concerns to Jacob Thompson would prove a challenge within itself, but he must address them. For now he pulled his hat over his eyes, leaned back, and within moments dozed into the soft, inviting arms of Martha O'Bryan.

46 – BACK TO JOHNSON'S ISLAND

Two days later Charlie waited outside Colonel Charles Hill's office. Only eight days until Chicago erupted. He questioned if his operation could evolve to coincide. No word from Canada for five days. The headquarters' door swung open. An athletically built blue clad soldier escorted by four others exited. A slender sergeant paused by the door and greeted Charlie. "Welcome, Mr. Cole. The colonel will see you."

A dark-haired officer with bushy muttonchops advanced. "Pleased to meet you, Mr. Cole. Captain Scoville speaks highly of you."

"Thank you, Colonel Hill. I appreciate your accommodating me despite your demanding schedule." Charlie looked over his shoulder toward the door. "Disciplining your men further disrupts a day I imagine."

After a thoughtful pause the colonel chuckled and motioned his guest toward a chair. Hill glanced at the door and offered a good-natured smile. "Oh that, let me explain. The gentleman exiting was not mine. Fact is we captured him, again, trying to escape." Hill clarified in response to his visitor's inquisitive expression following the word "again". "This is Charlie Pierce's third escape attempt. We caught him several months back tunneling out alone. Yesterday our guards caught Pierce and two others when they broke through the ground behind block eight. Must have forgotten we moved the west fence out another forty feet in July. This morning the offal cart driver fell asleep inside Pierce's block, with the aid of strong spirits I reluctantly might add. My man continued sleeping when someone yelled the garbage was loaded. Pierce requisitioned our man's coat and cap, quickly donned them, and drove past the sentinels guarding the gate which closed just when our driver ran past block two shouting at his cart, much to our Louisiana soldier's dismay."

"Captured in the wrong uniform, Colonel? Going to shoot him?

"God sakes no, but the enemy appreciates your concern. I've been on the frontlines myself. I accept, although without wholehearted support from some men stationed here who have not faced enemy fire, that a soldier has the duty to escape. Besides, an occasional attempt keeps my men sharp. And a capture always injects pride into our troops and reminds them of their critical responsibility."

"Have any escaped, Colonel?"

"None on my watch. I recognize from shear boredom some occupy their minds with escape plots. To my consternation, in early July a Lieutenant Murphy obtained a blue uniform and exited the compound with a forged pass. We apprehended him shortly thereafter. Word of schemes involving more than two men generally filters to us well ahead of the actual attempt." Noticing the sudden appearance of perspiration on his guest's forehead the colonel asked, "Mr. Cole, did I say something to upset you?"

"Forgive me. The thought of even several vengeful Rebels roaming our safe and secure vicinity alarms me. I hope these attempts are on the decline."

"As do I. Unfortunately we reduced rations in retaliation for the meager allowance the Confederacy provides our men. Off the record I believe Southern civilians and Rebel soldiers survive on a limited diet also. As of today all packages for Confederate prisoners shall be withheld too by order of Secretary Stanton. In several months the prisoners' gardens shall lie fallow. The dread of another cold winter surely shall force some of these thin-blooded men to attempt escape. I've heard them say that even after eating, their hunger pangs only momentarily subside. With limited rations they claim all warmth will evaporate their bodies come November and not return until May. More than hunger drives others to attempt escape. As final victory nears the Johnnies surely must experience apprehension as to the penalty that might be exacted especially for their officers' transgressions. I trust President Lincoln lets them down easy."

"You believe Lincoln will be reelected, Colonel?"

"Analyze the landscape. Bobby Lee's facing a general who, though respects Lee certainly is not awed by him. You think my prisoners feel confined. The Rebs in Petersburg are severely restrained. Something will give. As the Union military piles its weight against Southern defenses in Virginia the enemy's lines shall crack and then shatter. While Lee is the genius of mobility he lacks room to maneuver and also confronts an unintimidated foe, both of which drastically diminish his skills. And Atlanta rests precariously before Sherman's western boys. Enough of the battlefront. I believe you desire to educate some of our prisoners as to the benefit of acknowledging abolition."

"With your approval I wish to distribute these tracts." Charlie handed a pamphlet to the commander.

A cynical look crossed Hill's face when he realized the renowned abolitionist William Lloyd Garrison authored the writing. "Good luck. I'll assign a squadron of men to protect you."

"No need, I'm confident General Trimble shall control his men."

"That cantankerous old coot? As long as you occupy him I'm free from his incessant whining," Hill added before Charlie departed.

As Cole approached the gathering site, General Trimble, with the use of a cane, steadily ambled from his block. The general sarcastically snarled, "A loaf of bread would digest better than the abolitionist propaganda you wish to shower upon us."

One of the blue guards curtly replied, "If we offend you, sir, I suggest you find accommodations at another establishment." Hearty laughter roared from the remainder of the Yankees.

Cole turned to the blue detachment assigned him and begged a private word with the general. In a lowered voice he whispered, “Don’t appear to acquiesce to anything I say, but limit emotional disruption to maintain our chaperones at a desirable distance. When finished I’ll offer you several cigars. Inside the wrappers you’ll receive a summary of our plans. If practicable we’ll communicate in like manner in the future.” Cole nodded as if concurring with Trimble’s wishes and loudly said, “General Trimble, you give me your word you shall listen without interrupting, provided I agree to take three random questions at the conclusion of my lecture.”

“You have the word of a Southern gentleman and a Confederate officer.”

Charlie ascended the staircase leading to the second story of block four. On the third step he gazed down to the few men standing, while the majority of his audience lounged on the ground. A Rebel officer appeared with a chair for Trimble. When Cole began, the most pious of listeners could mistake him for an evangelist while the more secular of his attendees could just as easily confuse him for a snake oil salesman. “My former Union brothers, my incarcerated listeners, if anyone understands the meaning of freedom, it is you. You understand the demoralization of the soul accompanying the loss of one’s freedom.”

“Niggers ain’t got no soul,” heckled a gray clad man sitting in the front.

“Never had freedom to lose neither,” jeered another.

Trimble struggled to his feet, held up his hands, and motioned for silence until the speaker finished. He instructed those who could show no such courtesy to leave. Immediately a dozen men walked away. Charlie surveyed his reduced audience of perhaps only a score of prisoners and continued. In an act of subtle defiance one man pulled out his pocket knife and commenced to silently play mumble peg with another prisoner. The action inspired several Rebs to open their knives. One carved a black chunk of gutcha rubber. Another worked on an intricate ring from a mother of pearl shell. A third whittled slivers of wood from a piece of firewood. Several rows back another prisoner contentedly played solitaire oblivious to the speaker’s drone.

After twenty minutes Charlie concluded his lecture. "As agreed upon I shall answer three questions from our attentive audience." Pointing to a distinguished officer sitting beside Trimble, he said, "Your question sir, and for my own edification, please tell me the state you hail from and your rank in the Confederate Army."

The officer stood as if at roll call. "Lieutenant Colonel John Inzer, 58th Alabama. If the North would win the war, which won't happen, I question how the darkies would earn a living?"

Cheers followed the last comment. Charlie superficially answered Inzer's question, accepted and responded to the other two, and offered, "Some interesting tracts from a renowned gentleman might better offer facts to substantiate my oratory today."

Several dozen pamphlets disappeared from the stack. As the men walked away a Tennessee lieutenant was heard to say, "If'n it ain't used to start a fire I spose I can always wipe my ass with it," which brought a chorus of laughter.

Cole walked over to Trimble and loudly said, "General, I hope my talk in the least provoked thought and that you permit me more interaction in the near future."

"I hope in the very near future."

Charlie shook Trimble's hand and offered him two cigars wrapped in a sheet of paper just as the squad of soldiers advanced to escort the visitor.

A pudgy corporal with shaggy hair, graying stubble covering his face, and who exhaled a foul breathe, preceded his men by several paces. To Cole's chagrin he reached to confiscate the smokes. "Mister Whatever-your-name-is, we don't waste good baccie on the likes of him."

Trimble grimly clutched his parcel. Charlie interceded by stepping between the two. He smiled despite the corporal's nauseating odor which suppressed the stench drifting from the sinks. He reached into his pocket, removed a fistful of cigars, placed his other hand on the soldier's shoulder, and whispered, "I save the expensive one's for our boys. The stale ones I only give to barflies and Rebs."

The corporal snatched them, drew one along his nose, smiled and placed them into his trouser pocket without so much as a thank you.

"What about us, Ramsey?" begged one of the three privates with him.

Ramsey spit on the ground and bluntly stated, "Rank has its privileges."

Approaching the main gate Cole earnestly prayed a lead slug would find that uncouth bastard in eight days. Minutes later the *Little Eastern* glided over the calm waters with Charlie anticipating his return to the prison compound the following week. Colonel Hill personally invited him to attend the match between the Confederates team and the Southerners team for bragging rights as the best baseball players on Johnson's Island. The night of the contest also happened to be the tentative date for the liberation of prisoners, an unanticipated obstacle.

In block four Trimble and Inzer puffed away on their cigars. They secluded themselves as the general reread the message.

Tentative event 29 August. Weapons for you in short supply. Michigan shall be ours, then J.I., then Sandusky, then back to CSA. Repeat—only tentative. Will communicate to confirm or postpone.

When Charlie entered his room he tore open a telegram and attempted to read it while Mrs. Cole pressed her breasts against his back. Her nails seductively tingled along his neck.

"Damn it, Annie, not now."

Stepping around to face him she demanded, "What's wrong?"

"Operation in Sandusky's postponed until after Chicago."

"Are you sure?"

"My message reads,

Acquisition of Chicago property now a priority. Due to limited resources Ohio acquisitions delayed until mid September."

Her eyes gazed seductively into his as she rubbed against him. "Does this mean we'll be unable to spend our funds allocated to us so generously by your Confederacy?"

"My dear Mrs. Cole, I am sure that Textor & Lerch offers a few glittering trinkets to appease your desire. I shall perform my duty to insure that my funds do not remain unused. Now let us enjoy dinner, satisfy the cravings of my appetite, and leave this war business alone."

Stroking his neck she asked, "Dessert now or later?"

47 – ANOTHER SEPTEMBER

Beall's impatience grew with the operation's lengthening delay. He stared across the river to Detroit, another Union city begging for retribution. He reread the *Detroit News* account of the disaster in Georgia. His disheartened mood inhibited the flow of dispirited blood through his depressed body. John Hood evacuated Atlanta on September 1. Would Sherman and his hoard of barbarians pursue Hood's Army of Tennessee, or might they instead set their sights further south toward the active rail hub and humming industrial complex of Columbus where Martha resided? He instinctively yearned to rush to her side to fend off the invaders. His despondency increased after word arrived that Tom Hines received nothing but hollow promises from Vallandigham. The alleged thousands of men belonging to the Sons of Liberty failed to rally behind the operation to release 8000 prisoners from Camp Douglas. John earnestly hoped the plans for Johnson's Island might promptly be polished and moved to the forefront.

Upon his return from Sandusky, Beall had located Burley. The pair earnestly commenced interviewing prospective recruits. They sought between twenty and thirty trustworthy, dedicated men. If brazen talk solely identified such men then an ample surplus resided in Canada. Beall's thoughts returned to Cole. He feared Charlie's boastful talk and brave actions would simultaneously disappear at the sound of gunfire. Thompson had scheduled a meeting in Windsor with Beall and Cole tomorrow and hinted Hines might also attend, much to John's relief. Thompson implied several newcomers too might join the group. The fewer the better but the commissioner gloried in large audiences. Beall's spirits climbed with the optimism that the meeting indicated the mission breathed new life. With God's help they must succeed. Failure would only invite future decades of the guerilla warfare; something he promised Martha would never occur.

The following day Thompson introduced Hines and Beall to Godfrey Hyams. Without emotion Hines offered a perfunctory handshake to the newcomer before slapping Johnny on the shoulder and warmly pumping his hand. Hyams emitted an ominous aura to Beall.

"Where's Mr. Cole," questioned John, barely concealing his irritation.

"He's in Sandusky tying intricate details together while continuing to garner additional information and enlarge his growing circle of contacts," replied Thompson.

"With Annie Brown I assume," remarked Hines with a touch of disdain.

"Of course, our proper Mr. Cole cannot be without his Mrs. Cole."

The response confirmed Beall's suspicion as to the Coles actual relationship. Thompson looked to John. "Tomorrow you'll travel to Sandusky to meet with Major Cole and finalize plans for the operation. I've invited Lieutenant Bennett Young to join you. A third perspective might prove beneficial."

"Good man, Johnny. Served with him under Morgan," reassured Hines.

"Our tentative date remains two weeks from this evening. I'll remain in Windsor and await Captain Beall's return," added Thompson. "Then I'll travel to Toronto and draw some of the despicable Yankee spies in the area with me. God's speed, gentlemen."

About the time the meeting concluded in Canada, Charlie exited a train in Sandusky, having completed some important business in Port Clinton twenty miles to the west. To his surprise Annie waited in his room. "Thought you'd be gone my dear," he said as she advanced to welcome him. "I remember you seemed none too pleased that business would separate us these past several days."

Annie cynically laughed, "This isn't Jacob Thompson you're conning. He may believe you, but your excursion consisted of nothing but a damn hunting expedition at Winnie's Point."

"Winous, Mrs. Cole, Winous Point, an exclusive club with elite members. When Mr. Moss invited me to visit with one of his close personal friends I jumped at the opportunity to develop connections which might prove of great value to me. Though not in attendance, Mr. Jay Cooke holds a membership to the club."

"Jay Cooke, the millionaire financier?"

"The one and only."

She sarcastically asked, "With so much time delegated to conducting business and developing relationships did you even hunt."

"Of course, I needed to display my skills with the other well-bred gentlemen. Since I travel with no firearm the club furnished me the use of a beautifully balanced 10 gauge Lafever. I downed three mallards, four pintails, and I experienced a unique highlight by dropping an eagle."

"Eagle, how do you cook that?"

Charlie shook his head and laughed. "You don't eat it, you mount it."

"Well, where is it?"

"When mounted it shall be sent to me in care of the West House. I convinced everyone I might be a fixture in the area for quite some time."

She threw her arms around him, drew him close, and giggled. "You're such a tease. You probably never shot a thing, certainly not an eagle. Doubt if anybody shot an eagle for that matter."

He strutted indignantly to his carpetbag and unrolled a stained cloth holding a pair of feet displaying deadly talons. He also withdrew a handful of eagle feathers. "One of my companions took the head clean off his bird and generously allowed me these keepsakes since his trophy could not be mounted. But enough of my adventure. Let us enjoy a pleasant evening together before you pack. For the next week it's to my benefit that you to remain in Buffalo."

Late the following morning Charlie sat in his room casually talking with the newly-arrived Beall. Two sharp knocks echoed through the room. Cole creaked open the door to a stranger who glanced down the hallway before quickly stepping inside. They greeted a clean-shaven man of average height with thick, wavy brown hair. His high cheekbones, thickset jaw, and Roman nose set between his glinting dark eyes, defined a man of action and substance.

Before their business commenced Beall offered his condolences to Bennett Young for John Hunt Morgan's untimely death. A pained expression froze upon Young's face. "I regretfully receive your sympathy. Having myself hailed from the bluegrass, at a young age I developed an admiration for the general. The man seemed like a brother, although eighteen years my senior. His death could only be the work of spineless bushwhackers or lowly traitors scattered about that region of Tennessee." The Kentuckian's mood brightened when discussion turned to the opportunity for retribution. Young looked to Cole. "Colonel Thompson arranged this meeting so I could report directly to him as to modifications deemed necessary for our plan. I suspect we begin with the elusive key to the entire operation, the capture of the *Michigan*. For my edification Major Cole, please begin."

John admired the twenty-three year old cavalry officer's take charge demeanor. Cole seemed oblivious that the subordinate actually controlled the meeting, another concern for Beall pondering if Cole could command men.

Charlie responded in the tone of a pompous man bathing in the spotlight of center stage. "I've identified men on the *Michigan* sympathetic to our cause. I've also recognized men whose allegiance comes with a price tag. I realize I might be forced to utilize our shear numbers to neutralize those remaining loyal to the Union."

Young's furrowed forehead inquisitively expressed concern. "Please elaborate. Shear numbers? Captain Beall shall have thirty men maximum. My understanding is that you now have just one accomplice."

Oblivious to Young's skepticism Charlie offered a relaxed smile. "I'm currently addressing that deficiency. My lengthy list of local gentlemen ready to lay down their lives for our cause expands by the day. A large contingent of the Sons of Liberty and Knights of the Golden Circle reside in the area."

"Those organizations failed miserably in Chicago. What makes you believe they shall raise to the call here?" grilled Young.

"With Vallandigham's preoccupation with his quest for the nomination everyone became totally distracted. They now realizes the fall of Atlanta all but eliminates the possibility of a significant Southern military victory prior to the November election. Only unforeseen disaster will force Lincoln from Washington. We are the unexpected catastrophe."

"Your analysis of the manner in which we must achieve victory is astute. However, I am reluctant to place trust in northern organizations until they prove worthy. Regrettably we lack the time to gauge their value." Young turned to Beall, "What's your view, Captain?"

"If you're asking me if I have confidence in our so-called northern allies I say emphatically no! But I concur in the major's belief that we do enter the critical stage of this horrible conflict where a successful operation which brings the war to the North remains our only recourse. As a people we are reluctantly forced to conduct this war in a manner we deem dishonorable. The Yankees ignited the fires burning throughout the South. Now they must reap what they have sown. General Early burned Chambersburg this summer but the Yankees continue their inhumane war. I liken Chambersburg to the first plague the Lord unleashed upon the Egyptians. Our sacred duty calls us to unleash misery upon our unrepentant foe until pharaoh's heart softens. If Lincoln remains blind to the destruction awaiting his subjects the blood of innocent people soaks his hands, not ours, as God wreaks his vengeance through us."

Young stared momentarily at Beall, gently nodded his head, and said to Cole, "This is the steadfast determination we require to succeed. Unfortunately I fear the average northern dissident lacks that resolve. Mr. Cole, please, more details relevant to your capture of the ship," requested the young lieutenant, with the casual omission of Charlie's superior military rank.

Much of the bravado evaporated from Charlie. He carefully kneaded his words before speaking. "I concur that we face numerous obstacles against heavy odds but," Charlie Cole paused for his optimism and the twinkle in his eye to return. "The longer the odds the more valued the element of surprise." Both listeners leaned forward. "I've spoken on several occasions to Captain Carter of the prospects of my hosting a banquet in appreciation for the friendship shown me during my stay in Sandusky. His chief subordinates, Ensigns Eddy and Hunter, shall also feel obliged to attend. Though none of the three drink heavily, when I commence with a toast to the good health of President Lincoln, all present shall be obliged to drink. A second toast to the speedy culmination of the conflict results with further indulgence. My absent minded apology for neglecting that culmination brings Union victory, which shall cause more ingestion of the fruit of the vine." Playing to his attentive audience he delicately added with a wide grin, "My friends, the wine shall be drugged."

Broad smiles covered both listeners' faces. Young commented, "Extremely risky, Major Cole, so ambitious it just might succeed. Continue."

"I anticipate after drugging the senior officers and a goodly number of the loyal junior officers that a sufficient number of enlisted ranks, for a prearranged price, shall assist with the overpowering of the balance of the Yankee crew not on shore leave. I also consider discreetly providing concurrent entertainment for several dozen lower ranking men at an establishment called the Seven Mile House, which as you might assume, is seven miles south of town. My banquet shall be held either here at the West House or aboard the *Michigan*. Captain Beall, I'll require your anticipated time of arrival."

"I've targeted the *Philo Parsons,* which departs from Detroit at 8:00 a.m., stops at the islands along the way, and docks in Sandusky before 6:00."

Cole suggested, "If you delay rendezvousing with me until 7:00 or later we could proceed under the cover of darkness, providing her tardiness sounds no alarm."

"We shall operate within that timeframe, Major. Did I mention that the *Philo Parsons* is capable of transporting three to four hundred men to Canada afterwards?"

"Which brings us to another discussion," interjected Young. "I believe I am correct in saying that once we control the *Michigan* and her fourteen guns we possess the firepower to control the lakes. Is our role to free the prisoners and assist in their escape or is our mission to free the prisoners and release them to create chaos throughout the North?"

John could have sworn Charlie told him that the *Michigan* carried twenty guns.

Cole replied, "Mr. Thompson communicated that President Davis instructed him to release and aid the prisoners in their escape so that they could return promptly to fill our depleted ranks while randomly spreading chaos throughout the North."

The comment brought a quick response from Young. "No disrespect to President Davis, but the man's an inflexible idealist. We admire him for his enormous devotion to the Confederacy but we cannot allow his narrow thinking to interfere with this operation. This mission's been approved and postponed twice in the past two years because of unrealized concerns and idealistic principles. Our precarious military situation that dictates we inflict maximum damage upon the enemy in the brief period remaining before the election. Conveyance south becomes secondary."

Forgetting that imprudent concern for his own men led to his incarceration John emotionally pleaded, “We can’t just release them to fend for themselves in a hostile land!”

“Johnny,” replied Young, reaching over and placing his hand on the Virginian’s arm, “all three of us lived within the confines of a Yankee prison. True, the enemy inflicts severe deprivations on these men. But understand, if we force the Northern citizens to vote Lincoln from office we welcome George McClellan as the new United States commander-in-chief. The general was always heavy on talk and light on action. We’ll have a cease fire and prison exchange in no time. He’ll dump Grant. Abolition will disappear. And when we achieve our goal, how many Union soldiers remain on the lines with their homes and families in danger? By coincidence rather than design the next draft in Ohio is scheduled for September 19, the day of our operation.” Young stared intently into Beall’s fiery blue eyes and continued, “We must acknowledge that many men shall be recaptured, but if we strike hard and shorten this damn war tens of thousands of our boys held in Federal prisons will gain freedom! Hell,” he added with a cocky smile, “most the Yanks we’re holding in the South would pull for us if they knew our objective. You’re all for finishing this blasted war, aren’t you Johnny?”

Martha’s image appeared. He placed his free hand over Young’s. “That I am.”

Attention turned to liberating the prisoners once the Rebels commandeered the *Michigan*. Young looked to Cole. “Everything we plan is tentative in nature except our resolve. Neither I as I rode with General Morgan nor you Major Cole as you rode with Forrest, knew what we might encounter over the next rise or through an ensuing thicket.” Turning to John he added, “And you, Captain Beall, while at sea never assumed what might lie beyond the horizon. I pray we open the prison gates without firing a shot. Our best case scenario is to proceed to Sandusky undetected with our freed officers. There we’ll capture train stations, cut the telegraph wires, open the arsenal, borrow horses from the liveries, and fire the city with minimal interference."

Beall jokingly interjected, "Lieutenant Young, you say we as if you're joining us."

"Rest assured, in spirit, my friend. Another location beckons me to create mischief of my own shortly after your success, or to use your analogy, to bring forth another plague upon the merciless pharaoh."

"And if we fail to arrive in Sandusky undetected?" John asked knowing the reply.

Charlie Cole, charged with the electricity flowing through the room, interjected, "Then we utilize the wonderful vessel donated courtesy of the Yankees and lob shells from the bowels of hell directly into this fair city."

"And once we control the city?" asked John.

Cole walked over to his desk and returned with his log. Leafing through it he paused, smiled, and reentered center stage. "I've spent countless hours selecting individuals and buildings marked for destruction. Unbeknownst to me hundreds of escaped Negroes traveled to Canada through this abolitionist den. I've documented men involved in the despicable practice. Many such as Lucas Beecher are damned radical attorneys. Rush Sloane, a Republican bureaucrat now in Washington, deserves to burn in hell; the least we can do is turn his home into an inferno. Joseph Root lives on the same street. Homer Goodwin, another nigger-loving lawyer, lives just off Washington on Hancock. Before visiting him we must call on Oran Follett. Local rumor persists he influenced Lincoln to sack McClellan the second time. Extremely detrimental to our military fortunes. I understand the harlot he took for his wife offered refuge to escaped slaves in the safety of their basement. For good measure, steam engineer George Barney lives adjacent to the man who besides owning this ostentatious hotel is the son of a bitch who constructed the prison. And if time permits the bastard Leonard Johnson who leases his island for the prison and steals from the prisoner's as sutler earns a visit."

"Well done," commented Beall, "but those attacks on private citizens won't produce the terror I anticipate."

"Ah, my good man," answered Cole with a smile, "I save the best for last. We must destroy this imposing landmark of Mr. West's in addition to three other heavily used hotels—the Colton House, Farmers Exchange, and the Verandah. Norman Hall, an auditorium a block to our west down Water Street, hosted the escaped nigger Fredrick Douglass when he lectured here. We shall cauterize his stage. I've targeted four nearby lumber yards. Several blocks to the east Captain Monk operates his boat works where he built the *General Grant*. He deserves to pay alone for the sinful christening. Klotz and Kromer Engine & Shipbuilders designed the engines. Neither shall we forget the two banks on Columbus Avenue nor the post office on the corner of Market Street. Especially on that day we must burn the Water Street recruiting office, a block to the east on the third floor of the Reber Building."

"Did you miss any buildings Major Cole?" jested Young.

Missing the humor Cole answered, "Why yes, while we cannot assume this will go according to plan I suggest we also raid the four gunsmiths for additional arms. I recommend we locate and open liquor stores to fortify discontented residents who choose to join us in burning the vermin's nest." Charlie paused, tapped the side of his head with an open palm, and added, "I almost forgot, I've mapped drugstores for us to acquire incendiary materials."

"Major, who brings the matches, you or I?" interrupted Beall, exhibiting good-natured humor for the first time.

"After the town's ablaze it's important to evacuate in all directions," stressed Young as he stood. "Remember, our strongest ally the following day remains the panic induced into the Northern population. Colonel Thompson handsomely compensated select newspapers to spread discontent with the Lincoln government whenever the opportunity arises. Our operation certainly qualifies. Now I must discretely leave. I'll take the evening train to Toledo and on to Detroit. Although a bit of a risk exists, John wants to book passage on the *Philo Parsons* tomorrow to become familiar with the vessel, to which I heartily agree. My thoughts and prayers are with you both." Young cautiously opened the door, glanced to either side, and disappeared.

Guilt enveloped John as he struggled to sleep that evening. He visualized the prison's 2500 confined souls who might only briefly absorb the euphoria of freedom. Abandoned to their own resources, many faced the depression as they're recaptured within days. He feared the repercussions they might receive in retaliation for the punishment they exacted from Sandusky. Acknowledging that Young, Cole, and he each served time in Yankee prisons soothed his conscience. He recognized that duty too called the Johnson's Island prisoners. Young spoke of Davis's idealism but wasn't everyone naïve and idealistic in the beginning. John had viewed acts he never believed one man could inflict upon another. He witnessed the gradual deterioration of chivalry and honor with the dissolving of the old era of warfare. He wondered if he too would perform almost any act to shorten the war if the deed reunited him with Martha. He restlessly sought sleep while visualizing the horrendous sight of this panic stricken city the forthcoming night of his visit. Martha's radiant image finally drew him into a welcome slumber.

48 – HUNTING FOR RECRUITS

"Johnny, has it been two years since we shoved off on our first endeavor?"

"Aye, Benny, it has," answered John. "Half a million fine lads from both sides with unfulfilled dreams now eternally resting. How many more before this bloody affair ends? How many more! Might I join them before we finally gain independence?"

Burley comforted his friend with a firm hand on the shoulder. "You've often stated God sends us on our earthly journey with our first breath and only he knows where the road leads until he calls us back."

"A man is fortunate to have a noble friend to remind him so. Thank you, Mr. Burley. With that bit of reassurance our attention turns to the business of ending this sordid affair. The *Parsons* remains our best means of reaching the *Michigan*. She makes sufficient stops to allow our band to intermittingly board without creating suspicion. Our search continues for weapons. I suggest a knife, a hatchet, and two revolvers per man. This proves secondary to recruiting trustworthy men. We'll settle for two dozen men but three dozen's preferred if we deem them reliable. We must use diligence in offering details if we unknowingly allow Yankee vermin to enter our midst. All a man needs hear is that we prepare to strike the enemy somewhere on Yankee soil. Nothing else, although we might spread the word that we'll sail for two days before we reach our target, thereby confusing any charlatan attempting to determine our destination. I suggest we continue recruiting men from states whose homelands most severely suffer the Yankee's rape and pillage."

"Any news from your home, John?"

"Nothing specific. Lee occupies Grant at Petersburg while Early holds his own against Sheridan, who might be the worst of the lot of Yankee generals. Civilians residing in the valley suffer severe depredation from him. I pray God protects Mother and the girls. God willing, if we do succeed, next year with Martha at my side my primary concern shall be the price of grain and hogs, not the damn Yankees. Back to the present, how many of the men whom we approached in August remain committed?"

"A dozen in the least and every one claims a comrade eager to serve the cause, although more than likely some desire only the fame and riches to be gained in the process. As I recall several hail from Georgia. There's also a lad each from Mississippi, Tennessee, and North Carolina. The others never mentioned their origins. All are youthful except for a Captain Morgan, the only man owning a rank above sergeant."

"That seems a bit odd."

"Johnny, an officer's duty pulls him back to the lines the moment he gains freedom. Most men we've interviewed contentedly sit out the war in Canada unless something better comes their way."

"Benny," John blurted out in a fit of frustration, "do they expect we'll be attending a church social?"

"It is our responsibility to convey we face a perilous adventure, but with the clock ticking we cannot afford to scare any away either."

The two men remained silent comprehending the daunting task before them. Burley broke the stillness. "Our illustrious Colonel Thompson asks that we keep Mr. Hyams informed of our plans."

Beall slammed his fist on the table. A crimson flush filled his cheeks. "With half of Canada West knowing of our plans why not post a notice in the Yankee papers announcing our arrival time in eleven days." He stood and shrugged his shoulders. "We have a duty to fulfill. Let's complete our crew." With that the two left in search of men.

49 – ANOTHER VISIT TO JOHNSON'S ISLAND

Charlie shifted his weight from one foot to the other, impatiently waiting for the stockade's massive gates to open. One week to finalize details and bring plans to fruition. He'd lost several precious days of preparation during a crucial scouting mission. He had spent a pleasant evening in Mansfield before reboarding a train to become familiar with the rail routes leading south. While in Columbus he had peered through the fence enclosing Camp Chase's 8,000 incarcerated men. He endured the arrogant claims of local citizens boasting that the war's fortunes finally improved when native Buckeyes took charge. Grant and Sheridan subdued Lee in Virginia. Sherman captured Atlanta and continued his march to points unknown. Lincoln functioned competently only through the consul of two more Ohioans. Stanton directed the War Department and Chase utilized his fiscal prowess as he headed the Treasury Department. Charlie's frequent visits to the reasonably priced pleasure houses in the capital city compensated for the obnoxious locals he encountered.

Charlie cleared his mind for the present as he irritably waited for his damn Yankee escort. His temperament soothed as he basked in the steady breeze streaming from Canada which kept the skies overcast but the air comfortably cool and dry. Corporal Ramsey's opening of the gate brought Charlie back to reality. The agent gained solace confident that the stench within the gates would mask the nauseating aroma emanating from the offensive soldier.

"Morning, Corporal."

"Cole, you got any more of them cigars? They was good."

Charlie pulled several from his coat pocket to which the uncouth soldier whined, “Only two this time?”

“Sorry, lad.” Fearing confiscation of those prepared for Isaac Trimble, Charlie quickly added, “But I shall send a box of premium Havana’s to your attention tomorrow.”

“That’ll be just fine,” answered Ramsey curtly. Pointing to block four he added, “You can find your way to that damned Rebel general’s quarters. You gonna have another free-the-nigger revival?”

“Not today, only a friendly discussion in his quarters,” responded Charlie, before he strode alone toward the prison barrack. He entered the open doorway to find the same men sitting at the same table playing cards.

“Looky here boys, Mr. Yankee abolition returns to save our miserable, downtrodden souls,” taunted a balding prisoner facing Cole.

“Not quite, Lieutenant,” Charlie answered with a tip of his hat. “Is General Trimble in?”

“No, President Lincoln and his misses invited the general over for morning tea. What do you think?” Loud laughter followed Charlie into the next room.

Trimble, who reclined across his bunk, sat up and motioned the visitor to pull up a chair. “Thought maybe Richmond forgot us, Mr. Cole?”

“Not hardly, sir. Been fine-tuning plans and reconnoitering much of Ohio.” He slid his chair closer and lowered his voice. “A week from tonight you’ll be free. This may well be my last visit to finalize details.”

“Mr. Cole, please invite Colonel Inzer from the next room.”

Charlie opened the door opposite the one he entered and returned accompanied by the Alabamian. Besides being a competent officer, Inzer had also attended his state’s secession conference four years earlier, serving as its youngest representative.

Glancing to Inzer and then to Trimble, Charlie asked, “Do any of your men know of our operation?”

"Colonel Inzer and I keep this to ourselves. On two occasions we've ferreted out Yankee spies and can never grow confident more don't exist. We also trust that our officers bring more dedication to the ranks than enlisted men, not that enlisted men aren't loyal, but most officers are gentlemen conscious of their role in upholding the honor of the South. Still, an empty belly gnawing away at a man also erodes his adherence to the code of chivalry. Before the Yankees cut rations and halted incoming packages the men spoke in good humor of preparing rats as a delicacy. I dare say over the past several weeks as the rodent population diminishes, the men swear that none have been paroled, exchanged, or freed. Draw your own conclusions, Mr. Cole."

Color drained from Charlie's face as he visualized holding a freshly cooked rat by the long, disgusting tail above his open mouth. "May we return to the subject at hand gentlemen," begged the queasy visitor.

Both prisoners chuckled before Inzer commented, "Much too our chagrin we face a new variable in our equation. The Yankees fail to comprehend the acceptable labor that a gentleman should be expected to perform. We balked at numerous menial tasks assigned to us and refused to perform duties no white man should ever be expected to carry out, except maybe a newly arrived Irishman," added Inzer with a good natured smile. "To remedy the situation the Yankees in their infinite wisdom scheduled the transport of several dozen privates from the camp in Columbus to serve as laborers, although we shall encourage them to resist also. The Yankees might deviously plant spies attached to units with which our men lack familiarity. This provokes a dilemma, Mr. Cole."

"Prudence dictates you assume all are spies. Although we trust the Yankees lack astuteness to perform such trickery, deceitfulness does seem inbred within them. Then with whom do you intend to share our plan?"

"Perhaps a summary of your operation might better allow us to determine how many to involve prior to your assault."

"Our primary objective remains the release and transport of all prisoners including the weak or incapacitated. The passenger vessel Captain Beall utilizes to rendezvous with the *Michigan* could transport 600 men to Canada. Railways branch from Sandusky to the east, west, and south. Half a dozen lines radiate from Toledo's hub. Numerous lines also travel to Cleveland, Columbus, Cincinnati, Dayton, and Newark. This state's highly developed network allows travel to Indiana via four different railways. Three more lead to the Pennsylvania state line. While only three rail bridges cross the Ohio River between Steubenville and Cincinnati many routes terminate at the river. Strong Confederate sympathies exist in Ohio's far southern counties. I've also located a dozen liveries in Sandusky stabling over 400 mounts. Unfortunately, a handful of men might be forced to escape on foot, but I stress our primary objective remains the return of every one of our comrades south. However, if the opportunity presents itself we shall provide the fine citizens of Sandusky with a taste of their own Yankee medicine before we depart. Does this provide an adequate outline of our operation?"

Trimble looked to Inzer. "I propose we inform the men in stages. Tonight I'll begin communicating with colonels of our choosing besides the generals. In several days we'll identify others based less on rank and more on character. By dark on the 19th all but the fresh arrivals shall be informed regardless if those new prisoners be the privates from Camp Chase or newly captured officers. It goes without saying that the traitors in block one shall be excluded. We'll also inform those fearless souls contemplating escape to hold fast. No need heightening the enemy's senses."

Inzer broadly smiled. "That places Lieutenant Charles Pierce at the top of my list."

"As I recall he's the gentleman who attempted to drive out of the compound after he donned a Union jacket the day of my previous visit."

"One in the same, Mr. Cole," said Trimble with a chuckle. "His comrades say when trapped last fall at the

Rappahannock, he watched many of his fellow officers toss their swords into the river rather than offer them to the Yankees in surrender. Not Charlie Pierce. He gracefully removed his weapon from the scabbard when a Union major approached. He then elegantly grasped it in both hands, broke it over his knee, and asked the dumfounded major which half he preferred. These are the kind of men we need for your action, Mr. Cole."

Inzer added names of the impatient Lieutenants Odam and Jones plus the restless Captains McGibbon and Kennedy. We'll converse with Colonel Hundley this evening. We are aware of two men itching to escape. Unfortunately we acknowledge others desiring to escape keep such thoughts from everyone."

"Do you possess any armaments, General?"

Charlie learned lax security measures early in the war permitted early contingents of prisoners arriving to smuggle in loaded revolvers. Despite current regulations mandating the confiscation of all knives, except the pocket variety, incoming Rebels managed to conceal larger cutlery, including three Bowie knives. If necessary each man could be armed with a club. The three reconfirmed an orderly evacuation of the prisoners without gunfire must be a priority.

Charlie stood and cautioned, "If per chance gunfire erupts keep everyone inside until I open the gates. But if all goes according to plan we shall call with invitations for you to attend our farewell party for the city of Sandusky. God be with you, gentlemen," he said as he departed.

Back on the mainland Charlie opted for some relaxation at the Cosmopolitan Billiard Hall across from the West House. After perusing the sparse late afternoon crowd scattered about the site he commenced warming up alone at a game table with designs for drawing someone to join him. Several young males sitting at a table near the front window remained preoccupied with the members of the opposite sex promenading past on the sidewalk outside.

At a corner table a fit man in laborer's clothes occupied a chair, joined only by a half empty pitcher of beer. His eyes stared aimlessly into his frothy mug. Wearing his trademark friendly smile Charlie approached the solitary man. The loner seemed oblivious to his surroundings until Charlie pulled up a chair. "I could use some company. Mind if I join you?"

"Suit yourself, won't be much though."

"What's bothering you friend?

"Nothing you or anyone can rectify unless you possess an elixir to prevent Lincoln and his damn black Republicans from reelection." He reached for his mug and held it high before he added, "Forgive me, they're the Union Party this go round."

Charlie scanned the room. "I've always believed in the First Amendment but I assume many citizens in your fair city are not so forgiving, Mister…?"

"Strain, Abraham Strain."

"Pleased to meet you Mr. Strain. I'm Charles Cole of the Mount Hope Oil Company."

"Seen you around. Heard about you too."

Charlie cocked his head. "Just on honest man in town on business. I didn't realize I gained notoriety."

"With all due respect, Mr. Cole, a man doesn't travel with a woman such as yours and spend money as freely as you without garnering attention. I assume this war's filled your coffers?"

Comfortable with the local's acceptance of his cover, Charlie transitioned the conversation to his companion's source of discontent. The life long Democrat established himself as a skilled stone mason in Sandusky. His vocal discontent with Lincoln's execution of the war the first several years, coupled with the initial economic downturn, financially strapped the tradesman. In '63 and '64 Strain kept his thoughts to himself while he seized upon the skilled labor shortage. His melancholy sprouted from a realization that with Grant holding Lee at bay, Sherman controlling Atlanta, and Sheridan laying waste to the Shenandoah Valley,

Lincoln again placed one boot in the White House with the toe of his second resting on the open door's threshold.

"Does this mean, Mr. Strain, that you desire the Confederacy's independence?" Cole innocently whispered.

"Hell no! And that's what drives a man like me to spend an afternoon here when unfinished work calls. Many a good friend's gone off to fight Lincoln's battles. When I pray for the safe return of each I comprehend that every Union success keeps the Republicans in power. I advocate the Union remaining intact, although by better means than exhibited these past three years. Since I was born here the decent folks in the area at least treat me with civility, unlike poor old Rosenthal who's rumored to originate from Baltimore."

"A fellow tradesman of yours?"

Strain exhibited his lighter side and roared with laughter. "Heaven's sake no!" He shook his head back and forth displaying a huge grin. "Louis Rosenthal performing manual labor, and skilled at that? A speck of dirt has never touched the man's fingers anymore than a callous has grown on his well-manicured hands. Our clothier is a gentleman of the highest degree."

Realizing no support would be garnered from Strain, Cole tactfully excused himself after learning of Rosenthal's business location on Market Street. Charlie entered an establishment several storefronts east of Columbus Avenue. Behind the counter an immaculately dressed gentleman exhibiting prominent Yiddish facial features acknowledged him. While Charlie nonchalantly examined merchandise he casually conversed before attempting to draw the man into a serious discussion. "Appears this war's in its final stages, although understandably not to everyone's liking."

Rosenthal exhibited an inquisitive expression. "Sorry, sir, I don't decipher your statement."

Charlie delicately crafted his response. "I've encountered numerous men in your quaint city who would revel in Lincoln's defeat even if the event resulted in an armistice whereby, rather than the army, the statesmen would settle unresolved issues."

"I migrated from Maryland to distance myself from the turmoil while trusting that in His own time, God Almighty would compose the final chapter of this tragic drama."

Discovering that Rosenthal would prove no more of an ally than Strain, Charlie purchased a cravat and exited. When the door closed behind the visitor the storekeeper pulled a pad from beneath the counter. He needed to communicate with his long time friend Judah Benjamin. The secretary placed Rosenthal in this assignment concurrent with the initial plot in November of '62. His coded telegram to Baltimore would be carried by currier to Richmond. With only a week remaining, Charles Cole appeared decidedly unprepared for the operation.

50 – SUNDAY, SEPTEMBER 18TH

In Detroit, Acting Assistant Provost Marshal General, Lieutenant Colonel Bennett H. Hill, sat in his office overlooking the river. An informer visited him the previous day with a tale of an elaborate scheme to free Rebel prisoners before the election. He promised Hill that he would return with details that evening if he could induce those involved to divulge substantiating facts. The Union official stroked his chin while considering his options. An officer who overreacted to rumor lost credibility. A commander who ignored relevant information which would prevent enemy mischief would experience a sudden halt in his career. How much credence could a man place in riffraff betraying secrets for silver. Southerner and Northerner alike despised such Judases. He leaned back and continued reading accounts of Atlanta's demise from the current issue of *Harper's Weekly*. Hopefully the lowlife would slither into his office with valid details of the alleged conspiracy before Hill quit for the day.

In Sandusky, Charlie again reveled in Annie's company. His anxiety diminished with the knowledge that several dozen of the men who Bennett Young sequestered randomly drifted into town the past several days. Charlie utilized the newly arrived simpleton John Robinson to convey parcels containing coded messages to the boarding houses and cheap hotels where the men lodged. Sometime today Cole needed to finalize details for tomorrow's banquet. Despite the rainy morning Mr. and Mrs. Cole booked an outing on the bay. He abhorred boat excursions but acquiesced since she thoroughly enjoyed the water. He wanted her in an appreciative mood for their final night together in Sandusky. To enhance her disposition, he suggested after their vessel docked that they stroll to the

Euterpean's parlor to indulge in ice cream topped with appetizing late season peaches.

In Georgia, Martha nervously conversed with Fanny and Amelia in the Chamber's quaint parlor. John's fiancé frequently experienced uneasy feelings of apprehension which usually passed in moments. Today, due in part to the anxiety hanging in the air since Atlanta's fall, a cloud of concern shrouded her since she awoke from a restless sleep. Even a joyful church service's relevant sermon that pleasant late summer Sunday failed to lift her spirits. Her sister comforted her by reminding Martha that since John's departure four months earlier such feelings of despair occasionally visited, but those fears proved unfounded. Today's uneasiness created a disconcerting unsettledness.

In Canada, Beall and Burley rehashed details. The schedule for the *Philo Parson's* departure remained unchanged. They had finalized plans for procuring and dispersing weapons the previous day. The unknown character of their hastily assembled crew remained the enormous concern.

"Johnny, one can only test the water by jumping in head first. Tomorrow we dive in together."

Beall managed a smile before giving his trusted companion a masculine hug. "If the Yankees only knew that tomorrow they would face the duo of Bennett Burley, the fearless Scotsman, and John Yates Beall, the scourge of the seas, they would run up a white flag on the *Michigan*, throw open the gates of Johnson's Island, and evacuate Sandusky today."

Both men enjoyed a nervous hearty laugh before separating.

51 – 7:30 A.M., SEPTEMBER 19, 1864

Crisp morning air greeted the early arrivals at the Detroit wharf. Walter Ashley, the *Philo Parsons's* slightly-built part owner and bookkeeper, squinted through his spectacles toward the young fellow who had approached him early last evening. He requested an unscheduled stop at Sandwich, on the Canadian side of the river below Detroit, to pickup several friends including a lame gentleman. The group planned to disembark at Kelleys Island, the last regular stop before Sandusky. The veteran ship's captain, Sylvester Atwood, agreed with Ashley that a dollar was a dollar, even if it was a greenback. Bennett Burley, relieved to hear of the arrangement's approval, presented his ticket and wandered to the upper deck, partaking of the opportunity to inconspicuously survey the ship. By 8:00 the vessel departed with forty passengers including a noteworthy contingent of ladies, much to Burley's delight. At 8:20 his friends, including the lame gentleman, greeted their friend after the *Parsons* docked briefly to add the foursome. That group congregated on the aft deck thereby allowing the cabin to deflect the invigorating breeze.

Shortly after 9:00 the vessel reached Malden on schedule to board twenty men wearing common laborer's garb. Six of them lugged a battered trunk held together with random lengths of rope. Ashley waited impatiently for those rummaging through their pockets for the fare. They handed him an assortment of bills and coins to segregate. Should charge the degenerate skedaddlers extra, thought Ashley, in deference to the brave lads who honorably answered the call to duty, while these shirkers migrated back and forth between Canada. The travelers claimed their trunk carried construction tools for work in Columbus. None of his business, reasoned Atwood, confident Sandusky's customs house would inspect the chest. He now looked forward to three uninterrupted hours before the stop at North Bass Island. He glanced to the lower deck where the so-called laborers congregated. He noticed several stuffing crumbling chunks of stale bread into their mouths.

The bookkeeper entered his office pleased that the lowlifes possessed the decency to maintain a respectable distance from the ladies and gentlemen on the upper deck. Burley already commenced charming the fairer sex with his pleasant brogue as he turned the sheet music for attractive pianists. Beall smiled while observing his comrade scurry about to promptly tend to every woman's needs. By the time they reached North Bass at quarter past noon the debonair Mr. Burley in some manner had accommodated every unattached female aboard.

Earlier that morning, sixty miles southeast of Detroit, the brisk, clear morning skies hinted of the harsh northern winter's imminent return. Sprawled on a top bunk, R. H. McClung listened as the young Ohio private assigned guard duty on the wall behind block ten mimicked dawn's shrill crowing of a rooster. His crude revelry aggravated some men, but the country boy McClung enjoyed the touch of home whenever the good-natured Yankee welcomed in a new day. The past several months McClung responded in kind with an imitation of a hen's reply. Aware of tonight's escape, the prisoner cackled and smiled. The poor cock would crow to an empty henhouse tomorrow morning.

Late that morning Trimble joined a cluster of men reviewing their responsibilities for the evening. His wooden leg would force him to command from inside the barracks. Inzer would remain with Trimble until needed outside. Inzer requested Charlie Pierce to accompany him in the event gunfire erupted. The athletic soldier with a win-at-all-cost mentality quickly became a favorite of both Trimble and Inzer during the past week. They recognized in a crisis Pierce would coolly survey the situation and perform admirably. Pierce's fellow Louisiana Tiger comrade Captain Ellis, Tar Heel Captain William Norman, and Alabamian Colonel Daniel Hundley each received assignments to assault a wall if necessary. Arkansas Colonel Charles Matlock, although not in the best of health, demanded responsibility for the fourth wall. The assault groups would each fabricate three scaling ladders after candles extinguished at 9:00. Every contingent would be issued two revolvers. Inzer and Pierce would also carry one. Trimble would retain the unloaded weapons to dispense once they obtained ammunition.

After the gathering dispersed Trimble and Inzer secluded themselves and continued turning over every detail of the operation. "It's to our good fortune that the two large mess halls behind the east blocks open today," said Inzer in reference to the small mess kitchens being consolidated into the enlarged messes separate from the barracks for improved sanitation. "This permits mingling with greater numbers of men without alarming the Yankees who might otherwise suspect mischief. If small quantities of firewood for the heating stoves can be procured we'll obtain a goodly number of clubs without destroying the furniture." Inzer paused and laughed, realizing the furniture wouldn't be needed after tonight.

Trimble reiterated, "After dark, when we've informed the balance of the men of the escape plan, we must reaffirm the necessity of proceeding in an orderly manner. Communicating that Mr. Cole emphasized the primary objective is to obtain safe journey home for everyone should maintain calm. Orders must be established for systematic evacuation and transportation."

Inzer stared at the floor, scowled, and shook his head.

"What irritates you, Colonel?"

"Men who choose to disobey orders. We confided early with Lieutenant Odam to prevent any rash action on his part that might jeopardize the operation and yet he attempted an escape six days ago. Thank God he apparently succeeded.

I only pray that if captured he doesn't bargain us for his freedom."

"We move forward on faith. Let's us pray that nary a shot is fired tonight."

"With my blessing," replied Inzer, as he envisioned the carnage a round of grape shot from each block house gun would inflict upon a mass of men attempting to capture the guns. "Until this evening, General." Inzer departed to track the sun as it arced painfully slow to the west inch by inch.

Across the bay at the West House, Charlie rose at 8:00. Annie dutifully fulfilled her role as his spouse by rising with him. By 8:45 they secluded themselves in a corner of the dining room. In a hushed voice Charlie reviewed the coming day. "It's imperative you pack our trunks by midday so that you may board the afternoon train to Cleveland."

"And our funds? You really should allow me to carry them for safe keeping," she suggested with a soft, bewitching smile.

He responded with a sly grin. "You do remember our prenuptial agreement?" Her expression transformed into one of aggravation as he elaborated, "When I committed to this operation, Mrs. Cole, I promised Mr. Thompson I would personally safeguard all funds assigned to me with due diligence. Placing them in your hands most certainly breaks that pledge. Relax my dear, I shall provide you ample traveling funds to see you through in the event I'm delayed."

"Charlie, if you don't arrive there'll be hell to pay when I track you down. You know what they say about a woman scorned. But when you do arrive…," she seductively smiled.

He digressed with his difficulty in establishing a site for the banquet. In the early stages of planning he discarded thoughts of hosting the entire event a mile west of Bloomingville at the Seven Mile House. Captain Carter declined to attend any function at the West House on the pretext of leaving his ship unsupervised without himself or either Ensigns Eddy or Hunter aboard, but he graciously offered the *Michigan's* seldom used dining cabin. Total elimination of the Seven Mile House for even a small gathering for lesser sailors freed Robinson to travel to Kelleys Island and board the *Parsons* with three other Confederates.

Charlie rationalized that unanticipated interruptions could occur at the West House. In the event shots were fired local authorities might appear. Holding the dinner on the vessel limited the potential for unexpected interference but also required transport of the food and doctored wine. The logistical prerequisites allowed eight caterers to accompany Charlie, in addition to his trio of Mount Hope Oil Company invited guests. Captain Carter expressed no uneasiness with the explanation for the additional visitors. Charlie's only reluctance with his third option lay with the lack of a clear avenue of escape should plans unravel.

Annie returned to the room to pack while Charlie tended to other details. He stopped at the livery behind the West House. Charlie arranged for two mounts to be saddled and waiting after eleven that evening. He offered the rationale that he planned to depart the city the following morning but desired one more memorable ride along the waterfront with a local companion. The stable keeper, in his usual state of vacillation between hung-over and inebriated, accepted the request with the generous advance tip as completely plausible. Having never participated in a desperate fight Charlie desired the second horse as backup to carry him east regardless of the mission's outcome. Despite stating his intention to travel to Cleveland to await Beall's arrival in the morning with the *Michigan* at the gun works, Charlie planned to reach Buffalo and cross the border before nightfall, with or without Annie. All was fair in love and war, and war received preeminence the next few days. He walked from the stable to the Moss Brothers' Bank and closed his account, after which he waited for the day to unfold.

52 – CAPTURING THE *PHILO PARSONS*

Beall pulled his watch from his vest pocket… slightly after 1:00. The *Parsons* churned away from North Bass destined for South Bass, followed by two more stops before the scheduled termination in Sandusky. Captain Atwood held to his routine of disembarking to spend his evening at his Middle Bass home and reboarding in the morning on the vessel's return voyage. In his absence the first mate D. C. Nichols commanded the 150 foot side wheeler. At 3:45 the *Parsons* reached Kelleys Island. Only three men boarded instead of the expected four. Beall assumed the trio belonged to Cole and hoped that they remembered their armbands. Thirty minutes later the *Island Queen,* heading for a lengthy layover at Kelleys, passed within a hundred yards of the *Philo Parsons* now sailing away from the island. Beall watched over his shoulder as the *Queen* docked in the distance.

He searched for Captain Nichols whom he located near the front of the hurricane deck. Beall asked to speak to him on a matter of greatest importance. The two strode aft and paused near the towering smokestack exhaling its black cloud. Nichols's inquisitive expression transformed to terror when in a single swift motion Beall drew the Remington concealed beneath his coat, cocked it, and pressed the barrel hard into his captive's side. "I am a Confederate officer accompanied by thirty heavily armed soldiers. This vessel and all aboard are my prisoners. Any attempt to disregard my orders shall result in immediate deadly consequences. Am I clear?"

Nichols's profane response ended in midsentence with the revolver's muzzle pinching his flesh against his ribs.

When he witnessed Beall escorting the subdued captive, Burley, joined by David Ross, James Brotherton, and Rob Harris, advanced to Ashley's office. Responding to Beall's cue his men sliced the ropes securing the worn trunk. In seconds every man carried either a deadly hatchet or a glistening knife in one hand and a loaded pistol in the other. John Bristol encountered the fireman and demanded his surrender. The *Parsons's* fireman turned and fled. The opening shot of the operation rang out followed by a belligerent curse from the fleeing target who disappeared before a second errant shot could hit its mark.

Wheelman Michael Campbell left the pilothouse to investigate the commotion only to enter Bristol's field of fire. Campbell ignored the order to stand fast and scampered up the first three rungs of the ladder leading to the main deck. He looked over his shoulder and taunted, "Go to hell you damn pirate."

Bristol took careful aim at the scurrying form. Smoke clouded the confined area as another shot reverberated through the close quarters. The lead ball sped between Campbell's knees and smashed against the wall. The rush of adrenalin from the near fatal projectile vaulted him through the hatch. The ship's engineer, James Denison, exited the fireman's cabin as Campbell's legs disappeared from view. To his chagrin he witnessed a dozen men wearing black arm bands corralling passengers. Overweight and lacking the agility of youth, the engineer froze and raised his hands. The Rebels forced the male captives to descend into the fire hold. They secured the compartment by shoving pig iron over the hatch. With the aid of Bill Byland and Tom Major, Burley, to no one's surprise, escorted the ladies to the comfortable confines of the main cabin. Morgan, Odoer, and Duncan guarded the captain, engineer, and fireman.

In the cabin a mesmerized young lady batted her eye-lashes and exclaimed, "Why Mr. Burley, I had no idea that besides being such a charming gentleman that you're also a man of adventure."

The girl's aghast mother squeezed her daughter's arm. "The man's nothing but a filthy Rebel pirate," she snapped as she pulled her enamored lass away from the source of infatuation.

Burley could not resist tipping his hat and offering his assistance to any ladies in need during their unfortunate confinement. A sarcastic voice from the rear countered, "You can invite us to your hanging when our forces respond to this atrocious act."

Burley smiled and closed the cabin door, leaving Byland and Major to stand guard outside. He assigned Dr. Riley to join the detail while he strode to the pilot house to locate Beall.

Campbell surrendered minutes after his brief escape. He joined Nichols in the wheel house while Denison and his fireman resumed their tasks in the confines of the engine room. The vessel avoided channel traffic by floating east in the lake. Beall positioned the *Parsons* for a distant view of the *Michigan's* mast as he anticipated Cole's success. In ninety minutes the setting sun would provide darkness for the *Parsons* to slip through the channel.

53 – THE DREAM UNFOLDS

With everything progressing according to plan Beall wandered from the pilothouse in search of solitude to gather his thoughts. He tugged his hat down to his brows to shield his eyes from the sun's orange glare, and drew his coat tightly up to his neck to insulate his body from the dropping temperatures. He stared into Lake Erie's shimmering water as the engine's rhythmic thumping stroke harmonized with the thrust of the huge side-wheel splashing into the sea. The image of his beloved Martha gradually ascended from the depths to rest upon the water's surface. She lifted her head from prayer, looked up, and smiled. When her eyes met his, she gently pressed her lips against her clasped hands and tenderly blew him a kiss. If only she could be at his side this evening, albeit out of harms way. Together they would witness the beginning of the end of the Lincoln government and the end of the beginning of Virginia's march to freedom. Knowing her spirit accompanied him sufficed.

He gazed beneath the sea's calm surface while visualizing the turbulent scene about to unfold. By 7:00 darkness enveloped Ohio's northern coast. Beams from the lighthouses on either side of the channel shone brightly. The eastern finger of land jutting into the channel partially obscured Sandusky's lights. The *Michigan's* silhouetted masts remained stationary.

After thirty minutes of idling in the lake the *Philo Parsons* glided peacefully into the channel as she churned toward her 7:30 rendezvous with Major Cole. Visible to the west above the stockade fence, candles dimly illuminated second story windows in the prisoners' barracks. Bright light radiated from oil lamps inside the Yankees' quarters. When the *Parsons* neared to within five hundred yards of the Union warship Beall peered across the *Michigan's* deck for signs of activity. Nothing. Should he halt? Should he advance? Without the designated signal most would consider the latter action foolhardy; Beall viewed such a response as the fulfillment of his duty. He pondered his options when a light blinked twice from the *Michigan*. The signal mirror from the enemy ship! He pressed his hands against his chest to contain his rapidly beating heart. He stared intently. Two flashes again, a minute's pause, and two more flashes. A subtle smile curled his lips upward. Cole controlled the ship.

Beall spun around to search for Burley only to bump into him. "Two flashes, Benny! The ship's ours. Order Mr. Campbell to move slowly to the starboard side of the warship." While patting his revolver he added, "Remind him that a careless maneuver, intentional or not, shall be his last."

As they approached the *Michigan*, Beall noticed one of his men standing twenty feet to his left. He called for the crewman to follow. "We have a pleasant but necessary task before us." From the open trunk he solemnly removed a cloth bag. With a smile he removed the Confederate flag and turned to his companion. "Your name again, Son?"

"Barkley, Captain Beall, Henry Barkley."

"Mr. Barkley, you receive the honor of raising the colors of the first Confederate vessel to sail the Great Lakes. Something to tell your grandchildren."

The lad grasped the halyard. The stars and stripes dropped unceremoniously. Barkley efficiently removed the hasps connecting the U.S. flag and raced to the rail to pitch the contemptible rag overboard only to be halted by his leader. "Not so fast sailor, we may need that later." The young man tossed the American flag back on the deck and hoisted the stars and bars. Beall immediately subdued the erupting cheers. He reminded his men that over nine hundred Yankee soldiers awaited them on nearby Johnson's Island.

Soon the *Michigan* and *Philo Parsons* floated side by side. With revolver drawn Beall hopped over the rails onto the *Michigan*'s deck. Eight men from the *Parsons* followed. Four lifeless seamen, sprawled in pools of blood, lay scattered about the deck. "What happened to them?" Beall asked the first of man he encountered.

The short grizzled man pulled a Bowie knife stained with fresh blood and grinned, "Yanks didn't followed orders; you might say we disciplined 'em."

The comment brought a chorus of laughter from several other men apparently involved in the takeover. John momentarily yearned for bygone days when a life, even that of a damned Yankee, possessed value.

Charlie strutted onto the deck with revolver in hand and greeted his visitors with a pompous bow. "Captain Beall, so good of you to join us this evening. I would offer you a glass of fine imported wine but unfortunately my Yankee guests discovered several cases were, shall we say, a bit tainted?" More laughter ensued.

"It appears your plan proceeded as designed, Major. Did we suffer casualties?"

"No, but the Yankees lacked our good fortune. We dispatched five uncooperative seamen after we drugged the officers. Unfortunately Captain Carter and his two ensigns drank very little. For a brief moment our operation appeared in doubt. The Union seamen we hired proved especially reliable. I must say there is more value to gold than greenbacks. Unfortunately one of the chaps possessed a strong dislike for Ensign Hunter. The poor officer took a step to escape and his former seamen placed a bullet in the ensign's back without so much as a warning. The regrettable incident did improve the others' cooperation. Those who attended my banquet find themselves confined in the dining hall while the balance of the Yankee crew remains below decks. As too…"

Beall grew impatient. He learned from Bennet Young the ease with which Charlie became distracted. "With all due respect, Major, we must coordinate our next phase. Providence has been kind but we must hold up our end too."

"Of course. How do we proceed?"

"I suggest that Mr. Burley board the *Michigan* and assemble men to prepare the guns for action. You and I shall sail the *Parsons* and dock her at the prison wharf on the pretext of mechanical difficulties. That allows the warship to remain at a safe distance but within easy range for our makeshift gun crews to lend support. Perhaps we may convince Captain Carter to discourage the garrison's opposition."

Charlie recognized the peril into which the landing party prepared to descend. "Excellent plan, Captain Beall, but in the event of unforeseen difficulties I must remain on the *Michigan* to coordinate my men in the city."

Beall acknowledged the prerequisite for brave men in the landing force. He tactfully responded, "How unwise of me, Major. We shall be best served with you remaining on the warship to be among the first to disembark in Sandusky." Between Cole's followers and those recruited in Windsor, Rebel strength reached forty men excluding the Union sailors Cole bribed. Beall redistributed his men, reboarded the *Philo Parsons,* and set sail for Johnson's Island.

Captain Carter belligerently refused to support the Rebels and thus remained on the *Michigan*. Four men disembarked with Beall at the wharf. A squad of Yankee guards halted the men at the dock. Following a brief conversation one disappeared to locate an officer. The remaining trio cautiously observed the unexpected arrivals. Beall approached the soldier nearest him and motioned Morgan to join him.

"Pleasant night for sentry duty isn't it?" Beall asked the blue clad lad. Receiving an affirmative nod he reached into his pocket and removed a handful of cigars. "You boys care for a Havana?" The other two glanced over their shoulders wary of approaching officers before stepping forward to accept the offering. Several more of Beall's men joined the gathering. The first soldier relaxed and puffed away while gazing into the partly cloudy sky. The odor of tobacco smoke filled the air in the serene setting when the second man stuck a cigar into his mouth and leaned forward for a light. Beall's knife thrust excruciating pain into the guard's abdomen as it tore through tissue on its pathway into a lung. His wide unsuspecting eyeballs rolled to his forehead and vanished. Before the body hit the wharf Beall wrenched his weapon free and raked it across the next man's exposed throat. Spurting blood splattered the Rebel's forearm. The victim's grotesque gurgling ceased as his knees buckled and he too crumpled. At the same instant the second man's throat ripped open, Morgan buried his heavy hatchet deeply between the third Yankee's shoulder blades. His smoking cigar dropped beneath him on the wooden dock. Barely visible crimson trails led to the three bodies dumped behind crates and barrels. Three new blue clad sentinels with Southerners dialects stood guard armed with Spencer and Hankin carbines appropriated from the *Michigan*.

The fourth Yankee sentry reappeared accompanied by an officer and a squad of men. The lieutenant, wearing a blouse with an empty left sleeve, acknowledged Beall with a tip of his hat before bluntly asking, "What brings you here at this hour?"

"Boiler overheated. We cut her back and she started to drift. Afraid we'd leave the channel and scrape bottom."

The officer studied Beall closely. "Been stationed here over a year," he said staring at his vacant sleeve, "ever since Chancellorsville. Never seen you aboard the *Philo*. You new? Where's the captain?"

"Calming the passengers. The ladies became skittish and the dandies escorting them ain't much better. Me, I've been with the *Philo Parsons* since July. Assist Mr. Denison. I'm an apprentice of sorts. Hope to be an engineer some day myself. Already spent two years on the Atlantic. Fact is…"

The officer impatiently interrupted, "We'll ask Colonel Hill how he wishes to assist. Come along."

Morgan joined Beall on the path to headquarters while the sentry meandered back to his post on the dock. The escort disappeared fifty yards into the darkness when the fourth guard approached one of his comrades and asked, "You think we'll be putting up passengers tonight, Zeb?" He halted and exclaimed, "You ain't Zeb!" At the same instant the point of a bayonet touched his ribs.

"Be still boy or you'll join your brethren. Give me your rifle, and take off your coat, hat, and cartridge box." Looking down, the disguised Rebel added, "Shoes too."

"I'll fetch another boy to fill his uniform," commented another blue clad Rebel turning to reboard the *Parsons*.

The Southerner escorted his prisoner to the wharf where three dead comrades lay. Staring at their horrific wounds the Northerner turned, glared at his captor, and vented contemptuously, "You're nothing but a pack of murdering pirates! You killed three unsuspecting God-fearing men."

"Not so," contradicted the Rebel. He viciously shoved his bayonet into the young soldier's soft belly. He withdrew it, spit into the lad's ashen face, and smiled when the boy collapsed on the ground. He snarled, "We now kilt four. You damn Yankees burnt my barn. Before the night's over scores of you will pay for that transgression."

The Union lieutenant hesitated on the covered porch before knocking on the door of his post commander's quarters. After Colonel Hill appeared in full uniform the lieutenant explained the situation to Hill who put on his hat and escorted the visitors to headquarters. The squad of soldiers waited outside while Beall and Morgan followed the two officers inside.

Beall and Morgan drew their revolvers the instant the door closed. "I am a Confederate officer here to liberate your prisoners. Any resistance shall force us to resort to violence."

Hill cynically laughed. "The *Michigan* shall blow you to pieces before you leave the bay. Besides that passenger ship will only carry a small number of men."

"I regret I must place you in checkmate, Colonel, for I command the *Michigan* and we train her guns upon the island. You sir, shall be the one blown to bits."

Hill's eyes locked with Beall's. "I'll call your bluff. Guards!" the colonel shouted. Beall glanced to the door. The Union officer used the momentary distraction to dive at the Rebel leader. A ball from Beall's Remington ripped into the colonel's shoulder and sent him reeling against his desk. The lieutenant raised his only arm in surrender just prior to the door flying open with two pairs of guards rushing forward. Four shots reverberated through the office. Two men slumped to the floor. Two more shots echoed. A yelp howled from one surviving guard. He joined his comrade racing out the doorway to safety.

Inside the compound the rapid succession of shots served as the catalyst for the tense prisoners to storm the walls despite Trimble's precise orders to remain inside the blocks. A dozen rifle shots crackling from the catwalk dropped five Rebels. More prisoners flooded onto the grounds in their crazed thirst for freedom. Thunder flashed from the two blockhouse platforms. Canister balls splintered bones and shredded flesh but the flow continued surging toward the walls. Another round of musket fire exploded, barely impeding the cresting wave. Return pistol fire from the handful of armed Rebel marksmen toppled several sentinels headlong inside the stockade fence. A race ensued to confiscate, load, and fire the newly acquired rifles. From the bay flashes of light proceeded the explosion of two shells near the wall. Union cannoneers manning the stockade platforms confidently reloaded their pieces with the knowledge that the *Michigan* joined in suppressing the revolt. Another salvo of Yankee canister extinguished the flames of freedom burning within three dozen more Southern souls.

Encouraged by the devastation the four rounds of canister just delivered, the two crews methodically reloaded their Napoleons. As an artilleryman rammed the powder bag into the barrel of his big gun another flash of light from the south filled the skies an instant before an explosive shell obliterated the main blockhouse. Another round slammed into the fence fifteen yards south of the far blockhouse. Startled gunners fearing they would suffer a similar fate to their counterparts leaped ten feet to the ground. With the stockade guns silenced, shells exploded amongst the Union barracks. Weak from loss of blood, Hill remained stoically seated at his desk. Beall guided the colonel to the window to witness the devastation.

He gently rested his hand on Hill's shoulder. In a compassionate, rational tone the Rebel leader said, "The decision is yours. Your guns are silenced while ours maintain their deadly fire. You might say, Colonel Hill, that I have trumped all your cards."

A military officer defines his whole being by victory or defeat. Defeat translates to failure—failure to his nation, failure to his peers, failure to his men, and most of all failure to himself. Hill breathed deeply, sighed despondently, and ambled reluctantly to the corner of his office. He symbolically extended his sword to Beall who stared at it momentarily, pushed it away, and politely responded, "I appreciate the gesture, Colonel, but I don't want your sword." With a tinge of contempt he stated, "I do want our freedom."

"As you say. Did I hear your men call you Captain?"

"Yes Colonel, Captain John Beall, Confederate States Navy. Now, if I may assist you to the courtyard to inform your men of your decision I shall signal the *Michigan* to cease fire so that I may initiate evacuation of the prisoners. We'll also locate a doctor for you."

Morgan scampered to the wharf and fired three signal flares. The Rebel guns silenced. While tripods of surrendered arms with cartridge boxes filled the yard leading to headquarters the prisoners scaled the walls and opened the gates. A young Southerner working through the meandering swarm of released men observed Beall standing with Colonel Hill. He rushed to his liberator, tightly grasped both his shoulders, and introduced himself as Lieutenant Colonel John Washington Inzer, 58th Alabama. Lieutenant Pierce accompanied Inzer. The three recognized the necessity of regaining some semblance of order before the evacuation.

Inzer ordered Pierce to locate the senior officers from each block and to organize the men into manageable groups of 200 men. Captured rifles would be issued evenly among the blocks. Numerous Rebels took it upon themselves to requisition the captured soldiers' shoes since "the Yankees weren't going anywhere soon."

Beall cringed as Inzer said, "The men shall respond in good order since Major Cole communicated President Davis mandated that our first priority shall be the safe transport of every man to freedom. First allow me to determine our casualties."

As he followed the Alabama officer into the stockade grief overcame Beall. Tears seared his eyes. Dozens of mangled bodies lay strewn about within yards of the walls separating them from freedom. An exhausted white haired man limped over to the pair. Trimble expressed brief words of appreciation before addressing the task at hand. After surveying the maimed casualties they remorsefully concurred that perhaps two dozen men lay too critically wounded to evacuate. A far greater number had perished. Prior to the liberation sixty bedridden prisoners already occupied the hospital, some too weak to move. The gravely wounded and those severely debilitated from illness would all be left behind. Over one hundred wounded but mobile men along with forty moderately ill soldiers could be transported to Canada when the *Philo Parsons* departed Sandusky Bay. Inzer and Beall insisted Trimble accompany those men. The Rebels guarding the stockade would also board with them.

Beall requested that an ample number of prisoners with artillery or infantry experience board the *Michigan*. Captured Union seaman from the *Michigan* joined their army counterparts inside the compound. Inzer detailed a hundred men to guard the Yankees before he joined the initial flotilla to Sandusky. The *Parsons*'s captive passengers received paroles but remained confined on Johnson's Island while key members of the *Parsons's* crew remained to operate the vessel. Transporting evacuees to Sandusky solely on the *Parsons* would prevent the chaos that might ensue if the *Michigan* also poured scores of loosely supervised troops into the city. The warship under Beall's command would escort the passenger craft during the initial voyage and could later lend military support wherever needed. The Rebel brain trust assumed the barrage of cannon fire which terminated thirty minutes earlier had cast the city into a state of pandemonium. Hopefully many citizens already fled to the countryside. The lobbing of several shells into Sandusky would encourage the indecisive to hastily depart. During their walk to the Johnson's Island dock Inzer asked about Cole. Beall acknowledged that the major performed exemplary service by capturing the *Michigan*. He tactfully suggested that if conditions turned chaotic that Major Cole might be forced to evacuate Sandusky prior to the masses.

A sparse crowd of curious onlookers lined Sandusky's waterfront near the main dock. Local militia formed a makeshift line of defense on the wharf to observe the captured vessel's approach. As the two ships neared to within two hundred yards of shore seven of the *Michigan's* guns erupted. Six rounds splashed harmlessly short of the barricaded militia. One round slammed into the face of the wharf, splintering the heavy timber but causing little damage. Civilians evacuated their perches and became engulfed in the escalating turmoil in the frenzied city. A minute later a second salvo belched forth another rain of fire. The solid shot crashed into the rear stone wall of the billiard hall, pocking the building's façade with jagged marks, and encouraging the militia to retreat into the expanding confusion. Convinced the rapture neared two women fell to their knees in prayer before their husbands dragged them to their feet, hurried them to waiting carriages, untied the reins, and bolted away. The *Philo Parsons* churned past the *Michigan* to the vacated dock at the foot of Columbus Avenue. Beall ordered his warship nearer for closer observation. He grinned at the pandemonium before him. A handful of citizens remained transfixed in utter disbelief. Others choked the streets while darting from the invaders. Men fought over the possession of the few remaining buggies. A score of poorly clad locals smashed storefront windows with the rationale that the Rebs would take anything the pilferers left. When the ferry landed Inzer promptly detailed fifty men to guard the dock. Cole, who had transferred onto the *Philo Parsons* met Robinson on shore, and received confirmation that the telegraph lines had been cut and the locomotives had been captured at the first sound of gunfire. Inzer detailed another contingent to further secure the train engines. The detail discovered a captured Sandusky, Mansfield, & Newark engine idling in the Sandusky depot. Cole's emissaries had also confiscated a recently departed Sandusky, Dayton, & Cincinnati train just outside of town after the firing initiated. With the city in Confederate hands the train rolled back into town. In all the Rebels commandeered ten freight cars and eleven passenger coaches besides the two engines. Over eight hundred men could cram into those cars. More would climb onto the tops. The first trainload departed from the Railroad Street depot near Jackson Street soon after the *Parsons* second consignment of released prisoners arrived.

As the *Philo Parsons* shuttled back and forth Beall turned his attention to loading provisions from Johnson's Island storehouses onto the *Michigan*. As the *Parsons* paddled to the mainland on her fifth freedom voyage, exuberant Confederates roamed Sandusky's business district scouring stores for long deprived basic items. The hunt escalated into a divesting of the delicacies absent for consumption these many months. Saloon and liquor store shelves emptied. Smashed window glass glittered below the flickering gas street lights. Inzer ignored the appalling conduct only because the evacuation demanded his full attention. He directed his most recent arrivals to the train station. They reached the terminal to witness the caboose fading away beyond the Warren Street depot and disappearing into the darkness, destined for Mansfield. Realizing they must now fend for themselves, a handful of belligerent junior officers threatened to commandeer the *Philo Parsons*. Inzer ordered his guard detail to dissuade any would be boarders as the final contingent of prisoners arrived in Sandusky. Beall and Pierce had boarded the *Parsons* for the final shuttle into the city. They gathered with Cole and Inzer on the dock to hold council prior to Beall's return to Johnson's Island to the *Michigan*. The recent throng of former prisoners patiently remained nearby awaiting direction.

Charlie puffed on an expensive cigar as he removed a sheaf of papers from his coat pocket. "This page details the businesses we must put to the torch. This next sheet indicates establishments you shall destroy only if time permits while my third page identifies known abolitionists who deserve our attention. The final page maps escape routes."

Inzer glared at Cole. "Major, you assured General Trimble that you arranged evacuation for everyone. After the *Parsons* departs seven hundred men shall remain to fend for themselves."

Beall's presence forced Cole to blend his lies into half-truths. "My plans called for commandeering another train from Cleveland; however, it must have been delayed or halted east of town. In any case, I'm aware of numerous vessels docked along the waterfront if we locate capable pilots. The *General Grant* and *Little Eastern* both come to mind."

Beall scrutinized Charlie's fabrication. Better to expose the major or to avoid divisive conflict and offer support for Cole's spontaneous alternative? He tactfully suggested, "The skies are clouding but the waters remain calm. The small craft Major Cole speaks of should cross the lake providing the weather holds."

Despite Beall delicately addressing the issue Inzer recognized Cole's deceitfulness. If the major had been forthright Trimble and Inzer would have planned for such a contingency. Sensing Inzer's disappointment, Beall placed both his hands firmly onto the colonel's shoulders. "Disperse the remaining men in all directions. I regret a number shall be recaptured, or worse, but imagine the panic enveloping the Yankees. If four hundred men reach the South the Northern papers shall multiply the number tenfold. Remember two trains speed south as we speak. Although I deplore the barbaric atrocities the Yankees inflict upon our homeland I relish the reciprocating mischief your men might create," added Beall with a sinister smile. "When newspapers describe the transformation of this secure coastal city of Sandusky into a pile of smoldering rubble, thousands of Yankee troops shall withdraw from their lines in Virginia, Tennessee, and Georgia. Prison camps throughout the North must be reinforced. Troops shall be reassigned to lake cities while Washington desperately searches for the elusive *Michigan*. Enormous amounts of manpower shall be exerted to hunt for the hundreds of escaped prisoners. Northern voters shall demand action. Lincoln must oblige. General Lee may even resume offensive actions. When calm returns the Republicans will have been voted out and armistice talks shall commence."

Inspired by Beall's vision Inzer collected his staff and issued orders. The colonel urged Cole and Beall to escape. Cole readily acquiesced, mentioning the necessity of reaching Cleveland prior to Beall's arrival. Charlie disappeared, intent upon securing his horses before fellow Rebels absconded with them from the livery. Beall held back as he had in the Chesapeake, drawn by the obligation which compelled him to remain until he fulfilled his duty in Sandusky. Pierce led a score of men on the mission to raze the town. They entered Adams & Fay Drug Store across from the West House and departed with turpentine soaked rags to ignite the lumberyards along the eastern waterfront. Smoke flowed from Gilcher's complex, then Richardson's, then Alexander's. Along the way the Verandah Hotel caught fire. Several men torched Monk's dock after securing the *General Grant* for the Confederate armada. In short order flames shot through the Klotz and Kromer Machine Shop roof. Before returning Pierce ordered the black Republican *Commercial Register* burned, to the delight of the former prisoners who suffered through its slanted view of the war.

With Pierce rampaging through the east side of town Inzer detailed Captain Belenger down Water Street to torch the other end. Inzer ordered the West House spared for the grand finale. At the foot of Decatur Street, R.B. Hubbard, backed by seven loyal employees armed with rifles and shot guns, defiantly guarded his lumber yard. As the ghoulish band illuminated by the glowing torches neared, Hubbard cocked the hammers of two revolvers, pointed them maliciously at Belenger, and insolently shouted, "One step closer, Reb, and I'll send you straight to hell!"

"Aside, sir. Spare the lives of your men and yours as well."

"Over my dead body!"

Shots crackled. Hubbard's lifeless body crumbled to the ground with his self-fulfilling prophesy. His leaderless men raced to safety without turning to watch the flames devour their former place of employment. With the Rebel's obsession to return to burn the West House, the Colton House escaped destruction. Thomas West begged Inzer to allow a room by room search before igniting his hotel. The colonel offered his regrets but succinctly stated, "We've controlled your city for three hours. If your citizens lack the common sense to evacuate I shall not be responsible." He pulled West aside and whispered, "I suggest you return to your Washington Street home, evacuate your family, and remove any sentimental treasures, as we shall also visit your residence tonight."

With an expression seething with contempt West raced to Washington Street and disappeared. The odor of greasy solvents soaking the desk and carpet permeated the West House lobby. A flash of light preceded the crackling flames. The Southerners watched in awe as the gruesome fingers of eerie flames reached out in search of fuel. Inzer looked to Beall and all but ordered him to depart while Beall urged Inzer to accompany him on the *Michigan*. The colonel firmly embraced his liberator. "Thank you for our freedom, Captain Beall. We each have our duties." He abruptly pivoted and left the Virginian on the wharf.

Before boarding the *Michigan*, Beall paused and stared at the frenzied scene in Sandusky. Bedlam reigned in all directions. The infernos along Water Street brightened the business district as clearly as the midday sun. High clouds reflected the sinister flames, transforming the sky into a devilish canopy of billowing shades of red. Isolated citizens aimlessly roamed the streets. A hefty mob of Southerners followed Inzer and Pierce up Columbus Avenue while other disjointed clusters clamored for escape routes along streets and allies. Remnants of confused citizens further clogged avenues of escape. Much to Beall's chagrin a score of former prisoners remained downtown either drunk with pillaged liquor or intoxicated with newfound freedom. In either case they seemed oblivious to the ramifications of remaining in town.

After the Rebels smashed glass and flung flaming torches through the broken post office windows, Inzer ordered Pierce to fire the deceased Eleutheros Cooke's massive mansion before marching west along the green on Washington Row to Lucas Beecher's stately home. Pierce reunited with Inzer at the corner of Adams Street where the Folletts' imposing home faced Hancock Street. In a distraught state Oran Follett steadied himself on his front porch while he absorbed the fiery backdrop to the north. Three days earlier, surrounded by relatives and friends inside his elegant dwelling, his family celebrated his daughter's wedding. Follett's wife coaxed her husband down the exterior's curved stone staircase. As the pair boarded their carriage, a Rebel determined to requisition their buggy approached. He reached for the harness and he ordered the Folletts to disembark. The raider chided, "Serves you right for hiding escaped niggers."

Feisty Eliza Follett placed her hand on her husband's before he could release the reins. With the composure of a woman possessing the fortitude to confront Satan himself Mrs. Follett stared boldly at her mocker. "As with Job of old, the Lord shall restore all which I lose just as you shall incur the wrathful vengeance of a just God." Turning casually to her husband, she calmly announced, "We may depart now, Mr. Follett." In a hushed voice she whispered, "In an orderly manner, my dear. Show no fear." The arsonists watched the stately couple's horse trot away.

Twenty minutes later Pierce and Inzer parted at the green near Huron Street and Monroe. Every man for himself now. A fortunate few discovered mounts secluded in barns. Those on foot traveled in bands numbering upwards of a dozen or as few as two or three, all intent upon reaching concealment in the countryside by dawn's first light.

Meantime Beall had departed to rendezvous with the *Parsons* to confirm her readiness to evacuate the wounded and infirm capable of traveling. With an hour of darkness remaining Beall guided the *Michigan* through the channel with the *Parsons* and *General Grant* trailing close behind. Once in Lake Erie he set his course east while the other vessels sailed due north.

He visualized the headlines in the Yankee papers.

Prosperous northern city miles from the front burned to the ground by Rebel soldiers. Hundreds of escaped prisoners spreading wide path of destruction throughout Ohio. No Northern port safe from captured U.S. warship. Lincoln recalls thousands of troops to protect northern homelands.

If Martha could only...

Bennett Burley's firm hand shook his shoulder. Martha O'Bryan's image drifted away with the lake current. Beall prayed the unfolding events he envisioned would become reality in a matter of hours.

54 – FROM DREAMS TO REALITY

"Johnny, lad, where's your head. I called you by name twice. You stand like an icicle frozen to the deck rail. You ready for this?"

"Aye, as I've ever been. I foresaw our entire venture unfold as clear as the midday sun on a cloudless sky. Simultaneously beautiful and horrific, perhaps the true essence of victory in war. A pained scowl crosses your face, Mr. Burley."

"The *Parson's* crew, the bloody bastards that they are, inform me we carry only six or seven hours of wood before our boilers loose power. We might well be in the center of our grand operation and find ourselves dead in the water. Ample fuel awaits us at Middle Bass, but our appearance shall surely alert the locals that something's amiss. Nothing our lads can't handle but a hindrance all the same. If we steam west now we can well be fueled and turned back towards Sandusky in two hours."

"We have no alternative." Beall glanced at the descending sun, stared down at the wooden deck, and shook his head in utter disgust. "Inform the *Parson's* crew to proceed at normal speed. Remind them any attempt to draw unwanted attention indeed brings undesirable and immediate consequences to the offender."

As the bottom of the sun touched the western horizon the *Parsons* inauspiciously prepared to dock at Middle Bass. Gathering cirrus clouds reflected the glowing hue of the radiant orange ball, as nature prepared to officially welcome autumn in two days. Several curious dockhands reached for the lines to secure the craft. "What in blazes you doing back?" demanded a hand.

Beall sauntered forward, proclaimed the Confederate States of America controlled the vessel, and ordered the man to load wood from the stacks some twenty feet beyond the dock.

The local brazenly told Beall what he could do with the fuel, spun, and shouted an alarm. In moments several dozen aroused citizens appeared, half of whom carried assorted flintlocks, squirrel guns, revolvers, and shotguns. The Southerners lined their deck maliciously brandishing revolvers. Most of the locals never before stared down threatening gun barrels. Hearts on the dock beat faster. Stomachs tightened. Tense islanders nervously waited for one of their comrades to initiate retreat. No one moved. The Rebs stood firmly in place with their expressionless faces concealing an anxiety similar to that so vividly evident upon the islanders' faces.

Lorenzo Miller, known more for his impulsive actions rather than his analytical mind, stepped from his comrades and advanced toward the *Parsons*. "You pack of pirates best skedaddle before the *Michigan* hears what you done and blasts you out of the water."

Ross shouted back, "Next time you see the *Michigan* she'll be a flying the stars and bars. If anyone's going to be running it 'ill be you. Should be accustomed to that by now," he jeered.

Miller took another step and swung his shotgun around. A shot rang out. Miller yelped. His weapon thudded on the wooden wharf. His right sleeve dripped warm, crimson blood. While the soldiers maintained their steady formation waiting for orders the locals remained stationary, until the sight of Miller's bloody coat issued the signal for dispersal. As the retreating citizens moved away Captain Atwood pushed against the flow toward his vessel.

"What in thunder are you doing with my ship, and where's Nichols?" Atwood demanded as he strode to the water's edge.

"Safe," Beall answered, "as you shall be if you follow instructions. Perhaps until we're finished fueling it shall be best that you come aboard and remain with us."

As the civilian and Confederate captains conversed Tom Major shouted, "Captain Beall, ship coming this way!"

The Rebel leader glanced to the east to observe the dim outline of a side wheeler sailing toward them. Other than the *Philo Parsons* docked at this unusual time nothing appeared suspicious to the *Island Queen's* Captain Orr or her engineer Henry Haines. The *Queen* navigated along side the *Parsons* so the *Queen's* crew could leap to the deck of the *Parsons* and fasten their lines. A similar number of Rebels jumped to the adjoining deck. Orr intuitively sensed danger and unsuccessfully attempted to reverse his engines. Shots echoed through the harbor. Blood dripped from Haines's cheek and ear. The Rebels secured their second prize of the day. Beall discovered in the bargain they captured twenty-five members of the hundred day 130th Ohio Volunteer Infantry traveling to Toledo to muster out. Beall released Atwood to care for the paroled civilian prisoners from both craft while he followed protocol with the captured Union soldiers.

Beall retained crews from both vessels. No telling when experienced seaman might prove beneficial after the *Michigan* joined his fleet. Shortly after 8 p.m. the refueled *Parsons* towing the *Queen* departed Middle Bass Island. A pointed but short discussion ensued relative to the fate of the *Island Queen*. The Rebels opened her valves midway between Middle Bass and Kelleys Island, and released the tow line. The scuttled ship drifted north before sinking in nine feet of water on Chicanolee Reef south of Pelee Island. Retaining the *Queen* would have forced Beall to divide his crew, which might prove detrimental in the capture of the *Michigan*.

The inhabitants of South Bass Island curiously observed the troublesome activity on Middle Bass a mile across the harbor. One resident of South Bass, or Put-In-Bay, as many referred to the island, intended to distance himself from all conflict. His family suffered casualties months before the firing on Fort Sumter. John Brown Jr., searching for tranquility away from the horrific war many credited his father with igniting, found solace growing grapes on the Lake Erie Island. He'd lost his father and two brothers at Harpers Ferry; another brother died in Kansas. The old man's namesake suffered physical effects from violence in the west. Proslavery forces captured John Jr. in Kansas, beat him with fists and rifle butts, tied him behind a horse, and drove him twenty miles under the brutal prairie sun to a jailhouse in Tecumseh to await indictment for murders of which he had no part. He suffered a nervous breakdown from the ordeal, which perhaps saved him from participating in the fateful attack at the Ferry. Brown and his wife Wealthy seemed content to allow others to carry the banner while they tended their grapes.

However, during the previous December, Brown sent a lengthy letter detailing his fears of the plausibility of launching an expedition from Canada to free the Johnson's Island prisoners. Canada's southern most possession, Pelee Island, lay eight miles south of the Canadian mainland. He feared numerous Southern sympathizers resided on the island. If invaders advanced over the thick ice which formed early in the winter, a body of men could march via four sparsely populated islands after departing Pelee and travel only an additional seventeen miles to reach Catawba Island, the peninsula obscuring Johnson's Island from the lake. Following the sporadic gunfire he watched with other onlookers as the *Island Queen* departed Middle Bass Island behind the *Parsons*. Brown reluctantly felt a vindication for what many perceived as his unnecessary paranoia.

With John Brown Sr.'s blood boiling through his veins he joined parties of men gathering to spread the alarm to the mainland. The strong current which carried the *Queen* to her submerged resting spot in turn hampered the messengers. In time only Brown and three companions in a small boat maintained the fortitude to row to Catawba Island, although another band of stalwarts fought the cross currents to warn Kelleys. While the South Bass citizens prayed for Brown's strenuous journey across the lake they also buried their valuables in their yards.

Meanwhile the *Philo Parsons* steadily sailed toward her rendezvous with the *Michigan*. The Confederates navigated to the location east of Kelley's Island which they vacated earlier, and observed the vaguely silhouetted masts of the *Michigan* anchored off Johnson's Island. The *Philo Parsons* waited two hours without a signal before Beall ordered her to advance by hugging the coast. His apprehension magnified with the glaring realization that his crew never assembled as a unit before this morning. On deck they recently splintered into disjointed clusters of two, three, or five. The tentativeness of the schedule prevented the seeds of unity from germinating within the hastily assembled menagerie. Motive further dissected the crew. He feared too great a number joined for the riches to be derived from the plunder or ransom of Northern cities. Several of the better intentioned apparently lacked the intestinal fortitude to fight. For all Beall knew one or two might be deserters or draft dodgers who migrated to safety across the Canadian border. Regardless of the crew's motivation the responsibility fell to Beall to inspire his men. The absence of Cole's signal coupled with Nichol's fear of running aground added to the dilemma. Fortunately Morgan's commitment remained steadfast. Beall confidently left him guarding the ship's navigators and mechanics while he assembled the Confederate entourage.

"Gentlemen, as you are aware, we have yet to receive our signal confirming the *Michigan's* capture. However, Major Cole's well-conceived plan to incapacitate her is sure to succeed. The signaling device for communication very well could have malfunctioned. Perhaps at this very moment he stands atop the Yankee deck anticipating our arrival. He..."

A voice from the rear sarcastically interrupted. "Perhaps at the very moment your Major Cole may be miles away from Sandusky as either a prisoner or possibly even as a traitor."

The masses responded to the voice promoting extraction from their ordeal by echoing a chorus of agreement.

Livid with anger the enraged leader drew his revolver and strode forward to dispatch the mutinous traitor. Burley firmly grasped Beall's shoulder and softly whispered, "Let me talk to the lads." Beall's tenseness vacated as he nodded in acquiescence.

With his booming voice Burley bellowed, "Lads, though now in a close spot, the captain and I have squeezed through tighter ones against greater odds with fewer men, and I might add for lower stakes and smaller prizes. Once we board the *Michigan* the entire Yankee coast from Buffalo to Chicago is ours for the taking. Imagine! Erie, Cleveland, Sandusky, Toledo, Detroit, Milwaukee and everything in between awaits us. Just one of those cities shall provide each of us a comfortable life. A second prize makes us all wealthy men. Another I dare say offers riches beyond imagination."

He paused, stepped three paces nearer his audience, and lowered his voice to deliver his final salvo. "Men, this goes beyond the gold sure to come our way. Each of us at one time bound ourselves to serve a greater cause. When the foot of the Yankee despot dropped to crush God's gift of freedom from our very souls we donned the uniform and fell in behind the Bonnie Blue Flag. His heel now crushes us into the soil as we coil to fend off his attack. His boot weighs heavily upon us. I fear we may well hold the South's final opportunity to uncoil with the deadly strike which pumps lethal venom directly into the heart of our cursed enemy." In an even, deliberate manner he continued, "Brave warriors, forty years from now you can tell your grandchildren one of two stories. You may apologize for your failure to dispatch the cruel hoards who rule over you because you retreated one fateful September night deep in Yankee territory. But I trust you desire to claim membership within the bold band of Southern saviors whose names the Confederacy forever reveres for our audacious bravery along the Yankee's northern coast."

John exhaled. How he coveted the gift of charismatically inspiring men. He shoved his revolver into his belt. His thoughts returned to capturing the *Michigan*.

A different voice tartly rebutted, "If our army of several dozen poorly armed men on this wooden pleasure craft confronts the steel hulled Yankee battleship brimming with heavy cannon and manned by over 100 disciplined men there ain't gonna be nobody left alive to spawn any offspring to produce grandkids."

Beall's lifeblood drained. His impetus to fight vaporized. Then Martha's tender image appeared. His resolve returned. In mass they willingly rejected the call to honor. Individually would they acknowledge their own cowardice?

"Men, we fight this war for the individual freedom to independently choose for themselves. If you reject my request for attack I only ask that you willingly sign a document affirming your opposition so I may exonerate myself for failing to fulfill President Davis's orders."

Observing no violent objections Beall departed and returned shortly from Ashley's office holding a freshly written document. Adrenalin again pumped throughout his body with the knowledge his tactic would push his men to action. In an even voice he read the document.

"*We, the undersigned, crew of the boat aforesaid, take pleasure in expressing our admiration for the gentlemanly bearing, skill, and courage of Captain John Y. Beall as a commanding officer and gentleman, but believing and being well-conceived that the enemy is already appraised of our approach, and so well prepared that we can not by any possibility make it a success and having already captured two boats, we respectfully decline to prosecute it any further.*"[8]

"Those so desiring may advance to record their names."

Surgeon J. S. Riley stepped forward without hesitation. His movement enticed fifteen to follow. Beall glared contemptuously at each traitor as their pens ground his soul into the *Parsons's* deck. A dozen spineless cowards lacked the guts to even acknowledge their shortcoming. Turning his back in disgust he joined Burley to inform Morgan of the abortion. Had Beall reflected upon his prior experiences his animosity might subside. The costly running aground of the *Alliance* at the mouth of the Piankatank River remained in the distance past. He blotted from memory the stern refusal of his former crew, including his brother, to carelessly race for stacked muskets serving as bait by the Yankee guards aboard the ship transporting them to Fort McHenry. As the P*arsons* turned to the northwest Beall stared into the churning waters behind the paddle wheel and searched fruitlessly for the image of Martha O'Bryan. He feared he lost her forever off the Ohio peninsula sheltering Johnson Island.

55 – COLE'S PREDICAMENT

While the *Philo Parsons* sailed toward Canada, Cole waited aboard the *Michigan* not as the host of a grand banquet but rather as the unwilling guest of Captain Carter. The scheme unraveled the previous evening in Detroit with the reappearance of Assistant Provost Benjamin Hill's mysterious caller. Hill never confirmed the visitor's identity although speculation varied from a disenchanted former Confederate soldier, to a Union spy, or to possibly a Rebel agent trafficking Southern secrets to the North for a handsome price. In any case, on Sunday evening Benjamin Hill prudently telegraphed Carter and confirmed the validity of the previous day's message which hinted at the possibility of clandestine activity. In response to the initial message on Saturday, Carter planned to order Ensign Hunter to proceed to Detroit on Monday morning to lend support to Hill. He anticipated detailing Ensign Eddy to the West House on Sunday evening for surveillance of the hotel. Upon receiving the second telegram Carter cancelled Hunter's trip. If the Rebel's attempted to carry forth their bold plan he needed both of his capable ensigns in Sandusky. In Detroit the assistant provost, desirous of uncovering and obliterating the Confederate spy network, allowed the plot to unfold. Hill assumed the *Parsons* posed little threat to the Union warship.

Early Monday afternoon Ensign Hunter docked a small barge at the foot of Columbus Avenue. Experienced seaman might question Hunter's unorthodox docking of the clumsy launch with its bow pointed away from rather than towards the pier. He ordered a squad of armed men to remain with the vessel except for coxswain Turley who he ordered to follow at a safe distance. Hopefully neither Cole nor any co-conspirators caught a glimpse of the bungling seaman. Hunter entered the hotel and subtly surveyed the lobby. Out of the corner of his eye he caught sight of Sandusky's Provost Marshall Steiner, seemingly oblivious to his surroundings as he sat reading the *Commercial Register*. The lawman's presence steadied Hunter's nerves. The locals reputed Steiner to be an even-tempered man, with an innate grasp of combustible situations, who avoided the poor judgment which often led to unnecessary injury to innocent citizens. Hunter acknowledged the Coles standing near the front desk.

Charlie's congenial smile crossed his face with recognition of Ensign Hunter. The unsuspecting agent strode over to Hunter, leaving Mrs. Cole standing amidst four trunks and numerous traveling valises. "Ensign, how pleasant to see you. I didn't expect to encounter you until this evening." He turned and motioned for Annie, who dressed in a trim-fitting dark blue traveling dress. "Mrs. Cole, please greet the good ensign. Unfortunately my wife must unexpectedly depart, preventing her from joining us this evening."

"I'm afraid that shall not be permitted, Mr. Cole. In the name of the United States Navy I place you under arrest. You are to accompany me." Turning to Annie, Hunter tipped his cap. "Mrs. Cole, you shall remain here under house arrest."

"Ensign Hunter, I vehemently protest this outrage, although I appreciate you only follow orders as baseless as they may be!" Cole retorted.

Hunter placed his hand firmly on Charlie's shoulder and gently applied pressure to nudge him forward. "If all you claim proves forthright we best join Captain Carter so we may clear you." Provost Steiner casually rose to support Hunter.

Cole cast his eyes about the lobby, feigning concern for the visitors unaware of the drama unfolding. He softly whispered, "We certainly do not wish to create an incident which might bring harm to any citizens." Especially me, he thought. "Let us depart at once." He turned to Annie. "I shall resolve this despicable misunderstanding promptly so you may board your late afternoon train, my dear."

When they reached the small transport Steiner and Hunter each tightly grasped one of their prisoner's forearms and all but threw him onto the barge deck for the waiting crew to surround. About ten paces behind, coxswain Turley searched the perimeter for imagined intervention. He stared at the roof of the West House, envisioning a regiment of Confederate sharpshooters suddenly appearing to rein fire down upon the Union captors in an effort to free their cohort. When his eyes met Hunter's impatient glare he boarded.

"Gentlemen, may I offer you a fine cigar?" Charlie asked, as he reached into his coat pocket.

Either their unflappable captive was an actor, a liar, or an innocent victim, although based on the facts presented Hunter ruled out the latter. "Better hold on to those Mr. Cole. You might desire one before the noose drops over your neck."

Color drained from Charlie's cheeks momentarily before he regained his composure, smiled, and with his unassuming blue eyes looked to Hunter and Steiner. "I confess my transgression gentleman. Instead of only gathering information of the traitorous plot about to be hatched and immediately bringing the details to the proper authorities, I, shall we say, grew accustomed to the generous stipend which the Rebels provided me for my charade."

Hunter and Steiner already heard more than they cared, especially with the presence of the gossipy seamen. Steiner bluntly terminated the dialogue. "Cole, or whoever you are, save your story for the captain."

Once aboard the *Michigan*, Cole surveyed the situation. Sailors scurried about preparing for action. Never before had he physically fought his way out of a predicament. Not the ideal conditions to begin but the pressure from the Yankee vise squeezed him uncomfortably tighter. He called upon his innate talents to fabricate a whopper to extricate him from this mess. The edge of his lips curled upward as his mind commenced writing the script.

Under guard the prisoner marched to the captain's cabin. Through the open door he observed Captain Carter pacing nervously to and fro while Colonel Charles Hill, recently arrived from Johnson's Island, stood solemnly near the table. Charlie extended his hand as Carter approached. The captain responded to the gesture with a scowl, contemptuously ignored Charlie's hand, and motioned for everyone to be seated. Carter seethed with bitterness from the betrayal of their perceived friendship. "Mr. Cole, you have a great deal of explaining to do. Before you begin I must warn you that if the details of this scheme prove valid you could easily swing from the scaffold. While I am not empowered to offer concessions, any useful information you provide could deter the decision to hang you. I emphasis everything you say henceforth enters Colonel Hill's and my official reports."

The prisoner inhaled deeply. Number one priority, save his own neck. Next, avoid incriminating Beall. Finally, warn those in Sandusky of the unearthing of the plot. Charlie casually leaned back in his seat, rested his forearms with open palms atop the chair arms, looked directly into Carter's eyes, and with his charismatic smile began chapter one of his concocted tale.

"Let me backtrack to June when I visited Virginia. At the time I'd been exchanged and intended to return to Harrisburg and allow the inevitable conclusion of this war to methodically expire. While in Richmond I became acquainted with some mid level officials working for Secretary Mallory. They knew vaguely of plans to repay the Union for the transgression of the Dahlgren affair. Unbeknownst to me they forwarded my name to the War Department. Through no initiation of my own I received an invitation to participate. I reluctantly accepted, although my particular assignment seemed somewhat nebulous. Since I honorably signed the *Oath of Allegiance* prior to my parole, I conceived the design of infiltrating the Southern network, gathering key information, and communicating in a timely manner such knowledge to proper Union authorities.

Trusting no one I chose to conceal the information until the ideal opportunity presented itself, that occasion being tonight, Captain Carter, so together we might construct a trap and foil the invaders. As I've already confessed to these two fine gentlemen," Charlie said nodding toward Steiner and Hunter, "I regret I became dependent upon the flow of Confederate funds." He paused with a sheepish grin, "But I did take it upon myself to personally drain the Confederate Treasury."

"Mr. Cole!" Carter angrily interrupted before sarcastically demanding, "Enough of your noble deeds. Time is short. I need details now!"

Unaware of the precise nature of the Yankee's information Charlie innocently answered, "We coordinated activities in Sandusky. We were ordered to incapacitate the *Michigan* for some sort of assault to occur to free Colonel Hill's prisoners. Unfortunately Mr. Thompson remained tight-lipped as to the specifics. I'm unable to speculate as to all of the forces he intends to utilize. I learned at noon, unbeknownst to me earlier, that one hundred men shall arrive in town today."

Looking to Hunter, Carter ordered, "Have the prisoner placed in chains. We'll contact Stanton's office as to the manner he wishes to dispose of Mr. Cole."

Charlie asked, "Gentlemen, don't you desire the names of the local citizens whom Richmond requested I contact?"

"We're waiting Mr. Cole," snapped Colonel Hill.

"I've had discussions with John Williams as well as John Brown, both long time Sandusky citizens with Copperhead affiliation. Doctor Stanley offered me substantial support. I spoke with the architect Merrick concerning the location and condition of area bridges. A bricklayer named Strain also contacted me. The clothier Louis Rosenthal appears tied directly to Richmond." Charlie paused, pleased with his latest revelations. None of the dissidents possessed ties to him, or the Confederacy for that matter. As he assumed, the provost departed to arrest the alleged traitors. The excitement and rumors generated by those apprehensions would alert his fellow conspirators of impending danger and force them to lay low or flee town. For good measure Charlie added, "Feel free to collaborate my story with my associate Mr. Robinson." He knew his simpleminded courier would totally confuse his captors. In an act of total audacity, Charlie stood and smiled. "I assume I am free to leave now."

Captain Carter stared in disbelief at the man's impudence, shook his head, and tartly replied, "Yes, you may leave. Ensign Hunter, manacle our guest and quarter him in an isolated, secure area." After Cole's departure, Carter and Hill discussed efficient utilization of their combined forces to thwart the eminent assault.

"The man's lying through his teeth, Colonel. Can we believe anything?"

"Probably not, Jonathan, but prudence requires us to act as such. Provost Steiner's arresting the men Cole identified. Our forces must scurry to meet the 5:30 train if possible. We'll certainly screen all passengers disembarking from later trains."

Hill traveled from Johnson's Island via the ferry *Princess* with thirty men and officers only to land in Sandusky after the 5:30 train arrived. Several passengers spread alarm with the confirmation that perhaps fifty riders leaped from cars at the outskirts of town. At 6:00 Hill dispatched a segment of his force on the southbound Sandusky, Mansfield & Newark to meet the Detroit and Toledo train in Monroeville while he apprehended the scattered Rebels who inexplicitly jumped from the earlier train. To his relief, the men thought to be enemy insurgents proved to be laborers and mechanics traveling to Nashville for work. Cheap lodging existed on the south edge of town. Instead of riding to the station and hiking back to their accommodations they hopped off in the vicinity of the boarding houses. At 7:10 the train from Cleveland arrived without suspicious persons. By 8:15 Hill's contingent from Monroeville returned to report nothing unusual. Earlier that evening Colonel Hill telegraphed Detroit for the location of the missing *Philo Parsons*, now several hours overdue. He assumed Detroit authorities interceded that morning to capture the Rebel pirates and protect the innocent passengers. To his dismay he learned she departed on schedule. Before returning to his Johnson's Island headquarters he boarded the *Michigan* to update Captain Carter.

Both officers had responded admirably without waiting for orders from their superiors. Hill's stellar performance preceded a similar action by Carter. After debating whether to enter Lake Erie that evening the naval captain decided to commence his search for the missing *Philo Parsons* at morning's first light. No use taking foolish action and potentially grounding his ship. They concurred with the prudence of the *Michigan* remaining offshore from the prison until daylight. Due to the mutual respect each man held for the other, two typically uncooperative branches of the military worked in unison during the crisis. Hill bid his naval counterpart a good evening and disembarked to escort Cole to his new accommodations on Johnson's Island.

That evening twenty-five hundred Confederate prisoners anxiously awaited the arrival of their rescuers. By midnight men resting in their bunks randomly dozed off. By the middle of the night most of the prison population drifted to sleep. All but the most optimistic realized another long winter awaited. None knew that Charles Cole, their alleged savior, joined them as a fellow prisoner.

56 – THE MORNING AFTER

In the early morning darkness the *Philo Parsons* churned through western Lake Erie, destined for the Detroit River. Burley struggled to console his comrade. "Johnny, for reasons unbeknownst to us Providence chose not to bless this mission."

"Damn it, Benny, God provided a plan. Devilish deceit from vermin either in Sandusky or in Canada betrayed us. Had we sailed with men of the character we recruited in the Chesapeake instead of settling for these cowardly castoffs we would yet have overcome the deceit. Success awaited us tonight if each man possessed the heart to will us to victory," emphasized Beall with a thump of his fist against his chest. "After this futile attempt I question whether another such opportunity presents itself."

He turned away choosing to sooth his aching body and numbed mind with the sound of the methodical thrust of the craft through the water. By early morning the *Philo Parsons* lay scuttled in shallow waters with her valuables stripped and her prisoners released. The side wheeler's owners raised her and returned her to service within a week. Following the aborted rescue attempt the Rebels evaporated into the sanctuary of western Canada.

At 7:00 a.m. that same morning a civilian with unkempt hair and damp laborer's clothing, arrived at Johnson's Island accompanied by three weary comrades. Although thoroughly exhausted from the physical strain of the journey and constant exposure from the splashing surf, John Brown demanded to speak with Colonel Hill. Only from Brown did the colonel learn of the captures of the *Island Queen* and *Philo Parsons*. The post commander immediately telegraphed the new information to Major General Heintzelman, headquartered in Columbus. In the message

Hill included his incorrect assumption that Beall would return with two boatloads of invaders charged with the task of freeing the prisoners.

Inside the stockade walls prisoner McClung awoke to the sentinel's simulated rooster's screeching. The disheartened Confederate prisoner knew days would pass before the hen would acknowledge the dominant male bird.

Several miles to the north the *Michigan* steamed towards Kelleys Island. Nervous islanders feared that Rebel privateers commanded the warship. Upon the vessel's arrival only a crusty old salt braved the unknown and walked down the pier to investigate. He recognized Captain Carter, spoke briefly with the skipper, and watched the craft sail west. By midday the *Michigan* reached Detroit. With no sign of the Confederates or the missing vessels, Carter determined it necessary to return with haste to Sandusky Bay to protect the prison. On the return route they spotted the *Island Queen* submerged in shallow water. Fearful of running aground if he neared the *Queen*, Carter sailed to Sandusky Bay and arrived by late afternoon.

There he learned of War Secretary Stanton's incensed anger at the brash raid. The secretary ordered Major General John Dix, commander of the Army's Department of the East, to proceed to Buffalo to forward a firsthand report of conditions along Lake Erie's shore. By evening the drama subsided with the knowledge that the *Island Queen* and *Philo Parsons* both rested on watery floors.

With their respective slanted views, pro-Lincoln Republican and antiwar Democratic northern newspapers spewed forth headlines of the bold raid. Relevant stories lingered in the northwest, where rumors of new conspiracies periodically surfaced. On the east coast the headlines vanished as citizens foolishly believed that similar events would never occur in their secure section of the country.

57 – THE STRUGGLE CONTINUES

John moped in the solitude of his Buffalo hotel room. The frigid, dreary December weather permeated his worn body. The ill-fitting window chattered as wind gusts swirled snow about outside. The stark landscape epitomized his listless mind. Twice in recent months dastardly treachery snatched success from enterprising missions. In Sandusky a cowardly informer betrayed Charles Cole. Despite the duplicity, had dedicated men accompanied Beall rather than spineless mercenaries, he would have captured the *Michigan* and subsequently released the prisoners from Johnson's Island. Ensuing lies fabricated through the Republican press arrogantly claimed that the Yankees aboard the warship stood ready to obliterate the Rebel assault force.

October's subsequent adventure came nearer fruition. Beall convinced Jacob Thompson that Lake Erie's unprotected coast hung like an apple ripe for the plucking. With the commissioner's blessing Rebel agents purchased a Canadian steamship, the *Georgiana,* and even located an artillery piece. After shelling and sacking Buffalo the Confederate raiders would sail to Cleveland while laying waste to numerous shoreline cities. Along the way they would secure a second ship, divide their forces, and multiply the chaos. Beall, commanding the *Georgiana*, would then hug the Canadian coast as he advanced toward Toledo while the other vessel wreaked further havoc along Ohio's coastline. If the *Michigan* pursued the other vessel Beall would swoop into Sandusky Bay and at long last free Johnson's Island prisoners. Canada unfortunately bowed to U.S. pressure, increased surveillance of suspected Rebel agents, and located the *Georgiana*. Although nothing aboard incriminated the vessel, titled in the name of a Confederate sympathizer, the Canadians nonetheless impounded her.

Illegal seizure of civilian ships apparently had become sanctioned as well by the Yankee's neighbor across the northern border. Unaware of the ship's confiscation, Beall awaited her arrival, after which he would sail to join Colonel Robert Martin and Lieutenant John Headley. The trio escaped before Union spies apprehended them. During the period of heightened awareness the Canadians captured Burley. The papers debated the complexities of international law while the discussion of extradition ensued. A smile crossed John's somber face with the revelation that authorities believed they held the infamous Captain John Beall rather than Bennett Burley. To date no one discerned Burley's true identity.

Other Confederate cells hatched plots to the east. Bennett Young led a daring raid into the small border town of St. Albans, Vermont, a month to the day after Beall's seizure of the *Philo Parsons*. The raiders absconded with over $200,000 from three local banks and attempted to burn the town with the experimental incendiary, Greek fire. As he dodged civilian bullets on his hasty horseback retreat Young gleefully glanced over his shoulder to witness the plumes of smoke spiraling into the blue October sky. To his dismay he learned that the fires extinguished themselves after inflicting nominal damage. Young and many of his companions now awaited trial or extradition in Canadian jails.

The operation garnering everyone's attention in the east occurred on the November weekend following Thanksgiving. Headley, Martin, and several other accomplices smuggled forty bottles of Greek fire into New York City with the mission of burning six hotels. Barnum's museum also inadvertently became an impromptu target. The incendiary might better have been named Greek smoke since only minimal damage transpired. Collectively these activities germinated into a nettlesome source of escalating aggravation for the Yankees, and especially for Major General John Dix, Commander of the Union Army's Department of the East.

During this period of subversive activity only word of isolated, insignificant Confederate triumphs circulated northward while the elusive major victories prevalent in the past remained distant memories. After Atlanta fell Sherman dissolved into Georgia's countryside. Even the eternal Southern optimist understood no news meant good news only for the Yankees. John Hood's failure in Tennessee confirmed excellent division commanders who struggle when promoted to corps commanders most certainly shall fail when placed in independent command of an army, as evidenced by the unnecessary carnage suffered recently in Franklin. November's election returned Lincoln to power and significantly strengthened the hold of the radical Republican Congress. John had so hoped that future years of partisan warfare could be avoided. He witnessed firsthand the erosion of civilized boundaries in the conflict as he waged war, against his better judgment, with Rebel operatives in Canada. No defined structure; inflict damage upon the enemy and live to fight another day.

His current mission epitomized this manner of combat. Three of Morgan's former raiders involved with the failed *Georgiana* escapade rendezvoused with Beall in western New York, with the express purpose of freeing Generals Cabell and Marmaduke. The New York Central train rumored to be transporting the two prisoners on any of three days from Johnson's Island to Boston's Fort Warren passed through the region. They received vague instructions to halt the train, free the generals, and remove any valuables from the express safe. Orders prohibited confiscation of personal property from the passengers. Under no circumstances should civilians be harmed unless they attempted to interfere. During the prior two days the Rebels endeavored to derail the eastbound train without success. One final attempt remained.

The thin lines defining honorable warfare gradually blurred. Six months earlier John refused an assignment into the Confederate Secret Service fearing he might be ordered to blindly follow a path dictated by others. Today he followed men insensitive to the potential of collateral damage. He stared outside into the whiteout which obscured his view of the outside, much as this damn war masked his perspective of his inner self. He saw nothing outside; he felt nothing inside.

A sharp knock brought him to his feet. He welcomed the operation's commander. Colonel Robert Martin forced a smile while rubbing his hands together to regain warmth. Tight abundant curls hung to the top of his ears while more locks touched his forehead. A bushy mustache rested below his classic nose and high cheekbones. A narrow band of facial hair drooped from his lower lip to the base of his chin. Clean shaven John Headley entered next. His full head of dark brown hair resting on his collar concealed most of his ears. His eyes sparkled in anticipation of the evening's action. Eighteen year old Virginian George Anderson closed the door. He shuffled over the threadbare carpet while scarcely looking up. The subdued teenager seemed bored in the bleak surroundings and miserable in the unpleasant climate where fate deposited him. In early September the Yankees captured him amidst the ambush in Greenfield where John Hunt Morgan died. Anderson escaped the prison train carrying him to Camp Chase and gambled that striking out to Canada would prove safer than backtracking through miles of Union occupied territory to the south.

In his refined Dixie drawl Martin spoke. "Expected all of my fighting to be in the South and for only a year. Figured hell would freeze over before we'd be fighting the Yankees four years." He glanced outside and grimaced. "Looks like it has." His comment brought laughter from Headley and Anderson and a soft smile to Beall's worn face.

"It's near dark," commented Headley. "Time to meet the others and get to the sleighs."

Ninety minutes later three large sleds pulled to a stop at a rail crossing. Six men tossed snow covered blankets on the seats and dusted cold white flakes from their coats. A light snow continued but dropping temperatures slowed the accumulation. Headley lifted two sledge hammers from the sled's floor and handed one to a man whom he motioned to follow. The other four silently stomped their feet to force a steady circulation through their numb feet. Anderson, the shy youngster who seemed drawn to Beall, again gravitated near the soft spoken fellow Virginian. After searching in the dark for several minutes for the three loose rails they concealed yesterday, Headley illuminated the area with his lantern and shouted, "Found them. Give me a hand, fellows."

The men made easy work of dragging the first rail to the tracks. Martin finished securing it when a humming from the tracks announced the forthcoming passenger train. "Son of a bitch," mumbled Martin, extinguishing the lantern. "Hope one rail knocks her off the tracks."

The drone of the engine muffled by the blanket of snow preceded the clattering of metal wheels grinding over the tracks. The saboteurs raced to safety away from the derailing cars. The dark snowy sky obscured the rail secured across the tracks. The locomotive hit the obstacle, shimmied against the lone rail, and propelled the iron bar clattering to the side of the bed. The vibrating wheels held the tracks as the engineer applied the brakes to bring the train's wheels to a screeching halt. He again opened the throttle with the realization that with the inclement weather he best reach Buffalo as soon as possible. The disappointed raiders returned to town, dispersed, and agreed to reunite the following afternoon.

At the meeting they contemplated returning across the border by rail on the 9 p.m. Canadian Great Western. At Beall's urging most of the party instead individually walked over the suspension bridge while he inexplicably opted to ride the train with his shadow George Anderson. The pair separated inside the station to deflect unwarranted attention. John's tenseness diffused with the sound of the northbound train grating to a halt. He casually walked across the platform, climbed the coach steps, slid into a window seat, and breathed a sigh of relief. He reflected upon the mission's futility while comforting himself with the knowledge that he survived to fight another day. While glancing out the window and surveying the meandering travelers, panic enveloped him. George Anderson dozed on a dark oak bench inside the station.

John stared aghast. How would he rescue his young companion? In five minutes the train would pull away. If he disembarked both men might risk another day in Buffalo, plus increase suspicion if authorities recognized them the following night. If he woke Anderson local officials would realize the men who sat far apart in the station actually traveled together. Not wise either but his best option. He descended from the passenger car, reentered the station, and walked deliberately to the sleeping soldier. Placing his hand on the lad's shoulder he said, "Stranger, you mentioned you're traveling north. The train's about to depart."

The groggy boy replied in a distinctly southern dialect, "Gracious Johnny, thanks. I was gone to the world."

John grabbed the boy's arm to usher him to the waiting train when two men with drawn revolvers blocked their route. A short stout man with a Yankee nasal twang demanded, "Where you boys from and where you off to in such a hurry?"

John calmly answered, "Just a pair of Canadians heading home after several days business in New York."

"Traveling pretty late aren't you?" asked the other man, a tall lanky fellow. "With that secesh drawl and scruffy clothes you boys might be some of the Rebs who broke out of Point Lookout. What do you think, Officer Thomas?"

"Think you just might be correct, Officer Saule. Feared this war would end before we captured our first ones."

Realizing the consequences of revealing their true identities, particularly with the recent mischief in Vermont and New York City, John surmised a return to Point Lookout might be their most viable option. He cautiously raised his arms, shrugged his shoulders, dropped his head, and compliantly said, "George, looks like we'll be heading back to Point Lookout. Got to admit these last couple days have been a pleasant diversion."

The burley policeman opened John's coat and removed a loaded Colt. "Won't be needing this, Mr. Rebel businessman," Thomas said with a chuckle, as he pushed Beall toward an open door. Saule followed with Anderson in tow to the telegraph office for further questioning.

On December 18, three days after their late night capture, the duo arrived in New York City where authorities separated them. The heavy oak door with steel grating slammed shut behind John after he entered his eight by five cell. Light from the barred windows in the adjoining first floor room dimly illuminated his damp, uncomfortable accommodations. A mattress and blanket provided minimal comfort. An ample water supply and a waste sink served as his only other amenities. Spartan meals arrived at nine, three, and seven. Limited light allowed him to read from his common prayer book and testaments. Christmas dinner consisted of a cupful of bland rice, a thin slice of bread, and a small chunk of boiled beef. He pondered the basis for the delay of their transfer to Point Lookout.

On several occasions guards escorted him to unfamiliar properties showing signs of recent vandalism and arson. The authorities diligently strived to link him to November's fires. In one instance they placed him in a lineup between two police officers immaculately dressed in civilian apparel. Beall stood disheveled wearing the same dirty, rumpled clothing he had worn since his capture. They prevented him from even combing his grimy hair. He logically appeared the perpetrator while standing between the disguised lawmen.

Confined with the most despicable elements of New York City's population, he reaffirmed his conviction that the evil permeating throughout Yankee culture flowed from crowded urban centers to contaminate his pure agrarian civilization. The profane, lying, thieving lot simply regarded all mankind as enemies and fair prey. He endured prison with an undying commitment to his noble cause.

By the end of December, Beall acknowledged the near impossibility of a dramatic escape. Instead he subtly approached the jail's doorman, Edward Hayes, and offered him $1000 in gold, to be awarded by Southern friends residing in New York, if Hayes aided his escape. All the while the prisoner attempted to bribe the turnkey, the jailer inquired as to his captive's true identity. Neither man met with success.

During their stay at the Mulberry Street jail Anderson and Beall remained apart. Various officers questioned the pair individually but to no avail. A veteran policeman prepared to take his turn, confident of better results than his predecessors. Detective Kelso orchestrated events so that Andersen missed his meager meal while waiting nearly an hour in the cold, drafty hallway before being interrogated. The sparse noon dinner provided prisoners their major nourishment of the day. The boy entered the small, brightly-lighted room with only enough space for a stove, table, and three chairs. The policeman pushed his half finished bowl of thick soup to the side, wiped drippings from his beard with a red and blue checkered napkin, and said, "Sentiment in the city suggests you two gents had a hand in the arson. Every once in while folks talk of lynching the dirty sons of bitches who played the part. A shame too."

"What do you mean?" asked the squirming lad.

""'What I'm I telling you sonny is you don't have many options, and only one makes sense. If we take our time before sending you south to the Reb prison ya'll, as you people fondly say, just might freeze to death. Not a good way to go but better than being hoisted up a lamp post with a choking rope squeezing your neck. Generally the more you gag and kick the rowdier the crowd gets. Even if you avoid the lynch mob you'll end up back in that prison camp. A lad such as yourself has got to realize this war's about over." Kelso smiled, sat back, stroked his beard, and then leaned forward over the table. He rested his elbows on the worn wooden surface and pointed an index finger within ten inches of the youngster's face. "You boy, are on the losing side. Losers don't fair well. Rumor has it all you soldier boys who don't get executed will be sentenced to ten years of hard labor with a nigger overseer. That would be justice and a spectacle in itself."

The detective paused to allow his message to sink in. He relaxed his posture and continued in a friendly, mentoring tone, "Son, people understand how a young man gets caught up in the excitement of war. You left Virgini for the cavalry. Debonair uniforms. Fast horses. A pair of shiny Colt pistols with a glittering saber at your side. Probably joined with friends. How'd your journey end?"

Anderson stared at the table before barely bringing his eyes to meet Kelso's. His throat burned. He fought back tears. "Only rode with Morgan several months before the general got his self kilt in Tennessee. Yanks took me and shipped me up to Ohio, but I jumped the train figuring Canada to be closer and safer to get to." He shivered and added, "Didn't realize it would be a whole lot colder."

The interrogator rested his hand on the lad's arm and softly smiled. "Boy, I'd a been caught up in the glory too. I made foolish decisions myself at your age although none that would cost me my life. But you're young. You have two roads to travel. One leads to a new life, a new beginning. The other takes you down a way from which there is no return, one you don't want, do you?"

Anderson's head moved somberly back and forth.

A shocked expression crossed Kelso face. He slapped his forehead with his open palm. "Georgie, you must be starving! I caused you to miss your noon meal. Speak up! We're not the cold-hearted people you've been led to believe." The detective turned and bellowed, "Mr. Hayes, bring me a bowl of that hot bean soup with a nice piece of bread before our young friend here starves."

Moments earlier George sat outside—scared, hungry, cold, and worst of all alone from his own kind, constantly in fear of the swarm of crude city criminals. Hayes set the steaming soup before him with its appetizing vapor warming the boy's soul before the first spoonful reached his lips. He realized across from him sat the opportunity for freedom from his miserable cell and the strange sounding, horrible criminals.

In a pleading tone Kelso begged, "Not for me lad, but for you, tell us what you know of your companion?" The interrogator recognized that Anderson struggled with his divided loyalties. In an all-knowing paternalistic manner Kelso comforted his young captive. "I suspect your companion is an officer rather than a simple enlisted man. Georgie, because of his rank he's obligated by his Southern code of honor to remain mum as to his recent activities. His silence offers no aid to his cause; rather he only jeopardizes you both." Kelso paused before emphasizing in a low voice. "I give you my word as an honest, God-fearing gentleman that your cooperation performs a kind service to your colleague which his chivalry denies him."

Hunger had disappeared. Warmth had returned. How could George not trust this man? Good men existed north and south. Deep inside he acknowledged Beall's stubborn streak placed the captain in jeopardy. George grasped that he could perform this moral Christian deed and benefit his comrade without harming anyone. He leaned forward, lowered his voice, and naively whispered as if the words he prepared to utter would be repeated to no one. "The man you hold is Captain John Beall of Virginia."

"Beall, John Beall?" The puzzled detective inquisitively repeated the name until his eyes brightened. "John Beall, the raider who seized the steamer on Lake Erie, the boat called the *Parson Phillips*. Yes, that's it. Read about it in the papers.

Kelso stood and excitedly called the doorman. "Hayes, come here!" When the turnkey entered, the beaming detective slapped the lad on the back. "George identified our mute prisoner! He's John Beall, the pirate. Return Mr. Anderson to his cell. I must locate the commissioner! I'm sure he'll wish to deliver the news to the authorities himself." Kelso scurried out the front door leaving Hayes to discard George in his cell.

58 – ANOTHER YEAR

January 1, 1865, his second consecutive New Years Day in a damp, dismal cell. John anticipated that his futile attempt to bribe Hayes coupled with Anderson's betrayal of his true identity would lead to a transfer to a secure military prison, in all likelihood either Fort Warren in Boston or Fort Lafayette here in New York. Thoughts of Martha periodically entered his cluttered mind. Martha. He pondered if they would ever roam his estate's serene, rolling fields. The last four years had taken its toll on his worn body, his withered spirit, and his faded dreams.

He again stiffened his resolve to continue his commitment to Virginia's quest for freedom, to visit his aging mother, and to maintain his obligation to his comrades in arms. Yet these motivations paled whenever Martha's angelic vision appeared. He would fight to the last breath of air in his lungs and the final drop of blood in his veins to rejoin her. Absorbed with thoughts of her, he tenderly sang the verses he composed on the previous two New Years Days.

He searched for words to arrange the next stanza. Would it become the third verse with many more to follow as the epic ballad lengthened in unison with their years together? Or would his composition consist of only a trilogy of verses? Perhaps when he possessed a clearer view of his future he could compile a fitting stanza.

At day's end he wrapped snuggly in his thin blanket and curled tightly into a fetal position. He smiled as he humorously recalled his complaints of Jefferson County's chill winter nights. The coldest nights in Virginia warmed considerably compared to evenings in this Godforsaken climate. He drifted to sleep bringing his thirtieth birthday to an end.

Four days later Beall and Anderson shivered inside the unheated cabin of the small ferry hauling them to Fort Lafayette. Directly ahead, centered in the narrows separating New York's inner harbor from its outer harbor, a gloomy circular structure rose. Dreary clouds crowned the uninviting bastille amidst a colorless landscape. Black smoke curled from the boat's stack. Patches of crusted white snow remained in the shadows along the shore. Icy flakes randomly drifted from the sky. And gray, so many shades of dingy gray. The bottomless sea one hue, the depressing clouds another. An ominous tone tinted the portentous prison looming ever nearer. Nothing but insipid grays everywhere.

As they neared their destination Beall watched the towering cylinder transform into an irregular octagon with four slender walls connecting four massive planes. Two ominous rows of gun casements mounted within the fort's walls protected the narrow shipping channels. The fort's unique architecture also trained guns over land surfaces to either side. Following the fort's construction after the War of 1812 on two and a half acres of rocky shoal, her guns never fired upon enemy ships since the only subsequent conflict involved Mexico far to the south. To further protect the channel Forts Richmond and Tompkins on Staten Island flanked Fort Lafayette to the right while Brooklyn's Fort Hamilton protected the left. Modernized nineteenth century warfare transformed many of the armed castles into munitions storehouses, troop barracks, and with the civil war's advent, even into prisons. Since the conflict commenced the Yankees utilized Fort Lafayette as a retention center for political prisoners. In 1861 Marylanders, with their right of habeas corpus suspended, languished in the so-called Northern Bastille. Though designed to hold 50 prisoners, as many as 163 men suffered confinement within the walls.

The rolling surf thrust the craft into the wharf with a jolting thud. John stared at the drab half-century old stone walls towering thirty feet above. Blue clad troops ushered him through the sally port's massive reinforced oak doors.

The entourage marched through the opening cut into eight foot thick walls and proceeded onto a courtyard where the walls' interior surrounded an exercise square. A twenty-five foot paved walkway adjacent to the walls lined the inner perimeter which served as the boundary for the seventy foot square parade ground.

Only a sergeant escorted Beall into the post commander's office while the other guards remained outside with Anderson. General Martin Burke had served as on aid directly under General Winfield Scott in Mexico. He carried the reputation as a fair but mechanical officer who methodically followed his orders explicitly. After outlining the facility's general operating guidelines he unemotionally added, "I am instructed to manacle your ankles and wrists."

Beall erupted with anger and snapped, "Colonel, as an officer in Confederate States Navy I vehemently protest under the rules of civilized war!"

Burke raised his hands in resignation. "Captain Beall, over my years in the military, I've discovered the only law in warfare is the order coming from one's superior." He paused and added casually, "I suspect you may utilize the same defense before your time here concludes." John's inquisitive expression only disappeared when the colonel dismissed him to be taken to the blacksmith.

Fort Lafayette's conversion from a bastion into a prison appeared complete. In 1861 masons laid brick partitions in the sixty foot wide by twenty-four foott deep battery casements and added the necessary doors to adequately secure the newly created dungeons. Some of original thirty-two pound cannons remained mounted in several individual rooms. Burke assigned Beall to casement number two on the lower level. His modified cavern measured fourteen feet wide by twenty-four feet deep. The apex of the vaulted ceiling terminated eight feet above the floor. Three small loop holes through the walls allowed the permeation of virtual twilight into the cells during daylight hours. Regulations permitted circulation with other men housed in the four casements on the lower level while those confined above visited with prisoners in the upper enclosures.

Roger Pryor, Dick Page, J. D. Allison, and several other prisoners welcomed their new cellmate. Allison, a former Morgan's raider, grinned as he pointed to the straw mats strewn about the cold stone floor and offered Beall his choice of bunks.

John listened to Page's interesting background while he studied the officer's physical characteristics. General Richard Lucian Page's facial features distinctly resembled Robert E. Lee's. Page's snow-white hair, trim faded beard, and penetrating eyes presented a similar classical gentlemanly appearance although Lee possessed a thicker frame than his counterpart. Coincidently Page and Lee, both fifty-seven, hailed from Virginia. Page's lifelong U.S. Naval career ended with Virginia's secession when he entered the Confederate Navy. In March of 1864 Richmond commissioned Page a brigadier general responsible for both naval and land forces on the outer defenses of Mobile Bay. When Fort Morgan fell in August, Page journeyed from the gulf coast to Fort Lafayette where unbeknownst to him, he would linger until September the following year. Upon introduction Page politely smiled. "Unfortunately you missed our meager breakfast of a small piece of meat and a thin slice of bread, although you are invited to join us for a fine midday feast of the same, supplemented with a meager portion of bean or rice soup. Remember to save room for your slice of evening bread," he concluded with a wink.

Pryor stepped forward, bowed graciously, and with a wide grin offered, "Private Roger Pryor at your service." John stared momentarily at the man six years his senior. The native Virginian's receding hairline displayed ample long straight locks which he combed behind his ears, allowing hair to touch his shoulders. Sturdy cheeks framed his dominant nose. The former fiery publisher of *The South* trumpeted the militant cry for southern unification long before guns fired on Fort Sumter.

"Private?" John asked. "Last I heard you were a general. Now you're a private? And if so, what in the name of Dixie are you doing in this exclusive hotel for," John paused momentarily searching for proper words, "vocal northern dissents, high ranking Confederate officers, dangerous men like Mr. Allison, or alleged saboteurs such as me?"

Dick Page heartily laughed. "Answer the captain, Roger. Tell him who stripped your general's stars and broke you to a private. Repeat in full detail the dastardly deed you committed to send you here to protect all Yankeedom from your reprehensible act."

"I proudly acknowledge the individual who reduced my rank to private is…" Smirks covered everyone's face except John's, who quizzically listened. "I, I am that man." John's shoulders arched with surprise as his eyebrows furrowed in disbelief while Pryor explained. "Our division reorganized a year ago, leaving me without a field assignment. For six months I wrote letters, visited officials, and cajoled friends in my quest for a return to action. As you know, our military genius in the Richmond White House believes only men with a West Point pedigree deserve to command. Taking nothing away from Jackson, Lee, or Longstreet, one must recognize the academy too produced the likes of McClellan, Burnside, Pope, and our own Braxton Bragg. In any case, I've dedicated myself in one way or another to our quest for freedom long before the first shots fired. I grew impetuous, resigned my officer's commission, and enlisted as a private, to the chagrin of my wife Sara and many dear friends."

"And the deed leading to your incarceration, Mr. Pryor?"

"Please John, call me Roger. No need for formalities or titles especially since I'm the lowest ranking soldier present," he added with a chuckle. "I'm here for buying a newspaper."

"A newspaper?" John interrupted.

"Early one morning while I fulfilled my obligatory picket duty, I noticed a lad in blue across the way performing a like task. Being formerly in command, I assumed no officer to be awake at that hour of the morning, especially with November's chill filling the air. I offered my Union counterpart a plug of exceptional Virginia tobacco for a day old Yankee paper. Figured I'd be safe since the Federal got the best of the swap. Unbeknownst to me, the previous week another such transfer of goods terminated when for some reason Confederate officers captured a poor Northern picket. As you might suppose the Yankees schemed to one up our deed, so they set a trap for a Confederate officer. Possessing mannerisms of a fine southern gentleman I must have carried myself with the air of an officer. I found it rather humorous my enemy needed an officer and treated me as such while my own government refused such recognition. Apparently several well-read Union officers remembered my comments before the war while I served as a U.S. Congressman, which subsequently led to my deportment into the company of you fine gentleman in these luxurious accommodations. Enough of my adventures. Tell us about yourself, Johnny, though we somewhat know of the mischief you created over the years."

He briefly told of his wounding at Bolivar Heights, his maritime adventures on the Chesapeake and Lake Erie, and the events leading to his recent capture. "I must be an extremely elusive man. The second time I've worn these," he commented, extending his manacled wrists. "Don't know who ordered them."

"Probably not Colonel Burke. He only follows orders," Allison sarcastically replied.

"I'd wager General Dix issued the mandate," interjected Pryor before he detailed the major general's career. "Lincoln commissioned Dix in the summer of '61 to command the Department of Maryland with headquarters in Baltimore until the summer of '63 when he received reassignment to command of the Department of the East. He hurriedly traveled to his new headquarters in New York City to quell the July draft riots. He endured several embarrassing months but puffed up like a bantam rooster when he finally restored order. Then a year later a troublemaker like you kidnaps private vessels with the intention of commandeering the only warship on the Great Lakes. You waited only another month before purchasing and arming the *Georgiana*. The old codger endured more restless nights because those actions all occurred within his jurisdiction. But our boys weren't finished harassing him. Bennett Young robbed banks in Vermont in October. In November unnamed perpetrators set fires in Dix's own backyard. Two weeks after the fires, you created more mischief. I trust it accurate to assume General Dix probably just plain doesn't like you," Pryor concluded, with a sheepish grin.

"Very astute observation, Roger," Dick Page innocently added causing the casement to erupt with loud laughter.

John added to the abounding humor. "And Dix probably decided every deed John Taylor Wood committed along the shore while the general commanded the Department of the Maryland was my doing." With a rattling of his manacled wrist, John patted Roger's arm. "Why do we finally receive the belated recognition we seek at inopportune times from undesirable authorities."

Page smiled and sagely replied, "Another one of the idiosyncrasies of war, and politics I suspect." The day's conversation digressed into small talk as the prisoners coped with another mundane afternoon.

Two weeks later John received crushing news which he despondently shared with his cellmates. "I'm to stand trial tomorrow charged with being a spy and a guerrilla. I expected some sort of charges but certainly not these, compounded by such limited time to prepare."

Pryor placed his hands on John's shoulders, pulled him close, and humbly offered to serve as consul if the accused graciously allowed him to do so.

"It would be my honor to have you by my side," John said, with a warm smile. The men prepared the defense unaware the gifted attorney, Daniel Lucas, neared the end of his journey north to aid John with his legal battle. When Dan gained admission into the Canadian prison where he expected to find his friend he discovered the inaccuracy of the initial newspaper articles which mistakenly identified Burley for Beall. The deteriorated network of Confederate operatives provided Lucas with little aid in his search for Beall's location. Dix prudently suppressed word of the Rebel's capture to retard interference from Washington politicians and to prevent retaliation from Richmond. Lucas remained in Toronto sorting through farfetched rumors and scraps of information as he vainly searched for clues to his friend's fate.

59 – THE TRIAL

Shortly before 11a.m. on Friday, January 20, 1865, guards escorted the manacled prisoner to the site of the hearing at Fort Lafayette's Headquarters office. General Dix's military commission consisted of Brigadier Generals Fitz Henry Warren and W. H. Morris, Colonels M. S. Howe and H. Day, and Majors G. W. Wallace and John A. Bolles. Dix named Bolles judge advocate. John prayed for inner strength to displace his engulfing isolation. Late the previous day Assistant Secretary of War Charles Dana denied Roger Pryor the right to serve as Beall's counsel on the grounds that "under no circumstances can a prisoner of war be allowed to act as counsel for a person accused of being a spy."[9] Beall requested a postponement in order to either seek counsel, or in the very least prepare his own defense. The commission acquiesced and adjourned until the following Wednesday. Unfortunately John's choice of counsel, the renowned attorney James T. Brady, found himself involved in another case. Brady committed to defend Beall if the trial commenced a week later.

Major Bolles conversed privately with General Dix after the commission adjourned. "I am somewhat surprised you allowed another week's delay for Brady to defend Beall. The counselor possesses excellent skills," Bolles commented apprehensively.

"Perhaps in a civil trial, Major, but remember ours is a military affair. Mr. Brady's defense of Beall adds credibility to our investigation before we hang the marauding arsonist," answered Dix with a cynical smile.

"With all due respect, General," Bolles tactfully challenged, "the Rebel's not charged with arson."

"True. I sincerely doubt we ever obtain definitive evidence tying him to that malicious crime but he will not so easily elude responsibility for his other transgressions. We sequestered two witnesses unquestionably identifying him as the pirate leader during the Lake Erie raid in September. We have a creditable Buffalo police officer observing his seditious behavior in the train station. The doorman from Mulberry Street's jail revealed Beall's attempt to bribe his way to freedom with the aid of Southern sympathizers. Beall admits his acquaintance with suspected arsonists although he naturally denies involvement with them. And finally we have our coup de grace. Our interrogators vividly described to young Anderson the scene of the lad choking for breath while dangling from the rope squeezing life from his throat. He understands the option of cooperation offers far better prospects. Our boy, a member of Beall's own lair, provides a creditable witness testifying with firsthand accounts of the dastardly deeds orchestrated on the New York Central's rails. Our counsel shall insure the boy repeats in detail the heinous attempt, not once, but three times, to derail a civilian passenger train filled with defenseless woman, helpless children, and feeble old men." Dix added presumptuously, "It does my heart good to recognize we may spare the young boy the fate of the hangman's noose. I pray he rehabilitates and becomes a productive member of our new society." The men separated with Dix's request that Bolles contact him with further concerns.

John's optimism blossomed during his initial conversation with his defense attorney. James Topham Brady, just shy of fifty, cut his teeth in New York City courtrooms. At fourteen he served as junior counsel for his eminent father, attorney Thomas S. Brady. James gained admittance to the bar in 1836 at the age of twenty-one. By 1843 he advanced to New York's District Attorney. While many competent lawyers used the legal profession for a natural stepping stone into politics, James preferred the challenges of his chosen profession. In one of his more prominent cases before the war he defended New Yorker Dan Sickles, charged with the murder of the *Star Spangled Banner's* author Francis Scott Key's nephew, Philip Barton Key. Sickles painstakingly staged and orchestrated events consummating with Key's shooting. Brady received notoriety in his opening defense statements for the original introduction of the temporary insanity plea in court. The politically connected Sickles received a not-guilty verdict, wrangled a general's commission after the war commenced, and actively served the Union until he lost a leg on the second day at Gettysburg.

Competent in all fields of law, Brady functioned with exceeding proficiency in criminal defense trials. His short chin cultivated a small triangle of hair beneath his lower lip and bushy mustache above. His deep set eyes complimented his angular nose. His head of thick curly hair highlighted by dark features accentuated his charismatic presence. Several wisps of locks adorned his broad forehead which further conveyed a debonair gentleman with immense intellectual prowess. As a former law student, Beall eagerly anticipated observing his defense counsel in action.

Brady understood charisma counted for little in military proceedings. Ability to present an accurate interpretation of the law was always a priority, but especially in this case. In military trials political connections too often tilted the scales of justice. Although Brady had adamantly supported states rights initially, and later the candidacy of John C. Breckenridge in 1860, he had rigidly supported Lincoln since the attack on Fort Sumter. He trusted if the commission delivered an undesirable verdict that he maintained the political clout to render a reprieve from the supreme authority of President Lincoln.

The accused faced two defined charges, the first being "the violation of the laws of war." Four of the six specifications within this charge addressed his actions in Lake Erie on September 19 while the other two specifications addressed his actions in New York just prior to his capture. The other charge alleged "that he acted as a spy." The specifications from the second charge also referenced his Ohio and New York activities.

The prosecution sequestered five witnesses to testify. Brady acknowledged any witness whom he might call for the defense could face imprisonment and charges similar to Beall's. Eyewitness Walter Ashley, part owner of the *Philo Parsons,* testified first. He established the raiders wore civilian clothing without military insignia. He accused Beall and Burley of the petty theft of cash from his office. He failed to recall claims by Beall that the defendant represented the Confederate government.

Veteran Sandusky fireman William Weston, a passenger aboard the *Philo Parsons,* then took the witness stand. Weston reaffirmed much of Ashley's testimony, restated the marauders wore civilian clothing, and added no one saw a Confederate flag. He failed to recall if any of the party identified themselves as members of the Confederate military.

Niagara city police officer David Thomas concluded the first day's testimony. He described the capture in the train station, the contents of the carpet bag which Andersen and Beall shared, Beall's use of a fictitious name, and the Confederate leader's false tale of their escape from Point Lookout. Thomas reaffirmed both men wore civilian apparel.

The commission opened proceedings the following day by calling Edward Hayes to the stand. The Mulberry Street jail's doorman recited Dix's script as rehearsed. After Hayes stepped down from his brief testimony the commissioners settled into their chairs for George Anderson's lengthy but intriguing testimony. The lad stated he only became acquainted with Captain Beall the week prior to the fateful night of their capture. Anderson acknowledged that he and Beall remained separated while in the city jail. Anderson mentioned Headley and Martin, and identified the latter as the man giving the orders. The boy failed to recall any mention of instructions descending from the Confederate government. He innocently mentioned plans of taking money from the express safe which unfortunately planted seeds that the band functioning under the alleged auspices of the Confederate government actually operated as a band of mere train robbers. The commission dismissed Anderson and prepared to recess for the day.

As the introverted lad stepped down, his eyes accidentally met Beall's. Anderson instinctively struggled to break the gaze but Beall's despondent stare transmitted a message of forgiveness. The soul of a selfless man still resided deeply within the captain. Tears of guilt dripped down the boys soft, innocent cheeks. The lad passed John and whispered, "Forgive me." A responsive, gentle, affirmative nod magnified the grief consuming the youth.

The unbearable, enveloping shame suffocated George as he entered his cell. The guilt-laden lad carried the burden that for the remainder of his wretched life he would be branded a cowardly betrayer. He imagined the epitaph carved into his tombstone. "Here lies the body of the Judas Iscariot of the Confederacy." Judas Iscariot. George commiserated that the ancient charlatan betrayed Christ for thirty pieces of silver. George exchanged his own miserable existence, not nearly worth thirty pieces of silver, for John Beall's noble life. He opened his Testament. In the dim light he leafed through the pages until he found Matthew, Chapter 27, verses 5and 6. In the cell's dim light he read,

"*And he cast down the pieces of silver in the temple, and departed and hanged himself. And the chief priests took the silver pieces, and said, It is not lawful for to put them into the treasury, because it is the price of blood.*"

He looked at the rusted window bars. He reread the portion of verse 5 which said "*and hanged himself*". He removed his suspenders and reread the verse. No longer capable of sustaining his despicable life, he stood, tied one strap to a bar, and formed a noose with the other. The compassionate image of Captain Beall's forgiving blue eyes continued haunting George. The boy released the noose, dropped to his knees, and wept uncontrollably, allowing the day's emotions to escape through his eyes. He realized true repentance would only evolve from his commitment to a new life exemplifying the character of John Yates Beall, the man who sacrificed his own life so that his young charge might live.

The following day the court entered letters into evidence which Beall mailed days earlier to friends requesting support for his claims of innocence. Burke intercepted the communications and forwarded them to Dix. John wrote three letters dated January 22. The first correspondence he addressed to his close friend Daniel Lucas. Another he sent to his Jefferson County acquaintance Colonel Alexander Boteler. He directed the final epistle to Jacob Thompson. Dix never forwarded the appeals but instead maliciously utilized them for self-incrimination of the Virginian.

John's spirits soon rose when Brady submitted a copy of the defendant's March 5, 1863 Confederate Naval Commission, validated by a handwritten endorsement from Secretary of the Navy Mallory. Apparently Brady finally succeeded in notifying the Confederate government of Beall's precarious predicament. The six member panel concluded their proceedings on February 7. John returned to his cell while Brady returned to his law office to continue reviewing the case. As John awaited the verdict in the company of his cellmates the hours turned into days. The late afternoon's dim light on February 13 almost disappeared when Colonel Burke solemnly entered the dungeon and requested a private conference upstairs with Beall.

His cellmates heard the colonel say, "I have bad news Captain, but I know you are a brave man and can stand it."[10]

60 – THE QUEST FOR REPREIVE

Beall's ankle manacles scraped along the stone floor as he trudged beside a guard to the colonel's office. The commander motioned for his prisoner to be seated. The officer looked toward the doorway and nodded to the young soldier stationed just inside. The private took the cue, exited, and closed the door, relieved that he avoided the forthcoming conversation. Beall stared at the dull overcast sky through the window behind Burke. At this hour of day, in this depressing location, only melancholy filtered through the dingy glass pane.

The Union officer stared at the paper before him and looked up. Beall sensed the man's anxiousness to dispense the news but he also recognized the hesitancy to commence. Burke cleared his throat and spoke deliberately, without emotion. "Captain Beall, the commission rendered its verdict. They thoroughly reviewed all facts before them. Sometimes in war duty dictates we perform unpleasant tasks. I trust the commission experienced such."

Burke paused to collect his thoughts. Beall impatiently waited, desiring to avoid a lengthy philosophical rationalization for the rendering of the verdict's perceived justice. He brusquely broke the uncomfortable silence. "Colonel Burke, you stated that you possess dire news which your position requires that you dispense. For both our sakes get to the point so that we may conclude this unpleasant business."

Burke sighed, taken back by the prisoner's abruptness. He stared momentarily at the closed door while searching for appropriate words. He awkwardly perused the document, desiring to read the official wording. Finally out of frustration Burke bluntly stated, "It is my duty to inform you that you have been found guilty of all charges and are sentenced to death."

The fire flaring from Beall's rebellious eyes met Burke's sympathetic gaze. "The hanging's to occur here in your Bastille, I presume? How appropriate," the prisoner cynically commented. He pointedly demanded, "When?"

"This Saturday, the 18th. And General Dix requested a change in venue. Why? I do not know. In fact, the location remains undetermined," added Burke while holding up both hands to fend off further questions.

"Dix probably desires a site to accommodate a larger audience," John sarcastically but accurately speculated. "Are my cellmates aware of my fate?"

"Sensitive to your situation we removed your comrades to the upper battery so you may use your final days to settle your affairs, compose correspondence, and make your peace with God Almighty."

"I shall take full advantage to address the first two obligations. However, I long ago reconciled with my Maker. If we are finished, may I return to my quarters?"

With his duty fulfilled, Burke placed his hand firmly on Beall's shoulder and with sincerity said, "I so hoped fate might have treated you differently, Captain Beall."

Two men controlled by unwavering compliance to duty while wearing different uniforms stood silently, before Beall simply replied, "Thank you, Colonel Burke."

John entered the eerie solitude of his cell. He opened his Testament to Romans 8:28 and read aloud, "*And we know that all things work together for good to them that love God, to them who are called according to his purpose*." Next he leafed to Galatians 3:21. "*Is the law then against the promises of God? God forbid: for if there had been a law given which could have given life, verily righteousness should have been by the law*." He turned to Philippians Chapter 3: Verse 13. "*Brethren, I count not myself to have apprehended: but this one thing I do, forgetting those things which are behind, and reach forth to those things which are before*." He concluded with

Hebrews 13:5. "*Let your conversation be without covetousness; and be content with such things as ye have: for he hath said, I will never leave thee or forsake thee.*"

His mind raced through the duties he must accomplish within five days. He awoke the next morning with an array of concerns following the night of restless sleep. Martha's image constantly interrupted his thoughts. He hoped to complete all necessary tasks promptly so that his remaining hours could be absorbed with memories of her.

Nibbling on a crust of last evening's bread he stared at the pen and paper before him, complements of his benevolent host. With a sigh of relief he remembered he entrusted Roger Pryor with his diary two days earlier. He cringed at the thought of his journal falling into Yankee hands. Now his account could eventually document accurately the events leading to his fate.

With momentary peace of mind his attention turned to his correspondence. He addressed a letter to his former University of Virginia classmate and long time friend, James McClure, who resided in Maryland. John refuted his conviction for spying or committing ruthless guerrilla acts. He requested a reconciliation of his legal expenses to settle the account. He also documented his desire that his body be buried in New York City, "not to be removed to my native State till this unhappy war is over."[11]

He turned his attention to his younger brother. He disavowed the unjust Federal charges, verdict, and approaching execution. Assuming the role of consummate mentor he stressed kind treatment of vulnerable Yankee prisoners. He emphasized that he spilled blood only in conflict and never enriched his pockets by the plunder of war. He closed by instructing Will to care for their aging mother.[12]

After completing Will's letter John gathered his thoughts for his farewell message to Martha. He softly sang and reflected upon the first two stanzas.

It was only eight months ago, Martha
When you said you'd always be mine
At the bridge with the stream below, Martha
Rushing past the sweet scented pine.
Though our days were a precious few, Martha
In the tranquil land by the sea
I surrendered myself to you, Martha
For all of eternity.

Two years since I held you near, Martha
When cruel war again beckoned me
The loss of my comrades so dear, Martha
In our struggle to be free.
I sit tightly bound in chains, Martha
So that I cannot fight
But my devotion for you remains, Martha
My one sustaining light.

The troubadour struggled with the chore of composing his third verse, realizing it would also be the last. He futilely attempted to swallow the burning lump in throat as he grasped his pen.

They say very soon I too shall die, Martha
For crimes I did not commit
For the banner I held so high, Martha
Which my honor shall never submit.
To our Lord I shall soon flee, Martha
And his full glory I shall view
But my last thoughts on earth shall be, Martha
Of my undying love for you.

John's following day consisted of reading scripture while he interspersed reminisces of his past. He concurrently speculated upon the milestones he would miss with his abbreviated life. He ineptly pondered the mysteries of life in the hereafter. Late in the day Colonel Burke informed him of his transfer to Governor's Island the following day.

Before 9 a.m. a squad of Yankees escorted Beall from his cell for transport to his final earthly residence. During his march over the parade ground he defiantly saluted his fellow prisoners scattered about the exercise area. In sixty seconds he disappeared through the sally port and onto the waiting tug.

The small boat chugged through the narrows into the inner harbor, occasionally referred to as the upper bay. Beyond Governor's Island the southern tip of Manhattan jutted into the water. In the early stages of the American Revolution, colonial forces fruitlessly attempted to maintain troops on Governor's Island to dissuade English occupation of New York City. After the colonists evacuated the city the Redcoats held the island for the balance of the rebellion. During the new nation's erection of forts in the First Coastal Defense System, the earthen works of Fort Jay appeared on Governor's Island prior the end of the eighteenth century. During the fortification with the Second Coastal Defense System the rechristened Fort Jay became Fort Columbus as its earthen barriers transformed into masonry walls. Shortly thereafter the construction of Castle Williams in 1811 on the northern end of the island further fortified the location. Three ominous tiers of guns mounted in the circular stone structure menacingly threatened invaders. Despite a diminishing military role for fortifications of that vintage, the installation retained numerous responsibilities with the advent of the Civil War. Basic training for field musicians aged twelve and older continued as it had since the 1830's. Military supplies awaiting shipment filled storehouses. Numerous troops garrisoned in New York City called Fort Columbus and Castle Williams home.

The tug navigated to the dock along the east side of the island facing Brooklyn. Ironically, Beall disembarked on the same Governor's Island walkway which Union troops eagerly marched over four long years ago to board ships destined to supply Fort Sumter in the failed relief attempt to aid the doomed Charleston installation. Raw, abrasive air lashed him as he plodded toward the confines of the fortress which would house him until his execution. To the left he noticed the stately Commander's Residence, so named and so used since 1843. As he trudged on, the blustery western wind bit into his cheeks. Imposing Castle Williams rose to the right of Fort Columbus. The castle occasionally housed lower ranking Rebel prisoners but more often detained Yankee deserters. Nearing the entrance to Fort Columbus two sides of the diamond shaped corridor excavated into the earth separated at the apex and descended through the maze which converged at the drawbridge leading to the sally port. Fort Columbus, although a solid masonry fortification surrounded by a moat, exposed only a low profile in contrast to its towering circular neighbor, Castle Williams. From a distance only the roofs of the white two story brick barracks inside Fort Columbus peered above the fortress's thick perimeter walls. Inside the main gates spread a spacious parade ground flanked on all sides by sturdy brick buildings.

His guards escorted him to the right towards the north end of the east quarters, serving primarily as home to Company K, 29th U. S. Infantry. Still encumbered by chains, Beall stumbled down three steps onto a covered walkway adjacent to an interior hallway leading to three basement dungeons. In Beall's cell, stark walls transitioned into a low-arched ceiling. A simple cot, several chairs, and a table with candles furnished the cavern. Would the outdated fireplace provide any warmth in the drafty chamber? The inner door clanged shut. The tumbler clicked and locked, preceding the slamming and securing of the outer door. He dropped to his bunk, seeking a revelation as to how best occupy his remaining forty-eight hours.

Unbeknownst to Beall, President Lincoln was discovering the convicted pirate and saboteur, sentenced to hang two days hence, maintained ties to persons of great influence, or in the very least to individuals possessing access to powerful men. General Dix had successively suppressed the publicity of the trial and of the conviction, as evidenced by the obscure, vague articles which appeared in the press. Dan Lucas remained ignorant of the trial and of his friend's location. Reluctant to accept the verdict, other Beall supporters labored franticly to rotate the wheels of Washington's powerful inner circle to gain a reprieve. On February 17, one day before the execution, Lincoln's long time friend O. H. Browning presented Lincoln with a petition signed by ninety-one members of Congress, begging the president to commute Beall's sentence. Nearly sixty of those men represented New York, Pennsylvania, Ohio, Michigan, Indiana, and Illinois, areas where the majority of the recent covert Confederate activity transpired. Six U.S. Senators threw support to the cause. Men such as radical Republican Thaddeus Stevens visited with a request for Lincoln to grant a reprieve. The president, absorbed with the demands inherent with concluding the four year blood bath, devoted precious hours to this one Rebel prisoner. Lincoln attempted to toss the scorching hot potato into General Dix's hands for intercession. Dix skillfully lobbed it back. Beall's precarious fate hung midair between the only sets of hands authorized to commute his sentence. Late Friday evening, within twenty-four hours of the hanging, the stay of execution arrived.

61 – THE REPRIEVE

John awoke on the 18th in better spirits. Yesterday he received word that his mother traveled to visit him on this original date of his execution. In a despicable act of duplicity the Yankees portrayed the extension as a benevolent gesture which allowed a loving mother a final visit with her condemned son. In actuality Northern legal experts discovered technical irregularities which they wished to clarify before disposing of their prisoner. Although the rescheduled execution date of February 24 loomed only six days beyond, John relished the opportunity to visit with his mother and to share the numerous thoughts one regrets not communicating after the opportunity vanishes.

A rare bright mid morning sun joined Major Coggswell in escorting Janet Beall to the cell. After they entered the cell the officer politely tipped his hat and exited. Mother and son grasped hands and silently stared into each other's eyes. Each recognized the physical strain etched upon the other's face. John's fair skin, leeched by lack of fresh air, drew attention to the darkened shadows forming around his sunken eyes from his irregular sleeping patterns. Three months of poor diet had sucked the fullness from his face. This morning his defiant, fiery eyes emitted only warm compassion for his mother. His goatee and moustache, additions since his capture, also modified his appearance.

The number of furrows below Janet's eyes and upon her forehead had increased and deepened since they visited nearly three years ago. Her faded blue bonnet merged with her predominantly gray hair, covering locks which not so long ago had gracefully glistened with her matronly salt and pepper blend. Her dull tresses further evidenced the physical erosion of his emotionally exhausted mother, unable to protect her child from the fate before him. He seethed with contempt for his captors as he acknowledged his ordeal accelerated her physical deterioration. He released her hands and guided her to the chair and table which he earlier shoved nearer the inefficient fireplace. Mother's worn, ankle-length, green woolen coat, tightly buttoned to the neck, and her bonnet strings snuggly tied beneath her chin, compensated for the cold setting. John wrapped a heavy brown knit shawl tightly about his shoulders.

He seated himself across from her and firmly grasped her gloved hands. "On occasion I desired that you would not leave Virginia but now I am exceedingly grateful to see you. I understand that Mary travels to Washington to plead my case. I feared if Annie, Beth, or Janie accompanied you that my composure would be difficult to control as might well my anger with the Yankees. How are the girls?"

"They send their love. Annie swears she'll never look at the Yankee flag as long as she lives while Beth somberly keeps her thoughts to herself as usual. And Janie," Mother paused and smiled for the first time since her arrival, "Janie tells us all she'll latch on to a handsome young Confederate soldier and move to Cuba or Mexico to avoid living under the rule of the damn Yankees, as she always refers to them now, despite my disapproval of such profanity. I guess after four years of this dreadful war we've all changed," she said with a long sigh.

John's mind raced back to his grueling ordeal on Bolivar Heights. "Yes Mother, many of us have changed, but there exists an element of men who don't change. For them war provides the stage to exhibit their inbred Machiavellian character. The day the bullet ripped into my chest I witnessed the dreadful mutilation of dead soldiers, a scene which haunts me to this day."

"John, that's why our men fight so nobly for so long to fend off Yankee barbarianism."

"Very true Mother, but I regret you must learn that those desecrated bodies wore blue. The girls must never forget the sacrifices of our honorable men, but I trust Will shall confirm honorable men, living and dead, fought against us too. Unfortunately the men at the head of the Yankee government are devoid of such moral fiber. Without conscience they sanction and promote the uncivilized warfare raging through the towns, villages, and fields of the South. *Vengeance is mine sayeth the Lord.* In that I take solace. But enough of that. How are the Negroes? Do many remain?"

The younger ones, and the ones you acquired after Father died, fled to their promised land, as they refer to the North. We always provided ample food, proper clothing, and warm quarters, and only asked for fair production in return. Whenever serious mischief surfaced we followed Father's philosophy of humanely shipping the malcontents south instead of resorting to the lash. I suspect those who remain shall be hired by your brother. Oh, forgive me!" Janet moaned, placing her hand awkwardly over her mouth. "I should consult with you before making such plans."

John smiled softly at his mother while contemplating the folly of mortal beings. The grim reaper rescheduled an appointment with John in six days, yet Mother sidestepped the inevitable as if failure to acknowledge such might keep death from the doorstep. "Mother, we are blessed to have someone of Will's character to fill my role."

Tears trickled down her cheeks while she vainly attempted to maintain composure. A rambling procession of phrases spewed forth. "Four miserable years. All the deaths and maiming. So much destruction. So many lives with years never to be lived, or," she blurted as her sobs deepened, "so many young men with loves never experienced."

John never intended to speak of Martha with his mother, for fear the revelation would only intensify her sorrow. Thank God the opportunity appeared for him to divulge his relationship while simultaneously comforting Mother. A wide, contented smile crossed his face. The unfamiliar expression lacked the good natured grin which she had become accustomed to the past thirty years. He radiated an inner tranquility never before exhibited. He inhaled deeply while searching for the appropriate words to fittingly describe Martha. His face glowed as he tightly squeezed her hands. An impish smile covered his face. "You Mother, are responsible for my twenty-seven years without a soul mate."

"John, how can you say…? You said twenty-seven years, didn't you? You owe me a full explanation, now!"

He enjoyed the admonishing tone not directed toward him in ages. He chuckled recalling how for years the newly ordained master of Walnut Grove filled the void as the primary recipient for Mother's reprimands. John promptly commenced explaining before he received a good scolding. "Mother, throughout most of my life, I only encountered one woman who possessed all the qualities I deemed essential to qualify as my future mate. You are that woman. Remember how the fortunes of war took me to convalesce at the plantation of General Williams. During that time Mrs. Williams's two cousins sought sanctuary from Yankee occupation in Nashville. One of the women, for whatever reason, developed the same attraction for me that I held for her. She is neither flamboyant nor docile. She is firm yet compassionate. She understands my unspoken thoughts. She is the only person other than you with whom I share my innermost thoughts. Most importantly, we profess common Christian faith. And she is a true Southern patriot. In a moment of irrational bliss I offered to flee to Europe with her as my bride under the pretext of my participating in the war from there. She refused on the grounds that such behavior would lead to my shameful guilt and might even create a chasm between us. Her wise counsel, like yours, of course proved precise. Once the war ended we planned to settle in Virginia for our lives together."

Tears cascaded from Mother's eyes. No children yet married. Prospects dwindling for grandchildren. A wonderful daughter-in-law snatched from her before the joyous ceremony. All initiated by the condescending enemy who casually elected to extinguish her noble son's life. Tragically her boy would never experience the true bliss of a harmonious marriage.

He rushed to her side, knelt, and wrapped his arms securely around her. “Mother, shed no tears for me. I journey from this world to enter my eternal home with our Lord and Savior. I depart knowing that I die honorably for my country. I’m blessed with a loving Christian family. I’ve met and held the one woman God destined for me. If you must shed tears, shed them for yourself. Shed them for my sisters. Remember too my dedicated friends who fight tirelessly for Virginia. Save most of your tears though for Martha. For me, separation shall seemingly pass in seconds, but if she remains alone, as I fear she shall, our time apart shall consume her lifetime.”

“Martha, what a lovely name, the first you’ve spoken it. Describe her appearance.”

John smiled as Martha’s image came into focus. “Her sparkling hazel eyes shaped like almonds, her long glistening auburn hair, her classic cheeks and nose, and her slim mouth, all contribute to her tantalizing beauty. But these qualities pale in comparison to her inner magnificence which radiates from within and dwarfs all other woman, except you.”

Mother’s composure returned. Deep within her heart she knew her son experienced a real love, albeit one of short duration.

The visit continued for several hours with little of substance spoken, each contentedly absorbed in the other’s company. The two stood for one final embrace before the guard arrived to escort her to the ferry. On board, she morbidly reflected that this same boat might transport John’s remains for burial in this unwelcoming city. With the boat churning through the bay an inner peace descended upon her with her realization that her son accepted his fate as duty, that he harbored no bitterness, and that he did discover that special someone. Janet looked beyond, to that emotional day when she might meet her son’s betrothed, the woman who could be her daughter-in-law in spirit only. Today this unexpected knowledge sufficed.

62 – THURSDAY, FEBRUARY 23

When John awoke he cleared his mind as he finally realized where he lay. He'd been blessed with a deep sleep filled with pleasant dreams from his distant childhood. Now his thoughts returned to the present. He ate a simple breakfast as he prepared for his last full day, the surreal hours suspended between life and the scaffold. The white sands of his existence steadily flowed through the fragile conduit of the hour glass connecting the capsule of life to the chamber of death. While he waited stoically for the final granules to filter through he received comfort from numerous visitors, including one from long ago. Mrs. Algernon Sullivan now lived in New York City. She had followed with passing interest vague articles describing the trial of a Rebel spy, his guerrilla activities, and his death sentence. Mrs. Sullivan's sister had been John's schoolmate in Jefferson County. The sibling informed Mrs. Sullivan of the unknown prisoner's identity. After determined visits to Fort Lafayette, to Fort Columbus, and to General Dix, she finally received permission to visit. She departed with several locks of John's hair from which she delicately fashioned keepsake lockets for John's family and Martha.

The Reverend Joshua Van Dyke followed to offer spiritual consolation. Van Dyke, an acknowledged copperhead, commented shortly thereafter to acquaintances that, "The blood of martyr is the seed of the church."[13] John's classmate at the University of Virginia, Albert Ritchie, arrived in the late afternoon and remained until midnight.

Two hundred miles farther south in Washington sustained efforts continued to commute the sentence. A week earlier several close friends of Lincoln had conferred with the president while unsuccessfully presenting the document pleading for Beall's life. Today a barrage of visitors, sometimes alone and at other times in groups of two or three, sought audience with the president. The seemingly endless stream of petitioners exasperated a weary chief executive overburdened with the responsibility for ending the conflict which many referred to as Lincoln's war. He refused interviews with, among others, Mrs. Gittings and Montgomery Blair. The former, the wife of an influential railroad president, hosted Mary Todd Lincoln and her children the evening that Lincoln quietly sneaked into Washington prior to his first inauguration. Blair served as Lincoln's postmaster general throughout much of the war. In a cabinet abounding with egotistical men with their own agendas, Blair may have been the president's most loyal cabinet member. Later Montgomery's brother, Francis, did gain admission to confer with the president, but he too departed empty handed. Even Beall's renowned attorney and Lincoln supporter, James Brady, received rebuke at the door by Lincoln's personal secretary.

A unique trio of men did gain audience with Lincoln late Thursday. Roger Pryor accompanied John Forney and Washington McLean to the White House. McLean, the Democratic editor of the *Cincinnati Enquirer*, used his connections with Lincoln's former law partner, Joshua Speed, to gain Pryor's release from Fort Lafayette on February 19. Forney, the Republican editor of the *Washington Union* and a former associate of Pryor's, blended diversity into the group. After a brief conversation the visitors soon realized that Lincoln, ever the shrewd politician, correctly assumed that Pryor, shortly to be exchanged or paroled, might in a matter of days have occasion to meet with President Davis. The more adamantly the trio promoted Beall's case the stauncher Lincoln's resolve intensified to blame Davis for the prisoner's execution and all subsequent war deaths, for the Confederate president's stubbornness only forced pointless continuation of a conflict with the outcome all but decided. Pryor, personally committed to Beall's circumstance, pressed particularly vigorously, causing Lincoln to rise and walk over to his desk. The president shuffled through papers until he located and read aloud from Judge Advocate General Joseph Holt's report, "*Beall's last enterprise was a crime of fiendish enormity which cries loudly for the vengeance of* the *outraged law.*"[14] He then repeated General Dix's previously quoted declaration that, "a *want of firmness would be against the outraged civilization and humanity of the age.*"[15]

With those readings the threesome dejectedly departed holding only a promise from Lincoln that he would look into accommodating Pryor's exchange or parole. Moments later the White House clock struck twelve, signaling John Yates Beall's day of execution.

Several weeks thereafter Lincoln commented to those close to him, "I've had more questions of life and death to settle in four years than all the other men who ever sat in this chair put together. No man knows the distress of my mind. The case of Beall on the Lakes—there had to be an example. They tried me in every way. They wouldn't give up. But I had to stand firm. I even had to turn away his poor sister when she came and begged for his life, and let him be executed, and he was executed, and I can't get the distress out of my mind yet."[16]

Lincoln slept restlessly that night aware that Beall's Friday date with the executioner had arrived. Neither the president nor the nation could fathom that seven Friday's hence Abraham Lincoln would follow John Beall, but from the unscheduled meeting with an assassin, a murder some speculated might be tied directly to the Beall execution.

63 – FRIDAY, FEBRUARY 24, 1865

Near the end of a restless night the condemned swung his legs over the edge of his crude bunk and sat up. Throughout the evening an aching tooth throbbed in the rear of his lower left jaw. In the past he eased such pain with small doses of laudanum but now he refused to request the opiate medication. The Yankees would never accuse John Beall of drugging himself to sustain courage to face the gallows. During the intervals when he drifted to sleep, a disturbing, reoccurring dream interrupted his slumber three times. In the vision Beall stood outside the War Office in Richmond staring down the street to the fork in the road. Secretary of War Seddon had offered him a key position within the Confederate Secret Service, an assignment leading toward the left fork in the road. If he followed that route he would journey with men whose orders might not adhere to Beall's strict code of honor, the standard by which he had lived his entire life. The other fork, leading to the right, allowed him to blaze the way and select choices consistent with his own moral values.

Without hesitation he traveled to the right, a highway nonetheless littered with obstacles, including debris from failed attempts to free the prisoners from Johnson's Island and with wreckage from the unlaunched *Georgiana.* He unfalteringly advanced, holding high the crest of his noble ancestor, Rob Roy McGregor, along side the sacred Confederate battle flag, with both banners fluttering boldly in the wind. The harsh winter climate descended upon the unwelcome land through which he sojourned. Fatigue smothered his body. His banners faded and tore. He paused at another fork. To the right ascended a steep trail, laden with a deep covering of freshly fallen snow bearing no sign of travel. The other path, a level corridor which flowed to the left, exhibited recent footprints which cleared the way through the snow! He leaned his banners against a large rock and kneeled down to momentarily rest. He stared at the demanding road to the right. He glanced to the left and vaguely distinguished several gray clad figures who motioned him to follow. His weary mind urged his exhausted body to pursue those forms beckoning him. As he neared them he realized that instead of crisp gray uniforms they wore tattered rags without insignia—yet he methodically followed the five men.

He joined them piling steel bars across train tracks. A sharp whistle cut through the cold night. The train rapidly approached with the brightly lighted passenger coach windows outlining the silhouettes of harmless old men, innocent women, and helpless young children. He reached for his banners of honor to wave a warning of the looming danger. He searched frantically for the wooden staffs but to no avail. The train thundered toward imminent disaster. John awoke filled with panic, soaked with perspiration despite the chillness of his cell. His hand searched anxiously for the absent flags. His jaw throbbed. He drifted to sleep only to experience the nightmare twice more. His elbows rested on his knees with his hands supporting his weary head. The haunting truth overwhelmed him. If only he chose not to follow the path leading to the train tracks he would not be facing execution today. He silently prayed for forgiveness for the only dishonorable act he ever committed, the transgression which would claim his life.

With night's darkness slowly disappearing, he stood, stretched, and emitted a long yawn. Lack of sleep or nervousness? Irrelevant now. Within the hour the guard brought him fresh water and the clean clothes which he requested. The authorities acquiesced to his request that he be photographed that morning. He groomed himself carefully as he would have for his wedding day with Martha.

While he completed preparation for his portrait, James McClure waited impatiently outside General Dix's office. McClure's voice seethed with bitterness as he directed his anger toward the grizzled old sergeant standing guard before the closed door. "Does your general who rejoices on the day that he sends an innocent man to his death also revel in preventing the victim's friend from bidding a fond farewell?"

"Hardly so. He commands his department only in conjunction with direction from Washington."

"He's a paper-shuffling desk officer. What does he know about command beyond saluting his superiors?"

"Sonny," retorted the guard, "in the second war with the British, the general, at age fourteen, served as an ensign aboard a warship. After we whooped the English he switched to the army and spent many a day in the field for fifteen years. He holds that flag which represents the Union very dear. Anyone attempting to rip the banner in half becomes the general's personal enemy."

Before McClure could offer a rebuttal, a young lieutenant opened the door and invited Beall's friend to enter. Moments later McClure walked toward the dungeon escorted by the lieutenant. Major Coggswell met them at the steps and ushered McClure into a small room adjacent to Beall's, where Ritchie waited.

Ritchie smiled at the unexpected sight of his friend. "James, I feared the Yankees would block your arrival."

McClure shook his head in disgust. "Had to bow down to the emperor himself to beg these precious few moments."

"I'm sure you're referring to the sanctimonious son of a bitch, General Dix."

McClure nodded. "Dix had the audacity to say any hope now rests with the president, as if the general remains innocent of any involvement in today's shameful act."

"And Lincoln piously says Dix may dispose of the case in the manner he pleases, that the president shall not interfere. It is poetic this treacherous government moved the execution to Friday. The imagery is astounding. As the innocent lamb faces his oppressors, Pontius Pilate sends the prisoner to Herod, who returns the accused to Pilate. Without conscience Dix watches Lincoln wash his hands of the matter which seals John's fate. Neither man acknowledges his role in the crucifixion but nor is either bold enough to halt the injustice."

Coggswell silently stood at a distance ignoring their lamentations until he ushered the men into the cell.

Ritchie noticed a sparkling gleam in John's eyes as he compassionately embraced him. "With the ordeal before you, my friend, you offer a very poised presence."

John wrapped his arms around the other man and nodded to Ritchie. "Aye, that I am! Not many a man may bask in the knowledge that his final act shall be the honorable fulfillment of his sworn duty to his sovereign land with his repentant soul bared before his maker. I humbly kneel before my Lord willing to offer my life for the fair and just cause for which Virginia fights."

Tears welled in the eyes of John's comrades and trickled down their cheeks. McClure guided the conversation to times past when war existed only as a romanticized adventure which would circumvent their generation. Stories surfaced of escapades while the three attended the University of Virginia, bringing laughter into the dismal setting. John dryly commented that he should have completed his final year of law school. His friends chuckled as he innocently added that his dilemma proved the world needed at least one more skilled lawyer. Light conversation continued before Ritchie reiterated that Dan Lucas would be present if at all possible. John acknowledged his friend's responsibilities in Canada. Besides, John prophetically joked, the gifted writer must survive the war should he decide to elegantly write of today's events. McClure casually glanced at his watch.

"Is it noon yet, Jimmy?" John asked.

McClure silently nodded affirmatively.

"I imagine the escort to dispense with today's labors shall soon appear." John firmly grasped a hand of each man. In an even toned, solemn voice he thanked the pair for their years of friendship.

Reverend Weston, the Episcopal chaplain of the 7th New York Infantry, entered as if on cue. John's friends departed, permitting the pastor several private moments to attend to the spiritual needs of the prisoner. For the final time Weston read from a book of prayer. Together they rigorously sang John's favorite hymn, "Rock of Ages". Preparations continued until Captain Tallman, in charge of the proceedings, entered with U.S. Marshall Murray.

The Southern knight stands erectly, robed immaculately for his final battle. His dark trousers touch his polished boots. His pristine white shirt shows beneath his dark jacket. A solid black cravat below his rolled collar accentuates his attire. When Beall's escorts ask if he is ready he answers affirmatively and requests that the work be done quickly. As they approach with bindings to pinion his arms to his sides he quickly completes his attire by covering his hands with new saffron colored dog skin gloves. Tallman drapes a black military cape over Beall's shoulders. The marshal holds a rolled turban, the cap which shall soon be drawn down and become the black hood concealing Beall's face on the scaffold. The headpiece is placed atop his head. Its tassel dangles on his left shoulder. The prisoner follows the procession into the hallway. He pauses and looks to McClure and Ritchie. "Good-bye, Boys,….. I die in the hope of a resurrection and in defense of my country!"[17]

The entourage walks up three steps and falls in line with the guards and musicians waiting on the parade ground. Squinting, Beall acclimates to the bright sun directly overhead shining from the pristine blue sky. Ironically this same day Lincoln issues a pass to General Grant guaranteeing Roger Pryor safe travel through the lines to Richmond and home to Petersburg.

Captain Tallman heads the procession, Beall follows, and then Reverend Weston. Next in line stands Marshall Murray. Ritchie and McClure locate their designated positions. A company of U.S. soldiers flank both sides of the condemned. As the march begins the regular soldier's footsteps synchronize. Beall's feet fall into step with the drum's melancholy cadence. The procession passes through the sally port and over the bridge. Tallman leads one line of soldiers. Beall follows veering through the narrow corridor to the left. The other contingent advances through the cut to the right. Beyond the pathways carved through the earth, both bodies of men reform. They prepare to march up the rise to the right and then down the airy plane sloping gently to the scaffold. Upon reaching the shallow crest the procession halts. The musicians become silent. All is not ready at the execution site. Beall gazes across the panorama. General Dix, who so miserly limited visitation to the condemned, liberally issued an excess of four hundred passes to this gala event. John cynically smiles at the spectacle unfolding. He stares at the harsh reality of his fate. Until now only words defined his punishment. The tangible instrument of death rests hungrily eager to devour its next victim. To date the apparatus has extinguished threes lives: those of a slave trader, a Negro murderer, and a pirate.

After a nine minute delay officials signal the procession forward. The musicians again play their morbid dirge. John's legs move in unison with the blue clad soldiers, but in a surreal vision his soul remains anchored to the hilltop watching the parade march down the slope. It reluctantly reunites with his body at the base of the scaffold steps.

Ritchie and McClure walk to the front row of one side of the hollow square surrounding the scaffold. In disgust McClure stares at the killing machine. In a low voice he utters contemptuously, "Damn Yankees weren't content to let the body drop from sight. Used their crude ingenuity to build a device that will draw the body up to better display Johnny's poor corpse for all to view."

McClure refers to the new concept of seating the victim on the platform with the noose about his neck. Instead of the body falling through a trap door, weights attached to a slackened rope drop through the platform's door. The victim's neck violently snaps as the body jerks upward. The humane Yankee designers proclaim the neck instantly breaks, alleviating the potential for torturous strangulation.

Beall gracefully ascends the steps and seats himself. The prisoner stands for the brief reading of the charges by the post adjutant Lieutenant Keiser. John's irritation grows as the charges digress into a lengthy dissertation of Yankee justification for the travesty about to take place. Several minutes into the rendition he wraps his foot around the chair and draws it near so that he might sit. He smiles sadly at the words "insurgent State of Virginia." With Keiser's monotone voice droning on, Beall softly hums "Dixie", inaudible to even those nearby.

At the conclusion of the lieutenant's laborious tract John rises and bows his head while Reverend Weston compassionately bellows the benediction for all present to hear. Tallman asks the prisoner if he desires the opportunity for any last words. The proud cavalier calmly, firmly says, "I protest against the execution of this sentence. It is a murder! I die in the service and defense of my country. I have nothing more to say."[18]

The condemned sits again. In the short interlude of seconds before the hood drops over his face John lifts his eyes toward the South and visualizes his unlived years. Looking beyond the calm sea before him, his vision reaches the productive rolling fields of Walnut Grove with the peaceful mountains to the east. The internationally recognized Confederate flag billows in the balmy breeze atop the flagpole in the front yard. The scent of honey suckle fills the air. Janet Beall sits on the porch entertaining her grandchildren. Down the porch steps bounds Martha's slender form with arms outstretched to welcome her husband home. As she wraps her arms tightly around him she whispers words of her undying love for him. He squeezes her warmth tightly to him. He… Suddenly the black hood covers his face but her comforting presence still remains as he longingly whispers, "Oh, what could have been."

AFTERWORD

Since I was young, I've spoken of writing about nearby Johnson's Island. My initial concept evolved around the Civil War prison camp, with ample attention given to the plot to free the prisoners. In the process I learned that John Beall operated a farm in Jefferson County, Virginia, between present day Charles Town and Harpers Ferry, West Virginia. To my good fortune, my son spent the summer in 2005 interning at Harpers Ferry National Historical Park. My many visits to him allowed me to become acquainted with Beall through the local historical community. The book quickly transformed into a chronicle of Beall's wartime adventures and *Eyes Toward The South.*

During the fifty years following the war, numerous periodicals and books referenced Beall's experiences and untimely death. While publications such as *Southern Bivouac* offered a Southern interpretation, writers such as Isaac Markens attempted to produce an unbiased view. Daniel B. Lucas, Beall's lifelong friend, published the *Memoir of John Yates Beall* within months of the execution. Lucas, a renowned southern writer in his own right after the war, surely wrote his book in part to vindicate his dear friend. Between 1880 and 1901 the *Official Records of the Union and Confederate Armies* was compiled from Northern and Southern wartime documents. Little was written of Beall following Markens's work in 1911, until 1965 when Sandusky historian Charles Frohman released *Rebels on Lake Erie*, which locally rekindled an interest in Beall's daring albeit unsuccessful raid. Without the efforts of the afore mentioned works the documentation of Beall's life would be sketchy at best.

The good Lord led me to a variety of wonderful institutions, organizations, and people to further aid my research for *Eyes Toward The South.* The staffs of the Sandusky Public Library and the Follett House Museum provided unending support. In the infant stages of my research the folks at the Jefferson County Museum in West Virginia, especially Doug Perks, Susan Collins, and Jim Glymph, always warmly welcomed this inquisitive Yankee into their midst.. Kind people in Cascade and Dubuque, Iowa helped me unearth little known facts relating to Beall's summer in 1862. National park rangers at both Harpers Ferry and Governor's Island provided the insight which I've come to expect from the park service—excellent. The Filson Historical Society in Louisville, The Museum of the Confederacy's Eleanor S. Brockenbrough Library in Richmond, the Archives Department at the University of Kentucky, the Rutherford B. Hayes Presidential Library in Fremont, Ohio, and the Ohio Historical Society all graciously contributed direction and relevant information.

I would be remiss if I didn't thank Jane, Jake, Brent, Jill, and Chris for critiquing early manuscripts. Neither can I forget Pacer, who deserves a pat on the head for lying at my feet throughout much of the writing.

The array of data collected combines to document numerous events in Beall's life between 1859 and 1865. However, many undocumented gaps exist which necessitate connecting factual dots with the lines of speculative fiction. Everyday characters, such as Sue Ellen O'Brien, Seth Hendersen, Ashley Cooper, Timothy Murphy, and Major Carpenter are fictional, while many military and government officials generally are real. All dialogue is supposition. Most prominent events depicted actually occurred, with the exception of Beall's maritime journey from Mobile to North Carolina. At times, documentation became contradictory. For example, *The Memoir of John Yates Beall* states that Beall was released from Point Lookout in May of 1864; Confederate war records list his release date as March. I opted for the government records.

Viewed from the Southern perspective, Beall indeed was a noble warrior who gave all to his cause. As the conflict dragged on four long years, Beall suffered the physical and emotional drain inherent with war. While we question the motive for Beall's role in the attempted derailment of the civilian passenger train, we also acknowledge that he paid for that act with his life.

During the writing of *Eyes Toward The South* my objective remained to present an accurate interpretation of John Yates Beall and the events which shaped his life. After the book's completion the goal remains the same. If you possess knowledge which challenges the "historical dots," or if you have insight to offer into the "lines of speculative fiction," please e-mail me at rkoch@sanduskycivilwar.com., so that I may continue compiling his story. To view relevant pictures or to obtain a listing of research sources, visit www.sanduskycivilwar.com.

Thank you for reading *Eyes Toward The South.* I hope you received some of the enjoyment and education from reading about Beall that I did while writing about him. And remember—besides being a wonderful site to visit for recreation, Sandusky, Ohio abounds with Civil War history.

ENDNOTES

[1] *Harper's Weekly*, December 10, 1859, 794.

[2] *Ibid.*

[3] John T. L. Preston, letter to his wife written December 2 1859; published in the *Lexington* (Va.) *Gazette,* December15,1859.

[4] Stephen B. Oates, *To Purge This Land With Blood: A Biography of John Brown* (Amherst, Massachusetts, 1984), 351.

[5] *The War of the Rebellion: A Compilation of the Official Records of the Union and Confederate Armies* (Washington, 1880-1901), Series 1, Volume 29, 206.

[6] Larry E. Nelson, *Bullets, Ballots, and Rhetoric: Confederate Policy for the United States Presidential Contest of 1864*, (University of Alabama), 68.

[7] Thomas H. Hines, "The Northwest Conspiracy," *Southern Bivouac*, II (1886), 568.

[8] *Southern Bivouac*, 700.

[9] Isaac Markens, *President Lincoln and the Case of John Yates Beall*, (Buffalo), 3.

[10] J. D. Allison Diary, February 13, 1865 entry, Typescript, Filson Club Historical Society Library, Louisville, Kentucky.

[11] Daniel B. Lucas, *The Memoir of John Yates Beall: His Life; Trial; Correspondence; Diary; and Private Manuscript Found Among His Papers, Including His Own Account of The Raid on Lake Erie* (Montreal, Canada, 1865), 67.

[12] *Ibid.*

[13] *Southern Bivouac*, 701.

[14] Isaac Markens, *President Lincoln And The Case of John Yates Beall,* (New York, 1911), 10.

[15] *Ibid.*

[16] Carl Sandburg, *Abraham Lincoln:The Prarie Years & The War Years,* (New York, 1954), 671.

[17] Lucas, 80.

[18] *Ibid.*, 87.